T3-BNZ-912

ORGANIZATION THEORY AND THE
MULTINATIONAL CORPORATION

Organization Theory and the Multinational Corporation

Edited by

Sumantra Ghoshal

*Associate Professor
and Digital Equipment Corporation Research Fellow at
INSEAD, Fontainebleau, France*

and

D. Eleanor Westney

*Associate Professor of Management at
Sloan School of Management
Cambridge, Massachusetts, USA*

St. Martin's Press

First published in Great Britain 1993 by
THE MACMILLAN PRESS LTD
Houndmills, Basingstoke, Hampshire RG21 2XS
and London
Companies and representatives
throughout the world

A catalogue record for this book is available from the British Library.

ISBN 0–333–54622–9

Printed in Hong Kong

Reprinted 1993

First published in the United States of America 1993 by
Scholarly and Reference Division,
ST. MARTIN'S PRESS, INC.,
175 Fifth Avenue,
New York, N.Y. 10010

ISBN 0–312–07935–4

Library of Congress Cataloging-in-Publication Data
Organization theory and the multinational corporation/edited by
Sumantra Ghoshal and D. Eleanor Westney.
p.   cm.
Includes index.
ISBN 0–312–07935–4
1. International business enterprises—Management.
2. Organization.   3. Organizational behavior.   4. Corporate culture.
I. Ghoshal, Sumantra.   II. Westney, D. Eleanor.
HD62.4.O74   1993
338.8'8—dc20   91–47612
                                                              CIP

Contents

List of Tables and Figures

Tables

Figures

Acknowledgements

This volume had its origins in a panel for the annual meeting of the Academy of International Business in San Diego in October 1988. The Chair of the program, Donald Lessard, had chosen as the meeting's theme the challenge of building a stronger discipline-grounded theory base for future research in the field of international business. At his prodding, the two editors of this volume joined forces with Bill Egelhoff to organize a panel on 'Organization Theory and the Multinational Corporation'. The response from our colleagues persuaded all three of us that the topic warranted further development. We decided to pursue it by bringing together the scholars from the international business field who were working on organizational issues concerning the multinational corporation (MNC) and an equivalent number of organization theorists to explore together the potential contributions each field could make to the other.

We were fortunate to engage the interest of a number of leading contributors to both fields, who joined us at a Workshop on Organization Theory and the Multinational Corporation, held at INSEAD on 1 and 2 September 1989. The contributors to this volume – most but not all of whom are primarily researchers in the international business field – agreed to write papers that explored the potential synergies between the two fields. A number of leading organization theorists agreed to provide advance feedback to the authors and to serve as discussants for the workshop and as a collective resource for the overall project. Most of the time at the workshop itself was spent in small group discussions on the papers, and these discussions provided a further basis for the extensive revisions that produced the work included in this volume.

As editors, therefore, we owe our greatest debt of gratitude to the participants in the workshop: Howard Aldrich, Christopher Bartlett, John Daniels, Jacques Delocroix, Yves Doz, William Egelhoff, Cathy Enz, Michael Gerlach, Gunnar Hedlund, Jean François Hennart, Carlos Jarillo, Martin Kilduff, W. Chan Kim, John Kimberly, Bruce Kogut, Mitchell Koza, André Laurent, W. Richard Scott, Andrew Van de Ven, David Whetten and Sidney Winter. However, many other hands also lightened our tasks. Four of INSEAD's doctoral students acted as rapporteurs, providing the authors with detailed notes on the discussions: Carlos Cordon, Dana Hyde, Harry Korine and Gabriel Szulanski. Ruth Lewis of INSEAD managed the complex logistics of the workshop with unflurried competence and grace. Loretta Caira and Vaira Harik at

MIT provided invaluable help in preparing the manuscript, and Patricia Robinson aided the preparation of the lengthy bibliography. Our editors have proven to be extremely patient and understanding as one self-imposed deadline after another receded into the distance.

Finally, we wish to acknowledge the unstinting support – both administrative and financial – that we have received from INSEAD. We are particularly grateful to Ludo Van der Heyden, INSEAD's Associate Dean for Research at the time of the workshop and now its Co-Dean, who shared our enthusiasm for the project and provided the support that made it possible.

The participants in the workshop were virtually unanimous in expressing the hope that it would be followed by further opportunities for dialogue between the two research communities. We hope that this volume represents only the first step in the ongoing process.

SUMANTRA GHOSHAL
D. ELEANOR WESTNEY

Notes on the Contributors

Christopher Bartlett is Professor of Business Administration at the Graduate School of Business, Harvard University. He received an economics degree from the University of Queensland, Australia, and both a masters and a doctorate degree in business administration from Harvard. Prior to his advanced graduate studies he worked as a marketing manager with Alcoa, as a management consultant with McKinsey & Company's London office, and as general manager of Baxter Laboratories' subsidiary in France. His publications have appeared in the *Harvard Business Review*, the *Sloan Management Review* and the *Human Resource Management Journal*, among others. He is the author of *Managing Across Borders: The Transnational Solution* (with Sumantra Ghoshal) and co-editor of *Managing the Global Firm*. His interests have focused on the general management challenges facing large complex corporations.

Jacques Delacroix is currently an Associate Professor in the Leavey School of Business Administration at Santa Clara University. A native of France, Jacques Delacroix emigrated to the USA in 1963 and obtained his PhD from Stanford in 1974. From 1974 to 1978 he taught at Indiana University; from 1978 to 1983 he founded and managed an international business consulting company in San Francisco; in 1983 he joined the faculty of the business school at Santa Clara University in California. His recent research on organizational ecology has been published in the *American Sociological Review*, the *American Journal of Sociology* and *Administrative Science Quarterly*. His current interests centre on the application of the methods of organizational ecology to international management issues.

Yves Doz is the John H. Loudon Professor of International Management and Associate Dean for Research at INSEAD. He is a graduate of the Ecole des Hautes Etudes Commerciales (Jouy-en-Josas, France) and received his doctoral degree from the Harvard Business School, where he was an assistant professor from 1976 to 1979. His research on the strategy of MNCs, focusing particularly on high-technology industries, led to numerous publications, including three books: *Government Control and Multinational Management* (1979); *Strategic Management in Multinational Companies* (1986); and *The Multinational Mission: Balancing Local Demands and Global Vision* (with C. K. Prahalad, 1987). His research interests also include innovation and entrepreneurship in large, complex firms, and strategic partnerships and technological cooperation between companies.

William G. Egelhoff is Associate Professor of Management Systems at the Graduate School of Business, Fordham University. Previously he was on the faculty at New York University. He received his PhD and MBA degrees from Columbia University, and his undergraduate degree from the University of Texas. Prior to returning for his PhD, he worked in various planning positions with Esso and the National Distillers and Chemicals Corporation. His research deals with strategy and organizational design in MNCs. He has written a number of articles in this area and also a book entitled *Organizing the Multinational Corporation: An Information-Processing Perspective.*

Sumantra Ghoshal is Associate Professor of Management and Digital Equipment Corporation Research Fellow at INSEAD. He received his doctoral degrees in international management from MIT's Sloan School of Management and in business policy from the Harvard Business School. His research interests focus on the strategic and organizational challenges facing large, complex organizations, particularly multinational companies, and his articles have appeared in the *Harvard Business Review*, *Sloan Management Review*, *Strategic Management Journal*, *Journal of International Business Studies*, *California Management Review*, *McKinsey Quarterly* and *Academy of Management Review*. He has written two books: *Strategic Control* (co-authored with Peter Lorange and Michael S. Scott Morton); and *Managing Across Borders: The Transnational Solution* (co-authored with Christopher A. Bartlett).

Gunnar Hedlund is a Professor of Business Administration at the Stockholm School of Economics, and he has been a visiting scholar at the Wharton School, the European Institute for Advanced Studies in Management in Brussels, and the Graduate School of Business at Stanford University. His publications have appeared in *Strategic Management Journal* and *Human Resource Management* and, with Christopher Bartlett and Yves Doz, he edited *Managing the Global Firm* (1988).

Jean-François Hennart is Associate Professor of International Business at the University of Illinois at Urbana-Champaign. He received his PhD degree in Economics from the University of Maryland. He is the author of *A Theory of Multinational Enterprise* and has published extensively on transaction cost approaches to the international business firm, joint ventures and countertrade in such journals as *Management Science, Journal of International Business Studies* and *Strategic Management Journal.*

Martin Kilduff is currently an Assistant Professor of Organizational Behaviour in the Management and Organization Department at Pennsylvania State University. He received his PhD degree in organizational behaviour from Cornell University and until 1990 was a member of the faculty in the organization behaviour group at INSEAD. Recent publications have appeared in *American Anthropologist* and in *Organizational Behaviour and Human Decision Processes* (1991, edited by John Carroll). His current research includes a social network study of team interaction and productivity in Japanese factories (with Mark Fruin) and an investigation of cultural differences in institutionalization (with Reinhard Angelmar).

W. Chan Kim is Assistant Professor of Business Policy at INSEAD, which he joined after teaching at the University of Michigan, where he received his PhD in international management. He has published various articles in the area of global strategy, and economic and organizational analysis of multinational enterprises in such journals as *Sloan Management Review, Journal of International Business Studies, Strategic Management Journal, Management Science* and *Journal of Business Strategy.*

Bruce Kogut, who received his PhD from MIT in 1983, is Associate Professor of Management at the Wharton School and has been a visiting scholar at the Stockholm School of Economics, Science Center, and Academy of Sciences in Berlin. He has published on country competitiveness, the operating flexibility of the MNC, and the theory of foreign direct investment in such journals as the *Sloan Management Review*, the *Journal of International Business Studies*, and the *Strategic Management Journal*. His current work is on the internationalization of national industrial networks and the international diffusion of best practice.

André Laurent is Professor of Organizational Behaviour at INSEAD. He is a graduate of the Ecole de Psychologues Praticiens de Paris at the University of Paris - Sorbonne (with a degree in Sociology and a doctorate in Psychology) and of Harvard University's International Teachers' Program. He was an industrial psychologist with Pechiney in West Africa and spent three years with the Institute for Social Research at the University of Michigan as Research Associate and Study Director before joining INSEAD. His major research interests centre on the impact of national cultures on organizations and the management of cultural diversity in multinational firms.

Renée Mauborgne is Research Associate at INSEAD. Prior to joining INSEAD she was a Senior Consultant for Lux Management Associates in Greenwich, Connecticut. She has published several articles in the area of global strategy and the organizational aspects of the multinational enterprise in such journals as *Strategic Management Journal* and *Journal of Business Strategy*.

C. K. Prahalad is the Professor of Corporate Strategy and International Business at the Graduate School of Business Administration, University of Michigan, Ann Arbor. He received his BSc in Physics from the University of Madras, his MBA from the Indian Institute of Management, and his DBA from the Harvard Business School. He was Visiting Research Fellow at Harvard, Professor at the Indian Institute of Management, Ahmedabad, India, and Visiting Professor at INSEAD, France. His research and consulting interests centre around the role of top management in large, diversified MNCs. He has published widely on the subject in professional journals and has co-authored *The Multinational Mission: Balancing Local Demands and Global Vision* with Yves Doz (INSEAD, France), and his recent work on strategic intent and core competencies has been published in the *Harvard Business Review*.

John Van Maanen is the Erwin Scholl Professor of Organization Studies in the MIT Sloan School of Management. He has also taught at Yale University and has been a visiting member of various faculties for executive development programs, including the University of Hawaii and the University of Southern California. He has published a number of books and articles in the general area of occupational sociology. Cultural descriptions figure prominently in his studies of the work worlds of patrol officers on city streets in the USA; police detectives and their bosses in London; fishermen of the north-eastern Atlantic; and, currently, ride operators in Disneyland. His latest book is about ethnographic narratives and is entitled *Tales of the Field*.

D. Eleanor Westney is Associate Professor of Management at the MIT Sloan School of Management. She received a BA and an MA in Sociology from the University of Toronto and a PhD in Sociology from Princeton University. She has worked extensively on Japanese organizations, and is the author of *Imitation and Innovation: The Transfer of Western Organizational Forms to Meiji Japan* (Harvard University Press, 1987). Her research continues to focus on the processes of learning across borders, particularly in the context of the internationalization of R & D in large US, Japanese and European multinationals.

1 Introduction and Overview

Sumantra Ghoshal and D. Eleanor Westney

As an organization that operates simultaneously in many diverse environments, the multinational corporation (MNC) would seem to be promising territory for testing and developing organization theories, particularly theories about the relationships between organizations and their environments; and yet organization theory and the study of the MNC have not had a particularly close relationship. Organization theorists have rarely taken the MNC as an arena for study. Theorists who have focused on case studies of individual organizations have found the MNC's size and complexity forbidding, whereas those favouring large-sample quantitative studies have preferred to look at categories of organizations with much larger populations.

On the other hand, within the international management field the study of the multinational has drawn eclectically rather than systematically on organization theory. Other fields have dominated the study of multinationals: the explanation of the existence of MNCs by an economic paradigm (e.g., Hymer 1960; Dunning 1981 a and b; Rugman 1980a; Buckley and Casson 1986); the study of the effects of multinationals on society by political science and political sociology (e.g., Vernon 1971; Moran 1985); and the study of the behaviour of MNCs by paradigms developed in corporate strategy and business policy (e.g., Dymsza 1972; Stopford and Wells 1972; Daniels, Pitts and Tretter 1984; Prahalad and Doz 1987). With the possible exception of contingency theory, no paradigm from the major theories about organizations and environments has had a major impact on the study of multinational enterprise, and no research on MNCs has drawn significant attention from organization theorists. In a 1981 review article, Peter Evans asserted that MNCs offer a unique opportunity for organization theory (1981, p. 200) and deplored the 'inexcusable' absence of interest from sociologists in MNCs. A decade later, we can repeat virtually unchanged both his assessment of the great potential of a closer relationship between organization theory and the study of the MNC and his critique of the performance of both fields. The 'diverse literature . . . analyzing the MNC from a variety of disciplinary and theoretical perspectives' that Evans charted in 1981 has grown enormously over the last decade,

1

and yet it has gone uncited and largely unread by organizational sociologists.

This book is an effort to build a bridge between the two fields of macro-organization theory (theory focused on the interactions between organizations and environments) and international management. Its underlying premise is that research on the organizational aspects of MNCs can be strengthened by a more systematic grounding in organization theory and that the theory can be enriched by extension to one of the most complex forms of organizations currently in existence. This book begins to explore and assess the potential for synergy across the two fields.

THE ORGANIZATIONAL ANALYSIS OF THE MNC

In the 1960s, the MNC was defined by its offshore manufacturing: the first major research project on US MNCs at Harvard in the late 1960s defined a multinational as a firm that had production facilities in several countries, a definition that became standard in the international management literature. The emergence of global competition in the late 1970s and early 1980s stimulated a rethinking of this approach. Scholars have noted that this definition not only made it difficult to include in theories of the MNC the growing internationalization of non-manufacturing firms such as banks, advertising agencies and consulting firms; it also ignored the importance of firms extending other functions across borders, particularly distribution and service networks. The inadequacy of the definition was driven home by the success of Japanese firms, which often concentrated their production at home but made substantial overseas investments in sales, marketing and distribution to penetrate markets throughout the world.

The early focus on offshore production as the defining characteristic of the MNC was largely a result of the dominance of the economics paradigm in theory-grounded work on the MNC. Indeed, to this day the term 'theory of the MNC' refers to a literature grounded in an economics paradigm, as is the 'theory of the firm' in general. For economists, the MNC was a critical anomaly, which it has *not* been for sociologists of organizations. In a world of efficient markets, a firm would produce in its home country and either sell abroad through exports or contract out its proprietary know-how to firms in other countries for an appropriate fee. It is understandable, therefore, that the earliest and the most voluminous stream of theoretical work on the MNC has been driven by an economics paradigm (for overviews of this literature, see Dunning 1974; Calvet 1981; Casson 1987).

In this paradigm, firms extend their organizational boundaries across national borders in order to exploit firm-specific advantages for which there are imperfect markets (Buckley and Casson 1976; Dunning 1977, 1981 a and b; Rugman 1980a, 1981; Caves 1982). The work of the 1970s saw the parent organization as the generator of those advantages, which were exploited through overseas subsidiaries. Subsequent work has suggested, however, that the firm-specific advantages of the parent that gave rise to the initial expansion across borders may well erode over time and be replaced by emergent advantages derived from the multinational network itself (Kogut 1983; Dunning 1989).

This kind of work has moved more recent writing in this paradigm somewhat closer to a second stream of research on the MNC, which has its roots in the strategy–structure paradigm of Alfred Chandler, contingency theory, and a more intensive interaction between researchers and MNC managers. Early work in this paradigm (e.g., Stopford and Wells 1972) focused primarily on developing a typology of MNC structures and entry modes and on the problem of maintaining headquarters control over national subsidiaries (e.g., Doz and Prahalad 1981). More recent work has focused much more on the changing strategy and organization of MNCs in the face of increasingly global competition: that is, of growing interaction and interdependence across markets.

As Christopher Bartlett (1986) notes, the conceptual framework for this approach, developed at the Harvard Business School, was strongly influenced by the concepts of differentiation and integration of Paul Lawrence and Jay Lorsch. In keeping with the contingency theory model, the scholars working in this area made a typology of the environment a cornerstone of their approach. The strategy and structure of MNCs were portrayed as a response to two major environmental factors. The first included a number of the 'forces for global integration', including growing homogenization of markets and market segments across societies; the geographic dispersion of lead users; and the growing parity in technology among countries. The second category, 'forces for national differentiation', included state intervention to maintain a local presence in certain industries, distinctive tastes and preferences, and distinctive marketing and distribution systems.[1] The two forces were seen as orthogonal: in a growing number of industries, firms were seen as subject to simultaneously increasing environmental pressures for global integration *and* responsiveness to local conditions.

In keeping with the strategy–structure tradition, the scholars working in this area quickly moved to identify the organizational structures associated with these strategies. By the mid-1980s an increasingly widely used typology distinguished between MNCs whose organization was 'multidomestic', in which national subsidiaries focused on their local markets, carried out production and marketing activities locally and had a significant measure of autonomy from headquarters, and 'global' MNCs who concentrated their production and administrative activities in one location (usually the home country) in order to reap the cost and control advantages of economies of scale (Bartlett 1981, 1986). Increasingly, however, interest centered on the firms that were portrayed as facing simultaneous pressures for global integration and local responsiveness. The vulnerabilities of the global organizational structure had been revealed by the volatile exchange rates of the 1980s, which exposed a firm whose production was concentrated in one country to unpredictable variation in costs relative to revenues (Kogut 1985 a and b; Lessard and Lightstone 1986). As a growing number of global firms tried to disperse manufacturing activities in order to reduce their political risk and exchange rate exposures, multidomestic firms sought a division of labor among their subsidiaries that would enable them to capture greater scale economies within their multinational network. In other words, a growing number of multinationals seemed to be trying to move towards a model that combined elements of the strategies and organizations of both the global and the multidomestic. Academic work in this paradigm began to concentrate on the organization of this 'transnational' (Bartlett 1986; Bartlett and Ghoshal 1989), the 'multifocus' firm (Prahalad and Doz 1987), or the 'heterarchy' (Hedlund 1986), as it has been variously dubbed.

Whatever the disagreements on terminology, scholars working on MNC organization from this perspective seem to have developed an 'ideal type' of this new model of the MNC, with the following characteristics:[2]

1. *Dispersion*: the MNC has subunits in each major market, each major national technology system, and the home country of each major competitor. The capacity to innovate is dispersed, as well as the capacity to exploit innovations, and technological innovation is no longer the prerogative of the center.[3]
2. *Interdependence*: subunits are linked to each other as well as to the headquarters organization by cross-flows of people, technology and products, such that key activities are performed in the location with the locational or organizational advantage. The interdependence comes out of a growing distributed division of labor among MNC subunits, creating what Bartlett has dubbed the 'integrated network' configuration (Bartlett 1986; see also Hedlund 1986 for a similar model).

3. *Tight coupling of subunits*: given that a defining condition of global competition is the capacity to respond to a threat in one market by actions in another, each part of the MNC is expected to respond quickly to stimuli encountered in another part. This requires very close communication linkages and closely coordinated strategies and reward systems. It should be noted that this tight coupling of subunits is often accompanied by a much looser array of joint ventures and strategic alliances aimed at cross-unit learning.

4. *Cross-unit learning*: because the emerging international competitive regime is a dynamic one, in which continuous innovation is an essential condition of remaining in the industry (Stalk and Hout 1990), one of the potential advantages of the integrated multinational network is the capacity to transfer innovations originating in one part of the system to other subunits and to adapt and improve them in the process (Bartlett and Ghoshal 1989). An increasingly important role of subsidiaries is therefore to exploit the particular conditions of the local environment to foster innovations that can in turn be leveraged elsewhere in the MNC.

5. *Structural flexibility*: the current work in this field insists that organizational process is more important than any particular organizational structure in the globally competitive MNC and that, in the words of Chris Bartlett, 'the management process must be able to change from product to product, from country to country, and even from decision to decision' (1986, p. 384). Formal structure is less important than the shared values and perspectives of upper-level managers at headquarters and the subsidiaries, perspectives inculcated through shared socialization and cross-unit experience (Hedlund 1986; Bartlett and Ghoshal 1989). This makes arm's-length structural measures of the prevalence of the 'new' MNC organization much harder to derive, since they cannot be gleaned from organization charts.

The extent to which MNCs are in fact moving toward this 'ideal type' is currently being debated in the field of international management, a debate that is reflected in this volume in the contributions from Hedlund (Chapter 8) and Egelhoff (Chapter 9). There is some confirmation of the basic premise of the interdependent MNC network organization. Preliminary empirical studies have found an increase in intrafirm trade (Kobrin 1988; UNCTC 1989), which is one of the key empirical indicators of the emergence of the 'integrated network'. Moreover, recent managerial rhetoric increasingly echoes the language used by the architects of the transnational model (Harvey-Jones 1988; Ohmae 1990).

This evolving model is implicitly acknowledged in the changing definition of the MNC as accepted by the UN. In 1973, it defined the MNC as
an enterprise 'which controls assets [such as] factories, mines, sales
offices and the like in two or more countries'. The present definition is
far more complex, reflecting the complexity of the new model:

> an enterprise (a) comprising entities in two or more countries,
> regardless of legal form and fields of activity of those entities, (b)
> which operates under a system of decision-making permitting coher-
> ent policies and a common strategy through one or more decision-
> making centers, (c) in which the entities are so linked, by ownership or
> otherwise, that one or more of them may be able to exercise a
> significant influence over the activities of the others, and, in parti-
> cular, to share knowledge, resources, and responsibilities with others.

Finally, work on the MNC in the economics paradigm increasingly
incorporates at least the first four features of the model: dispersion of
innovation, interdependence, increasingly tight coupling of subunits and
cross-unit learning (see Dunning 1988 for a more detailed explication).

The interaction between the changing model of the MNC and
changing environments for international business raises the possibility
that macro-organization theory could contribute to understanding the
emergence and form of the 'new' MNC. However, before plunging into
the task of trying to build bridges between the two fields, we should
explore what has kept the two fields so far apart.

THE GULF OF SCEPTICISM: 'SHOW ME'

Structural factors, not simply intellectual differences, have operated to
keep macro-organization theory and the study of the MNC from
interacting. Modern organization theory (OT) has been dominated by
Americans, and ethnocentrism has characterized the theory, as it has
American business and society, and for many of the same reasons.
Enjoying worldwide hegemony, American corporations have developed
products in and for their US market and have had no reason to believe
that these products would not meet universal needs, tomorrow if not
today. Similarly, in the field of organization theory, studies focusing on
organizations and environments in Europe or South-east Asia have been
labelled 'area studies', whereas research on organizations in California or
Ohio has led to propositions that have been implicitly stated and
accepted as universal. Boyacigiller and Adler (1990) have recently
documented the many historical, contextual and structural aspects of

US academia that have contributed to this parochialism and have argued that, as a result, mainstream organization theory in the USA has remained focused on the domestic context and paid relatively little attention to organizational phenomena that stretch across national borders.

Moreover, organization theorists and international management scholars generally evolved in different institutional settings: the former in social science departments, the latter in business schools. Their leading scholars often belonged to different professional associations, read and published in different journals, and interacted with very different kinds of students and research settings. Few mechanisms or incentives operated to induce them to interact.

Both US hegemony and the institutional separation of organization theory and international management have changed significantly in the latter half of the 1980s. The increasing importance of worldwide competition and the cross-border interdependencies and linkages that have been both its cause and its consequence have made the international dimension more salient to all social scientists, and to organization theorists in particular (see Scott 1987a, for example). Growing numbers of organization theorists have moved into business schools, and the seemingly impregnable walls that have traditionally separated different fields in the centers of higher education and research in the USA have begun to give way to greater interaction and more flexible boundaries.

Although the contextual factors separating the two fields have been changing, however, there remains profound scepticism on both sides about the value of interaction and exchange. For the organization theorist, the scepticism has focused on the distinctiveness of the MNC as an organization: what is it about the MNC that makes it *theoretically* interesting? For the more phenomenologically-oriented MNC scholars, organization theory has, at times, appeared to be focusing rigorously on the uninteresting, developing little by way of concepts and tools that can illuminate the *complexity* of large multinational organizations. While acknowledging that benefits from cross-fertilization might exist, this scepticism has led each group to wait for the other to demonstrate the usefulness of its wares. Before making any investment in an alliance, both have set out the challenge, 'Show me!'

The Uniqueness of MNCs: The Debate over Degree versus Kind

Organization theorists, along with scholars from other disciplines, have derived some of their scepticism from the failure of international management scholars to define clearly what an MNC is and to articulate unambiguously the specific features that distinguish MNCs as a class of organizations and the theoretical import of such features. Few students of MNCs take the trouble to define with any precision the object of their inquiry. The definitions that are offered change over time, reflecting perhaps both changes in the nature and characteristics of the phenomenon and changes in the interest and focus of scholars. To the theorist, there is only one distinctive feature in such an organization: its activities span national boundaries. What is the theoretical import of this distinction? Economists and political scientists in the field of international business point out the many implications of transacting intra-organizational exchange across the boundaries of sovereignty: the multiple denominations of a firm's value given that its cash flows are in multiple currencies; the multiple denominations of external and internal authority; the multiple market structures represented in the variety of customers, competitors, suppliers and institutional contexts in different countries; and the differences in location-specific factor endowments in those countries. Other international management scholars highlight differences in social organizations, cultural norms and individual orientations across countries as additional sources of plurality inherent in multicountry operations (see Chapters 3, 11 and 12).

Are these differences a matter of degree, or a matter of kind? To the organization theorist, acutely aware of intracountry differences – particularly in a country as large and as diverse as the USA – the distinction of differences between Boston and Dallas, on the one hand, and between the USA and Canada (or even Germany), on the other, appear blurred.

Furthermore, even admitting the additional environmental and organizational complexity entailed in multicountry operations, it is not clear that this complexity contributes in any way to the task of building and refining theory. The objective of theory is to simplify by focusing on the essential and ignoring the rest. To the extent that a simpler empirical setting can allow for testing and enhancing theory, choosing a more complex setting is merely bad research design. Therefore the question of degree versus kind matters. If it is merely a difference in degree, the only rationale for the theorist's interest in the MNC is to delineate the range of variation within which a theory is robust. The MNC will be of particular interest only to the extent that the theory in question is focused on any of the specific variables or outcomes that are likely to be influenced by that variation. If, on the other hand, the MNC is indeed a distinct kind of organization, with characteristics that make existing theoretical models and paradigms inappropriate or inapplicable, then it would clearly provide the opportunity both for extending and enriching current theories and for building new ones. To many organization theorists, it appears that those in international management who study the MNC have so far failed to make this case.

Managing Complexity: The Debate on Rigor versus Relevance

Many of those who study MNCs, on the other hand, have been equally sceptical of the contributions that organization theory can make to their quest for developing a deeper understanding of the environmental, strategic and organizational challenges of multinational management. Given their phenomenological and often normative orientation, as well as their association with and affinity for senior management personnel in the largest and most visible MNCs, they have been uncomfortable with the assumptions, motivations and methodologies of the dominant streams in modern organization theory.

Their argument focuses on the issue of complexity. The integrated MNC is a particularly complex organization, the different parts of which are dispersed in very different contexts that are nevertheless increasingly interconnected. Such MNCs are internally differentiated in complex ways, yet integrated to respond to the interdependencies across the different organizational subunits. The complexity caused by such differentiation and interdependence has been at the heart of the efforts in the international management field to understand how MNCs function.

Faced with what they see as a need to analyze and understand the internal working of such complex organizations, international management scholars despair at what they see as a trend in organizational theory to move increasingly further away from the messiness of organizations, either by redefining the theoretical quest or by simplified assumptions about individual and organizational behavior. Organization theory has increasingly become more a theory of environments than of organizations, they claim. Their case studies of significant change in specific and non-randomly selected MNCs contradict the premise of strong inertia in many of the currently dominant approaches to organizational analysis, and their rich contextual observations of internal management processes and individual behavior in companies – many of them non-American – make them deeply suspicious of theories premised on the pervasive opportunism of the rational actor in transactions cost theories.

The Chapter by Yves Doz and C. K. Prahalad that leads off this volume presents a clear version of the critique as the authors present and justify their twenty-year efforts to develop a new and different paradigm to guide research on MNCs. Building on their extensive field research and consulting experience in a wide variety of US, European and Japanese MNCs, these two pioneers in the international management field first identify a set of requirements for a paradigm that can be helpful for analyzing these complex organizations. They then review seven major strands of organization theory to suggest that whereas most of the theories can be useful for some specific and relatively narrow set of questions, none is robust enough to serve as a broad conceptual map to guide MNC-related research. The authors then lay out the paradigm they themselves have evolved – the 'global integration/local responsiveness framework' – and suggest how this approach can meet many of the paradigmatic requirements they have identified.

Organization theorists can, and undoubtedly will, take issue with this review. The search for grand theory is not very popular at present, and for good reasons. Doz and Prahalad's review of the seven theoretical strands can also be blamed for being too broad-brushed and selective. Finally, the contingency flavor of their integration–responsiveness framework can invite all the criticisms of contingency theory that have been made over the years. However, the review does present in sharp relief the motivations and demands of those who study the MNC and thus puts forward a wishlist for the future theory-building effort that this book aspires to trigger. It also fosters a degree of humility and modesty in the bridge-building task, suggesting how much clearly remains to be done.

If Doz and Prahalad set up the challenges, the other chapters in this volume suggest ways in which these challenges can be approached. Each chapter attempts to develop a theoretical approach to the study of some specific aspects of MNC-related phenomena. Although the emphasis on theory and phenomenon varies among the authors, each attempts to explicate both the theory and the MNC context to which it is being applied. Most of the contributions deal with broad, overlapping issues, and they span levels of analysis. Yet, for the purpose of organizing the volume, we have categorized them according to a set of questions that has been fundamental to both fields and within which the synergies across the chapters appear most evident.

Following the introductory section containing this overview and the contribution by Doz and Prahalad, the book is divided into three parts. The first, containing chapters by Eleanor Westney, Sumantra Ghoshal and Christopher Bartlett, Jacques Delacroix, and Bruce Kogut, draws on a range of macro-organizational theories to describe and analyze *the environment and environment–organization interactions* of MNCs. The second part focuses on *organization structure and governance*. Agency theory, transaction cost theory, contingency theory, the theory of hierarchy and bureaucracy and procedural justice theory provide either the grounding or the point of departure for Jean-François Hennart, William Egelhoff, Gunnar Hedlund, and Chan Kim and Renée Mauborgne's contributions. The third and final section is devoted to the topic of *organizational culture and norms*. Martin Kilduff draws on structuration theory and the enactment perspective to develop a set of hypotheses about the formation, transmission and reproduction of organizational norms and routines within MNCs. John Van Maanen and André

Laurent investigate organizational culture both as a process and as a product and demonstrate, through a comparison of Disneyland in the USA and Tokyo, how culture flows and adapts through and in MNC organizations.

ENVIRONMENT AND ORGANIZATION–ENVIRONMENT INTERACTIONS

The emergence and rise to dominance of open-system models have made organization–environment interactions central to most strands of organization theory. Effective exchanges across the organization–environment boundary are key to an organization's survival, and the fit between its internal structures and processes and the characteristics of its environment influences the effectiveness of such exchanges. Although they may use different language systems, different criteria for survival and effectiveness, and different assumptions regarding flexibility, inertia and choice in adaptation to environmental changes, almost all branches of organization theory – including contingency theory, resource dependency, population ecology and institutionalization theory – appear to accept these fundamental propositions regarding organization-environment interdependencies (Lawrence and Lorsch 1967; Thompson 1967; Pfeffer and Salancik 1978; Scott 1987a; Hannan and Freeman 1989).

Virtually without exception, however, organization theorists have ignored or underemphasized the case of diversified organizations whose various constituent units are located in different business or geographic contexts. Each organization, in most paradigms, confronts a particular kind of environment. Most empirical work has also focused on single activity organizations operating in only one geographic area. Population ecologists have studied newspapers in Argentina and Ireland (Carroll and Delacroix 1982; Delacroix and Carroll 1983) and social service organizations in Toronto (Singh, House and Tucker 1986); institutional theorists have researched educational organizations (Meyer and Scott 1983; Tolbert 1985) and hospitals (Scott 1983) in specific parts of the USA; and proponents of resource dependency have analyzed organizational structures and processes in selected American universities (Pfeffer and Salancik 1978).

In contrast, the MNC consists of a number of national subsidiaries, each of which is located in a particular national environment. Each of these environments might share some characteristics with other national environments because of interdependencies and cross-linkages; it might also possess other characteristics that are distinctive. Existing theory can deal with this situation in one of two ways. It can either consider the

MNC as a single entity facing a common global environment or treat it as a set of subunits, each operating in a distinct environment that is independent of the environments of all other units. Neither view is satisfactory, for the first ignores the differences across national borders whereas the second ignores the similarities and interdependencies.

The problem of how to characterize the environment of MNCs and the consequences of the diversity and interdependence of various national environments on different aspects of organization–environment relations in MNCs lies at the core of the chapters by Westney (Chapter 3) and Ghoshal and Bartlett (Chapter 4). Westney focuses on institutional theory and, after an initial explication of this most recently developed of organizational paradigms, deals with two sets of questions. First, she asks how the study of MNCs might facilitate further development and enrichment of the paradigm. She believes that using institutionalization theory to study the MNC would force its advocates to deepen their treatment of three major issues: the analysis of the diversified organization that is a participant in several different organizational fields; changes in the boundaries of organizational fields; and the relationship between isomorphism and innovation. In turn, the analysis of certain key issues for the management of MNCs can be illuminated by the institutionalization paradigm, which views the MNC as an organization whose subunits are subject to two potentially contradictory sets of isomorphic pulls: those from the parent-dominated multinational organization and those from the local organizational field in each host country. She identifies three such key issues (the problem of standardization versus local tailoring in organizational structures and processes, the challenges of organizational learning across borders, and the relationship between host societies and the MNC) and suggests how institutional theory can facilitate a more theory-grounded analysis of current research questions and raise interesting and important questions that have so far remained unaddressed.

In Chapter 4, Ghoshal and Bartlett start with the same observation of diversity and interdependence among the national environments faced by MNC subunits to propose a model of the MNC as an internally differentiated interorganization network. Their conceptualization of organization–environment interactions in the MNC is also strongly influenced by institutionalization theory: the structure of the internal network within the MNC, they argue, is shaped by the relational networks among external institutional actors within and across the different national environments. Based on this conceptual model, they draw on recent developments in exchange theory and network analysis to propose a set of hypotheses that relate certain attributes of the MNC, such as resource configuration and internal distribution of power, to certain structural characeristics of the broader external network of all the key actors in the different national environments in which the MNC operates. Past research on MNCs, the authors claim, has at times been misleading beacuse of its focus on dyadic exchange among specific actors – typically the headquarters and one subsidiary – while ignoring the structural effects of the broader network. They identify a variety of new research directions that they see as necessary to develop more fully the network theory approach.

Whereas Chapters 3 and 4 highlight the potential synergies between institutionalization theory and research on MNCs, the next chapter by Jacques Delacroix does the same for a second influential paradigm in organization theory: population ecology. This contribution challenges Doz and Prahalad's contention that the utility of the population ecology model for the analysis of MNCs is limited to serving as a null hypothesis for studying organizational adaptation and change. Delacroix argues that important MNC-related phenomena can be both explained and predicted by using the very different conceptualization of environment-organization interactions in the ecology model: change in the organizational landscape results from replacement of some organizational forms by others through the process of natural selection, rather than from adaptation by existing organizations.

Delacroix, like Westney, provides a brief tutorial on the theory. He, too, presents a strong case for the potential synergies between the fields of organization theory and MNC-focused research. He identifies that contribution largely in methodological terms: to identify the extent to which organizational change is shaped by the selective elimination and replacement of organization forms versus the adaptation of individual organizations, survivor bias must be overcome through extended longitudinal studies of organizational populations. Cross-sectional research on one or a few chosen survivors will reveal adaptation as a self-fulfilling prophecy built into the research design. In arguing how MNC-related research can contribute to the development of the ecological approach, he suggests a theoretical extension that could have far-reaching consequences. For complex, multiunit organizations such as MNCs, adaptation can be a selection process in that selective elimination of parts out of a system may constitute a form of adaptation for the system as a whole. Thus, by letting specific underperforming subsidiaries 'die', the MNC can evolve and adapt to changing environments. This proposition, stated as a speculation in Hannan and Freeman (1989, p. 42) and applied to the MNC by Delacroix, can provide a powerful extension of ecological theory. MNCs – offering the maximum heterogeneity in organizational change – can serve as a particularly attractive testing ground for this theoretical formulation. Delacroix also illustrates how the ecology model can be applied to MNC-related research by demonstrating its capacity to explain the formation and disbanding of European subsidiaries of US MNCs during the period from 1903 to 1974.

In the fourth contribution on organization–environment interactions, Bruce Kogut begins with three of the most important and enduring questions in the field of international management: how firms internationalize, why they invest abroad and what factors contribute to their competitiveness. Kogut suggests that the answers to these three questions are inseparably intertwined: firms develop out of the socio-economic conditions of their home environment and, even as they internationalize, they remain imprinted by their early development in their domestic markets. With such a perspective, the analysis of the international expansion and competitiveness of firms becomes inseparable from the comparative analysis of organizations, which provides the basis for understanding the different imprints that firms from different countries carry into the international domain.

Starting from the empirical observation that competitive differences among countries persist for long periods of time, Kogut argues that countries differ in their organizing principles and organizational capabilities, and that these capabilities diffuse more slowly across national boundaries than across firm boundaries. Companies within the national environment come to share these organizing principles because of their involvement in interindustry networks within the country that leads to learning from suppliers and customers, because of competition that leads to learning from competitors, because a shared societal knowledge base allows them to identify differences in the practices of other domestic firms and therefore to discern what is to be learned, and because similarities in internal preferences and societal expectations make such learning relatively more feasible. Diffusion of these organizing principles has been relatively slower and more difficult across national boundaries because interfirm linkages have tended to be less dense internationally. The resulting differences in the organizing principles in different countries have led not only to different organizational capabilities of firms originating in those countries but also to differences in their learning capabilities, since these capabilities are tied to the same organizing principles. These national organizing principles, rooted in the social and institutional structures of countries, therefore influence how firms internationalize and how competitive they are internationally. Kogut raises the fascinating question of the extent to which growing inter-country linkages and the growing internationalization of firms will erode country differences in organization and management, leading presumably to an erosion of the barriers to international organizational learning.

ORGANIZATION STRUCTURE AND GOVERNANCE

As issues of organization–environment interactions have moved to the center stage of organization theory over the last two decades, internal organizational structure and governance issues in complex organizations have received relatively less attention. Although organization design and coordination processes were the key concerns of contingency theory and political models of power and control in organizations, they are less central to population ecology and even to institutionalization theory, although the latter tends to focus on isomorphism across structures rather than processes. In consequence, despite significant contributions by a few noted scholars, the concepts and tools of intra-organizational analysis have perhaps failed to keep up with the significant changes that have been occurring in practice.

In a few currently dominant theoretical approaches that do focus on internal structure and governance, such as transaction cost or agency theory, Chandler's description of the M-form organization still serves as the model of complex organizations. In this model, a complex organization consists of a number of more or less self-contained, semi-autonomous divisions, grouped according to some set of criteria such as product lines, technologies, distribution channels, geography or some combination of these under a corporate administrative structure. The distinguishing structural characteristics of the M-form, as described by Oliver Williamson, for example, are (1) the responsibility for all operating decisions is assigned to divisions and (2) the staff attached to the general office is primarily concerned with monitoring division performance, allocating resources among divisions, and making strategic plans.

Nohria and Ghoshal (1989) have argued that this stylized model of complex organizations does not provide an effective analytical framework for understanding the structural complexities of today's MNCs. One problem is that the model glosses over potential sources of variation in dispersed divisionalized firms. Allen (1978), for instance, has argued that a number of differences exist among firms that are ostensibly all M-form (differences in which of the firms' activities are centralized and which left to the divisions, as well as in modes of budgeting and control). Further, as Doz and Prahalad argue in Chapter 2, even within the same organization different divisions are often governed differently, with different levels of strategic and operational autonomy according to variations in their environmental context and strategic focus. However, by treating the divisions as independent of each other, the model also ignores a second key source of complexity in MNC structure and governance: interunit interdependence. As described by Doz and Praha-lad, different national subsidiaries of an MNC share sequential, reciprocal and pooled interdependencies with many other subsidiaries as well as with the headquarters. Assumptions that relationships must be either dependent or independent – common in theoretical analyses of centralization and control, for instance – are unrealistic in the MNC context.

These two limitations of the model contribute to a third: the model does not address a complicated issue concerning the level of analysis with which research on MNCs must cope. In the MNC, structural effects can arise from relational patterns at three different levels: the level of the subsidiary itself; that of the headquarters–subsidiary relationship; and the relational networks within the system as a whole, among the various organizational units including the headquarters and all the national subsidiaries. These complexities of organization structure and governance in MNCs provide the theme of the four chapters included in the third section of the book.

In the first, William Egelhoff draws on contingency theory and, more specifically, on the information processing perspective developed by Galbraith (1977) and others to propose a broad research agenda that focuses on modeling 'fit' between different aspects of the MNC's environmental and strategic context and different attributes of its internal organization design. Drawing on his decade-long empirical research on this topic, Egelhoff puts forward a conceptual framework based on information processing as a means of guiding rigorous and theory-grounded research on structural and governance aspects of MNCs. Unlike some of the other theoretical proposals contained in this book, Egelhoff's model represents an established and relatively mature line of inquiry within the field of international management research. His focus, therefore, is on developing more rigorously defined constructs and on fine-grained operationalization that can move this approach forward to greater explanatory power and more multidimensional and differentiated analysis of microstructures for different sub-units and tasks, as well as of the overall macrostructure of the corporation.

Jean-François Hennart's article on control in MNCs suggests an alternative theoretical formulation drawing on transaction cost and agency theory to analyze the same issues of MNC structure and governance. Although he uses these two well-established paradigms of organizational economics, his approach also represents a significant departure from how the two theories have generally been applied to MNC-related research. In contrast to a one-to-one correspondence between markets and price systems, on the one hand, and firms and hierarchies on the other, he distinguishes between methods of organization (the price system and hierarchy) and economic institutions (markets and firms). Both kinds of institutions can and do employ both methods of organization, though with differing emphases. The objectives of organizing economic activities include facilitating both exchange and cooperation among actors. Under different conditions the two methods of organization incur different kinds and levels of costs for facilitating exchange and cooperation. The choice between the methods of organization within complex firms is governed by the desire to minimize these costs. With cost minimization as his guiding principle, Hennart presents a number of hypotheses regarding different aspects of MNC structure and modes of governance for different kinds of tasks and different subunit contexts.

Whereas both Egelhoff and Hennart propose extensions and refinements in existing concepts of MNC structure and governance, Gunnar Hedlund suggests a more radical reconceptualization. He challenges the often implicit and taken for granted belief in the hierarchy as an efficient and effective mechanism for social organization and suggests that this belief is premised on assumptions of prespecification and stability of input, throughput and output processes; of pre-ordained and unchanging relationships among different actors within the system and between the actors and the total system; and of universality and one-way ordering in the relationships between the parts and the whole. These assumptions, however valid in Simon's famous example of two watchmakers in his classic defence of hierarchy, are inappropriate in the context of complex social organizations in general and the MNC in particular. Instead of the hierarchy – a concept carried forward from the past and from another field – Hedlund proposes a new model for the modern corporation: 'heterarchy'. The heterarchy is not a stable ordering of jobs, roles and transactions, and neither is it a particular structure or governance mode; instead, it is a mechanism for constantly selecting and adapting structure and governance mode. Hedlund reviews many well-known and well-documented characteristics of MNC organization to argue why his concept of the heterarchy is particularly suited for describing, understanding and analyzing complex multinational organizations, and he formulates a set of distinguishing characteristics for heterarchies that can serve as reference points and define the points of departure for future research.

The fourth chapter in this section also represents a significant departure from currently popular research approaches to MNC governance. Chan Kim and Renée Mauborgne begin from the importance of decision-making processes for effective governance in complex and dispersed organizations such as MNCs, and they draw on the fields of social psychology and law to explain the importance of procedural justice in maintaining commitment, trust and social harmony in such organizations. The authors share Hedlund's basic premise that hierarchical power has increasingly lost its effectiveness in mobilizing subsidiaries and in obtaining their cooperation in corporate goals and objectives. As the subunits have grown in size and complexity, and as dependence on the center and isolation from other subunits has been replaced by pervasive interdependence, procedural justice has become increasingly important in fostering a sense of community in the MNC's worldwide network of subsidiaries. Procedural justice, the authors claim, is what makes the difference between perfunctory and committed cooperation and is, therefore, the key to effective worldwide management, which often requires a subsidiary to sacrifice its own immediate gains for system-level benefits.

In Chapter 10, Kim and Mauborgne provide a detailed review of procedural justice theory and the empirical support it has received in the field of legal studies and define the various factors that contribute to the definition of fairness of process, as perceived by subsidiary managers. They present some empirical evidence to show the positive association and causal link between this perception of a just and fair process and higher-order attitudes of individuals, such as commitment and trust, and their overall satisfaction with outcomes. While emphasizing the potentially important and powerful contributions that this theoretical approach can make to the analysis of governance issues in MNCs, the authors also point out several limitations of this approach and suggest how they might be overcome in future research.

ORGANIZATIONAL CULTURE AND NORMS

The 1980s have witnessed a mushrooming of interest in organizational culture (Barley, Meyer and Gash 1988). Some theorists have seen culture as the middle ground between what they have perceived as overly deterministic models of behavior in and of organizations set forth in functionalist macro-organization theory and the overly voluntaristic models of individual behavior presented in micro-organization theory. Culture, in this model, serves as a bridge that offers at least a partial explanation of why people are in fact able to do things together in organizations. Organizations are socially constructed systems of meaning: they do not *have* cultures, they *are* cultures. As cultures, they help create the realities perceived by organization members which, in turn, serve as the basis for organizational action.

Others, with a more normative orientation, have seen culture as the glue that holds organizations together, in spite of the centrifugal forces generated by multiple and conflicting objectives, pervasive uncertainty and ambiguity, and increasing diversity and interdependence. Rational strategies of organizing, including normal structures and systems, are incapable of organizing such complexity. Culture, in this view, is a powerful managerial tool for creating integration, cooperation and alignment between individual and organizational interests.

From either of these perspectives the case of the multinational presents an interesting arena for concept building and empirical research. The multinational represents a theater of action at the intersection between two cultures: the culture or subcultures of the MNC organization and the culture or subcultures of the different countries in which the MNC operates. If culture is a socially defined meaning system that allows individuals to interpret organizational actions and to determine their own roles and beliefs with regard to those actions, individuals in MNCs must somehow reconcile the demands each of these two cultures places on the other. And the MNC, in turn, must take into account the processes and challenges of this reconciliation as it attempts to develop and protect a broader organizational and administrative coherence amid the diversity that exists not only among its employees but also among its customers, suppliers and others with whom it must interact in its operations around the world. The complex interactions among kinds and levels of culture in and around MNCs constitute the focus of the two concluding chapters of the book.

In Chapter 11, Martin Kilduff emphasizes the importance of routine behavior in organizations and argues that the MNC provides an interesting arena for research on the formation, diffusion and unintended consequences of the reproduction of norms and routines in complex organizations. One view of organizational culture, he points out, is as a set of social constructs negotiated between knowledgeable actors to anticipate and control the motivational and cognitive diversity in organizations. These constructs, however, which serve as the rules of everyday life in organizations, are often tacit and opaque to the members, including top management. As a result of this tacit nature of organizational routines, they are difficult to replicate, and their reproduction is accompanied by distortions and random variations. In the MNC, given the diversity of cultural premises of actors in different countries, these variations and distortions become particularly acute and difficult to control. As a result, when organizational routines are replicated in different parts of the MNC, perverse and unintended outcomes are as likely as the intended ones. Drawing primarily on micro-organizational theories of enactment and structuration, Kilduff suggests a set of theoretical anchors on which to base research on the micro-level behaviors of individuals and teams, which could lead to richer and more detailed understanding of the processes by which the norms that guide day-to-day actions in MNCs are formed and replicated.

In Chapter 12 John Van Maanen and André Laurent challenge much of the existing conceptualization of organization culture which, they claim, either trivializes culture by reducing its relevance to something thought to be fully controllable or enshrines culture as something impenetrable and unique. Culture, they argue, deals with patterns of thought and not behavior; it is a model *for* behavior, not a model *of* behavior. The student of culture must recognize that it is both a socially organized process and a collectively validated product.

This view of culture focuses attention on the flow of cultural influence across nations, a process in which MNCs play a key role. In all such flows, even when a direct replication or transfer is attempted, the meaning of what is transferred is always adapted. The foreign and the indigenous are combined into a new idiom that is consistent with the socially validated distinctiveness of the host nation and its norms. Van Maanen and Laurent illustrate this process of adaptation through an analysis of the Disneylands in the USA and Japan. Culture, these authors conclude, implies simultaneously both differences and similarities among people, and the concept of an organizational culture for large, complex and internally differentiated organizations such as MNCs has limited meaning except as a conscious managerial effort to describe to stakeholders how corporate officials would like their organization to be seen. Van Maanen and Laurent instead argue for analyzing culture deeper within organizations, where it is a felt reality of smaller units and thereby can provide insights into the complicated, divisive, unpredictable but lively processes of daily social life. Accordingly, they argue that research focusing on culture as the organization of diversity rather than as a structure of homogeneity is more likely to provide insights on how it is symbolically constructed, represented and used by different organizational groups.

POSTSCRIPT

It is not our objective to present a balance sheet of what the chapters in this book accomplish and how much progress, if any, they have made in the bridge-building enterprise. This book represents not closure, when such an assessment might be productive, but only a beginning. Our hope is that the book will trigger reflection and debate in the organization theory and international management communities – that perhaps it will generate some collaboration across the two fields – but above all else that it will stimulate mutual interest and further research that can benefit both fields.

Although the book is premised on the assumption that research on MNCs can enrich organization theory and that theory can, in turn, enrich research on MNCs, it would be overly optimistic to claim that the validity of this approach has been unambiguously established. Many key questions remain unanswered, not least of which is the speculation of Doz and Prahalad in this volume that the phenomenon of the MNC may be changing so rapidly that any effort to build systematic and durable theory about this phenomenon may itself be premature.

Yet some assertions can perhaps be made. The MNC is an important social institution. Collectively, MNCs account for over 40 percent of the world's manufacturing output and almost a quarter of world trade. About 85 percent of the world's vehicles, 70 percent of computers, 35 percent of toothpaste and 65 percent of soft drinks are produced and marketed by MNCs. A major source of research and development resources, they are an important vehicle worldwide for technological innovation and its diffusion. Their enormous social influence is manifest in the firestorm of debate raging in most countries in the world, including the USA, Japan and Europe, on the issue of national competitiveness in the new world order of growing interdependencies across national economies and in the central place that MNCs occupy in this debate. Their catalytic role in the growing density of cross-border linkages among nations and firms makes MNCs one of the major agents of organizational and social change in modern society. For organization theorists, continuing indifference to this organizational form may well amount to staying away from one of the main arenas that is influencing and even defining the processes of social change that lie at the heart of their discipline.

The model of the 'new' MNC implies that, however important the organizational history of individual MNCs and the national pattern of their evolution, MNCs face a common international environment that generates commonalities in the pressures for organizational change and the direction of that change, and they face challenges that are not encountered by comparable domestic firms. This model suggests, in other words, that at least in this regard MNCs constitute a distinct form or population of organizations, defined by their multinationality, and that in the new MNC, multinationality has implications for every subunit in the organization – including the home country organization – that cannot be ignored in organizational analysis. In broad terms, each subunit is influenced not just by its own environment but by the environments of other subunits. The very small number of studies of firms that explicitly analyze the effect of multinationality on organizational behavior (outside the international management field) suggests how radical an assertion this is.

If organization theorists have something to get from research on MNCs, however, we remain equally convinced that they have much to

give. Even if the chapters in this volume raise more questions than they
are able to answer, they do demonstrate the wide range of MNC-related
issues that organization theory can address and potentially illuminate.
Further, representing perhaps the serendipitous process by which the
contributors to this volume came together, the issues that are raised are a
small and unsystematic sample of the vast array of questions about
MNCs and their environments that can easily be generated for which
organization theory can provide a strong research anchor. For example,
the insistence of some international management scholars and corporate
managers on overcoming the inadequacies of the formal organizational
structure by socializing managers to deal with the contradictions as they
arise should generate some scepticism among organization theorists. The
formal organization chart may no longer capture the key elements of
structure, but the insistence on the importance of shared experience and
socialization processes as the solution to the strains on the formal system
suggests that the *social* structure of the emerging MNC is of critical
importance. The contribution that organization theorists make in
identifying crucial elements and indicators of social structure could be
of critical importance in understanding the evolving form of the new
MNC, if indeed it is as new as many in the international management
field believe.

Another issue that has yet to be directly addressed in the international
management literature on the new MNC is the extent to which the
tighter coupling of organizational subunits, the growing density of
interactions across the subsidiaries, and the postulated reliance on
coordination through socialization of upper-level managers will result
in increasing structural and process similarity across subunits. If this
occurs, one of the potential advantages of the MNC posited in the new
model – the range of internal variation across subsidiaries that provides
avenues for innovation and learning – will erode over time.

Turning to scholars in the field of international management, they too
must confront some disturbing questions. In spite of over two decades of
research, their efforts have not proved to be cumulative or consistent.
Part of the resulting frustration may well be ascribed to the changing
nature of the phenomenon, as suggested by Doz and Prahalad, and to
the double hermeneutic to which Kilduff alludes. But, at least in part, the
ability to make satisfactory progress in building a coherent body of
knowledge on the MNC may also be due to the lack of theory-grounding
and theory-building, as some international management scholars have
themselves asserted (Egelhoff 1988b; Dunning 1989). Irrespective of how
far this book has advanced the claim of macro-organization theory to
serve as an anchor of future research, the need for an anchor has, we
hope, been made evident.

Notes

1. The 'integration/responsiveness' framework originated in C.K. Prahalad's Harvard dissertation, 'The Strategic Processes in a Multinational Corporation' and was further developed by Yves Doz (1979) and Chris Bartlett (1979).
2. The following portrayal of the 'new' MNC is drawn from Westney (1990).
3. For a popular treatment of this issue see Ohmae (1990); for a more systematic discussion, see Prahalad and Doz (1987).

2 Managing DMNCs: A Search for a New Paradigm

Yves Doz and C. K. Prahalad

The increasing intensity of global competition (Porter 1986), the development of MNCs (Stopford, Dunning and Haberich 1980; Dunning and Pearce 1985), and the attendant academic and managerial interest in the role of the diversified MNC (Ghoshal 1987; Prahalad and Doz 1987; Bartlett and Ghoshal 1989) is too well documented to merit repetition. Although there has been a lot of debate on the nature of global competition and of the diversified multinational corporation (hereafter referred to as the DMNC), very little attention has been paid to the conceptual and theoretical frameworks used to analyze DMNCs and their management. Many attempts have been make to analyze aspects of the MNC starting from an established theoretical base: for example, Buckley and Casson (1986) and Hennart (1982) have attempted to seek a rationale for the MNC using a transaction cost perspective. Others (e.g., Dunning 1980 a and b, 1981b) have emphasized the need for an 'eclectic' theory explaining the DMNCs. We shall argue in this chapter that on the whole, scholarly research on the functioning of the MNC has suffered both from desire among some scholars to persist with existing paradigms and from other scholars' ignorance of what existing theories could bring them. Since existing paradigms, by the very nature of their underlying simplifying assumptions, are not fully able to capture the complexity and richness of the DMNC, and since discipline-based researchers have seldom taken the DMNC as an object of research, this discrepancy is not surprising.

The development of a 'process school' of research on the DMNC over the last fifteen years has led to the emergence of a new paradigm. This chapter positions this new paradigm and existing 'streams' of organization theory research *vis-à-vis* each other in an attempt to resolve the observed discrepancies between organization theorists and scholars of the DMNC. The argument is developed in three main steps. First, we will describe some basic requirements that a paradigm used in the study of DMNCs must satisfy. Second, we will analyze the dominant paradigms that have been used by researchers studying organizations (not necessarily DMNCs) and evaluate the adequacy as well as the adaptability of specific paradigms to the study of DMNCs. Finally, we will outline the search for a new paradigm and the contributions of a process school of research on multinational management.

THE NATURE OF THE DMNC AND THE SPECIFICATION OF A PARADIGM FOR RESEARCH

In this section, based on the empirical and inductive analysis of management processes in DMNCs, we attempt to establish how the complexity of the DMNC, as an organizational form, sets some distinctive requirements for any theory to be useful in analyzing, conceptualizing and explaining management tasks in the DMNC. Our purpose here is not to explain why the DMNC exists as an organizational form. Various researchers, starting with Hymer (1960) and culminating in Dunning's eclectic theory, have explained the logic for internalization of transactions and firm-specific assets in the DMNC. Our purpose in this chapter is to analyze management processes in DMNCs, and not to explain the boundaries of DMNCs as compared to other forms of organization of international investment and trade.

We see the essential difference between DMNCs and simpler organizations as stemming from the combined consequences of multidimensionality and heterogeneity. Multidimensionality results from the very nature of DMNCs: they cover multiple geographical markets with multiple product lines in typically multifunction activities such as sales, manufacturing, service, R&D, and so on. DMNCs therefore face the problem of structuring the interfaces among the multiple dimensions intrinsic to their activities. In turn, multidimensionality means that no simple, unidimensional, hierarchical solution to the issue of structuring the DMNC exists (Stopford and Wells 1972; Prahalad 1975; Beer and Davis 1976; Davis and Lawrence 1977; Doz 1976, 1979). Beyond the structural indeterminacy of DMNCs lies the need to handle multiple stakeholders, externally and by reflection internally, and multiple perspectives on choices and decisions. Simple concepts of centralized versus decentralized organizations break down in the face of strategic, structural and political multidimensionality, calling for more complex, 'multifocal' approaches that constantly reach trade-offs among priorities expressed in different dimensions (Doz 1979, 1986) and embodied in different management subgroups.

Heterogeneity results from the differences between the optimal trade-offs for different businesses, countries, functions and tasks as a function of a whole range of economic and political characteristics that differ between countries and affect individual businesses and tasks in quite varied ways. DMNCs are therefore very heterogeneous organizations. Any theory of organization that one sets out to apply to DMNCs must incorporate this heterogeneity. In particular, some businesses and functions may be much more 'global' than others, which are more 'local'. The advantages of globalization versus the need for local responsiveness and adaptations are quite varied across businesses, countries and functions. To be applied to DMNCs an organizational theory must therefore incorporate a differentiated approach to businesses, countries and functions and provide enough flexibility for different trade-offs among multiple dimensions to be made.

Except in advocating a matrix organization, which is another way to acknowledge structural indeterminacy, a structural theory of DMNCs has little to offer. One needs a theory that transcends the structural dimensions and focuses on underlying processes. Issues of information and control become essential. More than the formal structure, the informal flow of information matters. So do the processes of influence and power, such as how the trade-offs among multiple stakeholders and multiple perspectives are made.

If one considers the evolution of sources of competitiveness in global competition, the perception of the importance of information flows is reinforced. As competitors increasingly achieve parity in access to resources (including technology) in various parts of the world, sources of competitiveness shift from location-specific factors to firm-specific factors: that is, the overall organizational capability to coordinate the use of resources in order to respond to short-lived opportunities that may arise in many different parts of the world. The traditional stable international oligopolies, with a handful of 'friendly' competitors, are replaced by a quick succession of potential shorter-term monopolies, which only the more agile and discerning forms identify and exploit. Although this shift takes place unevenly across global industries (with financial services and electronics leading the way, and more stable, traditional products, such as tires, being less affected), it does suggest that researchers need to shift their emphasis from the physical infrastructure and the resource deployment of DMNCs to their information processing networks and to resource mobilization (Doz and Prahalad 1988; Martinez and Jarillo 1989).

Adopting an information network and organizational capability perspective, however, is not enough. The size and complexity of typical DMNCs, which often have hundreds of business units active in scores of countries, means that linkages and interdependencies can be neither planned nor centrally managed. Which linkages are going to be useful at a particular point in time for a specific task between two or more subunits is unpredictable, and probably needs to be self-adjusting. Management in the DMNC thus calls for providing decentralized, delegated decision contexts within which opportunities for linkages between subunits will arise at various points, levels in organization and times. In that sense, an interorganizational relation perspective may well be necessary to account for the polycentric MNCs (Ghoshal and Bartlett 1990).

This raises an issue of fuzzy boundaries. Relational contracting within the DMNC and with external partners, customers and suppliers has produced situations where the boundaries of the firm are no longer always clear cut and well delineated. A theory of DMNC management has to take this fuzziness of boundaries into consideration as well. Here again an interorganizational network perspective is appropriate.

The nature of this decentralized network management process creates a trade-off between repeatability and learning. For the DMNC organization to survive and keep its value to subunits, it must allow repeatability at a low cost (i.e., it must provide for routines and organizational memory that allow interaction patterns to be repeated); yet at the same time it has to invent, select and retain new interaction patterns when external conditions require an innovative response. This combination involves a delicate balance between institutional continuity and change capability.

In summary, considering the multidimensionality and heterogeneity of the DMNC has led us to specify particular demands on the DMNC organization and on its management tasks that an organizational theory of the DMNC has to take into account; these are set out below.

1. *Structural indeterminacy*: neither a single stable unidimensional structure nor simple concepts of structure, such as centralization and decentralization, are likely to be useful.
2. *Internal differentiation*: management processes need to differentiate between various countries, products and functions in the management process.
3. *Integrative optimization*: management processes need to foster varied decision trade-offs among multiple priorities expressed along different dimensions and represented by diverse groups of managers.
4. *Information intensive*: the importance of both formal and informal information flows as a source of competitive advantage and as an implicit structure in DMNCs is such that managing information becomes a central task of management.
5. *Latent linkages*: in a complex DMNC it is not possible to pre-specify linkages and interdependencies but only to facilitate the emergence of

appropriate linkages, as the need for them arises, in a decentralized self-structuring process.

6. *Networked organization and fuzzy boundaries*: this structure creates a need explicitly to incorporate partners, customers and suppliers' relationships, as well as networked relationships in the management tasks.

7. *Learning and continuity*: there is tension between the need for repeatability of interactions at a low cost and that for innovation and change.

These seven demands of DMNC organization and management derived from the multidimensionality, complexity and heterogeneity of the DMNC provide a grid against which to review various strands of organizational theory, and to assess how and to what extent they may contribute to an understanding of DMNC management.

THE APPLICABILITY OF ORGANIZATION THEORY TO THE STUDY OF DMNCS

Organizational theorists have very seldom taken the DMNC as their focus of investigation. They have, however, dealt with many of the issues that are germane to the DMNC and some that are conceptually similar. We will examine the contributions that theorists can make to the study of DMNCs from two standpoints: do contributions meet the seven criteria established above, and how useful are they in helping to conceptualize DMNC management processes?

The study of complex organizations has had a long intellectual history, to which many illustrious scholars have contributed. Any attempt to summarize this field must therefore be approached with caution and humility. By its very nature such an effort is likely to cluster different streams of intellectual effort, attempt to distil the basic premises behind the lines of inquiry and make generalizations. Furthermore, our brief review is made from a very particular perspective: to what extent do these theories contribute to an understanding of the tasks involved in meeting the specific demands of DMNC management, as outlined above? We recognize that risk but this attempt, with all its limitations, is an important part of building a new paradigm.

An implicit recognition of the complexity of the phenomenon under scrutiny – complex organizations – is the fact that there is no dominant paradigm that is used to study it. Over the last ten years, however, several streams have gained currency in the academic literature.

Economic Theories of Organization

The application of institutional economics theories to DMNCs has grown from two distinct but increasingly intertwined theories: transaction cost analysis and principal-agent theory (Williamson 1975, 1985; Williamson and Ouchi 1981; Arrow 1985). Arrow focuses on transaction costs in markets and explains organizations as a consequence of market failure, whereas Williamson focuses on transaction costs within hierarchies and also on the cost of control and compliance in organizations.

Transaction cost analysis provides a powerful point of departure for analyzing choices between institutional forms and thus can be used to establish the efficient boundaries of a DMNC (Dunning 1980b; Hennart 1982; Teece 1985; Buckley and Casson 1986). The usefulness of transaction cost analysis for research on management processes is limited by the simplifying assumptions inherent in the 'hierarchy' category and by its primary focus on single transactions as units of analysis. Thus, although transaction cost analysis does not formally violate the seven criteria established above, it is of limited usefulness for our purpose unless one adds to it reputational (Kreps 1984) and relational contracting (Dore 1983) dimensions.

Transaction cost analysis has proved useful in analyzing specific types of interorganizational relationships in a North American context such as relationships between US firms and their suppliers, vertical integration (Monteverde and Teece 1982; Stockey 1983), and joint ventures with rigorous constraints on the nature of the joint venture (Hennart 1982). Transaction cost analysis, however, does not explain relationships between Japanese firms and their suppliers, a relationship built on mutual trust and on a belief that the joint benefits (in contrast to self-interest) are worth pursuing in a 'win–win' framework over the long term (Dore 1983).

In fact, one of the most challenging management tasks in the DMNC is to make the assumptions of transaction cost analysis untrue: hence the emphasis on organizational culture, clan behavior, and control (Ouchi 1980), and on normative integration of managers in MNCs (Hedlund 1981). Transaction cost analysis, by its very assumptions about human beings and organizations, prohibits itself from addressing managerial issues.

Agency theory, on the other hand, is aimed at analyzing management control issues in various forms of contractual relationships between principals and agents and makes a useful contribution to the study of DMNC management. Agency theory does raise relevant managerial issues by casting issues of control in 'outcome' or 'behavioral' terms (Eisenhardt 1989). For example, the outcome-based model of control provides an interesting perspective from which to cast the problem of controlling subsidiaries, especially nationally responsive subsidiaries about which the headquarters may have very little information, whose behavior cannot be monitored easily and whose managers may not fully share headquarters' goals. Conversely, control over globally integrated subsidiaries may be seen as a problem in behavior-based control, as the relationship between specialized and interdependent subsidiaries can be based on the headquarters' substantive understanding of the tasks to be performed. In fact, headquarters may provide the skills needed at the subsidiaries. The task is to create greater goal convergence between headquarters and subsidiaries, which is often fostered by international mobility of managers, multidimensional measurement systems, and a desire to instil a shared sense of purpose. The dichotomy between outcome-based and behavior-based control is not new, remains quite simplistic, and certainly underemphasizes the non-economic dimensions of control. The simplicity of the binary choice it posits prevents it from exploring the more subtle blends of control and management approaches used in companies (Lawrence and Dyers 1983).

By emphasizing these non-economic dimensions, the literature on organizational culture that stresses clan behavior and control (Ouchi 1980) and normative integration of MNCs (Hedlund 1981) challenges the simplifying assumptions of the agency theory approach in a much-needed direction to include psychological affiliation models of control and goal congruence often ignored by the economic theories of organization, somewhat relaxing the assumptions of economic self-interest and rationality.

Further, agency theory implies a hierarchical relationship between principal and agent and assumes implicitly the centrality of headquarters. By treating the organization as a series of contracts, agency theory may not include the multitude of contingencies that arise in the management of DMNCs. As one tries to extend the agency theory framework to include a complex web of networked relationships, the researcher's task becomes extremely complex as the one-to-one nature of relationships, the simplicity of contracts and the clear identities of principals and agents tend to fade.

The increasingly related theories of transaction costs and principal–agent relationships both suffer too much from restrictive and culturally-bound assumptions to allow them to do more than raise managerial issues. Although they provide useful starting points from which to consider firm boundaries and control issues, their formulation of the working of an organization is too excessively simplified to be useful for management purposes.

Environmental Adaptation Theories

The issue of whether and how organizations adapt to their environment in order to succeed – or at least survive – has been central to organization theory for decades. Out of the very rich and diverse literature on organizational adaptation, which we cannot review *in toto*, emerge the themes of proactive versus reactive or even random adaptation and of the modes and processes of adaptation, which are studied at various levels of aggregation, populations of organization, organizational fields and individual organizations and their subunits. Since each of these levels is relevant to DMNC management research, as is the polarity between active and passive adaptation, we concentrate our analysis on three main streams of environmental adaptation theories: population ecology, institutional theory, and the differentiation–integration models of contingency theory.

Population·Ecology   Population ecology provides the 'null hypothesis' to strategic management of the DMNC: population ecology assumes that environmental resources are unequally distributed between 'niches' in the environment, and either an organization finds itself in a resource niche it can use or it does not, and it succeeds or falters accordingly (Hannan and Freeman 1977). Population ecology normally assumes strategic choices on the part of organizations to be unfeasible (Aldrich 1979), although some more recent developments now distinguish 'core' unchanging features of organizations and 'peripheral' ones which can change, creating the possibility of proactive adaptation (Singh and Lumsden 1990). From the standpoint of research on the management of DMNCs, population ecology is most useful when it stresses the difficulties that limit the feasibility of successful strategic redirection in MNCs (Hannan and Freeman 1989). Population ecology reports similar findings to those of some researchers of DMNC management processes when it stresses how overadaptation to specific environmental conditions makes reaction to changes in the environment particularly difficult (Aldrich 1979; Doz 1979; Prahalad and Doz 1987); however, the level of aggregation of the theory of population ecology – populations of organizations – tells us little about why or how companies fail to adapt, as compared to the management process literature (Doz 1979; Doz and Prahalad 1984; Bartlett and Ghoshal 1989).

The very fact that population ecology does not consider managerial issues but questions their relevance makes it a little unfair to apply our seven criteria of appropriateness to management issues to population

Table 2.1 The relevance of organization theories to DMNC management research

Criteria of relevance to DMNC management	Major streams of organization theory						
	Transaction cost	Agency theory	Population ecology	Institutional theory	Contingency theory	Power relationships and adaption	Organizational learning
Structural indeterminacy	Yes	Implicitly hierarchical	No	Yes	No, structure 'fits' the environment, except for matrix management	Yes, self-adjusting network of power relationships	Yes
Internal differentiation	Yes	Simplistic: outcome versus behaviour control	No	Yes, depending on influences	Yes	Yes, depending on external uncertainties	Yes
Decision trade-offs between multiple priorities	Narrowly defined self-interest not compatible; extension needed to include relational contracting	No, mainly dyadic principal–agent relationships	No	Not explicitly, but compassed in multiple 'fields'	Yes, at least on the part of some embody researchers (Lawrence and Lorach)	Yes, power 'games' embody multiple priorities	Yes, part of learning processes
Importance of information flows	Yes, but limited to uncertainty and asymmetry issues	Yes, but focused mainly on observability of behaviour and measurability of results	No	Yes	Yes	Yes, information is a key determinant of influence	Yes
Emergent rather than prescribed languages	Transaction patterns are not specified a priori. Hierarchies, however, are useful for interorganisational analysis	Yes, series of contracts but not encompassing multiplicity of linkages	No	Yes	Possible, but not specified clearly, although consistent with theory	Yes	Yes, result of learning processes
Fuzzy boundaries	Yes, well suited to the analysis of boundaries, but needs to be complemented to incorporate relational contracting	Yes	No	Yes, 'isomorphic' pressures to conform	Not explicitly	Yes, network of relationships in and out of the organization	Not explicitly, but not excluded
Repeatability versus change			Change capabilities are very limited	Yes	No	Yes, depends on network structure	Yes, central to theory

ecology: population ecology fails on nearly all criteria (see Table 2.1), but then population ecology never set out to analyze managerial behavior!

Perhaps, however, the population ecology theory can be made useful by shifting the level of aggregation at which it is applied to the inside of large complex firms, where it can provide a logic to selection and adaptation of subunits within the DMNC network, the network itself being considered as the population (Hannan and Freeman 1989; Delacroix, Chapter 5 in this volume). Focusing on selection processes within the firm, on the relative success of various geographical affiliates and product lines in different environments and over time under specified management processes and management system settings, can open an interesting avenue for research and use population ecology reasoning to study the adaptation of subunits to different environments under different management conditions.

Institutional Theory Considering subunit adaptations to differentiated local environments and to corporate management systems is roughly where institutional theory is most useful for research on DMNCs. The concept of organizational field (DiMaggio and Powell 1983) allows us to consider interactions, mutual awareness, information and patterns of competitive and coalitional behavior between organizations as determinants of their adaptation. This is clearly consistent in spirit with the early categorization work on MNC structures (Fayerweather 1960; Perlmutter 1969) and the more recent clinical studies of organizational adaptation to diverse types of multinational environments (Prahalad 1975; Doz 1976, 1979; Bartlett and Ghoshal 1989). By showing that some of the most interesting institutionalization processes may occur in organizations that straddle several 'fields' (Zucker 1987), institutional theory is also consistent with the observation on the part of DMNC scholars that 'multifocal' (Doz 1979, 1986) or 'transnational' (Bartlett and Ghoshal 1989) management processes both hold the most strategic promises and raise the most difficult managerial issues in the context of DMNCs.

At a second level of analysis, that of adaptation within firms rather than between institutions, institutional theory is also interesting. Both Meyer and Rowan (1977) and Zucker (1983) stress that organizations are powerful entities providing meaning and encouraging conformity in individual behavior. The fact that managers are subject to both corporate and external influences (see Chapter 3) makes the DMNC a particularly rich territory in which to apply institutionalization theory.

Although the current development of institutional theory is not specific enough (in its analysis and conceptualization of institutionalization mechanisms) to make it directly applicable in the management of DMNCs, it provides a most helpful theoretical base for researchers. For example, it allows the formulation of problems of headquarters–subsidiaries relationships and of the possible organizational implications of addressing national responsiveness and global integration demands at multiple levels of aggregation from the individual to the interorganizational level (Scott 1987a).

In summary, institutional theory is very consistent in its approach to organizational phenomena with the criteria we established. The dearth of explicit use of institutional theory in the study of DMNCs may reflect more the youth of the theory, the lack of discipline base for many MNC scholars, and the methodological and epistemological differences between institutional theory researchers and the clinical researchers working on the management of DMNCs. It seems, however, that as institutional theory develops further it will holds much promise for the study of DMNC management issues and processes.

Contingency Theory   Contingency theories of organization developed mainly in the 1960s (Woodward 1965; Lawrence and Lorsch 1967; Thompson 1967). Contingency theory clearly influenced research on MNCs. The early models of structural adaptation of MNCs to geographic and product diversity (Fouraker and Stopford 1968; Stopford and Wells 1972) are clearly examples of structural functionalist contingency theory applied to MNCs organizational forms. Research on patterns and modes of headquarter control over affiliates (Negandhi 1980, Chapters 6 and 7; Hedlund 1981; Negandhi and Baliga 1981; Doz and Prahalad 1984; Ghoshal and Nohria 1990), has also been clearly cast in a contingency model, although it considered the adjustment of subsidiaries both to their environment and to the culture and style of the parent company, thus raising issues of institutional isomorphism which are closer to the institutional school of organization theory. Researchers who focused on information flows and information processing capabilities of MNCs also clearly adopted a contingency framework (e.g., Egelhoff 1988), drawing largely on the work of Lawrence and Lorsch and on that of Galbraith (1973). Subsequent research by Bartlett and Ghoshal (1986, 1989) also clearly draws on the contingency framework, although the interpretation of their detailed analysis of nine MNCs draws on many strands of theory and remains phenomenological in focus.

Although the contingency theory of organizations, with its emphasis on differentiated responses to diverse environments and integration of action across environments, has had the most direct impact of all strands of organization theory on MNC management research, it leaves the issues of change and adaptation to new environmental demands, and thus part of the challenge to management research from population ecology, unanswered. Empirical research on contingency theory has been mostly static, seldom researching change processes. The most notable exceptions are Prahalad (1975), Doz (1976, 1979) and Doz and Prahalad (1981, 1987). The primarily static and functionalist views taken by most contingency theory researchers do not easily allow the incorporation of change processes in their theory, except at the broadest level of assuming that system dynamics apply to organizational change processes. Issues of empowerment, decentralization and the deliberate mismatch between organization and environment to create a state of tension that facilitates adaptation are all recent additions, and often challenges, to contingency theory (e.g., Norman 1976; Hamel and Prahalad 1989). A functionalist top management-driven perspective, in which adaptation is primarily organization design and development, begs the issue of how top management perceives the need for adjusting the fit, or for responding to new environmental conditions.

Further, an explicit use of contingency theory may lead to simplistic dichotomous thinking in considering the management of DMNCs: in particular, to polarizing one's understanding of MNC management into an opposition between responsiveness and integration categories when, in fact, a fusion is needed: that is, one needs to consider how to achieve both integration and responsiveness and to build on the dualities that result (Evans and Doz 1989).

Despite possible criticisms that contingency theory is static and encourages dichotomous thinking, it does meet most of our criteria, at least to an extent. Although contingency theory does not encompass structural indeterminacy – except in its extension to matrix organizations by Davis and Lawrence (1977) – it does provide for internal differentiation and multiple perspectives. It also stresses the importance of information flows – for example, the interfunctional integration in Lawrence and Lorsch (1967) – and the possibility of new emergent linkages in the management of interdependencies, rather than the presumption of linkages a priori.

Beyond the obvious applicability of a differentiation–integration framework to the managerial dilemmas of the DMNC, the language in which contingency theory was developed provided the intermediate levels/conceptual constructs that allowed us to bridge theory and the phenomenological approach to MNC management. The analysis of management processes and systems done by Lawrence and Lorsch (1967) provides a rich basis to study integration within complex organizations, and can be readily applied to DMNCs. In sum, contrary to the other, more abstract streams of organization theory, which seldom develop intermediate level constructs, contingency theory went a good part of the way towards process research and provided a relatively firmer and easier framework for scholars of the DMNC. In fact, one wonders whether contingency theory has not had an excessive influence on subsequent research and thus limited progress in research on the DMNC.

Power Relationships and Organizational Adaptation

The work of Crozier (1964) and Crozier and Friedberg (1980) provides an insightful analysis of organizations as networks of relationships in which 'actors' play self-interested and individually rational strategies in collective 'games' mediated by collectively accepted 'rules' and driven by the resources and constraints of the individual 'actors'. In particular, control over uncertainties affecting the performance of other members of the organization was seen by Crozier as a critical resource.

The network of relationships is thus never totally integrated or disintegrated. Organizations maintain a degree of cohesion and consistency *vis-à-vis* their environment through the regulation of internal antagonism (Astley and Van de Ven 1983). The game in the system of relationships balances tensions between integration and fragmentation. Its rules must be followed for the mutually beneficial association to continue, but players follow different personal strategies in the game depending on their own objectives and the resources they control.

In this perspective, adaptation to the environment takes place as those players most directly able to mediate dependencies with the environment for other players become more influential in the network of power relationships. Uncertainty brought by control over information is a key dependency, but other sources of dependence are also important (e.g., the ability to influence the environment's munificence). Structural inertia does exist, as in the population ecology view, but adaptation to changes in the environment may take place through an evolution in the game that reflects the changing relative criticality of various dependencies with the environment and brings more power to players best able to face these dependencies successfully. The adaptive capability of the organization depends on the density of the network of relationships. Very hierarchical organizations, with star and spoke patterns of communication and dependence, are not adaptive because the games they allow comprise relatively few strategies and cannot be changed easily. Organizations with more diverse linkages in their networks, in particular more lateral and diagonal rather than vertical linkages, are more adaptive. The network of relationships can reconfigure itself as new environmental contingencies become important. A system of relationships is therefore more or less 'blocked' or adaptive depending on whether its structure is narrowly hierarchical or not (Crozier 1964). This is congruent with earlier studies of the innovativeness and adaptativeness of organizations (e.g., Burns and Stalker's 1961 contrast of 'mechanistic' and 'organic' organizations).

In this approach power flows to players who control resources, irrespective of their hierarchical positions; the model thus posits no hierarchical system or collective goals, and so escapes the criticisms leveled by population ecologists at the strategic choice and deliberate environment–organization adaptation models. Adaptation takes place, or not, as a function of the structure of the network of relationships and of the external constraints in the environment (and presumably of how fast they change). Although individual rationality is usually assumed, organizational rationality does not necessarily follow. Information asymmetry, misunderstanding of the strategies of other actors and differences in goals among individuals allow for loose coupling and unstructured decision-making processes. Action can emerge and generate random variation in the system, which in turn helps its adaptation. Events can thus unfold and be incorporated into the relational system, which then in turn responds to them (March and Olsen 1980; Weick 1979).

By providing a very rich yet simple analytical theory of intra-organizational influence processes, the power dependence school addresses (albeit often implicitly) the seven criteria for a relevant theory of the management of DMNCs. Beyond these criteria, the power-and-dependence model holds a clear attraction for MNC management scholars, who have usually originated from a phenomenological rather than disciplinary perspective and have an applied rather than theoretical focus.

First, the power-and-dependence model's assumptions about human beings and the nature of organizations seem more realistic than those of other models, including the strategic choice model. The assumptions about human beings as purposively rational and self-interested but with differentiated personal goals and operating in a boundedly rational fashion are realistic to those familiar with organizational life. The assumption of an organization as a network of relationships among members of the organization, where uncertainty-reducing information is a resource and a source of influence, is also useful. In particular, it makes it possible to incorporate information-processing theories of MNCs (Egelhoff 1988a) into broader theory. The fact that the network of relationships may extend outside the organization to key players in its environment is also realistic.[1]

Second, the power-and-dependence model is seductive to MNC management scholars because it clearly holds application potential. It is both a theoretical and an applied model: that is, it can easily drive action. Analyzing and understanding the network of relationships that constitute the organization and discovering the strategics followed by participants in the games played along these relationships allow the researcher to start considering how the stakes and perceptions of the players can be modified and to simulate how changes in the rules of the game and in the active relationships in the network would affect outcomes (the overall behavior of the system of relationships). This is clearly a powerful set of tools for implementing actions in MNCs, in line with an applied perspective.

Gains in realism and applicability offered by the power-and-dependence theory, however, as compared to the other strands of organization theory applied to MNCs, come at the cost of a loss of simplicity and theoretical power. The detailed analysis of internal relationships, and the careful categorization of players (which do not easily match organizational lines) require clinical research of a very detailed variety not easily carried out by most organization researchers. Simpler models of power relationships in and between organizations (Dahl 1957; Pfeffer 1981), provide a less grounded argument than Crozier's but make the model's integration with other theories easier and more explicit. Pfeffer's work, for instance, introduces explicit contingency dimensions and can be seen as a detailed analytical approach to the solution of agency problems.

The influence of the resource dependence and power approach on scholars of MNC management is rather obvious. Early work on the responsiveness–integration dilemma in MNCs conceptualized the issue as one of relative power (Prahalad 1975) and discussed adaptation to contradictions in the environment as achieving a 'power balance' between geographic and product-line executives (Doz 1976, 1979). Work on matrix organizations in DMNCs used a rather similar set of premises (Davis 1974; Davis and Lawrence 1977). Thus the research on MNC management process has drawn extensively on the power-and-dependence literature. Similarly, issues of strategic control of affiliates have been using the power-and-dependency model extensively (Doz and Prahalad 1981; Negandhi 1980).

Although less explicitly connected to process research on DMNCs, the research on external power and dependence, in particular Pfeffer and Salancik (1978), is also quite relevant to research on DMNCs, models of external control and dependence being used, for example, by Prahalad and Doz (1980) in their study of different relational modes between headquarters and subsidiaries in DMNCs.

Organizational Learning and the DMNC

Of the various major strands of organization theory, the organizational learning literature is the only one to focus primarily on change and development. Although the discussion of environment–organization adaptation is common to all, other strands of the literature usually start from a static perspective and do not empirically address learning, change and development processes, with the exception of some recent institutionalization theorists (Scott 1987a).

This may be partly because most scholars of organization learning take the view that learning and development are essentially individual, but in the context of an organization, whereas other theories have a more aggregate view of learning, and ignore the issue altogether. Recent work stresses that learning involves adaptive processes at all levels of the organization (Levitt and March 1988), and that the institutionalization of learning takes place through organizational routines into which inferences about past successes and failures are embedded (Nelson and Winter 1982). Organizational routines then guide behavior. Levitt and March (1988) also point out why and how the concept of organizational learning itself is fraught with problems. Learning along a wrong trajectory leads to 'competency traps'. Inductive learning from experience by individuals is often far from accurate, largely because real causality linkages may be much more complex and interdependent than those inferred by observers and participants in an organization. Satisfying behavior leads to superstitious learning: that is, the first plausible explanation of successful outcome is accepted as true. Further, the assessment of outcomes as successful or unsuccessful may be very idiosyncratic and personal. Finally, the diffusion of results from learning in organizations is far from perfect, and learning results decay if they are not frequently used. Indeed, the process of deepening the knowledge of an organization (from information to understanding) often conflicts with the process of sharing such knowledge within the organization (Chakravarthy and Kwun 1989).

Although the organizational learning literature, as opposed to the individual learning literature, is still in its infancy, it holds tantalizing promises for the MNC management scholars. It has been loosely argued (e.g., Ghoshal 1987) that a key asset of MNCs is their opportunity to learn from multiple markets and multiple environments, in particular as they build differentiated networks to achieve such learning (Ghoshal and Nohria 1990). In our view, the applicability of the organizational learning literature is limited by its content-free nature: that is, the object of learning remains unspecified. In the context of the MNC the extent and process of learning may be quite different according to content. A lot of local autonomous learning may be vital to marketing success, whereas local experimentation and learning on safety of operations may be lethal if technical operations are invariant between countries. The blend of responsiveness and integration in various tasks drives the need for autonomous, localized learning and for sharing such learning in those tasks. Processes for learning may need to be different for geography-based learning, for learning about management systems and processes that have to reflect both integration and responsiveness needs, and for rather invariant disciplines, such as safety procedures. More research is needed on both organizational learning processes in general and their application to MNCs.

Overview

Table 2.1 summarized the preceding assessment of the major streams of research in organization theory from the perspective of strategic management in DMNCs. With the exception of population ecology, where the level of analysis makes our criteria less applicable unless one applies the theory to subunits within a DMNC (which was assumed in our treatment of population ecology in Table 2.1), most other streams of research do not contravene the seven criteria established at the beginning of our analysis. However, the managerial usefulness of these theories varies greatly.[2] Although they differ deeply in their premises, as well as in the levels of analysis they cover (see Figure 2.1, on the vertical axis), most streams of organization theory share a few key characteristics that make their applications to the study of management in MNCs somewhat difficult.

First, with the exception of contingency theory and of some recent developments of institutional theory, these theories fail to operationalize the theories into a model, or a framework, in terms other than the statistical. As a result they are relatively weak at the operational construct level: that is, the linkage between theory and empirical analysis (the horizontal axis on Figure 2.1). When the object of study is homogeneous groups of organizations that are relatively similar (e.g., local administrative units and agencies in public administration) and not excessively complex, it is indeed quite feasible to move between variable specification and measurement and theory directly, using simple statistical tests. This is clearly less feasible when dealing with heterogeneous groups of complex organizations, or when focusing on their management. Midrange constructs are needed to conceptualize and model the behavior (both strategic and organizational) of complex organizations and to be managerially relevant (Bourgeois 1979). In summary, studying large numbers of relatively similar, relatively simple organizations leads one to very generalizable theories, but these theories treat the organizations as a 'black box' and do not develop detailed knowledge of how organizations work. What is needed from a managerial research stand-

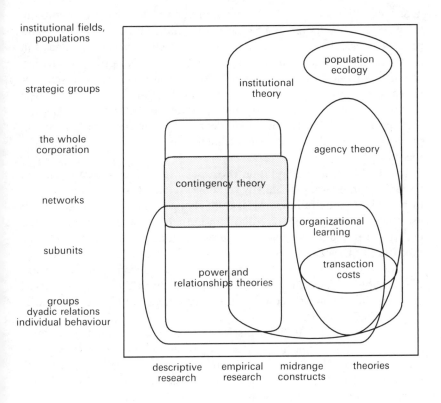

institutional fields,
populations

strategic groups

the whole
corporation

networks

subunits

groups
dyadic relations
individual behaviour

descriptive   empirical   midrange   theories
research   research   constructs

Figure 2.1   Levels of aggregation and theory development

point is a robust conceptual model of how the DMNC works: a model
that researchers and managers can play with to simulate reality.

Although we did not review it here, much of the literature on
multinational management suffers from an opposite but almost symmetrical problem. Although it is long on descriptive analysis, it is short on
theories and even shorter on midrange constructs. As a result, many
clinical studies of MNCs amount to little more than compendia of
descriptive case studies, and the few large sample studies focusing on
the management of MNCs often suffer from lack of conceptual and
theoretical integrity (e.g., Negandhi and Baliga, 1980). What is required
is a mid-range theory that bridges the gap between descriptive analysis
and theories and can span various levels of aggregation, from individuals
and small groups within MNCs to clusters of MNCs following conceptually similar strategies.

Second, the streams of organization theory, although conceptually relevant, need a more detailed way to address process variables and process issues. Key managerial processes, such as resource allocation (both financial and human) or conflict resolution processes within organizations need to be captured by the theory. With the exception of the models based on power and relationship analysis, organization theories usually operate at too high a level of abstraction to capture such processes. Furthermore, they do not, for the most part, focus on processes, with the exception of institutional, power, and learning theories.

Third, change and adaptation processes need more explicit attention. Organization theories are mostly static, geared to cross-sectional analysis rather than to longitudinal processes of change. Although it is possible to use these theories to analyze and conceptualize change processes, such use requires many intermediate steps of conceptualization, with the exception of the organizational learning and power/relationship streams.

Fourth, most theories of organization do not accommodate substantive variables: that is, they do not overcome the false dichotomy observed between context and process in the strategy literature. Context variables are captured, if at all, by abstract proxies.

Last, although the tests have seldom been made systematically, some aspects of organization theory may well be culture bound. For example, the assumption of self-interest and opportunism, critically important to transaction cost theory, may be deeply rooted in an economic and legal tradition quite specific to the professions in the USA.

In summary, the review of the main strands of the organization theory literature suggests the need for mid-range theories of the working of DMNCs, emphasizing constructs and frameworks and linking a potentially very useful set of theories with the often insufficiently conceptual and theoretical descriptive analyses performed by the observers and analysts of DMNCs. An effort at developing such a mid-range theory is summarized in the next section.

THE SEARCH FOR A PARADIGM

Our review of the various streams of organization theory research shows them to be implicitly suited to the study of the DMNC. Although none of them takes the DMNC as an object of study, they all address issues that can be transposed to the DMNC context: in particular, issues of part–whole relationships and of integration and differentiation in managing these relationships.

However, none of these theories allows a complete transfer to the study of DMNCs. We found these theories wanting on several key dimensions:

(a) importance of mid-range constructs to managerial understanding and action;
(b) attention to management process issues;
(c) attention to longitudinal change and adjustment processes;
(d) incorporation of substantive strategic and environmental variables, not just abstract categories of environments;
(e) need to avoid being culture bound, which may apply both to theories based on US views of economics (e.g., transaction costs) or, for example, to French views of organizational power (e.g., Crozier).

The Development of MNC Management Research: Towards a New Paradigm

Although early scholars of the MNC phenomenon (e.g., Fayerweather 1960; Perlmutter 1969; Wilkins 1970) had developed organizational process categories and identified the essential tension between fragmentation and unity in managing MNCs, the bulk of researchers' attention was then focused on economic and competitive models of the MNC, building on the seminal works of Hymer (1960) and Vernon (1966). It is only much later, following the development of contingency theory and the emergence of a process school of policy research (e.g., Bower 1970) that empirical research on the organization and management processes of MNCs started anew.

The line of research, starting with the work of Prahalad (1975), is united on the common theme of organizational processes and organizational capabilities in MNCs but focuses on various aspects of the general management task in MNCs. A full summary of the findings of this research is not the purpose of this chapter, but a few words putting the various contributions to that line of research in perspective may be useful. In particular, understanding the stream of process research on the management of DMNCs is complicated by the lack of discipline among researchers in the choice of labels to describe the concepts and in the language systems used. Further, the language systems used by individual researchers have also evolved over time as their understanding progressed. This can give a casual reader the impression of a lack of conceptual unity to the whole line of research.

Prahalad's research (1975) focused on the processes by which the management of a single business, not subject to intense host government constraints, perceived changing environment demands and responded to them by redirecting the attention of managers, refocusing the strategic direction, and realigning power and influence processes, consistent with the new environmental conditions. The work of Doz (1976, 1979) analyzed, on a comparative basis, the management processes used in several companies, and in several businesses in each company, to manage the tension between economic and technological pressure for globalization and integration and host government demands for responsiveness to national industrial policies. Doz (1979, 1980) then analyzed how differences in competitive positions between firms in the same industry affected their response to the tension outlined above. Bartlett (1979) compared the management systems and processes used in a sample of companies in industries differently affected by global integration and national responsiveness demands and also analyzed how different functions were affected by these pressures and further extended the understanding of redirection processes initiated by Prahalad (1975) and Doz (1978). Mathias (1978) compared redirection processes initiated by top management with processes emerging from tensions among middle managers in the organization without top management's playing an active role in the initiation of change processes. Bartlett then considered how what he called the 'institutional heritage' of a firm constrains the development of new capabilities and constituted a form of 'organizational inertia' that top management has to take into consideration (Bartlett 1981).

Ghoshal (1986) added a detailed analysis of innovation processes, stressing the existence of different patterns of interactions in the innovation process between affiliates and headquarters and among affiliates. This led to a more general analysis of DMNCs as differentiated networks (Ghoshal and Nohria 1990), and to the discussion of network theory as applied to DMNCs (Ghoshal and Bartlett 1990).

Finally, the research of Hamel and Prahalad (1990) led to reconceptualization of the basis for global competitiveness away from resource deployment to skill development and leverage, and both that work and that of Doz and Prahalad (1988) stress the importance of organizational capabilities in this process.

Simultaneously, but largely independently, a rather similar line of process research developed in Sweden which was based on the clinical analysis of the internationalization of major Swedish companies. Initially much of this work was concentrated on empirical tests of the validity of various propositions stemming from previous research (e.g., that a subsidiary's managerial autonomy would be inversely correlated to cross-shipments of goods between that subsidiary and other parts of the organization) or of grounded propositions stemming from detailed case studies of Swedish MNCs (e.g., Hedlund 1981). However, some interesting theoretical developments followed from the empirical research, in particular the concept of the 'heterarchic' DMNC (Hedlund 1986; Hedlund and Rolander 1990), emphasizing the geographic diffusion of corporate functions, a wide range of 'between market and hierarchy' governance modes and an emphasis on action learning and on variation, selection and retention processes in organizational adaptation.

Although this enumeration of issues, authors and research work may look somewhat disjointed, it is important to understand its cumulative nature and underlying logic. The process of research has been to start initially with relatively discrete, researchable building blocks, bounding both the territory researched and the complexity of the concepts and constructs developed. Each step then constitutes an attempt to challenge, extend and enrich the preceding steps by taking their findings to a broader more complex set of issues, and adding to the existing concepts based on a richer understanding of their applicability.

Although each research piece illuminates only an aspect of the managerial task in DMNCs, taken together the work of Prahalad, Doz, Bartlett, Ghoshal, Hedlund and Hamel provides us with a rich organizational theory of the DMNC, and with a detailed understanding of managerial tasks in DMNCs.

The emerging paradigm that results from this cumulative work has a few key characteristics. First, substance and process in a DMNC are captured using the same underlying framework. The underlying business characteristics can be mapped using the 'Global Integration–Local Responsiveness' (I–R) framework (for a summary, see Prahalad and Doz 1987). All the elements that contribute to the pressures for global integration needs, such as economies of scale, universal products, privileged access to raw materials, global customers, technology intensity and presence of global competitors, are supported directly in the literature on competitive dynamics and strategy. *The framework considers all factors that contribute to the pressure for global integration simultaneously, rather than one element at a time, as is common in the literature.* Similarly, pressures for local responsiveness needs, such as distribution differences, local customs, differences in customer needs, market structure and host government demands, also find support in the literature and are *considered simultaneously*. Further, the relative importance of the integration and responsiveness pressures can be used to *map industry characteristics*. The critical difference between this approach and traditional research approaches is that it explicitly recognized the need for integrative optimization between multiple and often conflicting pressures in a business. *Studying the process of balance across apparently conflicting demands is seen as more important than studying the management demands created by one element of the business (e.g., technology intensity) at a time.*

Second, the same framework can be used to chart the changing nature of a business, by evaluating the shifts in the relative balance among the forces that contribute to the integration and responsiveness needs and their impact on various key functions within a business (such as R&D, manufacturing, or marketing). Furthermore, one can analyze management systems in a DMNC, and in its various countries of operation, functions and businesses, and assess whether these management systems form a context consistent with the external demands, given business conditions and competitive positions.

The causes of enduring mismatches between external demands, strategic choices and management systems and the refocusing and realignment processes used to adapt to, or to anticipate, new environmental demands have been part of the emerging paradigm throughout (Prahalad 1976; Doz 1978; Doz and Prahalad 1981; Doz, Bartlett and Prahalad 1981 among others). *In that sense the emerging paradigm can be used both cross-sectionally, to compare industries, business strategies and management systems and processes at one point in time, and longitudinally to map out, analyze and understand change and adaptation processes.*

Next, *the basic unit of analysis of the paradigm is the individual manager, rather than an abstraction at a higher level of aggregation.* Thus the primary purpose of organizational processes – formal structure, administrative tools, decision making culture – can be conceptualized as influencing the mind sets or the *cognitive orientations* of managers, legitimating a currently dominant *coalition* of managers representing a certain strategy that is pursued, and representing the authority structure and *power* to allocate resources. Organization can then be conceptualized as consisting of these three subprocesses. We can make the following generalizations.

1. Formal structure in an organization (organization structure) is nothing more than a shorthand way of capturing the underlying subprocesses: managers' mindsets (and the attendant information infrastructure in the firm), a consensus on strategy, and power to allocate resources consistent with strategy. As a result, managers consistently desire to have 'pure organizations' (be they worldwide business or area organizations) because these pure organizational forms describe the three orientations of managers unambiguously (Prahalad and Doz 1987).
2. Managers believe that a matrix organization is complex, because in a matrix the three subprocesses – cognitive orientations, strategic

consensus, and power – are not aligned with the lines in an organization chart. Managers must understand the subprocesses in the matrix, independent of the formal structure. Irrespective of the formal structure, as shown in the organization chart, these three subprocesses continue and must be explicitly managed. Top managers must deal with the subprocesses and individual managers. This need to deal at the level of subprocesses in the organization makes a matrix complicated for managers who are not skilled at operating at the level of subtlety and detail.

3. Strategic change requires that managers change the cognitive orientations of a constellation of managers, gain a new consensus on strategy, and realign the relative power balance among the various groups involved in the interaction in the business.

4. Subprocesses in the organization can be effectively managed by the use of administrative tools such as planning, budgeting, information systems, rewards and punishments, training, career management and socialization (Doz and Prahalad 1984). The implication is that major strategic redirection can take place without a formal structural change.

5. The nature of interaction and the intensity of information flow between subsidiary and head office and across subsidiaries is a reflection of the strategic missions assigned to various units (Ghoshal and Nohria 1990). Even within a single business, all country organizations need not have the same strategic mission, and the differences will be manifest in the pattern and intensity of information flow. Patterns of information flow are predictors of the cognitive orientation of managers (which depends on the information infrastructure to which they have access), the strategic consensus process (i.e., where are the sources of tension, and who is involved in resolving the tensions), and the relative power balance to allocate resources.

Fourth, the whole paradigm is focused on mid-range constructs. It does not pretend to develop a universally applicable all-encompassing theory of organization but, much more modestly, to provide a set of integrative constructs allowing the observation, analysis, understanding and normative assessment of interaction processes between managers in DMNCs. As such it provides a mid-range theory, useful for linking strategic issues with theoretical bases (Bourgeois 1979).

Finally, it is not possible to ensure that a theory is not culture bound. It may be culture bound in its observations or in its observers. Scholars of DMNC management belong to a wide range of nationalities and cultures and have researched MNCs with a variety of home countries.

Several research contributions (e.g., Bartlett and Ghoshal 1989) have built cultural variety in their research design by systematically comparing US, European, and Japan-based MNCs. Although this design does not offer a full guarantee against cultural bias, at the very least it decreases the odds of bias due to cultural boundaries.

CONCLUSION: MNC MANAGEMENT RESEARCH AND ORGANIZATION THEORY: A MISSED OPPORTUNITY FOR CROSS-FERTILIZATION?

In the second part of this chapter we stressed that most organization theories were compatible with the characteristics that make the DMNC different from simpler organizations as laid out in the first part. It was not so much the features of the theories as the perspective adopted by the proponents of these theories which made their application to DMNCs difficult. Researchers studying the management processes of MNCs had borrowed more from organization theories than they, or for that matter organization theorists, are likely to acknowledge. Why such a surreptitious rather than explicit convergence?

Theoretical Dogma versus a Theoretical Phenomenology

We believe that organization theorists have remained too involved with the development of their theories, whereas many (if not all) scholars of MNC management have underexploited the theories available to them. The former have typically studied much simpler organizations than DMNCs, whereas the latter have often been engrossed in the complexity of what they studied and have failed to develop or borrow a sufficiently powerful conceptual framework to shed light on the observed phenomenon. As a result, the bridge between the MNC phenomenon and organization theory was not built.

Managerial versus Institutional Concerns

The difference in perspective between organizational theorists and scholars of the MNC also extends to the purpose of their theories: MNC scholars have usually undertaken to 'educate' practice (i.e., they have put managerial relevance before theoretical elegance). The converse is true of most organizational theorists. This difference made the dialogue more difficult.

Theory Building versus Theory Testing

By and large, scholars of MNC management have used data to develop their understanding of the phenomenon and then to illustrate their concepts to facilitate their presentation. There were essentially no attempts at propositions and hypotheses. Theory development progressed by attempts at refutation and by tentative extensions. Some researchers were not concerned with testing hypotheses (their priority being to provide a useful, insightful perspective on the MNC phenomenon rather than to delimit its exact contours or specify all its characteristics). Most deemed the testing of hypotheses premature or too difficult given the complexity of MNCs and the large number of control variables. As a result, the line of research lacks rigor in measurement techniques. The work of Ghoshal (1987) constitutes a useful shift of emphasis toward measuring and testing. Overall, it is only very recently that researchers have undertaken to test systematically some of the key propositions from process research on DMNCs (Chapter 10 in this volume). More of this work can be done now since the conceptual structure exists to enable scholars to understand the management processes in DMNCs.

Research Complexity versus Simplicity

Process research on the DMNC is complex, costly, and not always consistent with the funding and reward processes at many academic institutions. It is also demanding for the researcher, involving numerous interviews and process observations in many part of the world, which only skilled field researchers can carry out effectively. As a result, management process research on MNCs has taken place only at a relatively few academic institutions with a tradition for field research, abundant funding and a specific institutional interest in MNCs. The dearth of researchers has slowed down research progress.

A Consequence of an Elusive Phenomenon?

Observers have noticed that both the managerial cognitive maps and managerial tools within MNCs and the focus of attention of MNC scholars have shifted over time, without much clarity as to which influenced the other (or maybe they influenced each other over time). The underlying difficulty is the evolutionary nature of the MNC phenomenon itself. For example, the shift in MNCs from relatively long-term positions rooted in access to resources or in economies of scale to a succession of shorter-term positions built on intangible assets puts very different demands on management. The evolution of communication and information technologies may allow very different responses to existing problems and change management approaches. It is therefore not even clear that the search for a stable organization theory of the MNC is warranted. Perhaps researchers ought to satisfy themselves with addressing an evolving agenda of managerial issues created by changes in conditions for the success of MNCs and by the evolving technologies for their management.

Notes

1. For example, researchers on MNC management have observed that head-quarter–subsidiary relationships in the MNC could not necessarily be understood without an explicit analysis of the relationship with major customers and the governmental authorities of countries in which the subsidiaries operate. Country managers may use their privileged relationships with the local subsidiary's environment to limit the influence that headquarters, or other affiliates, may exert on its operations. Since the relationship is not transparent, such opportunities to leverage external relationships internally lead managers to seek out their environment in ways that increase their own influence in the organization. In so doing, they contribute to making the organization more responsive to the constraints and opportunities in the environment. Strategic choice is not central: it results from individual strategic choices made by individual players in selecting and adapting to their relevant environment.
2. Obviously most organization theorists would not consider managerial usefulness a relevant criterion of evaluation since they do not set out to analyze, enlighten or improve managerial behavior, but rather to analyze the behavior of organizations.

Part I

Environment and Organization–Environment Interactions

3 Institutionalization Theory and the Multinational Corporation*

D. Eleanor Westney

Over the last decade and a half, analyses of the strategy and organization of MNCs have increasingly widened their scope to incorporate detailed institutional portrayals of business environments. Relatively little of this work, however, has drawn on the simultaneously evolving body of sociological theory concerning the relationships between organizations and environments. Indeed, the two fields seemed to moving in different directions. As researchers into multinational enterprises focused their level of analysis on the study of businesses and product lines within the MNC, organization theory increasingly raised the level of analysis above the level of the individual organization to populations or fields. Scholars working on MNC organization tended either to remain within the 'strategy–structure' tradition of contingency theory or to move away from the detailed studies of formal structure that had dominated earlier work in favor of an emphasis on strategy and process, whereas macro-organization theory concentrated increasingly on structure (organizational forms, institutionalized patterns, the structure of networks) and paid less and less attention to strategy.

However, the two fields have more to say to each other today than such a superficial portrayal might suggest. Among those who study MNCs, the growing recognition that it is easier to develop appropriate international business strategies than it is to build organizational systems to carry them out is increasing the awareness of the potential contribution of organizational theories that analyze constraints on organiza-

*This chapter is based on a paper first presented at the Academy of International Business annual meeting in 1988. Its present form owes much to the discussions at the INSEAD workshop on Organization Theory and the Multinational Corporation in 1989, especially to the comments of Dick Scott, Chris Bartlett, Cathy Enz, Gunnar Hedlund and Bruce Kogut. Woody Powell also made some extremely helpful suggestions.

tional forms and structures. And the widespread sense that we have
entered an era of major shifts in organizational patterns in the highly
industrialized societies, shifts fostered by growing international competition and interpenetration and by rapidly changing technology, has
broadened the interest of business scholars in macro-organizational
paradigms and the interest of organizational theorists in analyzing large
complex business firms.

This chapter presents a brief explication of the most recently developed of the macro-organizational paradigms, institutionalization theory,
identifies some aspects of the paradigm where the study of the MNC and
of international business environments suggest the need for further
conceptual development in the theory, and sets out three international
management issues to which the institutionalization paradigm can make
a significant contribution: the problem of standardization versus local
tailoring of the organizational structures of subsidiaries; learning across
borders; and the relationship between the state and the multinational
enterprise.

INSTITUTIONALIZATION THEORY

Institutionalization theory begins with the premise that organizations are
social as well as technical phenomena, and that their structures and
processes are not shaped purely by technical rationality. But whereas
earlier critics of technically deterministic approaches to organization
tried to explain departures from technical rationality by looking inside
the organization (to factors such as informal social structure or power
relationships within the organization), institutionalization theory looks
first to the social context and focuses on 'isomorphism within the
institutional environment' (Zucker 1987, p. 443), whereby organizations
adopt patterns that are externally defined as appropriate to their
environments and that are reinforced in their interactions with other
organizations.

As W. R. Scott has pointed out, the analysis of organizations as social
systems was considerably slower to move towards this kind of open-
systems model than was the analysis of organizations as technical
systems (Scott 1983). In the latter field, the early 1960s witnessed the
development of 'input–throughout–output' paradigms that analyzed the
effects on organizational structures and processes of the organization's
interdependence with its environment in terms of resource inputs and
outputs. However, only in the second half of the 1970s did a distinct
paradigm emerge to address the social interdependence of organizations
and environments. While institutionalization theory is still at a relatively

early stage in its development, and there is only limited consensus on the details of its causal dynamics, some basic premises have emerged.

One is that the 'environment' is itself organized: that is, it is populated by organizations that have 'relationships', not simply transactions, and it is the source of normative pressures on organizations and of normative and cognitive constraints on their consideration of alternative structures, thereby influencing organizations towards 'isomorphism' (the adoption of structures and processes prevailing in other organizations within the relevant environment: Zucker 1987). In the vivid metaphor developed by Meyer and Rowan in one of the seminal pieces in institutional theory, the environment provides 'the building blocks for organizations' (1977, p. 345).

The nature of the environmental pressures toward isomorphism are still in the process of specification and elaboration. DiMaggio and Powell (1983, pp. 150–4) have proposed three categories of institutional isomorphism: *coercive* isomorphism, where organizational patterns are imposed on organizations by a more powerful authority, usually the state; *normative* isomorphism, where 'appropriate' organizational patterns are championed by professional organizations; and *mimetic* isomorphism, where organizations respond to uncertainty by adopting the patterns of other organizations defined as 'successful' in that kind of environment.[1] More recently, Scott (1987b) identified seven isomorphic processes. Three are analogues of the DiMaggio and Powell categories: '*imposition* of organizational structure' is equivalent to coercive isomorphism, '*acquisition* of organizational structure' to mimetic isomorphism, and '*authorization* of organizational structure' to normative isomorphism. Scott adds the '*inducement* of organizational structure' (where an organization that lacks power to impose patterns on other organizations instead offers inducements such as funding or certification); '*incorporation*' (where 'organizations come to mirror or replicate salient aspects of environmental differentiation in their own structures'); '*bypassing* of organizational structure' (where institutionalized and shared values can substitute for formal structure); and '*imprinting*' (period effects on organization, where an organizational form retains some of the patterns institutionalized at the time its industry was founded). 'Imprinting' has been explored at the industry level by Stinchcombe (1965) and at the country level by theorists of late development (Gerschenkron 1962; Dore 1973; Cole 1978) and by some recent work in international management on country effects on the competitiveness of firms (Kogut 1988 and forthcoming).

A recent formulation of institutional theory by Scott and Meyer (1989) provides a useful way of categorizing these seven processes. Scott and Meyer identify two major complementary strands of institutional theory, which are represented in these processes. One emphasizes the role of external 'institutional agencies' in the organization's environment, which try to shape organizations. Three of Scott's seven processes – imposition, authorization and inducement – share this emphasis. The other emphasizes the processes whereby those within organizations come to take certain externally validated organizational structures and processes for granted or to value them as ends in themselves. Acquisition, incorporation and bypassing share this emphasis on initiatives from within organizations, largely in response to sustained interactions with other organizations which share the same patterns and assumptions. The seventh process, imprinting, encompasses elements of both strands of theory.

Both sets of processes are reinforced by the fact that, as institutionalization theorists point out, the environment is not only external to the organization; the environment *enters* the organization. As Scott has pointed out: 'The beliefs, norms, rules, and understandings are not just "out there" but additionally "in here." Participants, clients, constituents all participate in and are carriers of the culture' (1983, p. 16). Organizations and environments 'interpenetrate', to use the somewhat awkward phrase used particularly by those interested in the ideational components of institutionalization processes (Zucker 1988). This interpenetration is the key both to environmental constraints on organizational change and to environmental pressures for the diffusion of organizational structures and processes.

For institutionalization theorists, the appropriate level of analysis for the environment is neither the society as a whole nor the organization-set of any single 'focal' organization,[2] but some intermediate level. The term applied to this level varies. Scott (1983) has identified four in the relevant literature: 'interorganizational field' (proposed by Aldrich 1972); 'interorganizational network' (Benson 1975); 'industry system' (Hirsch 1972); and 'organizational field' (DiMaggio and Powell 1983). Scott and Meyer have proposed a fifth: 'societal sector' (Scott and Meyer 1983). Usage in the institutionalization literature seems to be converging on 'organizational field', although the precise definition of this term has yet to be agreed. DiMaggio and Powell define it as:

> those organizations that, in the aggregate, constitute a recognized area of institutional life: key suppliers, resource and product consumers, regulatory agencies, and other organizations that produce similar service or products. The virtue of this unit of analysis is that it directs our attention not simply to competing firms, as does the population approach of Hannan and Freeman (1977), or to networks of organizations that actually interact . . . but to the totality of relevant actors. (DiMaggio and Powell 1983, p. 148)

While this definition sounds very much like the social analogue of the industry, there is one very important difference: the organizational field is a *social* structure in that it involves mutual awareness of the activities that they have in common (DiMaggio and Powell 1983).[3] It is also, more problematically, a *cognitive* structure, in which participants recognize other organizations as referents and as sharing a similar set of activities.

Thus the organizational field may be coterminous with an industry, as in DiMaggio and Powell's definition; on the other hand, it may be applied to a more circumscribed field such as a regional economy (Galaskiewicz and Wasserman 1989) or to a broader group of organizations such as the Fortune 200 (Mezias 1990). Therefore defining the boundaries of an organizational field raises significant methodological problems. A key element of the definition is mutual recognition of participants that they share the same activity clusters. DiMaggio and Powell have suggested that this process of institutional definition can occur through competition, regulation or professionalization; unfortunately each of these three can produce different definitions of the field boundaries. Given this, identifying the boundaries of the organizational field is, as yet, a time-consuming process, and Powell has singled this out as a major methodological problem in the institutional paradigm: he laments that 'surely we need more expedient methods [for determining the structure of an organizational field] than several years of field research' (Powell 1988, p. 131). It is a problem that is exacerbated when the researcher begins to analyze an organizational field in which key participants operate across national boundaries, as is the case for MNCs.

Another problem for the paradigm is the challenge of identification and measurement: that is, whether institutionalization is a dichotomous variable – institutionalized or non-institutionalized – or a continuous variable, subject to varying degrees of institutionalization, and also how one knows when an organizational structure or process is in fact institutionalized. A cognitive approach to institutionalization might suggest that it is dichotomous: after all, one either takes a pattern as given or one does not. An emphasis on the normative elements of institutionalization (patterns that are infused with value) would favor the concept of a continuous variable. In either case, the measurement problem is difficult, and institutionalization theorists of both stripes tend to avoid it to some extent by implicitly regarding widespread prevalence of a pattern as an indicator of institutionalization.

Institutionalization theory is increasingly portrayed as complementary to, rather than antithetical to, paradigms of population ecology and resource dependency. As DiMaggio has pointed out, 'most institutional theorists assume that the interest of organizations in survival leads them to accede to the demands of other actors (usually organizations) on which they depend for resources and legitimacy' (1988, p. 8). Institutionalization theorists also generally expect that 'isomorphism' will be particularly strong where organizations rely heavily on one organization within their field for key resources (DiMaggio and Powell 1983; Dobbin *et al.* 1988). Institutionalization theory can therefore be seen as sharing the population ecologists' concept of environmental selection, but expanding the criteria for selection and as sharing the interest of resource dependency in exchange relationships but focusing on social exchange.

We should not, however, overstate the commonalities across the three paradigms. While institutionalization theory shares with population ecology a strong interest in inertia in organizations, much of the empirical research using its framework examines the spread of organizational innovations within existing organizations. This is an area which many population ecologists consider uninteresting, because by definition such changes do not alter the core 'organizational form' (Hannan and Freeman 1989, pp. 79–80). And though resource dependency and institutionalization paradigms share an interest in the resource linkages across organizations, those working in the first have been primarily interested in how organizations act to control dependencies and increase their decision-making autonomy, rather than in isomorphic or normative pulls across those organizations. Indeed, the institutionalization paradigm raises the question of whether the basic assumption of resource dependency – that organizations are driven by efforts to reduce dependencies and increase autonomy – might not reflect the American institutional environment in which it was developed.

The institutionalization paradigm has other integrating elements that are perhaps more important. Over the last decade there have been repeated calls for organization theory to reconcile the apparently competing perspectives of environmental determinism and voluntarism (Aldrich and Pfeffer 1976; Astley and Van de Ven 1983; Hrebiniak and Joyce 1985). While institutionalization theory leans to environmental determinism, the processes listed above clearly span a range from strongly deterministic (coercive isomorphism and imprinting) to voluntaristic (mimetic isomorphism). The institutionalization paradigm also potentially spans the micro–macro divide that has long characterized organization theory. At the individual level it examines the 'taken-for-granted' character of much of organizational structure and process; at the macro level it examines the overarching structures of legitimation and ongoing reinforcement ('structuration').

Finally, in asking the question 'What causes similarity across organizations?', institutionalization theory deals both with organizational change ('why do organizations adopt certain structures and processes?') and organizational stability ('why are organizations slow to change their structures and processes?'). It is worth emphasizing that whereas previous paradigms have attributed the persistence of organizational patterns to 'inertia' and resistance to change within the organization itself, institutionalization theory emphasizes the reinforcing role played by the environment, particularly relationships with other organizations.[4] In analyzing the adoption of organizational innovations, some institutionalization theorists (see Zucker 1988) focus on what has been called the 'institutionalization project': the efforts of subgroups within organizations, or of external agencies to enhance the legitimacy of certain patterns by encouraging their dissemination throughout an organizational field.

Early formulations of institutionalization theory suggested that the paradigm did not apply to all organizations, and that it was more powerful in explaining organizational structures and processes in some organizational fields than in others. In consequence, earlier work on institutionalization has tended to focus on state subsystems such as schools (Meyer, Scott and Deal 1983) or on non-profit organizations rather than on business firms, on the grounds that technical efficiency criteria are less clear and less salient in these areas. However, institutionalization theorists have come to recognize that even those organizations in which technical rationality is presumed to be strongest are subject to significant institutional pressures (DiMaggio and Powell 1991). Some writers have pointed out that those subunits in business firms where it is difficult to draw clear causal linkages between the activities of the subunit and the overall performance of the firm, such as marketing departments and R&D laboratories, are more likely to be subject to institutional pressures than others, such as the factory (Meyer, Scott and Deal 1983). Researchers working in the institutionalization paradigm have been increasingly turning their attention to functions of business firms in which productivity and efficiency are difficult to measure, such as due process procedures (Dobbin *et al.* 1988) and intracompany training programs (Scott and Meyer 1989), on the grounds that these will be more subject to isomorphic pressures to emulate the structures and processes of leading organizations in the field than will functions in which there are clear performance indicators. Other analyses of business firms have focused on the role of state regulatory authorities or officially chartered agencies in endorsing or prohibiting certain organizational patterns (see, e.g., Neil Fligstein's 1989 study of the role of anti-trust regulations in the emergence of the finance-based model of the diversified firm, and Stephen Mezias's 1990 analysis of the spread of certain accounting practices in the Fortune 200).

The study of the MNC should be particularly fertile ground for developing institutionalization theory: the MNC operates in many institutional environments, and provides a context in which the nature and strength of isomorphic pulls within and across fields can be analyzed. The work of the past decade on the MNC has shown a growing appreciation of the importance of the institutional context and of the patterns in the way MNCs respond to that context. The MNC as an organizational phenomenon provides a locus not only for enhancing and testing some of the better developed areas of the institutionalization paradigm, but also for confronting some of its relatively undeveloped areas, as the following section suggests.

THE MNC CHALLENGE TO THE INSTITUTIONALIZATION PARADIGM

Turning the lenses of the institutionalization paradigm on the MNC brings into sharper focus several areas in which the paradigm itself needs further development. These include the analysis of the organization that straddles organizational fields; changes in the boundaries of organizational fields; and the relationship between isomorphism and innovation.

Organizations that Straddle Fields

The intitutionalization paradigm has to date largely avoided the challenges of analyzing the diversified organization that is a participant in several different organizational fields, even within a single society. In 1983, Meyer, Scott and Deal identified as one of the paradigm's unresolved theoretical problems the fact that 'our theory is formulated as if organizational environments were unitary, but educational organizations, for instance, produce different outputs under different controls . . . We need to consider both the fragmentation built into organizational environments and the way in which it is systematically reflected in organizational structures and processes' (1983, p. 63).

The study of the MNC makes the investigation of the organizational consequences of straddling fields imperative, and provides an unparalleled venue for empirical research on the issue. Most large multinational enterprises span both countries and industries, as Doz and Prahalad have emphasized in Chapter 2. As such, they are likely to be subject to a variety of different and potentially contradictory isomorphic pulls in the different environments in which they operate.

To date, the principal basis that institutionalization theory provides for analyzing these contradictions is derived from the conceptual and empirical work on organizations operating within a fragmented or pluralistic field, in which a variety of institutional agencies advocate different patterns (Meyer and Rowan 1977; Meyer, Scott and Deal 1983; Zucker 1987). The model so derived posits that organizations respond to incompatible or inconsistent isomorphic pulls by setting up formal structures to cope with or replicate the environmental pressures (e.g., corporate legal departments that are isomorphic with the law firms with which they deal, or public affairs offices in Washington staffed and organized by former public officials). When the environmentally-induced subunit or process is incompatible with other institutionalized patterns or with structures shaped by technical efficiency criteria, the organization responds by loose coupling across subunits. In some cases the coupling is so loose that the isomorphic subunit is functionally isolated from the rest of the organization, a situation that Meyer and Rowan (1977) call 'ritual conformity' and Hannan and Freeman describe as 'the organizational equivalent of smoke and mirrors' (1989, p. 94). Where loose coupling is not possible, conflict results. Organizations turn for conflict resolution to informal structures and human relations: 'The organization cannot formally coordinate activities because its formal rules, if applied, would generate inconsistencies. Therefore individuals are left to work out technical interdependencies informally' (Meyer and Rowan 1977, p. 258).

The relevance of this model to the 'new' MNC described in the introduction to this volume is obviously considerable. The growing interdependence and coordination across MNC subsidiaries makes less and less feasible the loose coupling that has hitherto characterized many MNCs, making it possible for them to vary their subsidiaries' structures to be isomorphic with local environments. Yet the growing pressures to strengthen local linkages with customers, suppliers and sources of technology raise the costs of rejecting local isomorphic pulls. As the institutional theorist would expect, the reaction of MNCs has been to eschew reliance on formal structures (Bartlett 1986, p. 384). The growing emphasis on 'creating a matrix in managers' minds' (Bartlett and Ghoshal 1989, p. 176) suggests that MNCs are responding to the problems of competing isomorphic pulls just as the theory would predict: by relying on individuals to deal with the contradictions. On the other hand, the MNC is too large and complex to rely solely on individual-level solutions; in consequence, they are turning to intermediate-level mechanisms (task forces, systems of socialization, mandated networks) that themselves are becoming institutionalized (Martinez and Jarillo 1989). Another response seems to be to broaden the scope of mimetic isomorphism: that is, MNC managers are widening their search for systemic solutions beyond what they have conventionally defined as their organizational fields.

The analysis of how MNCs respond to these conflicting pulls provides a most promising venue for deepening the paradigm. It also raises the following questions for research: at what point do inconsistent iso-morphic pressures generate forces for change within the field? If a large number of powerful organizations suffer from inconsistent isomorphic pressures, is 'de-institutionalization' an outcome, or are new patterns institutionalized that transcend or attempt to resolve the contradict-ions?

Changing Field Boundaries

If a single organization straddles two or more organizational fields, the researcher can focus on how the organization copes with different and potentially contradictory isomorphic pulls. But when a number of organizations cross the same organizational fields, do not the bound-aries of the field begin to change? Under what conditions would we begin to redefine the key issue as organizational responses to and involvement in changing field boundaries, rather than responses to participation in multiple fields?

While the institutionalization paradigm has encouraged numerous longitudinal studies of organizations and of the emergence of organiza-tional fields, it has generated relatively little analysis of changes over time in the boundaries of existing fields. But the study of the MNC makes such analysis essential. The changes most easily assimilated to the institutionalization paradigm are the cases of regional market integra-tion, such as the EC in 1992 and the North American Free Trade Pact. These involve the establishment of new formal regulatory agencies whose jurisdiction crosses national borders and the creation of a new cognitive space: the unified market, the single competitive arena, the shared playing field.

More challenging than the cases of formal regional integration is the question of whether 'global industries' constitute a case where the boundaries of an organizational field have changed and widened to cross national boundaries. The fact that in a global industry MNCs 'spread activities among nations to serve the world market . . . [and] coordinate among the dispersed activities' (Porter 1990, p. 54) means that subsidiaries in different countries are increasingly integrated across borders, either directly or through their parent organizations not just in one company, but in those companies which aspire to be 'major players' in the industry. A growing portfolio of business school cases analyze how certain industries were 'globalized' by the cross-border integration strategies of a major competitor. In the language of institutionalization theory, in such cases the behavior of one firm in straddling borders was emulated by other firms, resulting in a major redrawing of the boundaries of the organizational field.

Moreover, a global industry, to use what has become a standard definition in the international management field, is one 'in which a firm's competitive position in one nation significantly affects (and is affected by) its position in other nations. Rivals compete against each other on a truly worldwide basis' (Porter 1990, p. 53). The shared recognition of competitors from several countries that they are, in fact, global competitors operating in the same space fulfils one condition of DiMaggio and Powell's definition (1983) of an organizational field. This shared recognition is both demonstrated and reinforced by the recent popularity of global competitive benchmarking, in which an MNC attempts to measure its own organization and allocation of resources against those of its major competitors, whatever their home country. This interaction is intensified by the fact that, in many industries, supporting organizations (suppliers, banks, advertising agencies) follow their customers abroad and emulate their strategies (i.e., in globalizing industries they attempt to offer standardized services worldwide). In other words, institutionalization theory gives us reason to expect that global industries constitute organizational fields whose boundaries have come to transcend national borders and in which there are strong isomorphic pulls on structures and processes that are not fully accounted for by efficiency criteria. Among the challenges this poses for institutionalization theory is the analysis of how such changes come about and how the emerging isomorphic pulls relate to those in the older fields. It may be that the new fields affect only a small number of very large MNCs; on the other hand, they may constitute a fundamental re-alignment of field boundaries in ways that have broad implications for most of the organizations in the older fields. The focus on the large MNCs in the international management field has perhaps obscured the issue of how changes in those MNCs affect the very large number of organizations with which they interact.

However, there is an even more challenging question about the changing boundaries of an organizational field: do global industries *in toto* constitute a single organizational field? Clearly for many firms global competitive benchmarking has come to mean not only measuring the company against leading companies in the same industry, whatever their home country, but also against 'excellent companies' in any industry. The institutional agencies of mimetic isomorphism – the business press, consulting firms, academic organizations – themselves increasingly span borders in a variety of ways and foster the spread of shared definitions and models of the international or global corporation. For example, the London Business School, INSEAD in France, Canada's University of

Western Ontario, and other leading US and European business schools offer very similar executive education programs in international management and often informally exchange teaching faculty members to do so. Researchers in international management play a sensitive role in this process: the large MNCs grant them deep research access in exchange for insights into the company's problems. In their research roles, international managers cross industry lines in their quest for cases that will cover a variety of industries and business environments; in their roles as counsellors to MNC managers they extrapolate problem definitions and apparently successful practices across those lines.

It is becoming increasingly evident that MNC managers increasingly have a shared definition of what is the most desirable model of a modern multinational and the high value they place on being seen as global, international or transnational companies – whatever the most widely accepted term at the time – is one of the drivers behind 'globalization'.

Work by Meyer and Hannan (1979) on the emergence of isomorphic pulls within the post-war world system provides some conceptual guidance, but their analysis comes from an era in which the changes in the boundaries of organizational fields can be portrayed as the consequences of a set of international organizations that exported the 'rational myths' of the Western state system (particularly, in the post-World War II era, the USA) worldwide. The emergence of global industries since 1970 provides greater variety in the patterns by which the boundaries of older organizational fields elide: few are dominated by the MNCs from a single home country. One could, however, make the case that the institutional agencies of mimetic isomorphism remain dominated by the USA, even as the dominance of US corporations in global industries has been undermined. The challenge of analyzing the complexities of the emergence and the implications of global organizational fields is therefore an arena with particular promise both for the development of the institutionalization paradigm and for our understanding of the phenomenon.

Isomorphism and Innovation

Scholars working in the institutionalization paradigm have focused their research on how innovations spread across organizations, rather than on how innovations emerge. But the application of the paradigm to complex organizations that straddle fields and that play a major role in changing the boundaries of fields provides opportunities to use it to explain the emergence of certain kinds of organizational innovation. In particular, there are two types of innovation that fall within the purview of the paradigm: innovations produced when an organizational pattern institutionalized in one field is introduced into another, and innovations that emerge when conflicting isomorphic pulls produce new structures or processes that may, in turn, become more widely institutionalized through mimetic isomorphism.

One reason for the paradigm's lack of attention to the contribution of isomorphism to innovation is its relative neglect of the processes of mimetic isomorphism (or 'incorporation' to use Scott's term), or indeed of any form of isomorphism which is not primarily driven by external institutional agencies. One reason for this neglect is that mimetic isomorphism is much more difficult to trace through a field: it offers considerably greater scope for formal departures from the organizational model being institutionalized (the informal departures associated with ritual conformity may be present as well, but they are more likely to characterize isomorphism driven by external agencies). Some of the departures may be unintended and largely unrecognized: since direct access to the organizational model is often limited (especially when the model is a successful competitor), information is likely to be imperfect and even distorted. Information drawn from the model itself is likely to be idealized, as may information from mediating organizations such as consultants or the business press. Consultants or internal information gatherers are also likely to interpret the information on the model through the filter of their own organizational templates. Other departures from the model may be deliberate efforts to adapt a pattern originating in a different organizational field (another industry or another country) to the institutional landscape of its new setting (see Westney 1987 for a more detailed discussion of the interplay between isomorphism and innovation). Of course, not all departures from the model will be innovations; some, if not most, may be the result of efforts to minimize change by adapting the new model to established organizational patterns. But even here, the established patterns cannot remain unchanged; some innovations are likely to emerge.

The Japanese MNCs establishing production and research facilities in the USA provide a set of contemporary examples. Despite strong efforts to institutionalize many aspects of their work organization, supplier relationships and technologies in their US plants, the Japanese must adjust their practices to a different labor environment (which entails hiring and training women for heavy work on assembly line jobs in the car industry, for example, and the creation of more formal evaluation and grievance procedures). They must also adapt their supplier relationships to greater geographic distances and a different legal environment (see Fucini and Fucini 1990; Gelsanliter 1990). It is more than likely that in turn, the Japanese firms may in future try to 'learn from' and adapt some of the adjustments to their organizational patterns not only for their future plants in Europe but for their Japanese plants as well, as the Japanese institutional environment changes over time (with, for example, a shortage of skilled labor, which may necessitate the greater employment of women and the move to greater flexibility of rewards, and an increase in foreign component procurement). US firms, in turn, are learning from the Japanese transplants, a process which involves further adaptation of the patterns.

When organizational patterns cross fields, isomorphism produces innovation. The MNC provides an unparalleled venue for investigating this dynamic.

INSTITUTIONALIZATION THEORY AND INTERNATIONAL MANAGEMENT ISSUES

Standardization versus Local Tailoring of Organization

The debate over the globalization versus localization of MNC organization often takes place in murky conceptual terrain. 'Localization' can mean adding more value locally (*what* gets done), using local rather than expatriate or third-country managers (*who* does it), or adopting local rather than parent company organizational patterns (*how* it gets done). There is no clear logical linkage among these three facets of localization, but the assumption is often made that the more value the subsidiary adds locally and the more dominant the local managers in the organization, the more likely the subsidiary is to adopt local rather than parent company patterns (see, e.g., Rosenzweig and Singh forthcoming).

The extent to which MNCs adopt local organizational patterns in their subsidiaries is a continuing theme in the literature on managing the MNC, from Brooke and Remmers in 1970 to Ohmae in 1990. In fact, however, there are very few systematic analyses of the adoption of local versus standardized organizational patterns in MNC subsidiaries.[5] One longstanding framing of the issue is cultural (and highly normative): organizational structures and processes must allow for the distance between local national cultures and the cultural underpinnings of the parent MNC's organization (e.g., Hofstede 1980a and b). Work in this tradition tends to focus on the need for adapting the parent company's organizational patterns to the national culture of the local environment. Another approach is political: organization becomes one of the arenas for the struggles between the desire of local managers for autonomy and the headquarters' desire for control (e.g., Doz and Prahalad 1981). In this latter formulation, local managers' resistance to the imposition of externally mandated patterns is natural and relatively undiscriminating.

Both approaches, in the language of institutionalization theory, focus on 'coercive isomorphism' or the imposition of parent company patterns on the subsidiary organization, and on local resistance to such imposition. (This, in turn, raises for the institutional theorist the issue of levels of analysis within complex organizations: organizational isomorphism that, from the viewpoint of the top management of the organization, is mimetic – emulating successful organizations in the organizational field – can be seen by subunits, such as national subsidiaries, as coercive.)

Recent work has suggested that this question of standardization versus local tailoring of MNE organization can be better understood as the result of a larger range of potentially competing isomorphic pulls (Westney 1988; Rosenzweig and Singh forthcoming). The MNC organization is the source of strong isomorphic pulls towards similarity across the organizational structures and processes of subsidiaries; these pulls are not altogether a matter of conscious choice or imposition. Brooke and Remmers noted this in their classic study of the organization and strategy of multinational enterprise: 'The foreign subsidiary will naturally have a much simpler organization, but it is likely to mirror head office to some extent . . . This mirror effect may not be produced by instructions from head office, but by an almost unconscious development along the lines of communication' (1970, pp. 40, 41). And yet each subsidiary is also operating within a local organizational field that exerts a range of isomorphic pulls on its organization.

Putting the standardization/local tailoring question into the framework of competing isomorphic pulls from the environment helps to draw attention to the fact that local tailoring may not necessarily mean adopting patterns that are dominant in local organizations, just as 'standardization' may not necessarily mean adopting parent company patterns. A local organizational field may be populated largely by MNC subsidiaries, either because there are few major local competitors or because MNC subsidiaries define their field in terms of each other rather than local organizations.[6] In such a field, the 'local' patterns that are exerting the strongest isomorphic pulls may be those institutionalized in the MNC subsidiaries, rather than those institutionalized in purely local firms.

On the other hand, the model of the 'new' MNC tries to separate the issue of standardizing organizational patterns across the MNC system from the imposition of parent company patterns. To do so it draws on a stream of work on the MNC that follows Perlmutter's seminal model of the evolution of multinationals from ethnocentric (strongly shaped by home country patterns) to polycentric (each subsidiary shaped by local patterns) to geocentric (distinctive patterns that are shaped exclusively by neither home nor host country patterns but that develop overarching and emergent commonalities across the multinational's organizational system). These assumptions tend to be built into current thinking about 'transnational' or 'multifocal' firms (see Bartlett, Doz and Hedlund 1989). The MNC that must respond simultaneously to pressures to localize its products and its value-adding activities and to achieve the technical and economic benefits of close cross-border coordination and division of labour is portrayed as 'geocentric': that is, as one which must free itself from both home and host country patterns to create a distinctive 'transnational' (Bartlett and Ghoshal 1989), 'heterarchical' (Hedlund 1986 and Chapter 9) or 'multifocal' (Prahalad and Doz 1987) organization which is not subject either to strong home *or* host country effects. Since this perspective implicitly regards the primary loci of home and host country effects on MNC organization as the cultural socialization of managers and the kinds of behaviour that are evaluated and rewarded in the MNC, the 'geocentric' or 'heterarchical' organization can counter both home and host country pulls through intensive shared socialization and training and through appropriately designed evaluation and reward structures.

Home country isomorphic pulls on the MNC organization, however, may not be readily visible to parent company managers. What appears to the home country manager as 'the way things are done' (indicating a lack of awareness of genuine alternatives) or 'the way *we* do things' (indicating a belief that the patterns are company-specific rather than country-specific) often appears to locals as the product of the parents's home country. An observation by John Harvey-Jones, former Chairman of the British-based ICI, provides an excellent illustration of this phenomenon:

> Any firm with an American subsidiary must have experienced on the one hand a continued suspicion at the British end that the Americans wish to have nothing whatsoever to do with the main group and are interested in unilateral independence – regardless of the cost to the rest of the group – which on the other hand is mirrored with equal intensity on the part of the Americans, who are convinced that the sole aim of everybody outside America is to force them to operate in a way which is inappropriate in their country. No matter how many times you tell them that you do not wish to introduce British management into the USA they are convinced that every move you make is a step in that direction. (1988, pp. 160–1)

What may seem to the home country manager to be cultural paranoia (or a 'syndrome', as Harvey-Jones calls it) may actually be a more accurate perception of the institutional grounding of the parent company's organizational patterns than exists at headquarters.

Whatever the source of the standardization, however, it is possible to put the pulls for similarity across the MNC system into the context of isomorphism. In their article on MNC organization, Rosenzweig and Singh propose a two-dimensional typology of 'pressures for consistency within the MNE' and 'pressures for isomorphism with the local environment' that is analogous to the widely-used typology of integration and responsiveness (see Chapter 2). Indeed they explicitly assimilate their typology to the earlier one by hypothesizing that isomorphism with local patterns will be stronger in multidomestic industries than in global industries, because subsidiaries in the former are more dependent on the local environment. In global industries, they suggest, pressures for consistency within the MNC will mean that isomorphism with the patterns of the parent prevails over local pulls.

Underlying the Rosenzweig and Singh hypothesis identifying cross-border isomorphic pulls with global industries and within-country pulls with multidomestic industries is the assumption, drawn from institutionalization theory, that resource exchange between organizations generates isomorphic pulls on the dependent organization. The theoretical foundation for this assumption is the role of legitimation in interorganizational relationships: organizations that follow institutionalized patterns authorized by resource-providing organizations gain access (or perhaps preferential access) to those resources.

In subsidiaries that draw most of their resources from local organizations (presumably the case in multidomestic industries), adopting the patterns institutionalized in the local organizational field would contribute to the subsidiary's legitimacy and therefore to its ability to acquire the resources it needs in its local environment. Increasingly, however, managers in industries marked by global competition are being urged to foster the capacity of subsidiaries in key countries to become 'insiders' in the local technology, information, market and even political networks, regardless of the extent to which their activities are dominated by cross-border rather than local transactions (Ohmae 1990). Their success in doing so is dependent on 'the skilful management of boundary relations and conformity to the normative codes of the relational networks in which it participates', which is Powell's characterization of an organization operating in an environment subject to strong institutional effects (1988, p. 119). In other words, even MNCs in global industries can expect to encounter strong local isomorphic pulls. Moreover, as Brook and Remmers indicate, mimetic isomorphism with home country organization occurs even in multidomestic industries.

This is not to deny the premise that there are strong isomorphic pulls across MNC units engaged in a dense network of transactions with each other, but that premise can be made on efficiency or transaction cost grounds as well as institutional grounds: transactions are less costly in time and effort between organizations or subunits that are similar (see, e.g., Flaherty 1986 on the greater ease of coordinating production across borders when the subunits involved have similar organizational structures and processes). Efficiency and institutional arguments would agree with the hypothesis that cross-border isomorphic pulls within the MNC increase with the density of interactions across subunits. Where efficiency and institutional arguments part company is on the appropriate level of analysis and on the scope of isomorphic pulls. Efficiency arguments would examine individual organizations and organizational subunits, in the expectation that isomorphism is strongly associated with the density of interactions in that particular organization or function and would therefore vary greatly across the units of analysis. Institutionalists would advocate looking at patterns in the organizational field and across subunits, with the expectation that mimetic isomorphism would operate across organizations and across subunits and functions.

Learning across Borders

The view of the MNC as a 'learning network', in which successful innovations in management as well as in products can be transferred from one subsidiary to another (Bartlett and Ghoshal 1989), raises anew a longstanding issue in comparative organization theory: when is an organizational pattern that is established in one context transferable to another? The importance of this issue is increasing with the growing internationalization of service industries, especially financial services, in which such organizational technologies as task specialization, structures for communicating and adding value to information, and personnel development programmes are the core technologies of the firm.

It is a truism that the greater the similarity of contexts, the greater the ease of transfer. In the MNC, where the transfers take place across societies, the definition of similarity of contexts has in the past focused on national culture. To the extent that institutionalization theory also emphasizes 'the preconscious understandings that organizational actors share, independent of their interests' (DiMaggio 1988, p. 3), then the institutionalization paradigm may at first seem to involve primarily a recasting of the existing literature on culture into new terminology, giving employment to numbers of postgraduate students but doing little to further our understanding of the multinational enterprise or its contexts.

However, the institutionalization paradigm does make two important contributions to the discussions of learning across borders. One is that it provides a different way of defining and assessing 'context' by focusing on the organizational relationships affected by the pattern being transferred; the other is that it directs attention to the organizational field as a level of analysis.

Here again the Japanese transplants in the auto industry provide a useful set of examples that can easily be translated into the context of the institutionalization paradigm. Japanese firms like Nissan, Honda, Toyota, Mazda and Mitsubishi are strongly committed to work organizations that institutionalize highly flexible work patterns and the involvement of workers in continuous improvements and quality control. The means taken by these firms to have their US organizations learn from the patterns of their Japanese operations have been described at length in the business press and by industrial relations scholars. Location is a key variable: Japanese firms tend to locate their plants in areas where the institutionalization of current US auto industry patterns is weak or nonexistent. This has meant either areas where unionization rates are low and the labour force unaccustomed to assembly line work (such as Tennessee and Kentucky), or areas where high unemployment and plant closures have de-institutionalized existing patterns (such as the California NUMMI plant). They have undertaken extensive pre-employment education and screening, intensive socialization in Japanese production organization (including experience in Japan for considerable numbers of blue collar workers), and continuous reinforcement of the model through exhortation and ongoing training. The role of supplier networks has rarely been mentioned in this connection, but institutionalization theory suggests that assiduous Japanese cultivation of close supplier linkages either with Japanese subsidiaries or with US firms willing to undertake total quality control, 'Just-In-Time' delivery and close interaction on component development has a role beyond the assurance of quality that is usually adduced. The supplier network that the Japanese firms want is one which reinforces and institutionalizes the production organization of the branch plant, and they are willing to expend great effort to create such a network.

The experience of the Japanese auto transplants, interpreted through the lens of institutionalization theory, illustrates the major ways in which multinationals can reinforce the processes of learning across borders:

(a) re-creation of the home country organization-set to provide local reinforcement of the transferred pattern;
(b) 'countervailing legitimation': that is, highly visible bowing to *other* highly institutionalized patterns on dimensions that are less critically

important to the firm (such as Japanese firms' growing emphasis on 'good citizenship', including contributions to local charities and amenities);

(c) Challenge and 'de-legitimation', a direct articulation of an alternative and 'better' model of organization.

However, the case of the Japanese transplants suggests the importance of the insistence of the institutionalization paradigm on examining field effects. All three of these modes of reinforcing cross-border learning are made more feasible when the number of firms entering the local organizational field is significant enough to change the field itself. In the case of the auto industry, six Japanese companies have established production facilities in the USA in an industry where there are three local firms. A single organization entering a national organizational field overwhelmingly dominated by local firms will have a far more difficult time resisting adaptation to local isomorphic pressures.

The State and the Multinational Enterprise

The role of the state is a central focus of institutionalization theory (e.g., Meyer and Hannan 1979; DiMaggio and Powell 1983; Dobbin *et al.* 1988), as it has long been in work on the multinational enterprise. But the concerns of the two fields seem, at first glance, to be very different. Work in international management has focused on the role of the state in shaping what activities are carried out by the MNC within its borders; the influence of state policy on ownership strategy and industrial relations; and opportunities for MNCs to take advantage of their operating in multiple state jurisdictions by mobilizing one state (usually its home country government) to influence the policies of other states. In other words, international management has concentrated primarily on identifying the constraints on strategic decision-making and the strategic opportunities that various state policies generate for the MNC. The paradigm has been overwhelmingly that of strategic choice.

Institutionalization theory, in contrast, has been focused on the isomorphic pulls exerted by the state on organizational structures, usually (although not exclusively) beyond the realm of conscious strategic choice, and it has made the implicit assumption that each organization operates in an organizational field bounded by a single state. The state-induced isomorphic pulls identified have been:

(a) pulls toward isomorphism with state structures;

(b) pulls towards structures approved by the state but not necessarily incorporated into state structures;

(c) 'second-order' normative isomorphism induced by state-approved certification of professionals.

The strength of the first two kinds of isomorphic pull is posited to match the salience of the state in the organizational field. For example, a recent study of the institutionalization of grievance procedures and affirmative action programmes (a study that included both private and public sector organizations in the USA) found that 'linkage to the federal government is a significant factor in the elaboration of due process rights for both public and private organizations.' (Dobbin *et al.* 1988, p. 84). The 'linkage' referred to is primarily a resource linkage, where the government is a source of contracts or subsidies or of monopoly power (for the utilities, for example).

Two critically important areas where both isomorphism towards state structures and state-mandated isomorphism operate are internal control structures and interorganizational relations. Orru, Biggart and Hamilton (1989) suggest that there are powerful state influences on interorganizational relations (their own focus is on industrial groups in East Asia, but the argument has wider application). The state is the original 'multidivisional', multi-unit organization. Both its modes of coordination among its varied constituent parts and its modes of interacting with non-state organizations exert powerful isomorphic pulls on the modes of coordination in large, diversified non-government organizations and on interorganizational relations. This 'mimetic isomorphism' is reinforced by 'coercive isomorphism' imposed through laws and regulations. States which rely on arm's-length, formal, and largely statutory modes of dealing with non-state organizations tend both to provide an important model for interorganizational relationships and to reinforce that model through regulation (as in US anti-trust law and regulation of collusive interactions across organizations). States which themselves rely heavily on non-formal, densely interactive modes of influencing the behaviour of non-state organizations tend to have regulations and laws that mirror this mode of coordination (as in Japan).

One area of inquiry which would both increase our theory-based understanding of the organizational structure of MNCs and contribute to refining institutionalization theory is to explore under what conditions MNCs respond to such isomorphic pulls by engaging in one or more of the following:

(a) resistance to state-induced local isomorphic pulls in favour of isomorphic pulls from the multinational enterprise's internal system;
(b) substantial differentiation of organizational structure in different state-induced institutional environments;

(c)   ritual conformity.

There is yet another area related to the relationship between the state and the MNC to which institutionalization theory could make a major contribution: the impact of MNCs on society. This is an issue that is attracting growing attention (at last) in the USA, thanks to the recent increase in inward foreign direct investment, particularly from Japan. The analysis of MNC effects on society has primarily been focused either on the local or the home country economies (exploitation versus multiplier effects, 'hollowing out' versus returns on investment and the maintenance of globally competitive firms: see, for example, Dunning 1981b), or on political effects (Vernon 1971; Moran 1985). The organizational effects have been less systematically explored, largely because of the lack of a theoretical paradigm such as institutionalization theory can now provide.

There are two major dimensions of the potential impact of MNCs on organizational patterns within a society. The first is the MNC role in institutionalization. MNC subsidiaries in some countries can play a major role in establishing what Meyer and Rowan (1977) called 'the building blocks of organization'. To take just one example, Canada and Australia both have unusually low levels of investment of R&D in industry, compared to the other highly industrialized countries. Economic nationalists have blamed the high level of foreign ownership of industry; their opponents have considered this charge to be refuted by the fact that local firms have rates of expenditure on R&D that are very little higher than those of the foreign firms (see, e.g., Capon *et al.* 1987). The institutionalization perspective would suggest that the dominance of foreign-owned subsidiaries in both societies has been the major influence on the institutionalization of patterns of organization and expenditure in R&D, so that local firms are following patterns institutionalized by the MNC subsidiaries.

A second aspect of MNC influence on organizational patterns is 'de-institutionalization'. The introduction of new modes of organization in MNC subsidiaries can challenge the legitimacy of existing patterns: witness the role of US multinationals in Europe in the 1960s, or perhaps the current role of Japanese multinationals in the USA. The empirical investigation of the influence of MNC organizational patterns on the level and kind of institutionalization of organizational patterns within a society over time can both contribute to the debate over the impact of multinational presence and provide a counterweight to the current emphasis on institutionalized patterns as externally imposed on organizations.

A related area of interest emerges from another issue that has been receiving increased attention in the international management field: the role of the state in the advanced industrial societies in the context of the growing concern with international competitiveness and with the future of the world economic system. In the USA, anxieties over competitiveness *vis-à-vis* Japan seem to be fostering a newly cooperative relationship between government and business. In Japan, on the other hand, the gradually increasing movement of production offshore, government efforts to hold down public expenditure, and the fear of criticism of 'Japan Inc.' are reducing the leverage of the state over the business community. And in Europe, the movement towards greater integration within the EC has the potential for lowering the leverage of individual national governments over their business communities; whether a regional regulatory structure will emerge to exert control over business behaviour within the EC is still not clear.

One element of the increased concern over competitiveness in all three regions is the fear that institutionalized organizational patterns that have served the business community (and by extension the nation) extremely well in previous years have now become handicaps in international competition, and that some kind of intervention by the state is necessary to speed up the 'de-institutionalization' of those patterns and their replacement by more effective ones. In the USA, for example, the patterns under fire include managerial focus on short-term profits (fostered in part by the government's reporting requirements and by the organization of capital markets), the training of managers (both within the firm and in professional schools), and a decision-making process that is skewed toward the domestic market. The institutionalization paradigm provides at least the rudiments of a framework for interpreting some of these efforts at change, and the analysis of these efforts can provide an arena for deepening the paradigm's ability to deal with 'de-institutionalization.'

CONCLUSION

To date, institutionalization theory has provided an evolving framework of inquiry rather than a set of tested propositions. However, its relevance for some key issues in the international management field make it a paradigm whose development is important to the field, and some of its critically important unexplored issues make it a paradigm to which the study of the multinational can make a major contribution.

Notes

1. The parallels with Amitai Etzioni's typology (1961) of organizational control systems – coercive, normative and utilitarian – are striking, and not only in terminology. Etzioni focuses on the ways in which organizations induce compliance from their participants; DiMaggio and Powell on how environments induce compliance in structures and processes from participating organizations.
2. William Evan proposed in the mid-1960s the concept of the 'organization-set', an analogue of the 'role-set' in social pyschology, to describe the organization's 'interactions with the network of organizations in its environment' (1967, p. 178).
3. What is not yet agreed is whether the term 'organizational field' should be restricted to 'a set of organizations oriented toward some collective end' (Aldrich and Marsden 1988, p. 383), or whether the term can be applied to organizations with a common set of goals and which use each other as significant social referents. If the study of institutional isomorphism is to extend to business organizations, then clearly the less restrictive definition is preferable.
4. In fairness to the organizational ecology paradigm, we should note that Hannan and Freeman's discussion of organizational inertia also recognizes the constraining role of the environment (1989, p. 67).
5. One important exception is the work of Maria Arias, whose forthcoming dissertation at Yale, 'Multinationals and the Diffusion of Organizational Forms to Third World Nations', focuses on local and MNC isomorphism in human resource management practices in Ecuador's pharmaceutical industry.
6. There is some anecdotal evidence that this has tended to be the case in Japan: in some industries local subsidiary managers, Japanese and foreign alike, have tended to regard their major competitors in the markets and in recruitment as other MNCs, rather than large Japanese firms. In such cases, they tended (at least until recently) to collect market share information and engage in competitor analysis primarily on other MNCs in Japan (based on personal communications from MNC managers in the USA and Japan).

4 The Multinational Corporation as an Interorganizational Network

Sumantra Ghoshal and
Christopher A. Bartlett

As pointed out recently by Kogut (forthcoming), the late 1980s have witnessed a significant evolution of academic interest in the MNC. An important element of this shift has been a change in the focus of research away from the dyadic headquarters–subsidiary relationship in MNCs, or the specific decision of a company to invest in a foreign location, to the coordination tasks of managing a network of established foreign subsidiaries and analysis of the competitive advantages that arise from the potential scope economies of such a network.

This new research focus demands new theoretical, conceptual and methodological anchors. Analysis of international competition, for example, has already embraced a range of new theories such as those of multiplant production, multipoint competition and valuation of options to explore the costs and benefits of the MNC's geographic scope of activities (e.g., Teece 1980; Kogut 1983; Ghemawat and Spence 1986). This chapter advocates a similar adoption of interorganizational theory for future MNC-related research, albeit with some modifications to reflect the ownership-based intra-organizational ties that exist between the MNC headquarters and its different foreign subsidiaries. We believe that interorganizational theory, properly adapted, can provide new insights into a complex and geographically dispersed organizational system like the MNC, and our main objective here is to propose an initial formulation on how the concepts and tools of interorganizational analysis can be applied to fit this slightly different but analogous case.

To frame the context of our discussions, it may be useful to begin with an illustration. Figure 4.1 shows the simplest possible representation of N. V. Philips, a multinational company headquartered in the Netherlands. The company has its own operating units in 60 countries as diverse as the USA, France, Japan, South Korea, Nigeria, Uruguay and Bangladesh. Some of these units are large, fully-integrated companies

78

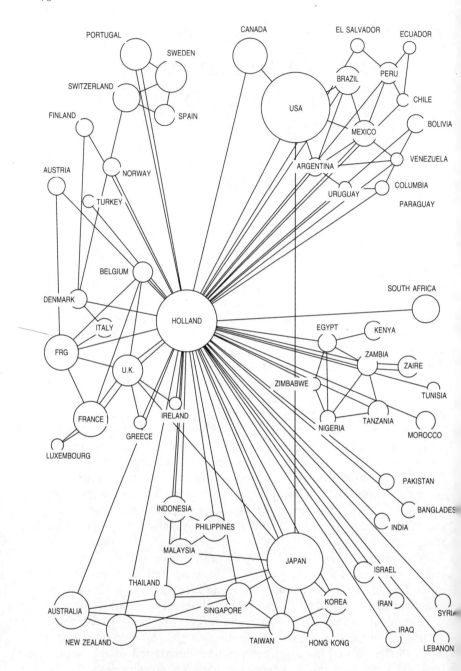

Figure 4.1   Organizational units and some of the interlinkages within N. V. Philips

developing, manufacturing and marketing a diverse range of products from light bulbs to defence systems. Such subsidiaries might have 5,000 or more employees and be among the largest companies in their host countries. Others are quite small, single function operations responsible for only R&D, or manufacturing, or marketing for only one or a few of these different businesses. Some of these units might employ 50 or fewer people. In some cases the units have been in operation for more than 50 years; a few began their organizational lives less than 10 years ago. Some of these units are tightly controlled from the headquarters; others enjoy relationships with the headquarters more akin to those between equal partners than those between parent and subsidiary.

With only minor alterations, Figure 4.1 could also be a representation of an American multinational such as Procter & Gamble, or another European company such as Unilever, or a Japanese company such as Matsushita Electric (see descriptions of these companies in Bartlett and Ghoshal 1986, 1989). In many ways our description of Philips is a generic account that characterizes many large MNCs. As suggested by a number of authors, MNCs are physically dispersed in environmental settings that represent very different economic, social and cultural milieus (Robock, Simmons and Zwick 1977; Fayerweather 1978; Hofstede 1980a); they are internally differentiated in complex ways to respond to both environmental and organizational differences in different businesses, functions and geographic locations (Bartlett and Ghoshal 1986; Prahalad and Doz 1987); and, as a result of such dispersal and differentiation, they possess internal linkages and coordination mechanisms that represent and respond to many different kinds and extents of dependence and interdependency in interunit exchange relationships (Ghoshal and Nohria 1990).

We believe that an entity such as any of these large MNCs can be more appropriately conceptualized as an interorganizational grouping rather than as a unitary 'organization', and that valuable insights can be gained into the internal structures and operations of such entities from the concepts of organization-sets and networks that are more commonly used for exploring interorganizational phenomena (Evan 1967; Aldrich and Whetten 1981). In particular, we believe that the concept of a network, both as a metaphor and in terms of the tools and techniques of analysis it provides, reflects the nature and complexity of the multinational organization and can provide a useful lens through which to examine this entity. We propose here a framework that conceptualizes the multinational as a network of exchange relationships among different organizational units, including the headquarters and the different national subsidiaries that are collectively embedded in what Homans (1974) described as a structured context. Further, following Tichy,

Tushman and Fombrun (1979), we visualize this context as an 'external network' consisting of all the organizations such as customers, suppliers, regulators and competitors with which the different units of the MNC have to interact. The main hypothesis we develop in this chapter is that different attributes of a multinational, such as the configuration of its organizational resources and the nature of interunit exchange relations that lead to such a configuration, can be explained by selected attributes of the external network within which it is embedded, and on which it depends for its survival.

A note of caution must, however, be sounded at this stage: because network analysis is a rapidly emerging and highly complex field of study and because of the considerable divergence in definitions and approaches that exists within this field, it is unlikely that this initial attempt to apply network concepts to the study of MNCs will be either complete or above reproach. In the concluding section of this chapter, we will discuss some of the limitations of the present effort and suggest how they might be overcome in future conceptual and empirical research. This chapter must be viewed, therefore, as an initial attempt to identify the possibility of developing a 'network theory of the MNC', rather than as a rigorous presentation of such a theory.

While the attempt formally to apply the interorganizational network perspective to the study of MNCs is relatively new, it should also be noted that the conceptual foundation for such an approach already exists in the international management literature. For example, Perlmutter's (1969) scheme for categorizing MNCs as ethnocentric, polycentric and geocentric organizations is clearly consistent with a network theoretic view. Similarly, the stylized models of MNC organizations developed by Bartlett (1986) and Hedlund (1986), the concept of a 'coordinated multinational system' proposed by Kogut (1983), and the application of the resource dependency model by Herbert (1984) for explaining strategy–structure configurations in MNCs have all been implicitly or explicitly grounded in the conceptualization of MNCs as interorganizational systems. While building on this foundation, the present chapter also differs from these earlier pieces in two important ways.

First, in most of these proposals, the structure and attributes of the MNC were explained as arising from the technical and economic rationality and constraints in resource allocation (Kogut 1983), or from the administrative heritage (Bartlett 1986) and cognitive orientation (Perlmutter 1969) of its managers. Our explanation focuses instead on the social and institutional structure of the environments in which the MNC operates. As institutional theorists have argued, the relational networks in the institutional environment play an important role in influencing the structure and behavior of organizations (Meyer and Scott

1983; Zucker 1988). The uniqueness of the MNC as an organizational form arises from the fact that its different constituent units are embedded in different national environments in which the structures of these relational networks can be, and often are, very different (Westney 1988). Further, in an era of expanding transnational linkages among individuals and organizations, these relational networks in the different countries are also increasingly interconnected among themselves in complex ways. These differences in national industry systems and the interconnections among them are central to our explanation of both economic action and administrative coordination within the dispersed system of the MNC.

Second, the concept of a network has so far been used in this literature mostly as a metaphor to describe and categorize MNC structures and to support normative arguments on the importance of lateral relationships, shared values and reciprocal task interdependencies for effective management of MNCs. While we believe that such a metaphorical use of the term has been useful for descriptive and normative purposes, this study represents an effort to move to the next step of theory-building by using network concepts to explain specific structural attributes of multinational organizations.

In the following section we discuss why, despite the intra-organizational ownership ties, a multinational can be legitimately conceived as an inter-organizational grouping, and draw on interorganizational theory to develop a conceptualization of the MNC as a network that is embedded within an external network. We then illustrate how this conceptualization might be applied to analysis of the extents of dispersal and specialization in the configuration of the MNC's resources, and distribution of power in the internal exchange relationships among its different units. Our arguments suggest a general model of the MNC as a differentiated interorganizational network, and this model is also described. We conclude by discussing some research implications that follow from our theoretical arguments and by suggesting some ways in which this interorganizational network perspective of MNCs can be improved and extended.

INTERORGANIZATIONAL THEORIES APPLIED TO THE MNC

Much of the existing theory and almost all empirical analyses of interorganizational networks have focused on interorganizational groupings that are not connected by ownership ties (e.g., Pfeffer and Salancik 1974; Bacharach and Aiken 1976; Van de Ven and Walker 1984). Before applying any of the concepts or empirical findings from such studies to the analysis of MNCs, it is first necessary to make a prima facie case that the ownership ties which exist within the multinational do not necessarily preclude the entire range of discretionary behaviors that are possible among interacting organizations that are not so connected.

A number of authors have argued that the linkage between ownership and hierarchical power (fiat) in complex organizations is much weaker than is often assumed (see, e.g., Granovetter 1985, p. 499). We believe that this link is particularly weak in the case of MNCs because of the large physical and cultural distances between the owned and the owning units. Case histories of extreme subsidiary autonomy have been well documented in the literature on multinationals: the refusal of North American Philips to sell the V2000 video cassette recorder developed by its Dutch parent, preferring instead to purchase from a Japanese archrival, is a good example. Even more dramatic, however, is the case of the British and German subsidiaries of Ruberoid which unilaterally severed all ties with the parent and, with the support of local financial institutions, ultimately secured complete legal independence. Such situations are relatively more common for MNCs headquartered in small countries, many of whose foreign subsidiaries often control more resources and contribute more revenues than the parent company. However, many such cases have also been observed in companies such as ITT and Unilever, even though the parents were headquartered in large countries such as the USA and the UK (Bartlett and Ghoshal 1989).

The efficacy of fiat is particularly limited in the case of multinationals not only because some of the subsidiaries happen to be very distant and resource-rich, but more so because they control critical linkages with key actors in their local environments, particularly the host government. To cite but one illustration, the Australian subsidiary of Ericsson, the Swedish telecommunications company, accumulated a very high level of R&D resources primarily because of a coalition between the local management and the Australian Post and Telegraph authorities that had as its principal goal the creation of a major R&D center in Australia. Subsidiary company links with local customers, suppliers and investors also contribute to the local management's autonomy. For example, following deregulation of the US telecommunications industry, the influence of the American subsidiary of NEC expanded significantly within the company, despite its relatively small size and short organizational life. This was so because of its role in building the company's relationships with the Bell operating companies which came to be viewed by NEC not only as major potential customers but also as its main contacts for joint development of new products.

We do not claim that the relationships between the parent company and the national subsidiaries in an MNC are identical to those among an interacting group of universities, or social service organizations or regulatory agencies. Some anecdotal evidence of extreme subsidiary autonomy notwithstanding, the parent company of a multinational typically enjoys considerable hierarchical authority. However, we suggest that the existence of such hierarchical authority does not necessarily lead to hierarchical power as the dominant or even the 'last resort' mechanism of control. Typically, in such large, dispersed and interdependent organizations, hierarchical authority coexists with significant local autonomy, and such a situation, we believe, is not inappropriate for the application of interorganizational theories.

For example, in one of the seminal articles on the topic, Warren (1967) developed a typology of interorganizational relationships that distinguished four ways in which members of an organizational field could interact: unitary, federative, coalitional and social choice. Table 4.1 summarizes the different attributes of each of these different contexts of interorganizational interactions. In our view the multinational organization lies somewhere between Warren's unitary and federative structures, both of which admit some level of hierarchical decision-making at the top of the inclusive structure. Further, even though the formal structure of MNCs may often resemble the unitary form, or what has been described in the literature as 'mandated networks' (Aldrich 1976; Hall *et al.* 1977), the actual relationships between the headquarters and the subsidiaries and among the subsidiaries themselves tend to be more federative because, contrary to the case of both unitary and mandated networks, issues of competency and power tend to be contested within the MNC and interdependencies among the units tend to be reciprocal as well as sequential (Ghoshal and Nohria 1990). This claim is consistent with Provan's analysis of different kinds of federation and his observation that the network characteristics of divisionalized firms are generally similar to those of independent federations (see Table 1 in Provan 1983, p. 83). As demonstrated by Provan, Beyer and Kruytbosch (1980), the interorganizational approach can be particularly useful for analyzing such federated relationships among units when the participants have only limited options for discretionary behavior and no opportunity to terminate the relationship.

Despite the broad theoretical scope of the interorganizational perspective as shown in Warren's classification of the field, empirical applications of this perspective have so far been limited to contexts that range from federative to social choice; interaction contexts that range from unitary to federative have been excluded from the domain of interorganizational inquiry and placed in the domain of intra-organizational

Table 4.1 Different contexts of interorganizational interactions

Dimension	Type of context			
	Unitary	Federative	Coalitional	Social choice
Relation of units to an inclusive goal	Units organized for achievement of inclusive goals	Units with disparate goals, but some formal organization for inclusive goals	Units with disparate goals, but informal collaboration for inclusive goals	No inclusive goals
Locus of inclusive decision-making	At top of inclusive structure	At top of inclusive structure, subject to unit ratification	In interaction of units without a formal inclusive structure	Within units
Locus of authority	At top of hierarchy of inclusive structure	Primarily at unit level	Exclusively at unit level	Exclusively at unit level
Structural provision for division of labor	Units structured for division of labor within inclusive organisation	Units structured autonomously; may agree to a division of labor, which may affect their structure	Units structured autonomously, may agree to *ad hoc* division of labor, without restructuring	No formally structured division of labor within an inclusive context
Commitment of a leadership subsystem	Norms of high commitment	Norms of moderate commitment	Commitment only to unit leaders	Commitment only to unit leaders
Prescribed collectivity-orientation of units	High	Moderate	Minimal	Little or none

analysis (Cook 1977). As such, the relationships between the diverse units of a multidivisional or a multinational corporation have rarely been examined from an interorganizational perspective.

Meanwhile, the limitations of applying traditional intra-organizational theory to the analysis of such complex and dispersed business organizations have become increasingly clear. As summarized by Nohria and Venkatraman (1987), the most critical of these limitations stem from the need in such analysis to provide a relatively clear separation between the 'organization' and its relevant 'environment'. As a result, 'the environment is typically viewed as an exogenous entity and is reified as a source of undefined uncertainties (e.g., volatility, resource scarcity, etc.) as opposed to being seen as a field of specific interacting organizations which locate the source of those contingencies' (Nohria and Venkatraman 1987, p. 2). The organization is seen as a well-defined collective and is assumed to be internally homogeneous, coherent and consistent.

> Therefore, it is typically described in distributional (e.g., organization chart, division of responsibility, authority, etc.) and categorical (e.g., centralized versus decentralized, mechanistic versus organic, differentiated versus integrated, etc.) terms as opposed to relational terms that focus on the actual interaction patterns based on both internal and external flows of products, information, and authority. (Nohria and Venkatraman 1987, p. 2)

In contrast to these limitations of traditional intra-organizational analysis, a dominant construct in most interorganizational theories is an exchange relation (e.g., Ax and By) which is defined as consisting of 'transactions involving the transfer of resources (x,y) between two or more actors (A,B) for mutual benefit' (Cook 1977, p. 64). The term 'resources' as used in this context includes 'any *valued* activity, service or commodity' (Cook 1977, p. 64) and therefore includes not only the flows of finances and products but also of technology, people and information. Furthermore, as Cook observes, 'the term actor in the theory refers not only to individuals but also to collective actors or corporate groups [thus making] it uniquely appropriate when organizations or subunits of organizations are used as the primary unit of analysis' (1977, p. 63). It is this suggestion of Cook that we adopt and develop here.

The Multinational as a Network: Constructs and Terminology

Let us consider a MNC, M, with operating units in countries A, B, C, D, E and F, and a focal organization in the corporate headquarters, H. For the purpose of analytical simplicity, let us assume that all the units of M

are engaged in a single and common business: i.e., M is a single-industry company. Note that H serves as a coordinating agency and plays the role that Provan (1983) described as belonging to the 'Federation Management Organization (FMO)' and, therefore, must be distinguished from the organizational unit, say A, that is responsible for operations in the home country of M, even though the two may be located in the same premises. By the term *multinational network* we shall refer to all the relationships and linkages that exist among the different units of M: that is, among A, B, C, D, E, F, and H.

Each of the national operating units of M is embedded in an unique context and, for any specific type of exchange relationship, has its unique organization-set (Aldrich and Whetten 1981). For example, the unit A can have existing or potential exchange relationships with a specific set of suppliers (s_A), buyers (b_A), regulatory agencies (r_A), and it competes for resources with an identifiable set of competitors (c_A). Collectively, the group consisting of $(s_A, b_A, r_A, c_A,$ etc.) constitute what we call the organization-set of A and denote by the symbol (OS_A).

Different members of the organization-set (OS_A) can be internally connected by exchange ties. Following Aldrich and Whetten (1981), we can define the density of (OS_A) as the extensiveness of exchange ties within the elements of the organization-set of A. Density measures the extent to which actors within the set are connected, on average, to one another (i.e., the mean relation from any one actor to any other actor). As suggested by Aldrich and Whetten, such a construct of density can be operationalized in different ways. For present purposes, we can choose the simplest of these ways and define it as the percentage of actual to potential ties among members of (OS_A). (The concluding section of this chapter includes a more detailed discussion on identification of boundaries and measurement of densities for the different local organization-sets.)

The density of such connections within the different local organization sets of A, B, C, etc., may vary. For example, it has been noted by many authors that the level of connectedness among different members of an industry group is significantly higher in Japan in comparison to some Western countries (see, e.g., discussions and the quotation from Lohr in Granovetter 1985, p. 497). Similarly, it has been shown in the literature that within the same national environment, the level of cohesiveness among customers, suppliers, competitors, etc., may be higher in certain businesses – such as construction (Eccles 1981), publishing (Powell 1985), textiles (Sabel *et al.* 1987) and investment banking (Eccles and Crane 1987) – than in others.

The different organization-sets of the different units of M may themselves be interconnected through exchange ties. For example, one of the supplying organizations in the local environment of A may be an affiliated unit of another MNC, and may have exchange linkages with its counterpart in the local environment of *B*. Similarly, the actions of regulatory agencies in one location (say, r_C) may influence the actions of their counterparts in other locations (say, r_D). This influence may be manifest in actions such as retaliation by r_C to what is seen as protectionist action of r_D, or deregulation of r_D to reciprocate or just emulate similar action by r_C (Mahini and Wells 1986). Such linkages may also exist among suppliers and competitors. In fact, much of the current literature on global strategy considers such cross-border linkages among customers, competitors and other relevant organizations as a key factor that does or should influence the behaviors of MNCs (this is a focal issue for a number of essays in Porter 1986).

Due to such linkages among the different local organization-sets, all members of all the organization-sets of the different units of *M* collectively constitute what we shall call the *external network* (Tichy, Tushman and Fombrun 1979) within which the multinational network is embedded. In the same manner as we defined the construct of density for each of the different organization sets of the different units of *M*, we can also describe the density of this external network as the ratio of actual to potential ties among all its constituents. To differentiate between these two densities, we shall refer to the density of ties within each of the local organization sets as *within density* and the density of ties within the total external network – that is, across the different organization-sets – as *across density*.

Our main thesis in this chapter is that different attributes of the MNC can be explained in terms of selected attributes of the external network within which it is embedded. Following the arguments of Benson (1975), the interactions within the different organizational units of the MNC are best explained at the level of resource exchange. This suggests two attributes of the MNC as particularly relevant to our analysis: (1) the distribution of resources among its different affiliated units, and (2) the structural characteristics that mediate internal exchange relationships within the MNC and continually restructure the resource configuration (Zeitz 1980). These two characteristics of the MNC and how they relate within and across densities will provide the focus of our attention for the remaining part of this chapter.

RESOURCE CONFIGURATION IN MNCs

Resources such as production equipment, finance, technology, marketing skills and management capabilities may be located in any one or more of the different units of *M*. By the term resource configuration we refer to the way in which the resources of M are distributed among *A, B, C, D, E, F* and *H* (we use the word 'resource' in the sense of Cook 1977, p. 64 to refer to 'any valuable activity, service, or commodity'). In some companies that Bartlett (1986) describes as 'centralized hubs', most of such resources may be concentrated in any one location, typically the parent company. For example, 90 percent of the manufacturing investments of Matsushita, the Japanese consumer electronics company, and 100 percent of its research facilities are located in Japan. In contrast, in companies such as Philips, Matsushita's European competitor and one that Bartlett categorizes as a 'decentralized federation', over 77 percent of total assets are located outside the company's home, which is in the Netherlands, and no single national subsidiary has more than 15 percent of the company's worldwide assets. This difference illustrates one aspect of resource configuration in MNCs that is of analytical interest, namely, *dispersal*, by which term we refer to the extent to which the company's resources are concentrated in one unit versus dispersed among the different units.

However, while both Philips and Electrolux (the Swedish home appliances company) have a relatively high level of dispersal in the sense that both companies have significant parts of their total assets distributed in a number of countries, the pattern of distribution of such assets is very different in the two cases. Let us consider their resources within Europe. For Electrolux, while the resources are dispersed, they are also very specialized: that is, the resources and associated activities located in any one country are of sufficient scale to meet the company's worldwide or, at least, regional requirements for that activity, thereby avoiding the need for carrying out the same activity or task in multiple locations. For example, Electrolux's washing machine factory in France produces top-loading washing machines only and it meets the company's requirements in that product category for all of Europe. Similarly, the washing machine factory in Italy produces only front-loading models to meet Europe-wide demand. Its research centers, product development laboratories and component producing units are all similarly differentiated and specialized. By contrast, despite considerable recent efforts to increase such specialization, Philips has five factories in Europe that produce identical or near-identical models of television sets, each basically for its own local market. In other words, the resources of Philips are dispersed on a local-for-local basis (Ghoshal, 1986): they are dispersed but undifferentiated, with identical resources being used by each unit to carry out essentially similar tasks in and for its own local environment. We refer to this dimension of resource configuration as *specialization*, and it represents the extent to which the resources located in each unit are differentiated from those in others.

Resource configuration in MNCs has traditionally been analyzed from an economic perspective, typically under the assumption that resource location decisions are based on rational, self-interested considerations such as the need for increasing profitability, gaining access to new markets or desired factors of production, protecting competitive position and minimizing costs and risks (for reviews, see Dunning 1981a; Caves 1982; Hennart 1982; Buckley and Casson 1986). Explanations of both dispersal and specialization have therefore focused on factors such as differences in costs of inputs (e.g., Stevens 1974), potential scale economies in different activities (e.g., Porter 1986), impacts of transportation and other 'friction' costs (e.g., S. Hirsch 1976), imperfections in information and other intermediate product markets (e.g., Magee 1977; Rugman 1980a), defence against opportunism (e.g., Teece 1986), and potential benefits of risk diversification (e.g., Lessard and Lightstone 1986).

Following Granovetter (1985), much of this analysis can be criticized as 'undersocialized' or 'oversocialized' conceptions that ignore the important and ongoing effects of surrounding social structures on economic behaviors of organizations. We present here an alternative framework that relates dispersal and specialization to the densities of interactions both within and across the different local organization-sets of the company. As suggested in the introductory section, our conceptualization is strongly influenced by the work of institutional theorists who have argued that the structure and behaviour of organizations are influenced by both technical and institutional factors (Meyer and Scott 1983), and that 'organizations compete not just for resources and customers, but for political power and institutional legitimacy, for social as well as economic fitness' (DiMaggio and Powell 1983, p. 150). While Meyer and Scott have been cautious in suggesting that business organizations belong to 'technical sectors' in which the economic need for efficiency and effectiveness in controlling work processes dominates institutional need for legitimacy, they have also contended that 'while the two dimensions (technical and institutional) tend to be negatively correlated, they are apparently not strongly so' (1983, p. 140). As suggested by Westney (1988), we believe that for MNCs strong needs for legitimacy and local isomorphism in each host country environment coexist with strong demand for efficiency within its worldwide system and, therefore, that the institutional structure of the environment (i.e., the attributes of the local organization sets and the external network) plays an important role in moderating the influence of technical and economic considerations. While different from traditional economic analysis, our arguments are much more consistent with the work of economists such as Porter (1990) and Kogut (1988), both of whom have shown the importance of interinstitutional structure in determining the competitiveness of different countries and companies in different businesses.

Effects of Within Density in National Organization-Sets

As Bower (1987) has shown through his in-depth study of American, European and Japanese companies in the petrochemical industry, the density of linkages among key players in a national industrial context greatly influences industry performance and company strategy. For a variety of economic, legal, sociological, cultural and historical reasons, some countries, such as Japan, are characterized by dense linkages among the suppliers, producers, regulators, customers and others involved in a particular field of industrial activity (Westney and Sakakibara 1985). Such linkages among the different actors may involve different kinds of exchanges, such as those involving funds, people or information, and they may be established and maintained through many different mechanisms, such as integrating governmental agencies, interlocking boards of directors, cross-holding of equity, institutionalized systems of personnel flows, long-term contracts and trust-based relationships, and mediating roles of organizations such as trade associations, banks, and consultants (see, e.g., the collected essays in Evan 1976). Bower's study shows how Japanese petrochemical companies were able to capitalize on these linkages not only to build entry barriers in the local market but also as a means of restructuring and rationalizing the industry.

In locations where the local organization-sets are densely connected, the implications for local units of MNCs are clear. As argued by Granovetter (1973), strong and multiplexed ties among the existing members of the national organization-sets will lead to exclusion from the sets of those who cannot establish equally strong and multiplexed ties with each member. Westney and Sakakibara's (1985) study on the R&D activities of Japanese and American computer companies illustrate this effect of within density in the local organization-sets. According to these authors, the Japanese R&D centers of some of the American computer companies could not tap into local skills and technologies because the absence of associated manufacturing and marketing activities prevented the isolated research establishments from building linkages with the local 'knowledge networks' that were embedded in the dense interactions among different members of the organization-set for the computer industry in Japan.

Where the linkages within the local organization-sets are sparse, no such barriers are created, as shown in the US Department of Commerce's account of the television industry in the USA in the early 1970s (Paul 1984). Absence of ties among producers because of rivalry and anti-trust laws, and their arm's-length relationships with suppliers, labor and government, created an environment that made it easy for Japanese producers to enter the US market with local sales offices importing finished products from the parent companies. However, when the American companies responded in a unified manner through the Electronics Industry Association, with the support of labor unions and suppliers, they were able to obtain government support on anti-dumping suits, and the resulting politically negotiated import quotas forced the Japanese companies to establish local manufacturing facilities.

We can, therefore, make the following propositions about the effects of within density on dispersal and specialization in the configuration of resources in a multinational. When interaction densities within the different national organization-sets are low, the social context exerts limited influence and intended economic rationality becomes dominant in resource configuration decisions. In this situation, therefore, the MNC will concentrate research, production, assembly and other similar activities based on consideration of potential scale and scope economies and locate them on the basis of 'resource niches' (Aldrich 1979) that may exist in different countries as a result of their comparative advantages (for example, R&D in the USA or Japan, manufacturing in Singapore or Brazil). As a result, its overall resource configuration will show relatively low dispersal and high specialization. When within densities are high, however, the company will be forced to fragment its activities and locate more of the different kinds of resource in each market so as to provide the variety that is necessary to match the structures of the local organization-sets. Consequently, in this case, dispersal will increase while specialization will decrease.

Effects of Across Density in the External Network

When the linkages across the different national organization-sets are sparse, the MNC's resource configuration follows the pattern we have described above based on consideration of the within densities alone. With high interactions across members of the different national organization-sets, this situation changes significantly.

Consider first the case of low within density and high across density. We have argued that low within density will lead to low dispersal and high specialization and the company will locate its resources according to the resource niches in different countries. However, with high across densities, many of these national resource niches tend to be eliminated because of freer flows. If technologies developing in one location can be accessed instantaneously from another, or if excess capital available in one environment can be borrowed in markets located elsewhere, there is no longer any need to locate specific activities in specific locations to benefit from access to local resources. Therefore, with high across density, resource seeking concentration will decline (although it will not necessarily be eliminated since regulatory and other barriers may selectively prohibit certain flows of people and products).

Consider now the case of high within densities coupled with high across densities. We have suggested that high within density will lead to high dispersal and low specialization because of the need for matching the structures of the local environments. However, when across densities are high, it is no longer necessary to establish a comprehensive range of resources in each market since exchange linkages can now be established across borders, without the need for complementary facilities on a location-by-location basis. In other words, with high across density, the logic of resource allocation for both high and low within densities becomes inappropriate. Instead, a completely different set of criteria emerges: in this situation, resource configuration is greatly influenced by the nodal characteristics of the complex external network.

Consider, for example, the situation when customers in locations A, B, D and E are strongly influenced by the standards and preferences of customers in location C. Bartlett and Ghoshal (1986) and Prahalad and Doz (1987) have described the existence of such 'lead markets' in many businesses, and their existence is predicted by the 'normative systems' that Laumann, Glaskiewicz and Marsden (1978) proposed as one of the modalities that influence the behaviors of members in a network. In such a situation, the MNC will tend to locate a significant amount of resources in C so as to be able to sense the demands of local customers and respond to them in a fashion that attracts their patronage. The level of resources in C will exceed what is required to match the needs for membership of the local organization-set (OS_C) and will instead be targeted to benefit from the greater role of C as a central node in the larger external network that is created by the linkages among (OS_A), (OS_B), (OS_C), etc. Given that for different activities of the MNC, different locations might emerge as the nodes in the relevant external networks, and that even for the same activity there might be multiple nodes instead of a single one, the consequence of increasing across density for the resource configuration of the company will be one of moderate dispersal (i.e., not as high as in the case of local-for-local distribution but higher than concentration only in countries offering specific resource niches) coupled with increasing specialization. Tasks will be divided into finer and finer segments so that each could be located at the appropriate nodal locations which, however, might well be different from those that would be predicted by the traditional considerations of comparative advantages or resource niches as applicable to those tasks.

Chandler (1986), among others, has documented that because of improvements in communication and transportation infrastructures around the world, increasing across densities have been a dominant trend that has affected a wide range of industries in the recent past. The observed consequences of this trend are entirely consistent with our arguments. For example, until the late 1970s, the telecommunications switching industry was characterized by high within and low across densities. Interactions among members of the industry were high within each country because of its status as a 'strategic industry' and the resulting coordinating role of the national governments. However, until the advent of digital technology, the industry was highly regulated in most countries and the need to synchronize the switching equipment with the idiosyncrasies of local terminal equipments constrained opportunities for cross-border linkages. As a result, the resources of most multinational companies were highly dispersed, with low levels of specialization. ITT provides a good illustration: each of its national subsidiaries in Europe had its own local facilities for product development, manufacturing and marketing, and the corporate staff, including the top management of the company, consisted of less than a hundred employees.

The context of this industry has changed significantly in the 1980s: while within densities have remained high, across density has increased substantially due to the emergence of digital technology and the growing trends of standardization and deregulation, all of which have facilitated cross-border integration among suppliers, customers and other industry participants. As a result, resource configurations of the producers have also changed. While the overall level of dispersal has reduced to a limited extent, the level of specialization has increased drastically. Ericsson, for example, has closed only a few of its factories around the world, but has converted many of them into focused manufacturing centers that produce a narrow range of components. Similarly, each of the laboratories of Alcatel, the company created by merging ITT and CIT-Alcatel, have now been given the mandate and resources to pursue a specific and well defined technology or development task, in contrast to the earlier situation when most of them operated quite independently, developing the entire range of products for their local markets.

CENTRALITY AND POWER WITHIN THE MULTINATIONAL NETWORK

Our preceding arguments on resource configuration in MNCs were based on a notion of isomorphic fit with the characteristics of the external network; we did not address the question of how such a fit is achieved. An MNC's configuration of resources at any point in time is the outcome of previous resource flows and, as argued by Benson (1975), the flow of resources within an interorganizational network is influenced by the distribution of power within the network. In this section we will suggest that within and across densities in the different national organization-sets of an MNC predicate the relative power of the headquarters and the national units, and that the nature of resource flows generated by the resulting distribution of power leads to the pattern of isomorphic fit we have described.

Effects of Within Density in National Organization-Sets

Applying Zald's (1970) political economy approach to the analysis of interorganizational relations, Benson (1975) suggested that an actor in such a network can enhance its power in dyadic relationships with other actors on the strength of its relationships with other organizational or social networks. Subsequently, Provan, Beyer and Kruytbosch (1980) provided empirical support for this proposal when they demonstrated that power relations within the network of United Way organizations were significantly modified by the linkages between the individual agencies and other elements in their local communities upon which the United Way depended for its survival. The dependence of the United Way on the local communities of its different organizations is in some ways akin to the dependence of the multinational on the local organization-sets of its different national units: just as dense linkages with the key elements of their communities enhanced the power of the United Way organizations, dense exchange relationships with the members of their local organization-sets can be expected to enhance the powers of the national units of the multinational.

It is inappropriate, however, to draw a direct correspondence between the United Way and an MNC because the central management organization of the United Way lacks the hierarchical power of the headquarters of the MNC. To incorporate this difference in our analysis, it is necessary to consider how hierarchical power might modify the interunit exchange patterns proposed by Benson.

We suggest that the efficacy of the hierarchical power of the headquarters to counteract the linkage-based power of the subsidiary is contingent on the density of interactions among members of the subsidiary's organization-set. When this within density is low, the potential power of the subsidiary is derived from its individual dyadic relationships. In this situation, the headquarters is more effective in counteracting the power of the subsidiary because it is potentially easier to have a 'direct control' over such relationships through mechanisms such as periodic visits by the headquarters staff. However, such direct control becomes more difficult in a situation of high within density in the subsidiary's organization-set. In this case, the subsidiary's power is not derived from an individual dyadic relationship, but from the web of exchange relations in the local organization-set of which it is a part. Remote control loses efficacy when 'localness', by itself, is the key requirement for maintaining the relationships. For example, in the case of the Australian subsidiary of Ericsson to which we referred earlier, extensive cross-licensing arrangements among all the producers, and the resulting close relationships among equipment suppliers, customers and regulators, was the main factor (other than distance) that impeded closer control of the local subsidiary from Stockholm and allowed the subsidiary to build up the high level of research and other resources.

Therefore, the positive relationship between 'environmental linkages' and power of the local unit of an interorganizational network proposed by Benson (1975) will remain operational in the context of an MNC under the condition of high within density. Following the arguments of Emerson (1962) and Cook (1977), the local unit will use this power to reduce its dependence on the other units of the network. Therefore it will bargain for, and obtain, a full range of resources so as to be able to carry out autonomously as many of its functions as possible. If all or most of the units of the MNC are located in environments of high within density, the consequence of this process will be a high level of dispersal of its resources on a local-for-local basis.

Effects of Across Density in the External Network

Recent literature on the distribution of power in social networks reveals two main sources of power in such collectivities (Fombrun 1983). First, power is an antipode of dependency in exchange relations (Emerson 1962), and accrues to those members of the network who control critical resources required by others but who do not depend on others for resources (Aldrich 1979; Pfeffer and Salancik 1978). Following Cook (1977), this might be called 'exchange power' to distinguish it from the second source of power which arises from structural rather than exchange dependencies. 'Structural power' emanates from the position of a member within the network; as shown by Lazarsfeld and Menzel (1961), it is an attribute that is induced by a member's context.

Our preceding discussions on power–dependency relationships within an MNC were based only on consideration of dyadic exchange between the headquarters and the national units. The situation changes when consideration of structural power is brought into the analysis. Structure of the external network now enters the calculation as an important variable since different members of the multinational network can potentially develop different levels of structural power based on their positions within the larger network of interactions among customers, suppliers, etc., across different countries.

Ignoring for present purposes the exceptions to the rule pointed out by Cook *et al.* (1983), the structural power of actors in a network can be assumed to arise from their centrality within the network (Lehman 1975; Laumann and Pappi 1976). As pointed out by Freeman (1979), the term centrality has been defined and used in the literature in many different ways. For present purposes, we can limit our attention to what Freeman describes as the point centrality of the different actors within the multinational network and also define the point centrality of each actor as a function of its degree (i.e., the number of other actors within the multinational network with which it has direct exchange relations). Following the arguments of Freeman, the headquarters enjoys the highest levels of point centrality when linkages among the subsidiaries are minimal. In a situation of extensive interactions among the subsidiaries, the centrality of the headquarters declines relative to those of the subsidiaries and the centrality of the different members of the network becomes dependent on the actual structure of such linkages. This becomes clear from a comparison of the three network structures shown in Figure 4.2 (each of which is reproduced from Freeman 1979).

High across density typically implies a high level of interactions among the subsidiaries of a multinational. As an illustration, consider the case of a manufacturer of automotive tires such as Italy's Pirelli. The company produces and markets car and truck tires in a number of countries, including the USA, Italy and Germany. It also supplies tires to the Ford Motor Company in each of these countries.

Until such time as Ford's local units in these countries operated relatively autonomously, with minimal coordination, there was little need for Pirelli's local units to coordinate their own activities with regard to their supply to Ford. However, as the interactions and coordination among Ford's operations in these countries increased, leading to internal comparisons of the prices, quality and support provided by common vendors (thereby enhancing across density, as relevant to Pirelli), Pirelli's subsidiaries also needed to enhance their internal coordination and communication, on issues of quality levels, pricing, service, etc., to prevent customer dissatisfaction (see Terpstra 1982). In other words, as a general principle, it can be stated that as across density increases, intersubsidiary linkages become more extensive and the centrality of the headquarters declines relative to other units.

Point centrality (degree)

	H	A	B	C	D
(a)	4	1	1	1	1
(b)	4	4	2	2	2
(c)	4	4	4	4	4

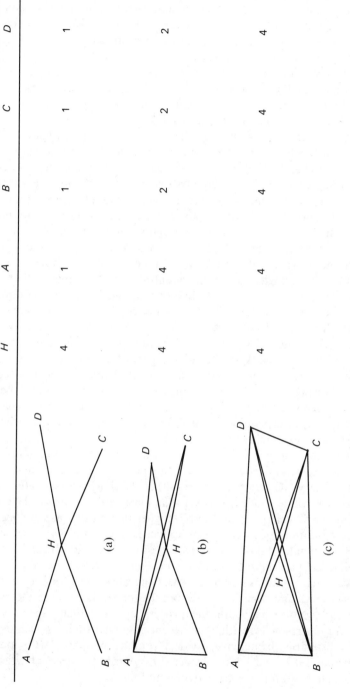

Figure 4.2 Centrality measure for three different network structures (reproduced from Freeman 1979)

More interestingly, however, under this condition, multiple points can emerge within the MNC with the same or similar degree of point centrality. Note that for the star-shaped structure, Figure 4.2(c), the headquarters and all the subsidiaries have the same point centrality, while in the hub-shaped structure, Figure 4.2(a), the headquarters has a very high level of point centrality compared to the subsidiaries. In Figure 4.2(b), however, while one subsidiary has the same point centrality as the headquarters, other subsidiaries have less.

An outcome such as the network structure shown in Figures 4.2(b) or 4.2(c) will follow from the existence of nodes in the external network. For example, for Pirelli, the USA, Italy and Germany may emerge as external nodes since these countries may be the headquarters locations for its major customers in these and other markets. Furthermore, only one of these external nodes (Italy) may coincide with the location of the company's own headquarters. Normative hierarchy in customer tastes and preferences (e.g., adoption by customers in other countries of a perfume or wine that is popular in France), and the advanced states of certain technologies in certain countries (e.g., ceramic technology in Japan, computer software technology in the USA and the UK) are some other examples of external nodes that can affect the point centralities of different units within the MNC. For the different activities of the MNC, different locations can emerge as the nodes of the external network; for any one particular activity, a number of different locations can possess such nodal characteristics. Consequently, following the arguments of Burt (1978), the multinational network will typically develop multiple centers with different internal coalitions and nodes corresponding to the different coalitions and nodes that may exist in the external network.

Therefore, in such a situation, the nodal units of the multinational will develop structural power and use this power to attract resources from within the MNC network. As a result, the level of dispersal in the MNC's resources will be moderate: lower than local-for-local dispersal (since not all units will emerge as nodes) but higher than in the case of concentration in locations of specific resource niches (except for businesses where a specific country enjoys a dominant position in all activities). Further, a high level of specialization will also develop in the resource configuration since nodal positions within the MNC network can be expected to vary by activities and tasks as a reflection of similar variance in the external network. Note that both the process and outcome aspects of this conclusion resonates with some recent empirical findings such as those of subsidiaries being given 'world product mandates' (Poynter and Rugman 1982) and 'global leader' or 'contributor' roles (Bartlett and Ghoshal 1986) for specific activities and tasks.

LARGE MNCs AS DIFFERENTIATED NETWORKS

Several highly simplifying assumptions were made in the foregoing discussions on resource configuration in MNCs under different conditions of local and global interlinkages. The enormous complexity of several disparate country-level organization-sets and the diversity of the heterogeneous international business environment were dichotomized into high–low categories of within and across densities. In reality, the levels of connectedness within and across the national organization-sets can be expected to vary across countries and groups of countries. Density of interactions across the national organization-sets may be high for the developed countries, or among regional groupings, but low in developing countries, particularly the more regulated and autarchic. Similarly, interactions among members within the national organization-sets may be high in homogeneous societies with a tradition of strong interinstitutional linkages, and low in countries where such linkages are discouraged through legislation, impeded because of societal heterogeneity or rendered ineffective because of poor communication infrastructures or the absence of linking institutions.

Therefore the configuration of resources in multinationals engaged in such businesses will be influenced by multiple criteria. In some locations internal interactions within the local organization-set may be high, but external linkages with other organization-sets may be low. In such locations, the MNC may provide all required resources in appropriate measures so that its local unit can build and maintain linkages with key members of its own community. The organization-sets in some other countries may be sparsely connected internally, but different elements of the local environment may be strongly connected with their counterparts in other countries. For these locations the MNC may create a resource structure that is concentrated and specialized, and in some cases the location of the specialized resources may reflect the desire to gain access to special resource niches, while in other cases the location choice may be motivated by the modalities in the external network. Finally, the organization-sets in a third group of countries may be characterized by high within and across linkages: in these locations, the MNC may establish all the complementary resources for integrated operating, but it may link these locations with others so as to provide leverage for the resources and achieve economies of concentration and specialization.

The overall resource configuration for a company like Philips, then, will reflect a mix of some resources that are dispersed among some units on a purely local-for-local basis (e.g., product development, manufacturing, marketing and other resources for the lighting business in India); some that are concentrated in different countries to access specialized local resource pools (e.g., the global scale audio factory in Singapore) and others that are concentrated in lead markets (e.g., development and manufacturing facilities for teletext television sets in the UK). Elsewhere we have described such a structure as the 'differentiated network', and have shown that a number of large multinational companies such as Procter & Gamble, Unilever, Ericsson, NEC and Matsushita are increasingly converging to this structural form despite the differences in their businesses and parent company nationalities (Bartlett and Ghoshal 1989).

Such a convergence is consistent with the theoretical arguments we have presented here. Following the arguments of Chandler (1986), one effect of worldwide improvements in communication and transportation infrastructures is the increasing interlinkages among actors, both within and across national boundaries. When such linkages are low, the influence of structural embeddedness is low and MNCs have a greater degree of freedom to locate their activities and resources to benefit from local resource niches and in line with the economic and technological characteristics of their businesses. Thus, in such situations, the resource configurations of different MNCs can be expected to differ as a reflection of those differences in their businesses and as a result of their freedom to exercise strategic choices. However, in the context of high within and across densities, such freedom is reduced because of the network influences: both dispersal and specialization now become essential, at least for the very large companies that have been the focus of our attention in this chapter. If within density is a country trait and across density is a world-system trait, the pattern of linkages in the overall structure of the external network is going to be increasingly similar for large MNCs, irrespective of their businesses. In other words, mimetic and normative forces of isomorphism (DiMaggio and Powell 1983) may be getting stronger as the world jolts along to T. Levitt's (1983) 'global village', and the observed trend of convergence to the differentiated network structure may be an outcome of these broader societal changes.

IMPLICATIONS FOR RESEARCH

In this chapter we have proposed a reconceptualization of the MNC as an interorganizational system rather than as an organization. This reconceptualization creates the possibility of applying exchange theory and network methodologies to the study of MNCs and has some important implications for future research on MNC-related issues.

First, at the aggregate level of macro-structural differences among MNCs, traditional analysis has tended to assume internal homogeneity within such companies. This has resulted in generalized conclusions at the level of the overall company based on empirical studies that have focused on individual actors or specific dyadic links. For example, a sampled group of American MNCs has been inferred to be more centralized than their Japanese and European counterparts based on analysis of the parent companies' relationships with their subsidiaries located in one region (e.g., Hulbert and Brandt 1980). However, as we have argued here, headquarters–subsidiary relations within an MNC can vary widely from subsidiary to subsidiary. The interorganizational network conceptualization can provide new concepts such as graph centrality (Freeman 1979) or hierarchy (Coleman 1966), which appear to be theoretically more appropriate for such macro-structural comparisons among internally differentiated and heterogeneous organizational systems such as MNCs.

Second, given such heterogeneity, macro-structural analysis alone may not be enough, and may need to be complemented with micro-structural analyses of these internal differences so as to build a more complete theoretical understanding of the ways in which an MNC functions. For example, in the differentiated network MNC, there is no formal macro-structure that 'fits' all parts of the company's heterogeneous environments. Yet it has to choose a formal departmental structure and might, quite arbitrarily, choose one that appears to be simple and consistent with its own administrative heritage (Bartlett 1983, 1986). Therefore not only might macro-structure have become more difficult to predict theoretically – as seems true, given the significant empirically-induced modifications to the Stopford and Wells (1972) contingency model proposed by subsequent studies of MNC macro-structures, such as those by Daniels, Pitts and Tretter (1985) and Egelhoff (1988) – but it might also have become a less interesting attribute to study precisely because of such indeterminacy. For example, contrary to the predictions of structural contingency, NEC, Proctor & Gamble and Unilever have not changed their macro-structures in over two decades despite some very significant changes in their business conditions. What have changed in these companies are the internal management processes: subsidiaries have assumed new and specific roles to respond to changing local conditions, and the headquarters' control mechanisms have evolved from ubiquitous 'company ways' to multi-dimensional perspectives that are applied differently to different parts of the organization so as to respond to shifting global contexts (Bartlett and Ghoshal 1989). The network approach is particularly suited for investigation of such differences in internal roles, relations and tasks of different affiliated units (e.g., through blockmodelling and analysis of functional equivalence), and of how internal coordination mechanisms might be differentiated to match the variety of subunit contexts (see, for example, the contributions by Burt in Burt, Minor and Associates (1983) on 'Distinguishing relational contents' and 'Studying status/ role-sets using mass surveys').

The same argument we made for structure can also be made for strategy. Discussions on company- or even business-level generic strategies and how they 'fit' generic types of competitive structures are too far removed from the reality of highly differentiated strategic approaches that can be expected in the various parts of the differentiated network organization. Instead, it may be more useful to explore the actual content of strategy in such complex organizational systems: network theoretic analysis of internal flows of resources, products, people and information might be more relevant for developing middle-range theories on resource commitment, decision-making, strategic control, normative integration and creation and diffusion of innovations in such companies (see, e.g., the application of network analysis in Carley 1985; G. Walker 1985; Burt 1987). In this chapter we have focused primarily on the hierarchical network relationships between the headquarters and the national subsidiaries of an MNC. Investigation of the lateral network relations among the different subsidiaries can open up avenues for similar fine-grained analysis of both the causes and consequences of horizontal interdependencies and synergy.

Finally, as has been shown in some recent contributions, the inter-organizational approach can be particularly useful for the study of another MNC-related phenomenon which is assuming increasing importance: that is, their forming complex webs of alliances and joint ventures with customers, suppliers and competitors (Harrigan 1985; Ohmae 1985). By focusing on relations among actors, the network analysis approach can provide both appropriate concepts and methodological tools for rigorous and theory-grounded investigation of the strategic and organizational aspects of such alliances (see, e.g., the contributions by Walker, Westney, and Hakenson and Johanson in Contractor and Lorange 1988).

Building a Network Theory of the MNC

The concepts and arguments presented here suffer from a number of shortcomings which need to be overcome before the network conceptualization can yield a useful and testable theory of the MNC. The necessary improvement and extension of these preliminary ideas will require both deductive theory building with more sophisticated use of network theory than has been achieved here, and also empirical studies to induce and test more fine-grained propositions and hypotheses.

First, our definitions of constructs such as within and across densities are too coarse since, as we point out in the concluding section, these densities differ for different parts of the total external network of any company. Such differences can be expected along both geographic and functional dimensions. For example, the external organizations relevant for the R&D department of a company may be far more interconnected across national borders than those that are relevant for the service department. Similarly, while within density, on average, may be higher in Japan than in the USA, there may be significant differences between the two contexts for different parts of the local organization-sets. One of the main attractions of the network perspective is that the implications of such differences can be explicitly included in both theoretical and empirical analyses, and the elaboration of these distinctions must be a priority for future research on this topic.

Second, we have considered exchange very broadly to include many different kinds of transactions involving products, information, affect and so on, without distinguishing among these different flows. As follows from the general arguments of Mitchell (1973) and Kadushin (1978), each of these different kinds of exchange can have some very different implications for the strategy, organization and management of an MNC; further, those effects are also likely to be interactive. Therefore, the next phase of theory development must explain the separate and joint effects of these different kinds of exchange.

Third, we have focused on density as the key parameter of the external network, since density appeared to relate most closely to the implications of social embeddedness described by Granovetter (1985). Furthermore, it is also a relatively simple construct that is easy to conceptualize and to measure once the relevant organization-sets and external network are identified (see below). However, density is not a complete description of a network, and it is possible that some other characteristics of the external network can significantly influence specific attributes of the MNC, therefore, for more complete development of the theory, it would be desirable to identify a set of parameters that completely and unambiguously define the external network, and then to explore the impact of each of these parameters on selected attributes of the multi-national. Recently, Krackhardt (1989) has proposed four parameters – connectedness, hierarchy, least-upper-boundedness and graph efficiency – as necessary and sufficient descriptors of a network, and his work provides some interesting opportunities for modifying and extending our theoretical arguments.

Finally, besides (indeed, before) such extension and refinement of the concepts, it might also be necessary to improve the specificity and precision in our definition of some of the constructs so as to facilitate their operationalization in empirical research. One key issue concerns delineation of the boundaries of the different national organization-sets, which is a general and widespread problem in network research (Laumann, Marsden and Prensky 1983). As suggested by Aldrich and Whetten (1981), the relevant organization-sets may well differ according to different kinds of exchange, and definition of the boundaries may therefore depend on the kind of exchange that is the focus of inquiry. In presenting our ideas here, we have been guided by the belief that these boundaries can be identified either through the naturalistic approach of a priori commonsense definition, or empirically, through measurement of structural cohesion (DiMaggio 1986). In the former approach, for example, all relevant suppliers, customers, regulators and competitors in any country can be pre-specified based on expert knowledge of the local structure of the business. In the latter approach, a broader population of potentially relevant members of the local organization-set may be identified through a repeated process of snowball sampling until sufficient convergence is achieved, and the organization-set can then be identified empirically from this population as the group of organizations that interact maximally with one another and minimally with other members of the population. Once all the relevant local organization-sets are identified by one method or another, the external network can be defined as the collectivity of all these local organization-sets.

Clearly, the former method for identifying the national organization-sets is the more convenient and it is our belief that experienced researchers should usually be able to pre-specify most of the relevant actors with sufficient accuracy. Some researchers, however, may prefer the latter approach for it avoids the arbitrariness of a priori selection. However, as Laumann, Marsden and Prensky (1983) have argued, neither approach is fully satisfactory, and some better way for delineation of the boundaries remains as another important topic for further reflection.

5 The European Subsidiaries of American Multinationals: an Exercise in Ecological Analysis*

Jacques Delacroix

Portentous and abrupt changes in the world economic order have recently rekindled public interest in the globalization of business. Students of international business thus face with renewed urgency the challenge of explaining the interaction between business organizations and their environment. This challenge is also an opportunity: large-scale environmental transformations constitute so many occasions to observe organizational reactions and proactions.

In this chapter, I use past transformations of the European business context to illustrate how organizational ecology, a leading paradigm in organizational theory, can be put to work to explore organizational responses to multinational environmental change. Specifically, I cast a retrospective look at the founding and disbanding of European manufacturing subsidiaries of American multinationals between 1903 and 1974. With this approach I show how the organizational ecology style of research lends itself to the testing of eclectic theoretical models of multinational organization and feeds research intuition.

THE MNC AS A PUZZLE

The existence of MNCs used to puzzle conventional, neoclassical economics. Why should the functions served by organizations headquartered in one country, but with subsidiaries or other dependent subparts in other countries, not be served as well by trade? Any organisation operating

* This chapter is an extension of an earlier empirical analysis with John H. Freeman, to whom I am thankful for a solid push-start. I am also grateful to Mark Makiewiez for cool, collected and competent research assistance.

in environments that are initially unfamiliar is expected to suffer learning and stumbling costs not imposed on indigenous organizations. Thus MNCs and all organizations of their kind are chronically at a competitive disadvantage. Consequently, manufacturing and other producing subsidiaries appear as poor substitutes for arm's-length imports and sourcing subsidiaries for exports.

The question asked by Anderson and Gatignon (1986), 'Why should true and tried mechanisms be replaced by comparatively clumsy organizational attempts to reach across national boundaries?', has received two broad kinds of answers from economics-oriented scholars. Some scholars, following Hymer (1970) and Kindleberger (1969), have argued that MNCs constitute organizational endeavors designed to pursue a firm-specific monopolistic advantage (Teece 1981) which would be dissipated if market mechanisms were relied upon. 'Beachhead' and 'headstart' (Kolde 1981, pp. 300–4) explanations fall more or less into the same conceptual category.

A second type of explanation tries to show that markets are the most efficient economic mechanisms *only* under certain conditions pertaining to perfect competition. Scholars belonging to this school of thought, traceable to Williamson (1975), and to McManus (1972), study the theoretical effects of relaxing certain assumptions on the likelihood that organizational solutions may be more efficient than markets (Hennart 1985, 1988, 1989). Transaction costs theory thus argues that some specific costs of trade, and of international trade in particular, are sometimes high enough to compensate for the costs of control and monitoring associated with organizational (or 'hierarchical') solutions (see Hennart Chapter 7, and 1989: also his 1988 case study of one industry; Klein, Crawford and Alchian 1978; Hill and Kim 1988; for a recent survey of findings and new findings, see Klein, Frazier and Roth 1990; for a different organization of the field, see Kogut Chapter 6).

The conceptual rigor that transaction costs theorists bring to bear on the question of why MNCs exist is great enough, and their empirical results persuasive enough (although few), for contending schools of thought to appear on the verge of extinction. (For a more sceptical account, see Buckley 1988.) Even firm monopoly arguments are in the process of being integrated into transaction costs theory. (See Hennart 1985, pp. 1–26, for a detailed discussion of transaction costs theory in relation to other theories of MNCs.)

Recent Developments in Organisation Theory

Organization theory has, thus far, had little to say about MNCs, in part because its conceptual tradition is largely blind to the special character of national boundaries (Carroll, Delacroix and Goodstein 1988). However, the recent evolution of this field points to the possibility that significant contributions will emerge. As recounted in Scott's thorough survey of the field (1987a), the older 'closed system' and 'open system' approaches, which focused on the internal structure and behavior of organizations, have been vigorously challenged by an 'open system' perspective which assigns priority to the relationship between organizations and their environments.

This new perspective has a special affinity with the study of MNCs, and it can complement the dominant transaction cost approach to the study of MNCs. Organizational theory, in turn, would benefit from paying attention to MNCs and to the work of students of international business.

Institutionalization theory (see Westney, Chapter 3) and organizational ecology are two important schools of thought within the open system perspective. Institutional theory, as its name indicates, emphasizes the importance of the institutional environments within which organizations must exist. Roughly, according to this view, organizations' structures and strategies are conditioned by their need to be viewed as legitimate, because illegitimate organizations are not ordinarily given the means to succeed. Institutions granting legitimacy include political institutions but are not limited to them. One central argument of institutionalization theory, which may be pertinent to the study of MNCs, is that organizational structures reflect a great deal of mimetic behavior. (Why invent new organizational forms which may be judged strange when there are plenty of already taken-for-granted models to emulate?) An underlying assumption recently developed in Meyer and Zucker (1989) is that many organizations are subjected to the vigorous market trials envisaged by economic theory either weakly or not at all. Not surprisingly, much (but not all) of the empirical evidence in support of the institutional perspective comes from studies of common-weal, non-business organizations (Aldrich and Marsden 1988, p. 381).

Organizational ecology is the other major open system school of thought. Organizational ecology (sometimes called "population ecology") is built around the concept of *structural inertia*. In the ecological view, organizations in general have little latitude for effective structural change (Aldrich and Marsden 1988, p. 380; Hannan and Freeman 1989, pp. 67–9; see Stinchcombe 1965 for a seminal substantive discussion and Kilduff, Chapter 11). Indeed, according to some ecologists (see, e.g. Carroll 1987), important structural reforms are often recipes for disaster and more likely to lead to organizational demise than to organizational adaptation, as assumed by managerial schools of thought.[1] Two major organizational ecologists propose further that structural inertia, and the attendant vulnerability, are not organizational pathologies. Instead, they argue, structural inertia is the predictable and mostly sound consequence of the role organizations are supposed to play in society (Hannan and Freeman 1989, pp. 72–7). As compared to both markets and other forms of social collectivities,[2] organizations are specifically expected to provide reliability of performance. This mandate in turn is served by permanence of structure. If organizations are supposed to be recognizably themselves, from day-to-day, in terms of their demeanor, clearly they should not be able to modify their structure frequently or rapidly.

The concept of structural inertia has important consequences for the way one goes about studying organizations. Given that today's organizations are different from yesterday's, it is necessary to explain change in the organizational panorama (Egelhoff, Chapter 8). Managerial schools explain this change as the aggregate result of individual organizations' efforts to cope with an environment that is both changeable and encumbered by competing organizations. To the extent that structural inertia is granted, this form of individual adaptation must be rare and contribute but little to organizational change. Instead, ecologists argue, organizational change occurs largely through the replacement of organizational forms by other organizational forms that may be either slight variants of the forms being replaced or completely different from them. Thus, for example, vacuum tube makers were replaced by transistor manufacturers with very little direct filiation between the two forms (Golding, 1971). The efficient mechanism of change invoked by organizational ecologists is therefore not adaptation but selective elimination, or simply 'selection'.[3] A selection viewpoint, in turn, necessarily requires a research interest in organizational dissolution. Correspondingly, the organizational ecology perspective is supported by a large and growing number of empirical studies of dissolutions or 'disbandings' pertaining to a wide variety of organizations. (For reviews that are useful but increasingly outdated, see Wholey and Britain 1986; Carroll 1988; Hannan and Freeman 1989.)

The counterintuitive logic of organizational ecology demands that a high replacement rate prevail within categories of organizations. If organizations seldom dissolve or if they are not replaced by new ones, selection cannot account for the observable organizational change. Several studies place this replacement rate at about 10 percent annually (Aldrich and Marsden 1988, p. 378). To detect the effects of such moderately high rates, in turn, requires reasonably long periods of observation; fairly deep longitudinal studies rather than cross-sectional ones. Consequently, organizational ecologists tend to study, over long periods, broad categories of organizations of the same kind. (See Hannan and Freeman 1989, and Carroll and Delacroix 1982, for studies extending over about 120 years and 175 years, respectively.) They call the latter 'populations'. In most cases, ecological populations are phenomenologically defined saturation samples covering every organization of the same kind which ever existed in a given locale.[4]

Recently, ecologists have begun to integrate arguments from institutional theory into both their theoretical models and their estimation models (see Hannan and Freeman 1989, p. 131, for example), a move not necessarily applauded by institutional theorists (Zucker, 1989). Some organizational ecologists argue that it is especially important to incorporate into ecological models variables capturing changes in the political environment (Carroll, Delacroix and Goodstein 1988).

DOING INTERNATIONAL MANAGEMENT RESEARCH WITH AN ORGANIZATIONAL ECOLOGY FRAMEWORK

Transaction costs scholars are sometimes perceived as adaptationists (Aldrich and Marsden 1988, p. 377) because they often write prescriptively, a habit imported from mainstream economics theory which tends to view organizations more or less as substitutes for *homo economicus* (for a constructive departure, see Hennart Chapter 7). Hence it appears as if they viewed the substitution of hierarchical, organizational solutions (e.g., the MNC) for cross-boundary market operations (imports and exports) as the result of conscious calculations by well-informed administrators (e.g., Kimura 1989, p. 297). This style of presentation seems to contradict what is known of market entry decisions. According to Robinson's (1978, pp. 374–5) survey, such decisions are seldom made with careful considerations. Kobrin, Basek, Blank and La Palombara (1980), show that entry decisions are seldom preceded by an adequate examination of the non-economic aspects of the host country environment.

Yet, it appears that the extent to which conscious choice presides over the choice of entry solutions, including FDI, is not central to the logic of transaction cost analysis. A selection perspective is just as compatible. In this view, firms that choose FDI when they should select other modes of entry, from a transaction costs standpoint, will suffer in the long run through inferior performance. Inferior performance, in turn, should lead to elimination, under certain conditions. However, this scenario lends itself to a realistic research strategy only if a long run is available for observation. (Arpan and Ricks 1986 show that there is great stability in the pattern of FDI in the USA between 1974 and 1984; Kobrin (1976) observes a similar pattern for American FDI in less developed countries.) Organizational ecologists have accumulated a wealth of experience in the manipulation of deep longitudinal data bases. Hence, empirical inquiry into international management matters may have something to gain from adopting some of the methodological practices pioneered in the social sciences by organizational ecology.

Scholars in all fields frequently call for more and better longitudinal studies (see, for example, Buckley 1988, p. 183; Egelhoff, Chapter 8). Ecologists have brought to this call a particular urgency by drawing attention to the possibility that cross-sectional studies may not only lead to imperfect results but to thoroughly fallacious ones. This theme, developed by Carroll (1984), Freeman and Boeker (1984), and Hannan and Freeman (1989, pp. 42–3, 92–3), among others, pertains in large part, to survivor bias.

In spite of vigorous but usually merely ritualistic denials that any generalization is intended, many studies of business organizations generalize on the basis of cross-sectional convenience samples (e.g., Cvar, 1986) or on the basis of shallow longitudinal samples.[5] With this practice, all organizations existing at the time of the study constitute the statistical population being sampled. The problem arises when scholars generalize unwittingly or implicitly from this sample to an undefined but much larger population extending far back in time. The population in existence at the time of the study is, in fact, itself a sample of the larger chronologically undefined population. The former is a very biased sample of the latter. Ecological studies have shown (Aldrich and Marsden 1988, p. 382) that survival is systematically linked to both organizational age and organizational size. Older and larger organizations are more likely to survive into the next time period than are younger and smaller organizations. The two effects are additive. Since the population in existence at the time of the study is composed in part of organizations that have survived from an earlier period, it is loaded with entities that are larger and older than the base population, at least. Thus users of cross-sectional samples are in danger of proffering generalizations about business organizations that are systematically biased because they do not take into account the effects of size and age on whatever they are studying. Note that drawing a perfect random sample from the population in existence at the time of the study does not solve this problem of survivor bias.

In general, survivor bias violates the fundamental logic of scientific inquiry which requires that we compare the effect of initial conditions presumed to be causal, on systematically arrayed different outcomes. In many cases, the outcomes of substantive interest are various conceptualizations of business success; hence, one wishes to compare a fair sample of successful organizations with a fair sample of unsuccessful ones. Keeping from consideration the many organizations that were so unsuccessful they did not survive,[6] in effect may eliminate the most important fraction of the test or treatment group. Only a longitudinal study based on all organizations of the relevant type that ever existed (or a random sample thereof) can completely eliminate survivor bias. Every effort in that direction will at least attenuate the effect of this bias and minimize the gravity of the fallacious inferences it implies.

A simplistic but not unrealistic example can help illustrate the seriousness of the problem. Suppose that we use a sample of 80 contemporary MNCs to assess the effect of giving intercultural training to Chief Executive Officers (CEOs) on some specified measure of market share. We find that 60 of the CEOs have received such training. We find further that of these, 50 preside over firms which have increased their market share over a given period of observation, while of the 20 CEOs who have received no such training only eight manage firms that have experienced market share growth. The overall picture is expressed in terms of percentages of the total sample as shown below.

	Training	No Training
Success	62%	10%
Failure	12%	15%

With such results, it would be tempting to state that intercultural training has a positive effect on, or at least, is positively associated with, performance as measured.

If we had opted for a more inclusive longitudinal study and collected the corresponding data, we might have found that the 80 firms in our sample were survivors from a cohort of 800 similar MNCs, all founded at about the same time. We might also have discovered that of the 720 MNCs that were disbanded before the period of the study of 80, 650 had CEOs who had received intercultural training. Keeping in mind that being disbanded is a genuine barrier to gaining market share, the relationship between cultural training and success would now appear as follows:

	Training	No Training
Success	6%	1%
Failure	82%	10%

With these more inclusive results, one would hesitate to assign any role to cultural training in achieving the form of success captured by market share gain.

Aside from reducing the probability of this kind of error, longitudinal designs give us a chance to build historical events explicitly into our models. This has both substantive and methodological advantages. As institutional theorists insist, and as international management research seeks to demonstrate, contextual events – especially those of a political nature – may affect the fates of business organizations.[7] Thus, Delacroix and Carroll (1983) show that political turbulence has a positive effect on the propensity to found newspapers, while Carroll and Delacroix (1982) show that newspapers founded under such conditions tend to be short-lived. In general, business organizations exist within a legal framework which is frequently modified in obvious or subtle ways (see Carroll, Delacroix and Goodstein 1988) by political developments. Thus it is not very useful to deploy treasures of ingenuity to uncover the economic causes of massive failure in an industry that was largely disenfranchised by parliamentary fiat (such as the wine industry in the USA during Prohibition). Instead, such a political variable should be explicitly incorporated into the estimation model so that it will compete with all other covariates for the variance available in the dependent variable. Historical and other macro-societal effects can easily be incorporated into longitudinal estimation models through the use of dummy variables. It is also relatively easy to study the combined effects of political and other factors by creating interactive variables around the dummy political variables. (For an illustration of these methods, see Delacroix and Carroll 1983, or Hannan and Freeman 1989, pp. 209–10 and Tables 9-1 and 9-3.)

Aside from helping to answer substantive questions, longitudinal designs can contribute to theory-building by palliating one of the built-in weaknesses of international management research. Such research is often also cross-national research, that is it makes use of the variability occurring naturally across nation-states because nation-states are especially bounded environments (see below). In the attempt to establish cause and effect relationships on the basis of this variability, research runs against an absolute limitation: there are only about 160 nation-states and the number for which reliable data are routinely available is much smaller. Hence it is important to make maximum use of those country cases for which there are data. One way to achieve this result is more extensive exploitation of information about those countries that are well-documented. (See Ragin 1987 for techniques especially appropriate to small numbers of cross-sectional investigations.) An alternative strategy is to make better use of changes occurring within those same well-documented countries. What is unobtainable through width of observation can often be reached through depth. It is possible to treat the history of individual countries as a ready-made laboratory offering variability in addition to that found across countries.

Thus, if we are interested in the effects of tariff barriers on the propensity to establish subsidiaries in the countries within the tariff barrier, for example, (a central question naturally derived from transaction costs theory), two research strategies are available. First, we can examine the frequency of subsidiary foundings in different countries with different level of tariff barriers. Secondly, we can locate tariff changes within the history of a given country or region and ascertain to what extent such changes are accompanied by spells of subsidiary foundings or, conversely, by a slowing down of such foundings. ('Accompanied' because, in this case, the effect may not follow the proximate cause; it may precede it since the efficient mechanism may be anticipated rather than realized tariff changes.) The empirical portions of this chapter below constitute an exploratory attempt to use the European Economic Community (EEC) as such a natural laboratory.

Note finally that it is possible to combine in the same research design cross-country and cross-time variability through recourse to pooled cross-sectional time series techniques, for maximum power. (For an introduction to such techniques, see Stimson 1985, and Sayrs 1989.) Thus, in addition to helping us use historical events to account for concrete phenomena, longitudinal approaches contribute to the construction of theories or systematic explanations about a class of phenomena.

The particular kinds of longitudinal design model pioneered by organizational ecologists are known collectively as 'event history analysis'. This is too technical a topic to be treated here. To summarize the advantages of such methods for international management research, it is enough to say that, with this mode of analysis, a case is one organization in existence for a given time period. This longitudinal approach improves upon more familiar panel models by placing at the researcher's disposal all the overlapping time subperiods available within the total period of observation of the study. Thus, the period 1950 to 1980 includes 1950 to 1951, 1950 to 1952, but also 1951 to 1953, etc. Any of these subperiods can be used, although not in the same estimation models. For a clear introduction to event history analysis, see Allison (1984) and Carroll (1983); for a more advanced treatment, see Tuma and Hannan (1984); for examples of applications, see Hannan and Freeman (1989).

How the Study of International Management can Benefit Organizational Theory

One of the central problems of organizational theory is as follows: how do organizational parts which have the potential to act independently of one another – unlike the parts of a watch, for example (see Hedlund, Chapter 9) – come to behave sufficiently in concert to benefit the whole organization? The word 'benefit' here is to be taken broadly; one weak interpretation of it is that organizations simply continue to exist as such, in spite of their great potential for dissolution, because of the centrifugal forces to which they are subjected. Organizational theorists have sought answers to this question through studying the mechanisms by which organizations cope with their diverse and diversely varying environments without falling apart (Aldrich and Marsden 1988). Curiously, organizational theorists' longstanding interest in environmental diversity is usually operationalized in terms of industrial sectors or institutional–political contexts and, more rarely, in terms of organizational fields of relevance to the focal organization. When diversity of operating conditions is examined from a spatial standpoint, inquiries tend to be limited to a domestic context (Aldrich and Marsden 1988, pp. 369–70). This is curious because for many purposes the greatest diversity of conditions encountered by a single organization has to be that faced by the MNC, an organization existing in a pluri-national context. This must be so because of the special nature of nation-state boundaries (Hennart 1985, p. 2; Kogut, Chapter 6).

The degree of difficulty encountered by complex organizations in coping with a heterogenous environment (or in remaining organizations) is a dynamic function of the degree of heterogeneity of the relevant environment. We can simplify the problem by ignoring the term 'dynamic' in the above statement (for a rigorous examination of this matter by organizational ecologists, see Freeman and Hannan 1983). What is left is the extent to which different subparts of the relevant environments exert different pressures on the organization. Relevant environments can be defined in terms of resource dependence or in terms of their capability to award legitimacy. Both angles matter to international management scholars. The simplest case might be that of a dyad on an island, abundantly furnished with creature comforts but facing lions inland and sharks in the sea. At the other extreme might be a complex organization facing different sets of constraints in a wide variety of locales with each constraint taking on different values in those different locales. A multinational environment is one where an organization (the MNC) faces the same basic sets of constraints in multiple locales where the constraints all take on different values.

A multinational environment comes very close to offering maximum heterogeneity because of the particular nature of national boundaries. National boundaries perform two functions which ensure that each national environment will be different from any other (from a business standpoint). First, they constitute obstacles to the free movement of goods, of capital and of persons and, to a remarkable extent of information; this last is accomplished through their monopoly over the attribution of hertzian space and occasionally by jamming communications from without and through censorship. Unlike all other kinds of social boundaries, the boundaries of nation-states are backed by force, insuring that these obstacles are more sturdy than any others. Secondly, nation-states intervene actively in social processes contributing to the homogenization of conditions within, and therefore, to heterogeneity across nation-states. They do this by erecting judicial systems which are the umbrellas under which most business transactions take place, by setting up more or less directly educational standards and programs, by supplying a more or less large fraction of the information on which the mass media has come to rely (when they do not exercise a monopoly over such media). The process of state-directed homogenization may have been more transparent in earlier times because it involved such dramatic practices as universal military draft, intended to mix recruits from different regions, but the strength of current processes may be no less. In addition, many nation-states, as the term indicates, were founded on the basis of pre-existing national (that is, cultural) groups: 'Italy,' for example, is a state of people speaking closely related languages. States usually do nothing to dilute the cultural singularity of their population and often act to strengthen it. Thus Japanese children are exposed primarily to Japanese history and French children to French history, which is probably not a random phenomenon.

The two sets of processes pertaining to the unique nature of national boundaries tend to reinforce each other to insure that the operating conditions an organization will encounter on one side of the border will differ markedly from the conditions it will face on the other side. Organizational theorists therefore should not fail to take advantage of the natural laboratory that the division of the world into nation-states offers to their inquiry, and of the wealth of empirical findings accumulated by students of international business.

The multinationalism of the world environment supplies organizational ecologists, in particular, with opportunities to test a variant of their central conceptual model. We saw above how organizational ecology favors a selection mechanism of organizational change over the adaptationist perspective implicit in all managerial, voluntaristic schools of thought. As we saw, organizational ecology focuses on selection mechanisms; however, the distinction between processes of selection and processes of adaptation does not have to be absolute. Hannan and Freeman (1989, p. 42) discuss the possibility that the selection of parts *out* of a system may constitute a form of adaptation *for* the system as a whole. MNCs give us a superior opportunity to test this formulation. Every subsidiary is a part of a larger organizational system which is subjected to the pressure of an environment which tends to be significantly different from the environments to which other subsidiaries in the same system are subjected. This is, again, because national boundaries, unlike most other kinds of social boundaries, circumscribe quite discrete environmental processes. Consequently, the configuration of organizationally relevant forces operating within one country is likely to be quite different, at any one time, from the corresponding configuration in another country.

Hence, the MNC as a whole is subject to a degree of environmental variation unlikely to be duplicated within a purely domestic environment. The proximate target of this environmental variation is each subsidiary in each individual country. The local (i.e. national) environment selects for or against the arrangement of parts this subsidiary constitutes by allowing it to be more or less successful, in conventional terms. 'Success' is defined in this context as simply the ability to make sufficient contributions to the whole MNC to be allowed to continue to exist as a subsidiary of the same particular MNC. It matters little whether the subsidiary goes bankrupt in a conventional business sense or whether its contribution is judged insufficient by the management of the parent company.[8] In either case, below this sufficiency threshold, the subsidiary is eliminated as a subsidiary. This act of selection may constitute an effective form of adaptation for the MNC as a whole in the sense that it achieves a better fit with the *global* environment than it would, absent the elimination of this particular subsidiary in its particular (national) local environment. This process of global adaptation through elimination of local subsidiaries, repeated many times for many MNCs, may also begin to explain the 'evolution' of MNC structure over time which has been the subject of much inquiry in the international business disciplines.

THE STUDY

Below, I present the results of an exploratory study of a population of European manufacturing subsidiaries of US-based MNCs. The chosen locale of the study is Europe, primarily because this part of the world constitutes a natural laboratory of the kind discussed above. During our period of observation, from 1903 to 1974, Europe underwent a number of well-documented crises and institutional transformations which may be expected to have consequences for the propensity of American companies to found and disband subsidiaries there.

Europe is a good site for another reason: most European countries in general, and those in the EEC in particular, have a relatively unambiguous pro-FDI policy. Thus the fact that we do *not* control for natural political variables in any of our models may not be as serious a weakness of design as it would be if the site were elsewhere. Among these transformations the creation of the European Economic Community and its progressive enlargement figure prominently. The changing membership of the EEC is itself a research opportunity. These transformations and their expected consequences are discussed below. Moreover, at a time when a new wave of forthcoming modifications of the EEC gives rise to numerous speculations in the press (*Wall Street Journal* 1989; Weihrich 1990), there may be some policy benefit in re-examining the effects that past changes in the EEC had (or did not have) on an important segment of American industry. Finally, such a study may throw some light on the behavior of American MNCs in general since the set of their subsidiaries located in Europe constitutes a large percentage of the total (W. H. Davidson 1980, p. 9). Nevertheless, the study is intended as an exercise only. It is a limited demonstration in the inductive mode of the application of ecological methods to conventional international management problems. The study is not sufficiently thorough or rigorous to give rise to trustworthy scholarly findings.

The subsidiaries' data are drawn from the Harvard Multinational Enterprise Study, 1979 version (HMES). (For a recent user of these data, see Kobrin 1988.) Although the HMES is much larger (see Curhan, Davidson and Suri 1977, and Suri and Hammett 1979 for a thorough description) I selected the 3372 American *manufacturing* subsidiaries located in Europe. The choice of manufacturing subsidiaries is in answer to a concern for rough comparability on some dimensions such as labor cost. For each subsidiary we have the date of founding and the date of disbanding and therefore the subsidiary's age at any time during the period of observation. 'Disbanding' is a conventional ecological term which simply means here that the subsidiary ceased being a subsidiary of a particular parent company. Thus, a disbanded subsidiary may continue to exist as an independent entity or it may have been sold to another company. The focus in this study is therefore on the relationship to the parent company although we are unable to link each subsidiary with its parent. However, we know for each subsidiary whether it was dissolved and liquidated or not. We also know whether a given subsidiary was founded as an acquisition or as a greenfield operation.

We begin with what ecologists consider a routine visual examination of the vital statistics of the population, so to speak. This is followed by a discussion of several longitudinal maximum likelihood estimation models.

Population Size, Foundings and Disbandings and the Transformations of Europe

Figure 5.1 shows the number of American manufacturing subsidiaries in simultaneous existence for the six founding EEC countries (West Germany, France, Italy and the three Benelux countries) and, separ-

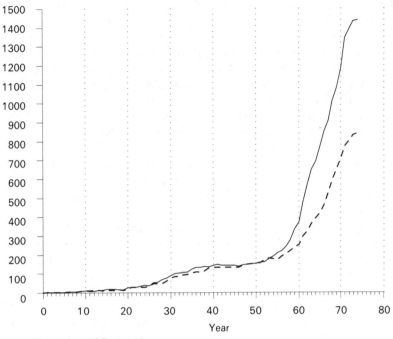

— Six original EEC countries
- - UK, Ireland Denmark

Figure 5.1   Number of subsidiaries in simultaneous existence

ately, for the three countries which joined the EEC in 1973 (the UK, Ireland and Denmark).

For the whole period 1903 to 1974, the two curves look remarkably alike. Neither curve would allow a casual observer to detect the occurrence of such momentous events as the Great Depression or even World War II. As observed by other scholars, there is a remarkable stability over time and this population of organizations is largely immune to many events that common sense would consider compelling. This observation converges with other ecological findings (see, e.g., Carroll and Delacroix 1982).

The curve pertaining to the three late-joiners, two of which are English-speaking countries, does *not* show an early rise in population. This contradicts the idea that cultural and other systemic-national properties play a more important role in attracting FDI than the more rational economic factors favored by transaction costs theory.

Both curves show a very sharp increase in the population of subsidiaries about the mid-1950s, the time of the creation of EEC (1957). This is partly, but only partly, in keeping with what one would expect.

There are at least three reasons why the evolution of the EEC should affect the propensity of American MNCs to found (or acquire) and to retain subsidiaries on its territory.

First, as the EEC dissolves its intra-community barriers and, as it absorbs new members, it becomes an ever-larger economic space. The two effects are additive; both lead to greater potential economies of scale in production (W. H. Davidson 1980, p. 9; Kim and Lyn 1987; Kimura 1989, p. 305.)

Second, the progressive adoption of the Common Economic Tariff (CET) raises fears, sound or not (W. H. Davidson 1980, pp. 13–14; Weihrich 1990), that hitherto accessible markets will become less accessible. An expected response is to substitute local production for exports (Franko 1974; Bartlett 1986, p. 372).

Third, as the EEC reduces its internal barriers to all kinds of transnational economic activities, its constituent nation-states must become more and more alike from the standpoint of business operating conditions (Guisinger 1989). Thus there is anecdotal evidence of acceptance of American auditing practices ahead of the formulation of EEC-wide practices. There is also anecdotal but forceful evidence that business actors from the several member states adopt English as a language of business: how else will a Dane and a Greek discuss an agreement? This convergence of practices gives rise to a potential for economies of scope also favoring physical presence within the EEC and thence to a numerical progress of subsidiaries as the preferred way to reach EEC markets. As these two examples illustrate, the homogenization of the EEC sometimes is achieved through a veritable American-ization which should make the EEC even more capable of supporting economies of scope, especially for American MNCs (Anderson and Coughlan 1987, p. 74).

The curve for the six in Figure 5.1 is compatible with these three convergent arguments. However, the curve for the three appears equally congruent, as if the advantages of the EEC in attracting FDI had been conferred on non-members much before there was any certainty that they would join. Another graph (not shown) indicates that Spain, Portugal and Greece, which entered the EEC only in the 1980s, experienced an upsurge in FDI at the same time as did all EEC members.

Finally, neither the final eradication of internal EEC tariffs in 1968 nor the admission of the three in 1973 is associated with any particular surge of population, in either curve; hence Figure 5.1 lends little support either to arguments concerning the effect of external tariffs (the CET) or to arguments regarding economies of scale or scope.

In Figures 5.2 and 5.3, we decompose Figure 5.1 into its constituent components, foundings and disbandings of subsidiaries, for the same two

120

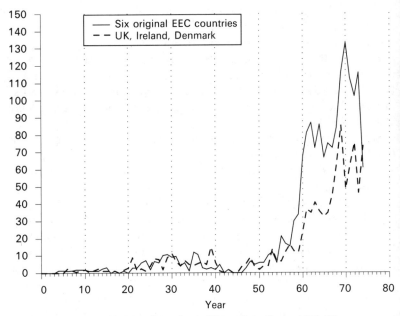

Figure 5.2   Number of subsidiary foundings, 1903–73

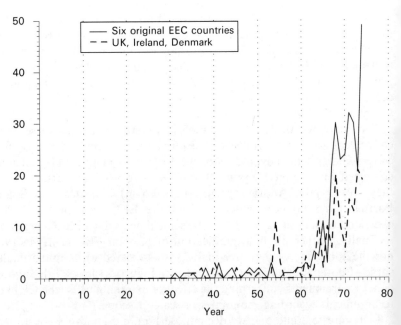

Figure 5.3   Number of subsidiary disbandings, 1903–73

sets of countries. In Figure 5.2, we do observe a marked decrease in foundings during World War II, but no clear evidence that the Great Depression deterred FDI in either group of countries. There is an upsurge in foundings in 1957–58 but, again, it affects approximately equally the six countries which were in the EEC at the time of the upsurge and the three which were not.

Figure 5.3, which shows the number of disbandings for the same two groups of countries, tells a somewhat different story. There is a small rash of disbandings in 1953, in the three only. This is compatible with scale and scope arguments if one is willing to see these disbandings in the three as involving a transfer of resources to the six, perhaps dictated by the impending formation of the EEC in 1957. There is no apparent upsurge of foundings in the six (Figure 5.2), however, that would correspond to this rash of disbandings in the three. At any rate the number involved (11 subsidiaries) is small enough to inspire caution.

This quick and admittedly crude visual examination does not command a powerful endorsement of three of the most common arguments seeking to explain the existence of FDI. This conclusion has heuristic value: it encourages us to direct our attention to other types of explanation. Although this visual test in no way demonstrates that these arguments are erroneous, it increases the plausibility of other types of explanation.

Imports and FDI: A Longitudinal Visual Examination

A central tenet of transaction costs theory is that trade and FDI are different means to the same end (e.g. Hennart 1988, p. 285). Although we lack data regarding the several intermediate forms (see Contractor and Lorange 1986), we may study the evolution of trade in various European countries according to their status *vis-à-vis* the EEC. Ideally countries which joined the EC earlier should experience a greater displacement of imports by FDI than those countries which joined later or which did not join.

In Figures 5.4, 5.5, 5.6 and 5.7, individual counties are paired according to the different timing of their status *vis-à-vis* the EEC. (W. H. Davidson 1980, p. 16 has also used paired comparisons.) Thus, France, a founding member, is paired with Spain, a third-wave joiner; likewise, the Netherlands and Portugal; Germany is paired with the UK, a second-phase joiner; Belgium, also a founding member, is paired with Austria, a steady non-member.

The left side of each graph shows the value of the imports into each country originating in the USA, expressed as a percentage of the value of total imports. The right side of each graph shows the value of imports

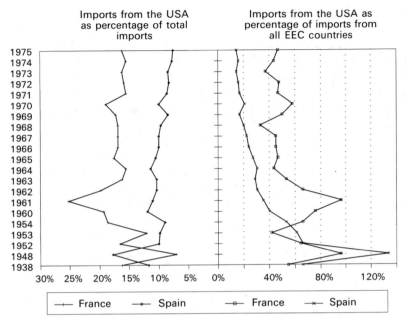

Figure 5.4   France and Spain

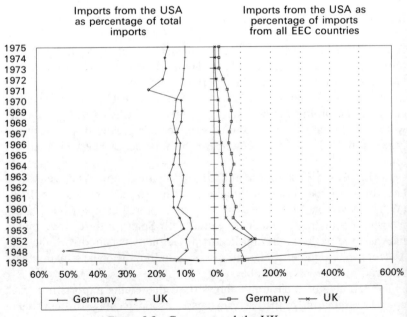

Figure 5.5   Germany and the UK

123

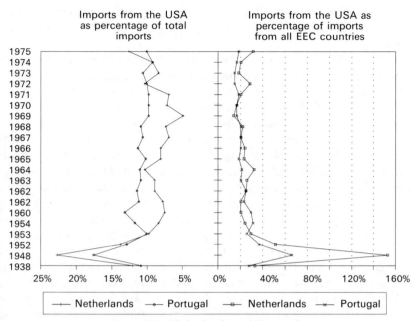

Figure 5.6   Netherlands and Portugal

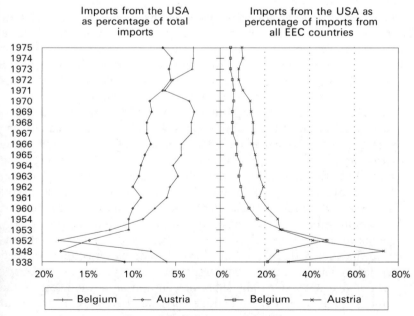

Figure 5.7   Belgium and Austria

into each country from the EEC, expressed as a percentage of total imports. All import figures are from United Nations International Trade Statistics.

Overall, the percentage of imports from the USA is remarkably stable over time, from the post-war period to 1975. This appears to be equally true for members of each pair, which does not lend credibility to the thesis that FDI displaces trade. The observation that France, Germany and the Netherlands did not decrease their imports from the USA as a result of early membership in the EEC is, in principle, compatible with this thesis. It is possible that the displacement takes the form of growth in imports which would have taken place had these countries not been in the EEC; however, this growth deficit interpretation would be more compelling if imports into the other members of each pair showed an increase in excess of those experienced by EEC members and early joiners. We observe no such differences in Figures 5.4, 5.5 or 5.6.

In the case of Belgium (Figure 5.7), we do see a decrease in the percentage of imports originating in the USA, from more than 10 percent to a little over 5 percent during the period. However, this small fall in American imports is easily matched by a corresponding fall in the American imports of Austria, a country similar in many ways to Belgium but one which never joined the EEC. Hence, we find that FDI may not replace trade at all in those countries where one would most expect it to do so.

The right side of the graphs points to a similar conclusion. For all four early joiners the value of imports from the USA expressed as a percentage of imports from all EEC countries declines considerably for the whole period. (This fact is somewhat obscured by the scale of the graphs.) However, the same is true of late joiners and of Austria. Thus imports from the EEC may have displaced potential imports from the USA (remember the left side of the graphs) in EEC countries but this is equally true for non-EEC countries. This fact is less compatible with the hypothesis that FDI displaced trade than with the idea that the EEC exerted its import pull not only upon itself but also on surrounding countries. This same observation is also compatible with an explanation which leaves no room at all for the EEC as an institutional arrangement: Europe as a whole rebuilt itself after the war and the close trade relations one would expect on the basis of propinquity and of historically determined national specialization simply returned. It would be interesting to find out if the post-World War II trade patterns approximated their late nineteenth-century counterparts.

The above discussion falls short of constituting a valid test of the relationship between FDI and trade for several reasons. First, visual examination is not sufficiently precise. Secondly, Figures 5.4, 5.5, 5.6 and

5.7 do not show every possible combination of countries; there may be hidden bias in the selection studied here. Third, as mentioned earlier, forms of entry intermediate between FDI and trade should also be examined as they might modify thoroughly these provisional conclusions.

In the next section, we examine the disbandings of subsidiaries with maximum likelihood logistics estimation models, and test a series of eclectic models, incorporating hypotheses and variables derived from ecological theory.

Disbandings of Subsidiaries: Logistics Models

Model Form

Table 5.1 shows six time series logistics regression models of the kind routinely used in organizational ecology. In each of these models, an observation (or 'spell') is a given subsidiary in existence in a given year. The dependent variables are the likelihoods of being in one of two states, such as disbanded or not, in a given year. The covariates (discussed below) are an eclectic mix suggested by various generalizations derived from organizational ecology and from various international business perspectives.

This modeling technique allows the investigator to manipulate the amount of time elapsed between the event of interest and the manifestation of its purported cause: thus, all the models in Table 5.1 comprise two covariates ('disbanded previous year' and 'founded previous year'). measured one year before the event of interest. The same variable could have been measured ('lagged') two, three or ten years before the event of interest. This latitude gives the investigator the chance to incorporate time in substantive fashion into models. This has both theoretical and heuristic advantages: theoretically, it allows for the testing of hypotheses regarding the length of time a given process requires; heuristically, it permits one to get a feel for the proper time specification of a process for which such specification is not theoretically formulated. Time lag manipulation carries a cost in terms of spells, however. Since each spell incorporates a time-period dimension (here, a year), any increment in lag shortens the total number of spells available for estimation.

The relationships between covariates and the dependent variables are expressed in terms of Beta coefficients. To each such coefficient is associated a conventional statistical significance level. In addition, a Chi-square coefficient associated with each model expresses the probability that the configuration represented by the whole model could have been obtained randomly. The Chi-square coefficient, however, is not

Table 5.1 Maximum likelihood estimations

	Beta coefficients (Standard error in parentheses)		
	Model 1: Likelihood of subsidiary disbanding in a given year	Model 2: Likelihood of subsidiary being sold in a given year	Model 3: Likelihood of subsidiary being liquidated in a given year
Age of subsidiary (years in existence as subsidiary)	-0.011** (0.004)	-0.006 (0.006)	-0.011 (0.007)
Greenfield versus acquired (dummy, '1' if greenfield)	-0.556** (0.090)	-0.349* (0.222)	-0.939** (0.139)
Number of foreign subsidiaries controlled by parent companies	0.037** (0.015)	0.024 (0.019)	0.069* (0.023)
Number of subsidiaries of American multinationals disbanded previous year	0.124** (0.008)	0.128** (0.011)	0.114** (0.014)
Number of subsidiaries of American multinationals founded previous year	-0.097** (0.012)	-0.125** (0.017)	-0.072** (0.018)
Subsidiary in existence 1902–38 (dummy, '1' if yes)	-2.227** (0.307)	-1.883** (0.418)	-2.048** (0.457)
Constant	-2.079** (0.074)	-2.170** (0.107)	-1.924** (0.106)
Chi-square	431.58 (DF = 6)	235.66 (DF = 6)	190.96 (DF = 6)
Number of observations	8512	4383	3474
Number of events	817	425	372

	Model 4: Likelihood of subsidiary being liquidated in a given year	Model 5: Likelihood of subsidiary being liquidated in a given year	Model 6: Likelihood of subsidiary being liquidated in a given year
Age of subsidiary (years of existence as subsidiary)	0.005 (0.008)	0.005 (0.008)	0.003 (0.008)
Greenfield versus acquired (dummy, '1' if greenfield)	−0.168 (0.0178)	−0.073 (0.181)	−0.055 (0.184)
Number of foreign subsidiaries controlled by parent companies	0.031 (0.031)	0.017 (0.032)	0.066* (0.034)
Number of subsidiaries of American multinationals disbanded previous year	0.048** (0.017)	0.008 (0.021)	0.016 (0.022)
Number of subsidiaries of American multinationals founded previous year	−0.071** (0.020)	−0.050* (0.021)	−0.011 (0.022)
Annual increase in unit labour cost	0.069* (0.023)	0.078* (0.023)	0.048* (0.241)
Subsidiary in existence 1957–67 (dummy, '1' if yes)			−1.493** (0.296)
Constant	−8.347**(2.48)	−8.709*(2.165)	−4.912* (0.296)
Chi-square	36.22 (DF=6)	46.50 (DF=7)	87.51 (DF=8)
Number of observations	1118	1118	1118
Number of events	169	169	169

* significant at the 0.05 level.
** significant at the 0.01 level.

equivalent to the R-square of multivariable, 'OLS' regression, for example. There is no convenient way to use this quantity to determine the amount of total variance explained by the model. Instead, Chi-square is used in nested models to evaluate the statistical significance of the incremental variance explained by the Beta coefficient associated with a variable added to a previous model.

Variables

Each of the models in Table 5.1 incorporates the following variables derived from organizational ecology theory.

Age of subsidiary measured as the number of years elapsed since the founding of the subsidiary. This included testing whether the liability of newness discovered with respect to many kinds of independent organizations (Hannan and Freeman 1989, pp. 81–6, pp. 245–70) also obtains for dependent organizations such as subsidiaries. Age has also been recognized as an important variable by some students of international business (Kogut 1988, p. 329; Li and Guisinger 1990.)

Number of subsidiaries of American multinationals disbanded the previous year. This variable simply captures the effect of unmeasured factors which are thought to affect adversely but specifically the category of organizations under study. Thus this variable can be viewed as a signal of bad times for American manufacturing subsidiaries. Another argument for including this variable is that every disbanding of such an organization frees resources for others of the same kind and might therefore have a negative effect on the disbanding rate. This argument is especially cogent in this case since many of our disbandings are sales to others.

Number of foundings of American subsidiaries in the preceding year. This variable is intended to capture in a fluid way the degree of legitimacy of such organizations. The underlying argument is that it is more difficult to make the decision to disband an ailing or controversial subsidiary at a time when other MNCs (possibly in the same industry) are founding new ones. There are both judgmental and strategic versions of this argument. First, it may be difficult for decision-makers to go openly against the current. Second, an MNC may retain a subsidiary of dubious usefulness in order to occupy the ground, so to speak, against competitors, local and domestic.

Both the number of prior disbandings and the number of prior failings are lagged one year to express the fact that we expect proximate but not instantaneous causation in these models. These two variables have been used in other studies with different specifications, including curvilinear ones. In general, these studies point to an empirical generalization supporting the general idea that the variables matter. For a theoretical discussion and application, see Delacroix and Carroll (1983, pp. 277–9) and Hannan and Freeman (1989, pp. 141–2 and pp. 207–16). For a more recent utilization, see Delacroix, Swaminathan and Solt (1989).

These three variables, together, constitute a base ecological model of subsidiary disbandings. It would have been helpful to include in this base model a measure of subsidiary size. Organizational ecologists have found strong support for the thesis of 'liability of newness'. It would be useful to discover whether the idea that smallness kills while large size almost confers immortality also applies to formally dependent organizations such as subsidiaries. Students of international business appear to have shown little interest in the issue of size of subsidiary, perhaps because of the definitional assumption of the dependence of subsidiaries (for exceptions, see Horst 1972; Swendenborg 1979; Kimura 1989). Yet the study of the link between subsidiary size and the propensity to liquidate may be an elegant if indirect empirical approach to the question of control: does their dependent status protect subsidiaries against the liability of newness generally afflicting organizations? If it does not, how much managing does the parent company management do?

The next two covariates are suggested by international business theory. Many scholars in the field consider parent company experience an important factor of success (Horst 1972; Swendenborg 1979; W. H. Davidson 1980, p. 13; Anderson and Goughlan 1987, p. 80; Terpstra and Yu 1988; Hennart 1989, p. 16). Since success seems to require continued existence, it is proper to include such a variable (measured as *number of subsidiaries held by the parent MNC*) anywhere in the world.

Finally, all models include a dummy variable expressing whether a subsidiary was *acquired* (bought) or whether it is a *greenfield operation* (coded as '1'). As Hennart (1988, p. 372) puts it, 'Taking over a firm involves transforming personnel into employees'. This diffuse but significant cost is not incurred by greenfield subsidiaries. Yet, greenfield implies a greater degree of control (Hennart 1989, p. 13). Other international business scholars have also used the distinction between greenfield and acquired subsidiaries (Caves and Mehra 1986, for example).

We also take *labor* cost into consideration both as a proxy for general level of economic development and because Hennart (1989) warns against ignoring different production costs in different countries. This variable expresses the annual increase in manufacturing labor costs across European countries with the value of the index in the year 1980 serving as a base of 100.

Finally, dummy variables representing time periods are incorporated in several models. This is done in an attempt to capture important phases in the economic and institutional history of Europe and of the EEC. The coding of the historical dummy covariates is based on Harrop (1989) and on Hudson, Rhind and Mounsey (1984).

Discussion of Findings

Model 1 conforms substantively to both organizational ecology and to international business theory. As was found previously for several different kinds of organizations (see Hannan and Freeman 1989 for a review), older subsidiaries are less likely to disappear than new ones (liability of newness). In addition, for foreign subsidiaries as for other kinds of organizations, there are good times and bad times. Subsidiaries are more likely to disband in periods when many like organizations disappear. They are less likely to suffer the same fate during periods when many like organizations are founded, presumably because the socio-economic environment is propitious to such organizations at such times, or because of mimetic decisions by parent company decision-makers. The fact that greenfield subsidiaries are less likely to disband, while subsidiaries controlled by experienced multinationals are more likely to do so supports a traditional viewpoint based on the presumption that executive governance is effective. It implies that multinational executives know what they are doing. The covariate, *subsidiary in existence 1902–38*, is included to denote a period of moderate to high protectionism in Europe. Note that its negative effect on disbanding exists over and above the effect of simple organizational age since the latter variable is controlled for in Model 1. This negative effect indirectly lends validity to the common practice of responding to trade barriers through FDI. This finding indicates that trade barriers protect foreign-held enterprises as well as indigenous ones. All variables in Model 1 show coefficients significant at or above the .05 level.

Models 2 and 3 disaggregate the dependent variable in Model 1 according to mode of disbanding. Model 2 shows the equivalent of Model 1 but only for those subsidiaries that were sold. Model 3 shows the same model for subsidiaries that were liquidated. A subsidiary is considered liquidated when its functions cease completely. Hence, liquidation is the organizational disbanding of the *subsidiary*. By contrast, the sale of a subsidiary is an ambiguous event because a sale may be precipitated either by the relative success or the relative failure of a business entity.

Model 1, 2 and 3 must be compared cautiously because they are estimated over different numbers of cases. Nevertheless, some interesting patterns emerge. Most notably, in Model 2, the age dependence of disappearance has vanished. The sign remains negative, suggesting that older subsidiaries may be less likely to be sold than younger ones. However, the relevant coefficient is not significant. In Model 3 the negative effect of age on the likelihood of liquidation only reaches the 0.10 level of significance. However, it is quite possible that it would reach the 0.05 level if this model were based on a larger number of observations and of events. Both findings cast a doubt on the idea that subsidiaries are as subject to the liability of newness as non-dependent organizations; hence, they imply effective control. Yet liquidation, a fairly sure expression of failure in the conventional sense, may be responsive to age, as we have seen, which implies that subsidiaries are subject to the same process as independent organizations.

Separating events according to mode of disappearance also throws some additional light on the role played by parent company experience, represented by the number of subsidiaries controlled. This variable has no significant effect on the likelihood of subsidiary sale but a significant positive effect on the likelihood of liquidation. This strengthens the assumption in Wilson's (1979) study that managers tend to be attached to the organizations they create. In this perspective, managers from a more experienced multinational are more likely than others to confront the tough decision to liquidate. This also implies control. The effects of all other variables are the same in Model 2 and 3 as in Model 1.

Model 4 shows the results of a best effort to incorporate conventional macro-economic variables into a basic liquidation model. Liquidation is selected as the most interesting mode of disappearance because it implies failure of the subsidiary, although possibly successful adaption at the level of the whole MNC. In this model, unfortunately estimated over quite a small number of observations, the age dependence of liquidation has vanished completely, as have the effects of greenfield and parent company experience. However, the positive and negative effects, respectively, of prior disbandings and foundings remain intact in spite of the reduction in the number of observations. This finding (unsurprising to an organizational ecologist) underscores again the sturdiness of the basic ecological model, in spite of the disappearance of the age effect. Model 4 includes a variable expressing the rise in unit labor cost. This variable has a strong positive effect on the likelihood of liquidation. This implies a rational economic managerial approach to subsidiaries rather than blind selection. Hence the finding lends support to the idea that liquidation of subsidiaries may be deliberate adaptive strategies enacted by MNCs.

With the visual examinations of patterns of events, we found that there is a possibility that the creation of the EEC accelerated the rate of foundings of American subsidiaries. Below, we pursue this idea with estimation models of the propensity to *liquidate* subsidiaries in EEC versus non-EEC countries. The importance of the EEC may reside either in the fact that it is perceived as an environment especially propitious for American MNCs, or that apprehensions about the CET erected around the EEC compelled American MNCs to found subsidiaries within the EEC which they would not have founded otherwise. Model 5 shows an attempt to introduce the existence of the EEC into the preceding Model 4. It comprises a variable which stands for having been in existence during the period 1957–67 when most of the intra-EEC tariff barriers were removed and the CET was gradually installed. The negative significant coefficient associated with this variable indicates that the EEC was a propitious environment. The Chi-square difference between Models 4 and 5 is significant at the 0.05 level. This favors the first explanation outlined above against the argument that the existence of the EEC merely forced American MNCs to have subsidiaries in that part of the world. All other coefficients in Model 5 are as in Model 4, except that number of disbandings in the previous year ceases to be significant. This is as we would expect since this variable stands for the relative benignity of the environment, a factor we incorporated into the model via the variable, *in existence in 1957–67*.

Model 6 replicates Model 5 with two changes. A dummy variable is included to capture the consequences on the probability of liquidation of being in existence during the period 1968–73, immediately preceding the admission of the UK, Ireland and Denmark. The inclusion of this variable swamps the previous effect of number of subsidiaries founded in the previous year. This suggests that the considerable enlargement of the EEC improves the perceived attractiveness of this entity, as the removal of internal tariffs did before.

In Model 6, we can improve on Model 5 further by excluding from the parent company experience variable all subsidiaries *not* located in the EEC. This suffices to restore this variable's significance (which was lost in Model 5) and re-inforces the idea that there is a link between tangible experience and the willingness to liquidate. This finding also encourages the speculation that it is the economies of scale or scope offered by the growing EEC, rather than avoidance of the CET, that results in the wish to have subsidiaries in Europe. If concerns about the CET predominated, experience in Europe specifically would not play a stronger part in liquidations than multinational experience in general. This is because any MNC executive understands trade barriers while it takes specialized geographic experience to comprehend economies of scale and scope potentials.

The Chi-square differences between Models 6 and 4 on the one hand and Models 6 and 5 on the other are both significant at the 0.01 level. Model 6 is the most powerful model constructed thus far.

Finally, we may note with interest that the large jump in Chi-square associated with the introduction of one historical dummy variable (in Model 5) and the even larger jump associated with the addition of another historical dummy variable (in Model 6) strongly suggest that students of multinationals rely on arbitrarily selected periods of observation only at great peril.

DISCUSSION

The estimations, performed in the ecological manner discussed above, fall short of resolving any important theoretical issues. However, considered together they constitute an economical way to select certain research directions against others. This style of modelling can be viewed as a quick means of feeding the research intuition. In particular, event history analysis gives the researcher a convenient but fairly rigorous means to question received wisdom. This is true, as well, for those who have no interest in selection processes.

The evolutive nature of this mode of analysis (see the changes from Models 1 to 6) also allows the researcher conveniently to assess the likelihood that hypotheses derived from quite disparate bodies of theories may complement one another or, conversely, be incompatible with one another. This style of research thus holds two kinds of promises: first, it promises to help free us from the habit, firmly implanted in the social sciences, of talking past one another; second, this style of research contributes to the realization of the dream of making theory truly incremental via the accumulation of legitimate empirical results.

Common wisdom has it that large multicase studies belong in research which already benefits from a high level of rigor. This seems a corollary to the view that case studies are a good approach to phenomenological understanding. However, the first idea may be short-sighted. An organizational entity taken in isolation may be quite different from the same entity considered in its large numbers. Hence the observation of many organizations of the same kind, even if it is done over time, may be necessary to the acquisition of an intuitive understanding of the *category* of entities that is both concrete and realistic. Large scale studies of whole populations may thus play a role similar to that traditionally advocated for case studies.

One may raise a reasonable objection to this research strategy prescription: it is very onerous, in money and in time, to collect the kind of large data set used by organizational ecologists. However, the latter's universal experience seems to be that, 'Seek and ye shall find'.

Moreover, large detailed longitudinal data sets can usually be used repeatedly. (Glenn Carroll advised me at the time of this writing, in 1990, that he was undertaking a new study based on our Argentinean and Irish press data set, collected in 1979.) Finally, the collecting, beating into shape and exploitation of such data sets foster cooperative endeavors. This is especially true at a time when major professional associations (the American Sociological Association, in particular) have decreed that authors of published articles must share their data more or less without restriction.

Students of international business reared in a managerial, voluntaristic atmosphere may find the working assumption of ecologists regarding selection absurd, repugnant, immoral or 'too horrible to behold' (as one of my colleagues puts it). Kogut's extensive and detailed discussion (Chapter 6) shows that there may be little philosophical incompatibility between these approaches that is fundamental. Actually, it is easy to view strategic management as the application of managerial skill within the area of freedom left by non-managerial processes, or by processes not under the control of managers. There is no reason why this rudimentary model of reality cannot be tested with the methods presented in this chapter. At any rate, it seldom makes sense to expel history from the study of social phenomena (Kogut 1988), either from a theoretical or from a policy viewpoint. It is sensible to incorporate it explicitly in empirical models.

In general, it is useful to keep in mind that event history analysis models can be used very eclectically, on both sides of the equation. Thus, in principle and given data availability, one could incorporate into such an analysis factors designed to capture Ghoshal and Bartlett's (1988) propositions on the innovations subsidiaries contribute to parent companies. (Perhaps they thereby stave off their own or the parents' selection out of the relevant population.) On the other side of the causal arrow, event history analysis and, in general, organizational ecology research strategies, lend themselves well to the study of transition processes which have captured the attention of international business scholars, such as the transition from purely domestic expansion to the several modes of foreign expansion that are the subjects of transaction cost theory.

Notes

1. The seemingly more commonsense managerial schools of thought which favour an adaptation stance tend to rest on few hard findings. This is especially true of adaptationist perspectives applied to business organizations. Thus, Boyd and McSween's exhaustive (1988) survey of published,

multi-case empirical studies shows a 'weak' link between the practice of strategic planning and measures of performance.

2. Note that this explanation of the role of organizations differs markedly from the explanation embedded in transaction cost theory. Nevertheless, the two conceptualizations are not incompatible.

3. It is essential to remember that selection, which applies to groups of organizations, is different, and even conceptually incompatible with individual adaptation, although the two mechanisms for change may exist side by side in the real world.

4. For an example of such a population, see Delacroix and Carroll (1983). For a discussion of the delineation of organizational populations, see Hannan and Freeman (1989, pp. 48–65). Aldrich, (1979), constitutes a good introduction to organizational ecology thinking. See Carroll (1988) for a collection of empirical studies in organizational ecology.

5. Although this way of doing things is most noticeable in practitioner-oriented works (e.g. Peters and Waterman 1982), it is not difficult to find instances in scholarly journals.

6. It is true that success as well as failure may lead to elimination, as with many acquisitions. This poses a technical problem, discussed by Freeman, Carroll and Hannan (1983), without impairing the soundness of this reasoning.

7. See Yves Doz (1984) on the importance of government policies. Note, however, that the intuitively obvious importance of political factors is not necessarily strongly supported by empirical research; see, for example, Kobrin's (1976) cross-sectional empirical study.

8. There is some indication, see Li and Guisinger (1990) who cite Stobaugh's (1970) study, that American MNCs are quite reluctant to save their subsidiaries from business failure.

6 Learning, or the Importance of being Inert: Country Imprinting and International Competition*

Bruce Kogut

An unfortunate development in the study of MNCs has been the separation of comparative management from the theory of foreign direct investment (FDI). The narrow effect of this separation has been to neglect the development of an understanding of how the country of origin influences the capabilities of firms and their domestic and international competitiveness. In fact, as argued below, FDI is the expression of the differential organizing capabilities of firms across countries.

The wider effect has been to impoverish organizational theory as well as the theory of the MNC. To a surprising degree theoretical efforts have been directed towards sustaining an argument that the blandest international comparison would falsify. At the same time, an unfortunate amount of effort has been invested in developing a theory of the MNC that duplicates, with varying degrees of success, well established principles in organizational theory.

It is a common complaint of outsiders to a field that they cannot make sense of its research program, or paradigm. Indeed, the panoply of theories in macro-organizational studies is often bewildering, ranging from resource dependency, to organizational ecology, to institutionalism. Curiously, the field of international management has generated over 30 years a rather well worked out research program based on the Dunning (1979) trinity of ownership, location and internalization (OLI) advantages. Yet research on the economics of the MNC has, perhaps by the

* I would like to acknowledge the comments of Jacques Delacroix on the draft, the roundtable discussion chaired by Sidney Winter, and the patience of the editors, Sumantra Ghoshal and Eleanor Westney.

very force of its success, not been matched by corresponding gains in developing a predominant view of the organization of firms that span borders.

One of the most promising areas of dialogue between the fields of international management and organization theory concerns the pivotal question of the bias of the country of origin on the capabilities of firms, or populations of firms, to learn and adapt. This question lies at the foundation of three major areas of study in international management: how a firm internationalizes, the effect of the home market on firm-specific advantages leading to FDI, and the transfer of new practices across borders. All three areas share a common assumption that the firm develops, much as Bendix (1956) and Stinchcombe (1965) stressed, out of the socio-economic conditions of its home environment.[1] Even as the firm internationalizes, it remains imprinted by its early developmental history and domestic environment. In this light, the tendency to separate the study of the international firm from comparative management is in fundamental contradiction to the implicit recognition of the conceptual interdependence of the two fields.

The common assumption of the significance of the early bias of the home environment presents a thorny patch of issues when the assumption itself becomes the focus of inquiry, for to what extent does the institutional context influence the creation of organizational forms and capabilities? And if different national contexts generate organizational forms that differ in performance, why is there such slow convergence to best practice? In this process of convergence, what are the relative weights assigned to selection (through firm entry and exit) and to learning?

These questions are, clearly, also central to the organizational literature on learning, population ecology and institutionalism. The following pages seek to show the benefits of estabishing a broader dialogue between organization theory and the theory of the MNC by establishing the elements required to address these questions. Ultimately, a theory of organizational learning, whether within or across countries, is the study of firm's knowledge and its inertia. The central problem analyzed below is the extent to which a portion of this knowledge is contingent on the country of origin.

The first section identifies three problems of longstanding interest in international management and argues that their analysis requires a comparative management perspective. The next section sets out the view of the firm as competing on organizing principles (i.e., *how* it organizes its activities), and argues that these principles are influenced by the prevailing templates of organization in a society. We put forth the view that FDI is the extension of organizing principles across borders.

The subsequent section, then, turns the tables and asks what theories of organization can learn from this definition of the problems in international management. Finally, the implications for the study of the MNC are examined.

PROBLEM ONE: GENESIS

Without question one of the most troubling areas of analysis in the field of international management is explaining the origins of institutions and their differences across countries. This problem has not gone unnoticed in the relatively ahistorical literature on the theory of FDI. Hymer (1960), for example, wrote:

> Why do firms of different countries have unequal ability? In part, it is due to the fact there is an unequal distribution of skills among people. The population of every country is a sample of the universe and the particular distribution of skills will vary from country to country for no other reason than this. In part it is also due to the chance discovery of a gold mine, a valuable formula, or Scotch Whisky.

Hymer states an explanation that strikes deep similarities with the notion of random genetic drift, or what we can call technological drift. Technological drift is here used to mean that the historical accident of an innovation behaves like a mutation in a small community, leading to a potential increase in frequency by a process of path-dependent diffusion. As outlandish as this seems, it should be recalled what a powerful effect the wheel had on Indo-European civilization following its discovery in Sumeria. Yet, while the necessity of the wheel would certainly demand its innovation, the Aztec and Mayan civilizations did not apparently adopt it. Indeed, Hymer seems to have understood well the implication of his reflections, as he writes, 'This consideration of historical accident comes into play whenever it is true that a firm's ability in a given year depends on its past activity' (Hymer 1960, p. 76).

Of course, no matter how intellectually engaging an explanation resting on path dependent drift may be, it is, sociologically, an inadequate and unsatisfactory theory. After all, the Aztec toys used wheels; it was not lack of discovery, but of the social process of adoption. An economic speculation might be that the use of slave labor reduced the attractiveness of adopting the wheel. Indeed, the relative factor bias explanation is the cornerstone of Vernon's (1966) theory of the product life cycle of international trade and investment.[2] It would seem that, whatever might have been the relative factor costs in Mexico, adoption of the wheel would have had substantial benefits. In fact, the Samuelson objection to the bias-induced theory of innovation is, by the principles of rational choice, devastating: why should a firm care about relative costs, he argued, when the objective function is to minimize total costs and, thus, the costs of any factor of production? Moreover, to return to our earlier example of the wheel, the demand for its discovery would surely be phenomenal in any civilization. Demand alone does not seem to be sufficient. In short, the Vernon notion of biased innovation is a convenient but unexplained assumption.

This perspective is also explicit in the influential ideas of Burenstam Linder (1961). In Burenstam Linder's original identification of the importance of intra-industry trade, exports are the extension of the home market network overseas. The multinational enterprise arises out of the initial variation in country environments that influences entrepreneurial endeavors and cumulative investments. Although Burenstam Linder sketches an explication of the firm as consisting of cumulative capabilities moulded by the home environment, it is not grounded in a general theory of organizational capabilities.

PROBLEM TWO: LOCATION AND OWNERSHIP ADVANTAGES

It should be recalled that the traditional explanation for the rise of the MNC and its international expansion has emphasized the importance of intangible assets (e.g., technology, product differentiation). These assets must provide a sufficient advantage to the firm to more than offset its disadvantage in competing against local firms in their home markets. At the same time, the intangibility of these assets discourage arm's-length contracting for the familiar reasons of market failure. This traditional argument does not, however, suggest an explanation as to why certain countries should own a substantially larger share of FDI than indicated by their share of the world's income. We have thus come full circle back to the problem of genesis.

Another way to approach the question of genesis is to eschew direct explanation, and instead develop a taxonomy of location factors influencing the ownership advantages of the firm. Such an approach is given in Dunning (1979). He argues that comparative advantage encompasses a broader spectrum than simply factor costs of labour and capital, since location influences the economics of the resident firms. Analytically the task is to link 'the type of ownership advantages particular countries are most likely to generate and sustain and then relate these to the resource and market requirements of particular industries' (Dunning 1979, p. 280). For example, Dunning speculates that large and standardized markets will lead to larger firms due to the reaping of scale economies and product diversification. Furthermore, technological advantages are likely to be created in countries where governments sponsor innovation and research.

This argument is appealing and sound. It is possible, of course, to come to other conclusions while accepting the overall logic. As a case in point, Dreze contends that firms from small countries must concentrate on fewer standardized products in order to compete effectively on world markets.[3] Whether the handicap of a small national market or the abundance of a large home market leads to standardization and larger firm size are two conflicting predictions, which, prima facie, seem equally plausible.

The empirical evidence on this question is mixed, as the variance in size distributions across countries indicates. If we compare, for example, the upper percentages of the distribution, the variation is remarkable.[4] The USA and the UK prove to have substantially larger corporations than Japan or Germany, a pattern going back to the earlier part of the century. Even within the same industries, the differences are striking. According to Fruin's (1989) calculations, there is considerable disparity in the size of leading American and Japanese firms in the auto, electronic and chemical industries. In 1987, General Motors had 813 400 employees compared to Toyota's 64 329; IBM, 389 348 to Hitachi's 76 210; and Dupont, 140 145 to Asahi Chemicals' 15 595.

A good deal of the explanation for the difference between the USA and Japan lies in the prevalence of subcontracting practices in Japan.[5] It is not compelling to attribute these variations to size differences of the economy, especially when we consider the extent of the export market which Japanese corporations serve. Instead these differences in the size distribution appear to be the result of long-term historical developments in the two countries.

An understanding of the differential performance of US and Japanese corporations, it would seem, cannot be derived by comparing individual corporations. The degree of vertical integration in the USA stands in stark contrast to the role of interfirm relationships in Japan. One suspects, as the study of Westney and Sakakibara (1985) has shown, that a comparison of Japan and the USA would also reveal strikingly different institutions regarding science-based ties to universities and research centers, internal and external labor markets and organizing principles. The concept of ownership advantage is difficult, in many respects, to separate from the wider institutional linkages binding firms into national industrial networks.

PROBLEM THREE: INTERNALIZATION

As noted earlier, theories of FDI frequently rely on the notion of intangible assets that are easier to transfer through the firm than across markets. The intangibility assumption is critical, as it suggests that the firm has a cost advantage in transferring this knowledge within its ownership as opposed to within a contractual or market context. A misleading form of the argument states that this transfer has the characteristics of a public good and it is the public good characteristic, via the well-known argument of Arrow, that leads to market failure. A more plausible rendition is simply that the marginal costs of internal transfer are lower than those of the market and the incremental saving is greater than the incremental costs of doing business abroad.

One avenue by which to explain why the internal marginal costs are lower is to appeal to the differential incentive properties of organizations and firms. As this perspective is well laid out elsewhere in this volume (see Chapter 7), we do not need to repeat the argument. Let us turn, instead, to a discussion of the effects of the country of origin on contracting.

In this regard, one of the striking results of an international comparison is the high variance in institutions across countries, ranging from differences in the degree of subcontracting to union activity to the internal organization of the firm. This variance is at odds with the ahistorical abstraction of the transaction costs or internalization approach, for why should economic institutions not evolve similarly to resolve the problems of opportunism under uncertainty?

A simple but elusive answer is that the degree of opportunism differs across countries. In a lecture, the anthropologist Clifford Geertz described an island culture where the prevailing practice was to conceal one's purpose and to respond to questions deceptively. A country filled with liars is likely to develop institutional mechanisms by which veracity might be tested, or be forever stalemated. And, somewhat similarly, Ronald Dore (1983) has argued that the conventions of trust in Japan, backed by an extensive social network, lead to lower degrees of opportunism and, hence, a greater willingness to rely on long-term relationships among so-called arm's-length partners.

A more detailed institutional analysis would point to a comparison not only of the dilemmas of market exchange among countries, but also of the internal characteristics of firms. We have, in fact, come remarkably far in understanding these issues better. The studies of Lincoln, Hanada and McBride (1986) point to different authority and decision characteristics between Japanese and American firms. Interestingly, commitment levels in the firms from both countries were relatively high, despite different incentive systems. (One suspects, in passing, that Hennart's polar attributes of shirking and cheating may not fully capture the affiliative needs of the individual to engage in purposeful activities within an organized and stable context.)

The literature on internalization and transaction costs may, with sufficient fine tuning, be able to explain differential performance of countries on the basis of national variations in contractual and organizational incentives; certainly, the work of Aoki (1988) and North (1981) are impressive examples of such efforts. But this fine tuning should not obscure the fundamental point that these differences exist due to historical developments and social characteristics unique to the country of origin. Neither should we fail to observe that such practices, even though they are widely believed to be causally responsible for differential performance, diffuse slowly, if at all.

A COMMENT

It seems surprising that studies of the MNC should have neglected so strongly the implications of the country of origin for the analysis of the central problems listed above. Part of the explanation is that studies of FDI and, though less so, the MNC have rarely been comparative. Since Hymer – and in spite of his parenthetical comments cited above – the question to be answered has been why FDI flows vary across industries, not the question of what the country patterns are in FDI. The nature of the answer has been, except for occasional outlier studies such as that by Aharoni (1966), to treat firms as largely homogeneous, but responding differentially to the market and demand conditions of their home countries.

Let us, briefly, follow a different avenue, suggested by Nelson and Winter (1982), that begins with the view of the firm as consisting of a set of capabilities, or competences, as embodied in a stock of knowledge. This stock of knowledge is developed cumulatively. Due to differences in their experiential histories, the cumulative learning of firms displays considerable heterogeneity.

From this simple description, the lower marginal costs of internal transfer of intangible assets across borders reflect the the accumulation, or sunk investment, in a specific set of capabilities within a firm. Organizations are social communities in which individual and social expertise is transformed into economically useful products and services by the application of a set of higher-order organizing principles. Firms exist because they provide a social community of voluntaristic action supported by a set of organizational capabilities that are not reducible to individuals (Kogut and Zander forthcoming).

For the sake of exposition, consider the implications of this view for a firm that seeks to maximize its value through costly and bounded search under uncertainty. This costliness is a function of the distance of the new technology from the current technology being employed by the firm. Because knowledge of current technologies can be used to increase the probability of success in searching in related technologies, it pays to search in the local neighbourhood. Clearly, the above behavioral description provides a better match to the argument of Vernon and Burenstam Linder than the inconsistent story of relative factor bias.[6]

From this perspective arises a central claim: that is, direct investment is simply the extension of the organizing principles and capabilities of the firm across countries. The drawback of the inherited schema of the OLI (ownership, location and internalization) approach has been the failure to spell out exactly the ownership advantages of the firm. Intangible assets represent the accumulated capability of a firm to advertise, to adapt products, or to produce cheaply. The theoretical challenge facing the theory of the firm is to understand what are the abilities of organizations to carry out these activities. Before determining the boundaries (e.g., whether a technology should be licensed or not) it seems logical that we first need to understand why this technology would be better created and exploited in one organization as opposed to another.

These are large issues that cannot be addressed here, other than to note that the type of capabilities will vary across countries. This variance will, in part, be attributable to the effects of a common history and environment (what Westney calls 'isomorphic pulls') on firms. But it is also, and this is a point that should be emphasized, because part of the capabilities a firm enjoys consists of its relationships with other firms and institutions. In the early history of firms, the predominant factor in these relationships is that they are usually contained within the borders of a single country.

The remaining pages trace out the implications of this perspective.

INSTITUTIONALISM AND IMPRINTING

When Robert Solow received the Nobel prize in economics for his seminal work in growth theory, the Swedish economist Assar Lindbeck posed the question of whether the real sources of growth are less proximate than costs of inputs and the productivity in the process of transformation. Solow answered that clearly the institutions of education, government services, etc. are critical; nevertheless the consequences of these less proximate economic activities could be best analyzed by the principles of economics.

It would be hard to imagine, though, the heroism of the economic assumptions required to explain the variety of institutional arrangements among countries. An aggregation of firms' heterogeneous productive capabilities to a generic production function is itself an assumption that has not been without its critics (see, e.g. Nelson and Winter 1982). Similarly, we can assume, without more discussion, that the heterogeneity of institutional arrangements – why countries do not adopt optimal institutional structures – would prove a troubling issue.

Part of the problem is that bias towards the *status quo* is strongly underestimated. Most people do not ponder whether they could trade their parents, or their children, if only markets were to exist. Instead, they become attached to their idiosyncratic characteristics; a 'charming rascal' is the oxymoron by which many parents are consoled.

Norman O. Brown (1947) noticed that in mythology, cultures tend to impose their world on the heavens. The Greeks saw the gods fighting among themselves as if they were city states; the Persians imposed a royal hierarchy on their stories of divinity. Divine order is the projection of the human polity on the heavens.

That individuals have templates of how activities are organized is a powerful force in the replication of social structure.[7] Unquestionably other mechanisms of institutionalism (as described by Westney in Chapter 3) play significant, perhaps at times dominating, roles. The coercive role of the state is well documented, from Kemal Atatürk to Peter the Great; the state's ability to induce change by incentives is exemplified in the policies of Meiji Japan to Bismarck's Germany. Indeed, Weber, who clearly emphasized the role of ideas as becoming 'common to whole groups' of individuals – as he stated in the *Protestant Ethic* – also stressed the importance of the government as an agent of change from 'on high' (see Weber 1946).

However, coercion, and even imitation, would not be needed in the absence of normative obstacles to change. While some of these obstacles may reflect the rational resistance of agents who would suffer by change, it would be hard to explain mass movements on the basis of economic self-interest. We should not forget Marx's frustration over the false consciousness of workers to see their 'true' interests.

There is no optimal arrangement of human affairs or organized economic activity that can serve as a template because social knowledge is evolutionary and embedded in the social relationships that prevail. The history of Utopian movements shows that contrarian ideas enacted in a hostile or indifferent social setting do not take hold. Capitalism grows,

Eisenstadt noted, when commercial elites are not isolated – as the overseas Chinese in Indonesia are – from the larger community.

That organizational forms reflect the social context of the times of their foundings is a widely held, but understudied contention. The frequency of organizational births is certainly influenced by economic conditions and/or the munificence of critical agencies, be they governments or charitable organizations. When new industries are born (such as biotechnology) new firms invariably take the structure of incumbent organizations in their environment as their template. The recipes by which activities are organized are likely to be far more persistent than technologies *per se*, because they are expressions of enduring social relations.

There is a frequent confusion in the writings on the ecology of organizations regarding new technologies and new organizational forms.[8] Foundings may represent the inducement of new entrants into an industry due to the arrival of new technologies, and the rate of entry will be influenced by such factors as the degree of competition and the availability of resources. But these foundings, though competing on new technologies and for resources, are likely to share the organizing principles prevailing in the wider society (see Kimberly 1975). Indeed, once a start-up firm begins to grow, its reliance on the collection of technological skills of individuals shifts to the important task of creating organizing recipes. These recipes, such as bookkeeping, divisionalization, hiring and promoting, are adopted from the current agreement on what constitutes best practice.

It is not so much that firms are inert as that social structure is enduring. Firms learn, but in the context of what they *can* know. The disposition of the availability of knowledge is structured by the structure of social relations. What firms know is determined by their position in an industrial network.[9] Whether a firm has a tie (either directly or via intermediaries) to a set of university centers conditions its information and its potential to learn of new scientific discoveries. Localized search and learning is not an activity that occurs in some abstract plan of theoretical possibilities, but is embedded, in the sense of Granovetter (1985), in the available information set (i.e., in the structure of a firm's environment).

A critical question, then, is the extent to which the vicinity surrounding a firm's position in a social network is largely national or international. In order to learn, there must first be new lessons to be taught. International competition is interesting exactly for the reason that it presents new templates of organizing principles. Though these templates have national origins, the growth of cooperative and competitive relationships in an international network of firms and institutions changes the content of information available to firms, permitting the diffusion of national practices across borders.

As a result, we come to a conclusion that differs from a narrow ecological perspective. We do not see firms as strictly inert, but rather as learning within a prevailing social structure. Some structures promote relatively rapid learning, others are less receptive. Let us turn, then, to examining how an international comparison throws light on the perennial and falsely stylized debate on adaptation versus selection.

LEARNING AND ORGANIZATIONAL ECOLOGY

It is easy to underestimate the importance of learning if firms tend to be born with similar templates. What appears as inertia reflects the similarity of organizational forms at birth and of developmental histories within fairly homogeneous (national) environments. This similarity is clearly violated in environments characterized by international competition and hence we should expect to find more striking examples and trends of learning among a population of firms of diverse national origins. But, before turning to the international aspects, we consider first the abstract argument.

The link between learning and inertia is, to varying degrees of explicitness, central to most theories on organizational learning. The article by B. Levitt and March (1987) on theories of organizational learning identified most approaches as falling under either adaptive or imitative behavior.[10] These theories generally share the property of being cybernetic: that is, they formulate the problem as bounded search with feedback.[11] It is easy to see this principle in operation in the formulation commonly used by March for trial and error learning, $Ft = Ft-1 + \alpha(F^* - Ft-1)$, where learning is described as gradual convergence of the current state F to some goal F^* at a learning rate α.[12]

Though Levitt and March focused only at the organizational level, this cybernetic view, as Steinbruner (1974) has noted, also fits learning at the population level, where the learning dynamic is Darwinian selection. In the population ecology literature, convergence is to a hypothetical number of homogeneous firms that can be supported by the environment. It is important to realize that the learning and hazard rates are roughly symmetrical, with the former representing convergence to an optimum from below (i.e., the number of firms learning best practices grows to approach some limit) and the latter, representing – if I may argue in a heuristic way – convergence from above (i.e., the number of entrants are in excess of the surviving number, with the total population declining to the same hypothetical limit).[13] The population ecology literature usually specifies the convergent number of firms empirically, such as the estimate of the asymptotic limit in the Makeham specification of the hazard models or as estimated solutions to the Lotka–Volterra equations.

Both the adaptive and selection view of change ignore, in their crudest formulations, the role of guided learning: that is, learning from others whether by imitation, consultancy or cultural institutions (e.g., schools). Given the existence of large consulting firms, guided learning seems to be, to say the least, significant. While the earlier equation of adaptation appears to include these wider considerations, the mechanisms by which guided learning occurs are not characterized by a simple feedback loop of trial and error (or trial and selection in the ecological description).

It is not hard, however, to relate the models to each other. In the adaptation model, α, the rate of adaptation, can itself be a function of how many other firms are engaged in a similar activity (see Herriot, Levinthal and March 1985; Stiglitz 1987.) Thus the rate of adaptation is influenced by the possibilities of externalities through an undefined mechanism of imitation. Or, to use the cybernetic language of Argyris and Schon (1978), if attention is switched from loop one (learning to do a task better) to loop two (learning to choose which tasks), F^* may also be set by an adaptive formulation tending to best practice among a firm's plants or among the firms in an industry (Herriot, Levinthal and March 1985). Imitation, therefore, can affect not only the rate of adaptation, but also the selection of the goal.

It is, in fact, difficult to reconcile the extreme assumption of limited trial and error learning to the results of most studies on the diffusion of innovations. As the studies of Rogers (1971) and many others have shown, communication plays a critical role in the diffusion of new innovations. Imitative channels are also created through the interchange of buyers and suppliers (von Hippel 1988). Firms which are sufficiently endowed with the ability to recognize shortfalls in performance are arguably also capable of comparing their performance against competitors in the industry.

Even though the population ecology models are seemingly remote from adaptive and imitative theories, a selection model is not necessarily incompatible. There is no intrinsic reason why selection can itself not be influenced by the varying learning abilities of the individual firms. The variation of the hazard rates faced by individual firms may well be a function of their differential abilities to learn from each other, just as size, generalism or specialism and other covariates are allowed to shift the hazard rates.[14] A population of firms may be driven to homogeneity by selection pressures, but these pressures are not inconsistent with heterogeneous capabilities of learning and imitation.[15]

To date, population ecology models have considered externalities among firms largely in the context of competitive effects created by density dependence. Whereas some kinds of externality may arise through communication and cooperation and promote group survival, density dependence is usually interpreted as representing competitive pressures forcing a population to some finite number of firms. But it may also arise, somewhat intriguingly, by firms inferring best practice from observations on firm survival. Through subsequent trials, stochasticity can be separated from differential capabilities and the reduction in noise to signal leads to more accurate appraisals of the true causality between firm characteristics and survival chances.[16]

The importance of learning by imitation or by instruction has tended to be neglected in the literature on ecology and adaptation. It is possible that learning is underestimated because firms within the same nation are more similar at birth and hence have less to learn from each other. At the same time, the sources of differences in their efficiencies are easier to identify and adopt as there is less noise (due to their similarity) to confound the search for best practice.

To take a favored industry as an example of learning, the inertia of large corporations to change is frequently illustrated by noting the failure of firms such as General Electric and RCA to succeed in semiconductors. But a simple international comparison raises challenges to this claim, as it is the large companies, such as NEC, Mitsubishi and Hitachi, that dominate Japanese (and world) production. Although not innovators in the original technologies, these companies showed striking capabilities for imitating major breakthroughs from the very start of the industry (Tilton 1971).

The international setting is interesting in another regard, for it illustrates also the difficulty of learning when the requisite institutional mechanisms are not well developed. This difficulty is greater when new organizing practices must be learned, as opposed to the imitation of technologies, because these practices are likely to be embedded in the social network and values of individual countries. In this sense, the learning of new organizing principles is both more transparent and yet more difficult, across the borders of a country than of a firm (see Kogut forthcoming for a more extended discussion). It is because learning across borders is difficult and because country differences in capabilities pose survival threats at the community level (i.e., the ability of national firms as a group to survive) that the process by which foreign practices are adopted often becomes institutionalized by governments. A recent example is the US Malcolm Baldridge Prize for quality, a clear response to the Japanese Deming Prize. In the next section, we turn to examine one important mechanism by which best practice is transferred internationally: namely, the MNC.

THE MNC

Theories of organizational learning are applicable to many issues important to international management in addition to competition among countries. Certainly, one of the most promising topics is learning to learn and the MNC. In this case, the MNC is no longer seen, as in the theories of Vernon and Burenstam Linder, as a repository of its national imprint; instead, it is an instrument whereby learning is transferred across subsidiaries which are responding and adapting to different environment pressures.

In this regard, Westney has identified the interesting question. What happens when an organization, isomorphic to its origins, extends into new environments? It is interesting to note how the failure to frame the question in this manner detracted from the study of the receding importance of the country bias on the organization of the MNC.

From the studies in the tradition of Stopford and Wells (1972), we know that organizational change occurs when thresholds (e.g., the proportion of international sales of total sales) are broached. Moreover, the type of structure that is adopted appears to reflect a firm's 'strategy'. Global product divisions tend to accompany technology-driven firms; and area divisions tend to characterize marketing-driven firms in mature industries. But these structural changes still reflect adaptations of organizational structures moulded by the home bias. The adaptive response for the American multinational was how to adjust the organizing principle of profit accountability for business in international markets. The solution was simply to enlarge the heuristic of divisionalizing the company to include international responsibilities.

This adaptive response, as has been often noted (see Hedlund, Chapter 9), was less prominent among European MNCs. European corporations tended to be organized along informal ('mother–daughter') lines, with far looser accountability. In fact, to the extent that international divisional structures were adopted, their adoption reflects an imitation of American practices more than an outgrowth of indigent European organizing principles. Whether this imitation was greater among European MNCs than among European firms in general is an important question for the understanding of the process by which practices diffuse among countries. But the relevant point here is that there is no question that European firms first grew internationally on the extension of European organizing practices across borders. Organizational change reflected a searching for a solution in the neighborhood of established best practice.

This stylized contrast of the American MNC operating on tight measures of accountability and the European company relying on decentralized informal control has been confirmed in many studies (see Chandler 1962; Pavan 1972; Channon 1973; Dyas and Thanheiser 1976; Franko 1976; Chandler and Daems 1980). It points to the importance of the home market conditions in imprinting the early developmental structures of resident firms. Some of these conditions reflect the technological requirements of different countries, as best expressed in the studies of Chandler and his students. But other conditions, such as the role of the state and educational institutions, have not been well studied, possibly because so few scholars have been willing to tackle comparative studies of business firms across borders.[17]

Whereas we have well documented histories of how firms learned to do business internationally, there are a number of other, more subtle, issues that have not been examined. One issue is explored in Chapter 3: namely, how a foreign subsidiary integrates itself, and is integrated, into the local social structure while remaining integrated within the multinational structure of its parent. For a perspective that views the firm as searching for models for its organizational structures and processes within an embedded set of social networks, the MNC presents an unusual case of a firm that belongs, with vary degrees of membership, to multiple national networks.

A second issue is the operating flexibility of the MNC. As a normative statement, it is logical that a firm competing on the extension of home market practices to foreign countries could subsequently enjoy the advantages of exploiting its network of subsidiaries on a multinational basis. This argument, given in Kogut (1983), was meant largely as a corrective to the prevailing view that FDI should be understood as a problem facing a firm investing overseas for the first time, even though the data showed that most investments were made by existing MNCs. In fact, the network of subsidiaries provided a firm with incremental learning (inclusive of foreign practices) and the option to coordinate operations flexibly in response to difficult-to-forecast events (e.g., exchange rates, innovations or government policies).

An emerging argument is that country advantages also serve to pull FDI. The traditional view has been that firms may choose to source raw materials or cheap labor in foreign markets. However, due to the work of Cantwell (1989) and others, there is also recognition that the technological leadership of certain countries can attract FDI. Empirical evidence is also provided by Kogut and Chang (forthcoming) in their study of the pulling of Japanese investment into the USA.

Over time, this perspective has broadened into more ambitious claims on the capabilities of firms to capitalize on best 'organizational' practice, no matter where it occurs. This does not necessarily constitute a third issue – it may be a variation on the themes of flexibility and variation in national types – but it has received considerable attention in its own right. In this form of the argument, the MNC is a conduit of best practices resident in diverse countries. It had long been noted that multinational practices influence local environments. An outstanding example is Dunning (1986),who finds that practices of Japanese MNC in the UK diffused more rapidly by the threat of competition than by isomorphic pulls among suppliers and Japanese buyers, a finding that underlines the significance of the joint presence of competition and learning.

The novelty of the more recent contentions in the organizational literature is that the international firm itself is influenced by the local environment, an influence not limited to the subsidiary but potentially extended to the whole corporation. There is little question that there are important cases whereby, say, the practices of quality control were transferred from Japan to other countries by non-Japanese MNCs. There is also growing evidence that a set of organizing principles has evolved that allows for cross-border flexibility, an evolution empirically in support of the idea of operating flexibility. But the organizational implications of how subsidiaries can constitute an integrated entity when regulated by organizing principles influenced by the local environments are still murky.

In Chapter 9, Hedlund suggests that national variations can be accommodated by a system where subsidiaries are given rein to develop unique resources, as long as they are harnessed to a coordinated international strategy. He clearly has in mind how the European mother–daughter structure has been coupled with greater degrees of integration to exploit national variations under a system of global coordination. In Chapter 4, Bartlett and Ghoshal have a vision of a firm as a set of subsidiaries nested in their national networks and yet forming an integrated network internal to a firm.

It is hard to evaluate the success of these early efforts in characterizing the organization of firms whose early imprinting has dimmed in importance. Part of the problem is probably that organizational theories in general have downplayed the capabilities of organizations to design themselves and to respond positively and flexibly to uncertainty (but see Starbuck 1983 for an important exception). It is not surprising, though, given the complex demands of operating across national borders, that questions of organizational design have been of paramount importance in international management (see Chapter 2). A bit of coordination across these differentiated fields might shed light, in both directions.

CONCLUSIONS

A conference meant to bridge organizational theory and international management should be able to arrive at a formula that will please everyone: that is, that comparative country studies can shed important light on the robustness of organizational theory. Questions such as the effects of density dependence in Japanese industries can, it would seem, lead to the rethinking of our theories.

The opportunity to do such studies is slipping away, however, because the world economy is so much more integrated. Immanuel Wallerstein's comment that the dilemma of the world system is that economies are integrated, but the political order is not, represents an incisive but, until recently, a misleading observation.[18] Economies have been, historically, integrated largely through transactions, monetary and physical. The transnational linkages of organizations and institutions, though often of substantial economic value, have been, up to the last three decades, dwarfed by the predominance of national, if not regional and local, institutions.

Yet the major changes in the past 30 years point in the direction of Wallerstein's observation. Even in one of the most autarchic of countries, the USA, foreign trade (including both imports and exports) is over 20 percent of the gross national product. The share of manufacturing total domestic sales by foreign affiliates domiciled in the USA in 1986 was over 10 percent (Graham and Krugman 1989). When we turn our attention to smaller countries, the share of sales by foreign affiliates in the national economies of France, the UK and Germany for 1986 was 27 percent, 20 percent and 18 percent, respectively (Graham and Krugman 1989). In industries where spatial competition is important, American restaurants can be analyzed independently of German establishments: even those of Van Nuys, California, independently of those in New York. If the industries, however, are semiconductors, computers, biotechnology, financial services and cars, the time is already past where industry borders can be safely assumed to be coterminous with those of countries.

If our focus is only on counting things, then it is easier to miss the importance of the international dimension. In Table 6.1, the number of new entrants in American industry is compared against the number of only foreign entrants.[19] Clearly, the foreign entry count is insignificant by this measure, but it should be kept in mind that the size of foreign entries tends to be of an entirely different magnitude.

Table 6.1   Total and foreign entries in the USA

	1976–77	1978–79	1980–81	1982–83	1984–85
Total entries	1 543 319	2 186 501	1 588 145	1 690 859	2 202 739
Foreign entries	526	952	1 990	1 668	1 984

Source: Small Business Administration unpublished data; US Department of Commerce, *Foreign Direct Investment in the United States*, various years.

Partly, this difference is due to the simple fact that MNCs are very much larger than the average American firm; their entries are, thus, large on average. For example, FDI in US assets amounted to $40.3 billion in 1987. As total entries for that year are estimated at 1219, the average size is over $33 million. The primary explanation for the large size of foreign entry is that acquisitions accounted for $33.9 billion of total investment, a striking figure when it is considered that the share of entries by acquisition represents less than 50 percent of the total.

Yet the challenge is far greater than widening the scope of data collection. The studies on the MNC have already made some contributions to the organizational literature, from internalization theory to the effects of the country environment – inclusive of governments – on organizational development as well as on the behavior of MNC. However, there is far more to be done. The apples are hanging in the orchard. The outcome is guaranteed to be less eventful than the first transgression, but consequential nonetheless.

Notes

1. See Kogut (1987) for a discussion of environmental imprinting and traditional theories of FDI.
2. This theory states that firms innovate in response to relative costs (e.g., they substitute expensive labor with new capital equipment) and to demand characteristics (e.g., a liking for luxury goods). (See W. H. Davidson 1976 for the cross-country evidence.) As these innovations saturate the home market, the myopic bias of the firm to serve only the home market erodes, first by exporting and later by investing overseas.

3. This point is made in an often cited, but little read, article. I have not myself been able to attain it and rely on the consistency of other writers' accounts.
4. See the listing in Chandler (1990) and Fruin (1989).
5. See Nishiguchi (1989) for a discussion.
6. For a formal model of bounded search consistent with relative factor bias, see Winter (1981).
7. This idea of a template is related to Meyer and Rowan's (1977) description of the cultural foundations to institutionalism. See also Scott (1987b).
8. See Scott (1987a) on the distinction between administrative and technological cores.
9. See Kogut, Shan and Walker (1990) for an examination of the consequences of this claim on the recreation of cooperative patterns in the biotechnology industry.
10. As the following discussion is not meant as a review, the reader is referred to B. Levitt and March (1987) for citations to the relevant literature.
11. In fact, the schema used by B. Levitt and March (1987) (i.e., learning mechanisms, interpretation, memory and intelligence) is strongly reminscent of Deutsch's adaptation of cybernetics to political organizations.
12. In studies in the organizational literature on learning, an error term is usually neglected, as it is also neglected in the population ecology specifications of the hazard model.
13. Of course, the exact dynamic which drives selection may vary from this account, but essentially this described symmetry between learning and selection provides the right intuition. Note that the proper analogue to the equation describing adaptation is the standard variation on evolutionary fitness.
14. Similarly, transaction cost considerations can be subsumed in this perspective, whereby firms are viewed as differing in their abilities to manage contractual dilemmas.
15. These issues are carefully worked out in the sociobiology literature. See Boyd and Richerson (1985) for a summary and analysis. The models of Nelson and Winter (1982) also explicitly allow for a mixed dynamic of learning and selection.
16. See Bohn (1988) for a model of noise to signal in the context of learning in factories.
17. Of course, Chandler's *Scale and Scope* (1990) stands out as a remarkable exception but, in many ways, succeeds most in showing the need for a better understanding of the institutional histories across countries.
18. Wallerstein (1979), as cited by Scott in discussion during the conference.
19. This table is dedicated to Howard Aldrich. The data for FDI, which are identified by the Department of Commerce from public sources, are described in Kogut and Chang (forthcoming); the overall entry count is from Small Business Administration listings derived from Dun and Bradstreet. The total number of entries from 1974 to 1988 is 10 524.

Part II

Organization Structure and Governance

7 Control in Multinational Firms: the Role of Price and Hierarchy*

Jean-François Hennart

How do firms manage to perform their functions efficiently? How do they constrain individual behavior to make it compatible with the overall goals of the firm? These age-old questions take on new significance in the context of the MNC (see, for example, Brooke and Remmers 1970; Doz and Prahalad 1981; Hedlund 1981, 1986; Prahalad and Doz 1981; Baliga and Jaeger 1984; Gates and Egelhoff 1986; Bartlett 1986; Welge 1987; Egelhoff 1988; Bartlett and Ghoshal 1989). In MNCs the problem of control is particularly acute. Geographical and cultural distance increase the cost of establishing control, and make it difficult for MNCs to secure the cooperation of their foreign affiliates. Overcentralization of decisions leads to paralysis, while excessive decentralization results in chaos (Doz and Prahalad 1981).

The issue of control in MNCs has elicited a considerable volume of empirical research. A recent survey of coordination mechanisms in MNCs lists 85 empirical studies undertaken since 1953 (Martinez and Jarillo 1989). Yet, in spite of this significant effort, our knowledge of control mechanisms in firms remains fragmentary. For example, Gates and Egelhoff (1986, p. 72) report that 'researchers have generated inconsistent hypotheses . . . and reported inconsistent results' concerning one of the most salient issues, that of the determinants of centralization (the extent to which decisions are taken at the headquarters of the MNC).

The goal of this chapter is threefold. First, it will sketch a theoretical structure that will clarify some of the concepts used in the study of coordination mechanisms in firms. One of the main building blocks of

* An earlier version of this paper was presented at the workshop on Organizational Theory and the Multinational Corporation at INSEAD on 1–2 September 1989. I thank Yves Doz, Gunnar Hedlund, John Kimberly, Steve Kobrin, Guido Krickx, Andy Van de Ven, Keith Weigelt, Sidney Winter and especially Kathleen Saul for their helpful comments.

this framework is the distinction between *methods* of organization (the price system and hierarchy) and *economic institutions* (markets and firms) that use those methods. A second building block is the argument that the price system and hierarchy can be regarded as substitutes. The price system can be used in firms to overcome the basic flaws of hierarchy, while hierarchy can alleviate the most glaring defects of the price system. This theoretical framework will then be applied to some of the control issues studied in the organization theory literature of the MNC, such as the relationship between the degree of centralization and the extent of interdependencies between the parent and its foreign affiliates. I shall show how the framework developed here explains some of the paradoxical results found in previous studies.

A THEORY OF ECONOMIC ORGANIZATION

The framework developed here, based on Hennart (1982), draws from transaction cost and agency theory, but differs from both to some extent. It posits that organizations are designed to minimize the cost of organizing exchange and cooperation, and that competition in the product and factor markets leads individuals to organize themselves under the form of organization that minimizes these costs.

The major insight of transaction cost theory is that firms and markets are alternative institutions devised to organize economic activities. If one accepts this premise, then to understand the nature of organizational processes within firms one must ask two separate questions. First, what must be done to organize economic activities: that is, what are the tasks that both firms and markets must perform? Second, how do firms differ from markets in the way they perform these tasks?

What is Involved in Organizing Economic Activities?

Economic institutions (such as firms and markets) exist to organize cooperation. Cooperation between individuals can be productive for two reasons. First, some tasks require more capabilities than can be provided by a single individual and consequently can only be achieved by pooling the efforts of two or more people. Individuals also have differing abilities, and cooperation through trade allows individuals to exploit those differences by making it possible for each to specialize in tasks for which he/she has a comparative advantage. In both cases the utility that individuals receive from cooperating exceeds what they could achieve through their solitary efforts.

Although cooperation is productive, achieving it involves costs; these costs (which we call 'organizing costs') arise from people's 'bounded rationality' and from their 'opportunism' (i.e., their self-seeking behavior). Three tasks must be undertaken to achieve cooperation.

1. Individuals must be told that their interaction will be profitable.
2. The benefits from cooperation must be shared among the cooperating parties. Cooperators can be expected to invest resources to increase their share, an activity which may be rational from the individual's point of view, but which is wasteful in the aggregate because it reduces the benefits to be shared. The gains of cooperation must therefore be divided between the parties in a way that discourages bargaining.
3. The division of the gains of cooperation (the sharing rule) must be enforced. Failing this, cooperation could not take place or would not last. Achieving cooperation therefore requires carefully devised techniques that reduce information, bargaining and enforcement costs.

In contrast to this view, neoclassical economics assumes that the three tasks that must be performed to obtain cooperation are performed costlessly by both firms and markets. What economists call 'the theory of the firm' starts by assuming that this problem is solved (Alchian and Demsetz 1972). In reality, and as argued above, all economic institutions experience costs in performing these three tasks. At any point in time, some potential gains of cooperation will be forgone because the gains from such cooperation are too small to warrant the establishment of institutions to organize it. Individuals will have to give up the gains of trade and specialization, and we will observe subsistence farming, self-insurance and home production of clothing and food. The greater the potential gains from trade, the larger the amount of resources expended to achieve cooperation.

Prices and Hierarchy are Two Possible Methods of Organization

It is important at the outset to distinguish between 'method of organization' and 'economic institution'. The price system and hierarchy are two methods that can be used to organize economic activities. They are alternatives in the sense that they use different coordinating mechanisms which result in different biases. Consequently, for a given interaction (transaction), they entail different levels of organizing costs. Each mode will therefore have a comparative cost adantage in organizing a particular set of transactions.[1] Firms and markets are economic institutions. These institutions generally use a mix of both price and hierarchy, although the mix in firms is heavily biased towards hierarchy, while markets predominantly use the price system. As we will show, the choice between organizing a transaction within the firm or having it organized through the market (the make-or-buy decision) can be represented as a choice between using the price system and using hierarchy. Furthermore, the same analysis can be used to decide whether to organize an activity *within a firm* through prices or through hierarchy.

Let us first consider how the price system and hierarchy are viable ways of organizing cooperation. To simplify the exposition, assume that there are no transaction costs. This makes it possible to distinguish between the method of organization used and the actual performance of these methods of organization when organizing costs are positive.

We have seen that organizing exchange and cooperation requires that individuals be informed of their interdependence, rewarded for cooperating and discouraged from bargaining. Prices can perform these three tasks. Prices inform individuals about opportunities for cooperation. The information structure of a market is fully decentralized, with prices conveying to all participants information on every one else's needs and desires, allowing them to act in a way that maximizes social (and individual) utility.[2] Prices also act as sharing rules that allocate the gains from cooperation. When markets function perfectly (i.e., when there is a large number of buyers and sellers), these sharing rules become exogenous. Individuals do not have the power to change them, and bargaining is discouraged. For example, the gains obtained by having farmers specialize in food production and workers in the construction of farm machinery are divided between these two groups through food and agricultural machinery prices. Prices also meter and reward perfectly an agent's behavior. The gross rewards that individuals receive are a direct function of their output multiplied by market prices.

In the absence of organizing costs, a hierarchy would also perfectly organize economic activities. We define hierarchy as a *method* of organization, and hence 'hierarchy' is *not* synonymous with 'firm' or with 'upper managers', as popular usage would imply and as defined by Hedlund (Chapter 9). Hierarchy as defined here is characterized by centralized information and the use of behavior constraints. While information is decentralized with prices, it is centralized with hierarchy. The hierarchical method of organization channels all the information possessed by individuals (employees) to a central party (the boss) who assimilates all this information, draws up consistent plans, and retransmits information to employees in the form of directives. If individuals have 'unbounded rationality', this method is as efficient in making optimal joint decisions as the decentralized system of market prices.

In a price system individuals collect their own information, make their own productive decisions, and are rewarded by their output measured at market prices. By contrast, under hierarchy the individual relinquishes to a central party, the boss, his or her right to make decisions concerning the allocation of his or her own resources (such as his or her labor-time and effort), and instead agrees to do as told, within the constraints established by social custom. The answer to the question 'Why do employees agree to have their behavior directed by the boss?' is that their reward under hierarchy is independent of their output. They are therefore less concerned about being ordered to perform tasks that do not seem to maximize their income than in a price system where their income is directly related to the tasks they perform. A hierarchical system does not reward employees by their output measured at market prices, but by their obedience to managerial directives. In other words, firms use behavior constraints to organize cooperation; employees are paid a fixed amount for following orders. Employees will be less concerned about the tasks they are ordered to perform than they would be under a price system because they will not bear the full monetary consequences of poor decisions.[3] Consequently, it will be possible for the boss to assign tasks by fiat.

Markets and Firms in the Presence of Positive Organizing Costs

In the real world, both the price system and hierarchy will experience costs in informing parties, in curbing bargaining, and in enforcing sharing rules. However, because these two methods are fundamentally different, they will experience different levels of organizing costs for a given transaction. Let us first consider the costs incurred by a price system in informing parties, before turning to those involved in enforcing the terms of transactions.

Information

The price system communicates information to all interacting parties. That information must by necessity be condensed, for otherwise the information needs of the system would be overwhelming. In a society consisting of n independent parties, organizing activities through prices requires $1/2(n^2 - n)$ two-way communication channels, as every individual must communicate with all others. By contrast, hierarchy only requires n two-way channels since all messages are channelled through a central party (Williamson 1970, p. 20). Whenever price information has to be supplemented by complex descriptions, transferring information to all parties rises dramatically with an increase in *n*. As Arrow (1974) pointed out, prices are concentrated information: in one number is expressed all that is needed for parties to make the appropriate production and consumption decisions. But this presupposes that the characteristics of the goods are known to all. Knowing that grade A butter sells for $4 a pound or that virgin aluminium grade P1020A costs 65 cents a pound is useful to guide behavior; knowing that cars are 50 cents a pound or that Old Masters paintings are $5 per square inch is of little use because the latter two goods have an infinite variety of attributes. With bounded rationality, individuals will not have a perfect knowledge of the characteristics of goods transacted. Prices will no longer perfectly describe all of their relevant dimensions. In some cases, they may provide 'wrong' signals that will mislead economic individuals, leading them to overconsume (underproduce) underpriced goods and underconsume (overproduce) overpriced ones.

When prices fail to act as efficient guides to behavior, a decentralized system may be efficiently replaced by a centralized one. A decentralized system requires individuals to gather all the information they need. If the compact information provided by prices needs to be supplemented by extensive additional information, then centralizing information is efficient. It may be desirable for each individual to specialize in the collection of a limited type of information and to transfer the information to a central party, the 'boss'. The boss can then synthesize that information, make decisions, and send directives for execution. This is the essence of the hierarchical solution.

The benefits of hierarchy are especially noticeable in rapidly changing environments. Since information and decision-making are concentrated in the boss, decisions can be made by a single person. Decisions can be imposed on employees by fiat, because their income does not depend on what they are asked to do. The price system, on the other hand, rewards parties in proportion to their output. When the price system works perfectly, prices are exogenous and bargaining is impossible. In conditions of imperfect competition, however, prices are no longer exogenous, and parties to the exchange will resist changes detrimental to their interest unless they are fully compensated. Hence, when the environment is changing rapidly, a real-world price system is at a disadvantage relative to a hierarchical system. The time spent communicating the information to all concerned and resolving disputes may be such as to make adjustment to new conditions impossible: by the time an agreement is reached, further adjustment may be needed. By contrast hierarchy allows the boss to quickly respecify the system through fiat (Williamson 1975).[4]

There are, however, two major problems with the hierarchical solution. First, information collection and decision-making are dissociated. In a price system individuals can be expected to use the idiosyncratic information they have acquired in the course of their activities to increase their income (Hayek 1945, p. 521). Under hierarchy employees have less incentive to become informed and to transmit to the boss information on how to maximize the employer's income because they will not be directly rewarded for doing so.[5] Even if employees faithfully transmit everything they observe, information can be lost as it is transferred across hierarchical levels. The information loss may be voluntary or involuntary. Involuntary distortion results from encoding/ decoding gaps (Williamson 1970). Involuntary distortion occurs because employees can be expected to distort information in ways that benefit them. With a constant span of control, an increase in the size of the firm will result in more hierarchical levels. The larger that number, the higher the information losses incurred by hierarchy.

Enforcement

Prices provide appropriate signals to guide behavior if they reflect the social value of goods and services. In reality, bounded rationality makes it costly to measure outputs. It will not pay for market traders to measure outputs perfectly because better measurement incurs increasing costs. Traders will invest in measurement up to the point where its marginal cost is equal to its marginal benefit. Consequently market participants will be able to alter the terms of trade to their advantage without a corresponding loss of revenues.

Consider a farmer who contracts for a fixed price to have fertilizer spread on his field. One important dimension of performance is the uniformity of application. If the fertilizer has not been uniformly applied, the crop in some parts of the field may suffer burns while in others it may fail to grow. Since an even application of fertilizer takes more time and effort than an uneven one, a subcontractor paid a fixed amount for the job will be incited, if detection is costly, to apply fertilizer in a quick, and therefore uneven, way (Roumasset and Uy 1980). To protect against this eventuality the farmer could carefully measure performance. He could sample parts of the field after application and calculate the weight of fertilizer per square yard. This, however, is likely to be very costly since the fertilizer may dissolve quickly into the ground.[6] In this case, the cost of using the price system is the cost of measuring perforance plus the cost due to cheating (the cost to the farmer of a reduced crop due to uneven application). More generally, high measurement costs will make it possible for individuals to cheat. Individuals will supply too little of what is desired and too much of what is not. Hence the costs of a price system (from the point of view of the reward function) will be the cost of measuring output plus the cost of cheating that will result from imperfect measurement. We call these 'cheating' costs.

Where the cost of measuring output and the consequences of doing it imperfectly are substantial, as in the case above, it may be cheaper for both parties to use a different method of organization: hierarchy. Rather than expend resources to measure output in all of its dimensions, it may be desirable to change the behavior of individuals by reducing the incentives they have to cheat. This can be done by breaking the connection between output and rewards. In our case, the farmer can hire the subcontractor who applies fertilizer and promise him or her a fixed sum of money per unit of time, on condition that he or she follows orders. Since the salary no longer depends on output per unit of time, the farm hand has less incentive to spread fertilizer unevenly.

One unavoidable consequence of this decoupling of output and reward is that, while it reduces cheating, it also reduces incentives to work. Self-employed individuals who slack or decide to take the day off pay the full cost of their behavior in the form of reduced income. Since their rewards are no longer tied to performance, employees will have incentives to shirk, that is, to break the promises they made to obey managerial directives. How much shirking will take place will depend on the extent to which the employees' objectives differ from those of the boss. If effort is painful, employees will have incentives to reduce the effort they devote to their tasks. More generally, employees who shirk will act differently from how they would if they were self-employed. Note that shirking does not necessarily mean loafing: it can involve doing the work too well. Bosses will therefore have to expend resources to direct and monitor behavior. In our example, the farm hand will have fewer incentives to exercise effort to get the job done as quickly as possible if he is paid on a time basis than if he is paid by the task. Because of diminishing returns to monitoring, it will not be profitable for the farmer to eliminate shirking completely, and some residual amount will remain. As a result, 'shirking costs' are the sum of the costs of monitoring behavior and of those of bearing the residual amount of shirking.

From Method of Organization to Economic Institutions

The argument so far is that prices and hierarchy are two different methods of organizing economic activities. The solutions they provide to the problem of information, bargaining and enforcement are radically opposed. While hierarchy centralizes information, the price system decentralizes it. A decentralized information structure avoids the losses

due to information transfer, but it experiences the problem of suboptimization if prices do not provide the 'right' information. Hierarchy's
solution is to centralize information, but this reduces the incentives
individuals have to collect information and can also lead to information
loss.

The price system also solves the problem of rewarding useful behavior
in a way that is quite different from that used by hierarchy. The price
system motivates individuals to maximize output, but the system's
efficiency is limited by the cost of measuring output in all its dimensions: individuals can be expected to cheat, underproducing those
dimensions of output which use positively priced inputs.[7] Hierarchy
solves the problem of cheating by decoupling reward from (market-
measured) output, but this solution requires control of behavior. Since
such control is costly, it generally will not pay to monitor perfectly, and
employees will relax their effort (they will shirk).

Since the price system and hierarchy provide different methods of
organizing economic activities, they tend to result in different levels of
organizing costs for a given transaction. In our previous example,
measuring the quality of the output (the evenness of fertilizer application) costs more than specifying and monitoring behavior (how the
fertilizer should be and is applied). In that case, the farmer will hire an
employee to spread the fertilizer rather than use the market to contract
for that task. Inversely, the price system will be used when output is
relatively easy to measure, but behavior is difficult to direct and monitor.
Such would be the case for home workers, who toil in dispersed locations
and are therefore costly to supervise.

So far we have described two methods of organization, the price
system and hierarchy. What is the relationship between these two
methods of organization and the economic institutions of firms and
markets? A simplistic answer is that firms are institutions which use
hierarchy, while markets use price signals. In fact, both firms and
markets use a mix of both methods of organization for reasons shown
below. However, the example of fertilizer application shows that the
essence of firms is the employment relationship (i.e., the imposition of
behavior constraints). It is by imposing behavior constraints (and
simultaneously relaxing price constraints) that the cost of uneven
application of fertilizer is reduced. Hence the use of hierarchy (behavior
constraints) is the distinguishing mark of firms. The use of pure
employment contracts, in which the employee is rewarded entirely in
relation to his or her obedience to managerial directives, is widespread in
firms.

The level of shirking may grow in some activities more than propor-
tionally as behavior constraints replace price constraints, so the firm may

then introduce price constraints alongside behavior constraints within the employment relationship. Consider the sales function. Commercial success requires coordination between the manufacturer and his sales force. There are two main ways to achieve this coordination: the firm can either use the price system (contract with sales representatives paid on the value of sales made), or use hierarchy (hire employees paid on a time basis). The choice between those two options depends on the comparison of two types of cost: sales representatives will maximize effort to 'move the goods', but may also fail to supply outputs that manufacturers find costly to measure, such as customer service (Anderson and Oliver 1987). When the latter is important, firms rely on employees to do the selling. Because their salary is now independent of performance, these employees will probably be less energetic in making calls. If the cost of curbing shirking is very high, paying employees in part through commissions can increase their incentives to make sales calls and may provide a cheaper method of control than hiring additional supervisors to monitor their behavior. Hence a mix of both modes of organization may be, in some instances, the least costly way of organizing the sales function. Firms generally use a mix of price and behavior constraints which varies with the nature of the tasks involved. What defines the firm is a *relatively heavy emphasis* on behavior constraints; markets, on the other hand, are characterized by the *predominant* use of price constraints.

CONTROL PROCESSES WITHIN FIRMS

This section describes in more detail the control processes used in firms. The discussion will focus on the relationship between the employer and the employee first at the task level, then at that of the subsidiary.

Control of Employees

In the hierarchical method of organization, the boss tells employees what to do and rewards them in relation to their obedience to orders. Since employees are paid a fixed amount, the information they collect in the course of their work no longer benefits them directly. Because of this reward structure, employees can be expected to be less motivated than self-employed individuals to gather and to make use of relevant information. Hence in order to be able to voice or draft clear directives to guide their behavior, the boss needs to know what the employee must do to generate the desired output. In other words, bosses must know the employee's production function. In some cases bosses can acquire this knowledge if they spend the necessary resources. In others, directives for the effective execution of tasks cannot be drafted in advance, for efficient production requires situation-specific decisions. In Ouchi's (1979) terminology, tasks are not 'programmable'.

The extent to which the boss knows (or can know) the employee's production function, together with information on the relative level of shirking costs versus cheating costs, can be used to categorize the various types of control mechanisms used in firms. Table 7.1, adapted from Ouchi (1979), sumarizes the argument. Firms can use three types of control, depending on the degree to which management has an information advantage over employees, and on the level of shirking costs relative to cheating costs.

Table 7.1   Employee control modes used in firms

Cheating costs/ Shirking costs	Management knowledge of the worker's production function	
	Higher than workers	Lower than workers
High cheating, low shirking	1. hierarchy	2. selection and/or socialization
Low cheating, high shirking	4. no interaction within the firm	3. price control (e.g., piecework)

Source: Adapted from Ouchi (1979).

Cells 1 and 2 correspond to behavior control. As argued above, this method of control is useful when all dimensions of performance cannot be easily specified *ex ante* and measured *ex post*, so that rewards based on outputs would generate high cheating costs. It may then be cheaper to control behavior. There are, however, two ways of imposing behavior control. The first one is the method described so far, hierarchical control (cell 1). Hierarchical control consists of explicitly telling employees what to do, and in observing their behavior to ascertain that they are following orders. This control can be exerted personally by the boss, or impersonally through bureaucratic rules and regulations: what Child (1973) has called a 'centralizing' and a 'bureaucratic' strategy of control. In a fundamental sense, those two modes of control are similar: they aim at specifying behavior (i.e, *how* employees must act). Hierarchical control will be used when two conditions are met: the employer knows well the employee's production function, and the cost of shirking is less than that of cheating. For example, machine-paced processes, such as assembly lines, make monitoring easier because the productivity of employees is indicated by their behavior. Using piece rates on assembly lines would be dysfunctional because workers would fail to cooperate and would abuse the machinery. Additionally, assembly-line processes make it difficult to separate the productivity of one employee from that of the others. Firms tend therefore to use hierarhical control for such processes.[8] The costs of using hierarchical control are likely to rise dramatically with geographical dispersion (which raises monitoring costs) and with idiosyncratic tasks, because how to perform these tasks cannot be specified in advance.

In some cases workers have an information advantage over management, and output is difficult to measure and price in all its dimensions, a situation characeristic of 'professional' work (cell 2). Efficiency requires that employees be left free to make production decisions, yet output is difficult to measure. The solution then consists of aligning the objectives of the employee and those of the employer. This can be accomplished by (1) selecting employees who have the same goals as management; (2) investing resources in persuading employees who may have different goals to internalize the employer's values so that they act without external constraint in the employer's best interest (Ouchi 1981a, pp. 414–15).[9] These two strategies are often combined.

The first of these two strategies makes direction and monitoring unnecessary since employees will perform as required out of their own self-interest. An example would be to hire student athletes to do maintenance work; they would exercise anyway, but now they are paid for it (Pratt and Zeckhauser 1985). Firms can also attempt to persuade employees with divergent goals, through indoctrination and socialization, that 'what they want to do is the same as what they have to do' (Kanter 1972, p. 1; see also Van Maanen 1975). If the firm is successful, employees will voluntarily choose not to shirk. This method, which Baliga and Jeager (1984) call 'cultural control', economizes on information and monitoring costs.[10] Socialized employees need not be monitored, and they do not have to be given specific answers to specific problems: they only need to be inculcated with the goals or philosophies of the organization. They can deduce from these the rule appropriate for any situation (Ouchi 1981a, p. 421). Because employees are given a general rule to guide their behavior, they have no need to seek orders from their superiors in unexpected circumstances. Hence the system is much more flexible than hierarchical control. Because employees now espouse management's goals, few resources need be invested to measure performance or to monitor behavior. Rewards can be tied to the dedication of the individual to the group and to his or her length of service, facilitating further socialization.

Worker selection and indoctrination involve very substantial up-front costs. Compared to hierarchical or price control, more resources must be devoted to selection, to training, to communication and to social interactions so as to impart the philosophy of the firm to the new recruits. Socialization strategies can be cheaper to implement if employees are recruited from a culturally homogeneous society. Investment in selection and socialization will pay off only if the employee remains with the firm for an extended period. This, and socialization in general, tend to create an inbred group of employees, intolerant of differences, and unreceptive to outside ideas, increasing the risk of 'groupthink' (Janis 1972). Creative types do not do well in organizations with strong socialization strategies, as shown, for example, by the difficulties experienced by IBM in developing in-house software (Depke 1989).

In both cells 1 and 2, the employer exercises behavior control (explicitly in the case of hierarchical control, implicitly through internalization in the case of socialization). The third type of control (cell 3) is output-based in the sense that the reward of the employees directly relates to their individual output, but not to the way they have achieved it. We call this price control. This mode of control is efficient when the employee's knowledge of his or her production function is better than that of the boss and when all dimensions of employee performance are easily measurable. Directing the behavior of the employees and rewarding them for following orders would be inefficient in that case since the employees know better than the boss how to achieve management's goals. The employees will be more productive if left free to choose the best course of action and if their shirking is curbed by reintroducing a market mechanism linking rewards to outputs. This type of control takes the form of bonuses, piecework and commissions.

The benefit of using price controls within firms is that, given positive monitoring costs, they elicit greater effort.[11] They also harness the capabilities and the knowledge of the employee, and make control possible without the need for management to know the production function and to monitor employees closely. Output-based rewards thus save on managerial capabilities. Unfortunately, unless all dimensions of performance are measured and priced (or constrained), maximization of effort may also lead to maximization of unwanted side-effects:[12] for example, paying piece rates for picking crabs (for extracting their meat) will incite workers to extract only the easy-to-remove back meat and to leave claw-meat in the shells. This tendency is easily checked by weighing the picked shells and deducting from the picker's earnings a penalty proportional to the weight of the shells. This discourages pickers from leaving too much meat in shells. In this case, the ability to control suboptimal behavior makes it possible to use piece rates. On the other hand, application of fertilizers on fields is done on a time-wage basis under hierarchical control because it is difficult to determine whether or not the chemicals have been applied uniformly, and because the consequences of uneven concentration can be substantial (Roumasset and Uy 1980).

Finally, it should be noted that the relative cost of using each form of control will vary across transactions within a given firm, and not just across firms, as the characteristics of tasks change. Thus employees in some departments of a store may be paid through commissions (price control) while others receive a straight salary (hierarchy).

Control of Subsidiaries

The analysis just presented can be used to explain not only the pattern of control over individuals but also control at the level of the firm's subsidiaries (Table 7.2). If the performance of the subsidiary is difficult to gauge, and headquarters knows better than the subsidiary what has to be done, then hierarchical control will be implemented (cell 1). Decisions will be made by HQ and the subsidiary will be told what to do. If HQ goals can be internalized by the management of the subsidiary, then control can be achieved through socialization (cell 2). Bartlett and Ghoshal (1989, pp. 163–4) describe how Unilever, like many Japanese MNCs, uses socialization as its main control mechanism. As an alternative, control can be achieved through prices by setting up the subsidiary as an independent profit center (cell 3). By choosing appropriate internal transfer prices, the firm can elicit the same behavior as it would through direct behavior control. If output is measurable, and HQ has less knowledge than the subsidiary manager about how to achieve the desired outcome, then leaving subsidiary managers free to maximize the subsidiary's profits (and rewarding them as a function of those profits) will achieve better results than specifically directing their behavior with directives from HQ. Then local managers will be induced to make use of their specialized knowledge for the benefit of their subsidiary, and thus for that of the firm. In addition to control advantages, establishing the affiliate as a profit centre also has informational advantages over hierarchical control, since it relieves HQ of having to learn how to operate locally and economizes on the amount of information that has to be sent to and received from affiliates. Transfer prices take the place of frequent complex directives, and the profits achieved by the subsidiary serve as the single, yet all-encompassing, measure of performance and the basis of the manager's rewards.

Table 7.2 Subunit control modes used in firms

| Cheating costs/ shirking costs | Headquarters' knowledge of the unit production function | |
	Higher than local management	*Lower than local management*
High cheating, low shirking	1. hierarchy 'centralization'	2. selection and/or socialization
Low cheating, high shirking	4. no interaction within the firm	3. profit centers

The practical problems and limitations involved in setting up price controls provide a good illustration of their costs and benefits and show why their use in firms is necessarily limited. To maximize their personal income, managers will maximize the profits made by their units. In the process, they will maximize the use of underpriced inputs or the generation of underpriced outputs (as was discussed above). For example, if the impact of the subsidiary's reputation on that of the firm cannot be quantified by HQ, and if the rewards of subsidiary managers depend only on the annual profits made by the unit, then they can be expected to engage in activities that maximize yearly profits even if those activities damage the firm's reputation. To make a price system an efficient method of control, all inputs and outputs used and produced by the profit center (including intangibles such as reputation and experience) would have to be correctly priced to reflect their cost and benefit to the firm as a whole.

Our model has shown that perfect pricing is an impossible task. If all interactions between the firm's subsidiaries could be priced then there would be no benefits to intrafirm organization. Activities are internalized within firms because market prices fail to organize at least one of the interdependencies. In consequence, not all intrafirm interdependencies can be correctly priced. Incorrect pricing of inputs and outputs will induce managers to suboptimize. Suboptimization is equivalent to 'cheating' as defined above; it means that employees will take advantage of the imperfection of the system used to measure their output.[13] To reduce unwanted side-effects and to encourage the production of desirable ones, HQ will supplement transfer prices with hierarchical constraints designed to organize unpriceable interdependencies. A subsidiary manager may be told to maximize profits, but he or she will have to follow specific rules concerning ethical behavior, worker safety, pollution control, employee turnover, etc. However, as more and more hierarchical constraints are introduced, the advantages of profit centers will decline. HQ will have to expend costly resources to send more directives to the subsidiary and to collect more information on compliance. Subsidiary managers will see their autonomy decline, decreasing their incentive to work hard and show initiative. They will shirk more. Both the informational simplicity and the motivating virtues of profit centers will be lost.

We would expect the relationships between HQ and subsidiaries to be a mix of the three control techniques described above and to vary with the headquarters' knowledge of the subunit's environment and the degree to which interdependencies between the parent and the subsidiary can be measured and constrained through prices. Non-priceable interdependencies organized through price controls will lead to cheating (suboptimization). On the other hand, imposing hierarchical constraints lowers the incentives that subsidiary managers have to show initiative. The optimum control system should balance those two sources of cost, shirking and cheating (suboptimization).

SOME OBSERVATIONS ON THE MODEL

How does the model developed above compare with agency theory and with organization theory approaches to the problem? In contrast with some agency models (Eisenhardt 1985), the model presented here makes no assumptions about differences in risk aversion between the employer and the employee and consequently does not address the risk-bearing consequences of control strategies. The model also diverges from agency theory in specifying the cost of control as the sum of the resources spent to impose a particular method of control plus the cost of the unwanted side-effects that result from using this method.

In contrast to standard organization theory (OT) which emphasizes the information aspects of control (Galbraith 1973; Egelhoff 1988a), the model emphasizes its reward aspects. This difference in emphasis is particularly important in the case of 'price control', an important component of our model which is downplayed in the OT literature.[14] Martinez and Jarillo's (1989) review of the OT literature on control lists the eight most common mechanisms of intrafirm coordination identified by OT researchers. Price control, as defined here, is not cited.

The neglect of price control is surprising, given its extensive use in firms. About one-quarter of all workers in US manufacturing industries in the mid-1970s (and 23 percent of all farm labor in 1959) worked under some type of price controls (Seiler 1984). Even at upper management levels, price control incentives in the form of bonuses made up 31 percent of the total compensation received by executive vice-presidents in 1986 (Reibstein 1987). Many firms also see in price controls the remedy for 'bureaucratic failures': that is, shirking. The recent trend has been towards increased use of price controls in the form of intrapreneurship schemes and of generalized commission schemes in department stores (Dunkin 1989).

Although Martinez and Jarillo do not mention price control, they do list output control, which they define as being based on the evaluation of files, records and reports submitted to corporate management, and which they equate with 'bureaucratic control' (Child 1973). Output control may resemble price control, although there are important but subtle differences between the two. Egelhoff (1988b), in a very thorough study of control mechanisms in MNCs, determined the extent of output control by measuring the frequency with which a number of performance measures (e.g., sales to specific accounts or inventory levels) had to be sent to HQ. This concept differs significantly from price controls. Although price controls are a form of output control, since a price system rewards output, not all output controls are price controls. Price controls establish a clear link between rewards and output. They ensure that agents will not shirk and will use their privileged knowledge to the employer's advantage. They are informationally economical because they save the employer from having to collect extensive information on the employee's production function.

Output controls can differ from price controls for two reasons. First, some organizations collect output measures which have no direct influence on rewards, and hence on employee motivation. Second, the term output control is sometimes applied to intermediate outputs. Observing the levels of many intermediate outputs approximates to monitoring behavior. For example, HQ may ask a subsidiary manager to report the level of salaries for its sales department and may intervene if the manager fails to cut the overall wage bill by 10 percent by the time of the next report. This is tantamount to telling him outright to cut the wage bill by 10 percent (the straight behavior control method). Thus the way organization theorists have defined output controls leads some to consider behavior control and output control as complements, while in our model (and in agency models) they are substitutes (K. Eisenhardt 1985).[15]

One important limitation of the model developed in this chapter is the lack of a time dimension. The model is implicitly a one-period model. No consideration is given to experience rating in firms and in markets. For example, repeated observation of the behavior of employees increases the employer's ability to control shirking. Similarly, market traders who expect continuation of the relationship may refrain from cheating so as not to jeopardize future dealings.

APPLICATION TO MNCs

The three control techniques of hierarchy, socialization and price control are used in varying proportions by MNCs to control their foreign subsidiaries. Hierarchical control over subsidiaries is exercised through visits from HQ personnel to the subsidiary and/or from subsidiary managers to HQ, written and oral directives sent to the subsidiary, and requests for information. When communication costs are high, socialization strategies may be the only way to control far-flung subsidiaries. In earlier days, family members were sent abroad with full authority to manage the foreign arm of the business. Later, these family members were replaced by a small corps of trusted home country managers (e.g., the 'Dutch Mafia' of Philips), who ran the subsidiaries. Increasingly, socialization is being used to develop a corps of both home-country and foreign country nationals (Edstrom and Galbraith 1979). Bartlett and Ghoshal (1989, Chapter 10) document the efforts of some MNCs to create such a cadre through extensive training and job rotation.[16] Lastly, MNCs often set up subsidiaries as profit centres and reward their managers on the basis of the profits of their subsidiaries.

Cost and Mix of Methods of Control for Foreign Subsidiaries

Extending our model to the MNC raises two main questions. First, how does doing business across national boundaries affect the level of organizing costs? Second, how does it affect the mix of control mechanisms used? Each of the three control modes will be more costly to implement in an international than in a domestic setting. Consequently, the lowest-cost mix of modes used to control foreign affiliates will be more costly than that used for domestic subunits.

Hierarchical control will be more expensive to implement internationally than domestically because geographical distance makes behavior more difficult to observe. Cultural differences make communication more costly: the need to be explicit and the chances of distortion are greater. Furthermore, foreign environments are likely to be substantially different from their domestic counterpart, so that employees posted to foreign countries will have a substantial information advantage over HQ, making centralized direction less efficient. In fact, up until recently, the length of time it took to refer decisions to HQ and receive an answer made centralization an extremely costly proposition, and led MNCs to rely heavily on 'on the spot' decisions.[17]

Operating internationally also increases the cost of socialization. Hofstede (1980a) has documented the presence of significant national differences in beliefs, behaviors and attitudes concerning work. Those differences must be bridged when doing business abroad. The cross-cultural interface can be set at various levels. If locally hired managers run the foreign subsidiary the cultural barrier lies between HQ and subsidiary managers. The cultural homogeneity of the management corps can be kept intact by sending expatriates to run the foreign subsidiary. This shifts the cross-cultural interface from the parent–subsidiary level to within the subsidiary, between the local labor force and the expatriate manager. Using expatriate managers makes it possible to socialize the management corps, but it shifts the cross-cultural problem at the subsidiary level: using expatriates tends to damage relationships with local suppliers, customers and host country governments. Local employees may resent expatriates because they receive higher pay and fill positions to which they would otherwise be promoted. Running the subsidiary with local managers, on the other hand, will automatically raise the costs of socialization by diluting the homogeneity of the employee pool. Thus imposing explicit or implicit behavior constraints costs more internationally than domestically.

The costs of using price constraints would seem to be less affected by distance. As argued earlier, prices are very condensed signals. The cost of communicating prices is not much greater across countries than within a country. Ouchi's finding (1978), that quantitative measures of output are less subject to distortion than qualitative measures of behavior when transmitted across hierarchical levels, supports this view.[18]

If it is true that internationalizaion increases the cost of imposing behavior constraints more than that of setting price constraints, then interactions that would be organized within firms in a domestic context will be handled through the market (or not at all) when they involve agents located in more than one country. Although this proposition has not been empirically tested, there is some evidence that the use of market processes to exploit knowledge is much more common internationally than domestically. In their study of licensing contracts, Caves, Crookell and Killing (1982) noted that licensing was much more frequent internationally than domestically.[19]

Our assumptions about control costs also imply that the mix of techniques used to control foreign subsidiaries should be biased towards greater use of price control than that used for domestic subsidiaries. One testable implication is that a greater proportion of foreign subunits than domestic subunits should be run as profit centers. This, too, is an area in need of empirical verification.

Centralization and Interdependencies

The explicit consideration of the full menu of methods of control used in firms could help explain some of the conflicting results found in the study of organization processes in MNCs. Consider first centralization and its determinants. Centralization is one of the fundamental dimensions of the design of large organizations. It refers to the extent to which HQ makes decisions (we have called this hierarchical control). Organization theorists have argued that interdependency among the subunits of the organization constitutes an important determinant of centralization (Van de Ven, Delbecq and Koenig 1976; Tushman and Nadler 1978). According to Egelhoff, interdependencies increase the need for information processing. Centralizing decisions at HQ is one way to tackle this increased information load, as 'centralization provides coordination and integration across the interdependency' (Egelhoff 1988a, p. 131); hence the extent of centralization in MNCs should be correlated with the degree of interdependence between the subsidiary and the rest of the organization.

Egelhoff tests this hypothesis by calculating the degree of centralization of decisions in marketing, manufacturing and finance, and correlating centralization with nine measures of interdependency. As shown in Table 7.3, the results are mixed. Of the potential 27 correlations between the degree of centralization and the extent of interdependencies, only six are significant at .05 (one-tailed test) and have the right sign (two are significant, but are incorrectly signed).

The theory proposed in this chapter suggests some explanations for these results. Egelhoff argues that efficiency requires that *all* types of interdependencies be organized through centralization of decision-making at HQ. The model we have sketched suggests, however, that not all interdependencies require coordination through hierarchical control. Exercising behavior control from HQ requires collecting a tremendous amount of information on local conditions and on the extent to which managers of foreign subsidiaries follow orders. If some interdependencies can be mediated through prices, HQ will economize on the need to gather information and to monitor behavior. HQ needs only to specify appropriate prices to govern interfirm interdependencies, and let the subsidiary operate as a profit center. Centralization will be low even though control may remains high. Only interdependencies that HQ cannot easily price will be organized through direct behavior control. For example, HQ is unlikely to make operating decisions for the

Table 7.3   Correlations between centralization scales and strategic and
environmental conditions

Measures of interdependency	Centralization in:		
	Marketing	Manufacturing	Finance
Marketing information dependence	0.21*	0.24*	0.10
New manufacturing information dependency	0.01	0.14	−0.19
Day to day manufacturing information dependency	0.11	0.15	−0.06
New product design dependency	−0.10	0.16	−0.25**
Product design change dependency	0.10	0.27**	0
Intracompany purchases by subsidiary	0.08	0.14	−0.24*
Intracompany sales by subsidiary	0.27**	−0.01	0.24*
Sales dependence	0.11	0.03	0.19*
Size of subsidiary (subsidiary size/parent size)	0.19	−0.19	0

* $p < 0.05$ (one-tailed test)
** $p < 0.01$
Source: Egelhoff (1988a), Table 7.2.

subsidiary, such as how to price its products, unless it purchases these
products from the affiliate (creating interdependencies) and there are no
existing market prices to guide the transfers (i.e., the interdependencies
are not priceable). Dependencies that are priceable include intracompany
transfers of commodity materials and of standard technical knowledge.
On the other hand, a subsidiary's use of a parent's trademark or of its
guarantee in borrowing funds is difficult to price; hence the parent will
find it desirable to establish procedures to be followed by the subsidiary
in order to maintain the quality associated with that trademark and to
specify the uses to which borrowed funds must be committed: that is, HQ
will impose behavior constraints on the subsidiary manager.
    Another factor weakens the link between centralization and interde-
pendencies. As argued above, behavior control can be explicit (hierarchical control) or implicit (socialization). An MNC faced with
interdependencies which cannot be organized by prices need not resort
to hierarchical control (centralization): it can instead socialize subsidiary
managers so that their decisions align with those that would be made by
HQ. Hence the connection between interdependencies and centralization

is not as direct as hypothesized by Egelhoff. Price control and socialization can act as substitutes to centralization. That Egelhoff found few correlations between centralization and measures of interdependency may reflect reliance by the MNCs he studied on these methods of non-hierarchical control.[20]

Autonomy of Affiliates

Our theory of MNC control also throws light on the concept of autonomy of foreign afiliates. Researchers typically measure autonomy as the locus of decision-making: if HQ makes the decisions, the subsidiary is said to have little autonomy (Hedlund 1981; Welge 1987). The concept is clear, but its interpretation is more ambiguous. Decisions made by a perfectly socialized manager may be indistinguishable from those made at HQ. This will also be true for those made by an 'autonomous' manager responding to a correctly specified system of transfer prices. Autonomy measures the relative use of hierarchical control (Table 7.2, cell 1) as opposed to socialization (cell 2) and price control (cell 3), but it does not necessarily reflect the subunit manager's degree of responsiveness to local conditions and to the needs of local stakeholders.

Is Decentralization Desirable?

The explicit consideration of price controls in firms also suggests new ways of looking at modern management methods. Consider the following parallel between profit centers and piecework schemes. Both have the same goal: to motivate the employee to apply effort and initiative when output is relatively easy to measure and the employee has an information advantage over management. Yet, while decentralizing management to subidiaries and rewarding their managers on the basis of subsidiary profits (setting up a multidivisional structure) has generally been considered a major advance in management (Chandler 1962; Williamson 1975, 1985), the piece rate system has been seen in a very different light. Piece rate schemes have been said to 'absolve managers of the responsibility and costs of exploring, designing, and supervising craft labor processes, which are typically complex and arcane' (M. Brown and Philips 1986). This was certainly the point of view of Taylor and his Scientific Management schemes aimed at replacing price controls by behavior controls. This required management to invest in knowing the worker's production function (through time-and-motion studies) but the pay-off was a significant increase in productivity (Edwards 1979). This suggests that decentralization, especially if it consists of having locals run the MNCs' foreign subsidiaries, may be a way to avoid learning how to operate in foreign countries, a way to avoid management, in fact. If so, the recent decline in the use of expatriates by US MNCs, a decline which has been attributed to the inability of US managers and of their families to adapt to conditions abroad (Kobrin 1988), may reflect the inability or the unwillingness of American MNCs to compete in increasingly global industries.

CONCLUSION

Organizing economic activities to capture the gains from joint effort and/ or from specialization constitutes the main task of all economic institutions. Firms and markets are two broad types of institutions devised to perform these tasks, and they therefore face similar problems in achieving their goals. Because in liberal societies individuals are free to choose the institution that will organize their interdependence, the use of firms to organize economic activities will hinge on their relative efficiency *vis-à-vis* markets. A theory of the methods of control used in firms must therefore be able to explain why firms are more efficient than markets. It must be a general theory of organization.

This chapter develops such a theory. The theory explains both the advantages and the drawbacks of firms as ways to organize economic activities. The same factors which explain why firms are chosen over markets also account for the relative mix of mechanisms of control used in firms. Framing the study of the control processes used in firms in this broader perspective has two main advantages. First, it allows us to consider the full range of control mechanisms used in firms (including price controls, which have been curiously downplayed in organization theory). Second, it explains how and why these mechanisms are combined in firms so as to minimize organization costs. The theory helps explain some of the paradoxical results found by researchers studying control processes in MNCs and advances a number of testable propositions.

Notes

1. If one assumes some degree of competition, one can expect the most efficient mode to dominate the less efficient one, and thus the mode actually chosen to organize the transaction should match that predicted by this theory. The model is thus applicable to those cases where institutions are not sheltered from competition by collusion or govern-

ment intervention. It has, therefore, greater applicability in competitive industries than in government bureaus.

2. Note that they do it 'in complete disregard of the decision of others, or even the existence of others' (Demsetz 1988). This is because prices reflect perfectly the social consequences of each agent's actions.
3. Since poor decisions may result in the disappearance of the firm, employees will bear some of the consequences if they have firm-specific skills and if the costs of moving to another firm are high.
4. This explains why democracies tend to delegate power to the executive branch in times of war.
5. Indeed, in some firms they may be punished for bearing bad news.
6. To simplify the exposition I am abstracting here from reputation effects. With bounded rationality, the probability of losing reputation due to dishonest behavior will never be 1, and can in fact be remarkably low. In some cases, however, reputation effects may be high enough to discourage dishonesty.
7. In our example, they will underuse effort in applying fertilizer because effort reduces their utility.
8. For a fascinating case study, see M. Brown and Philips (1986).
9. We are considering here strategies of control within the firm. An alternative strategy is, of course, to subcontract the activity (to let it be organized through the price system).
10. See also Ouchi (1979) and Durkheim (1933).
11. Clark (1984) quotes the results of a number of studies comparing the hourly rates of pieceworkers with time workers in a number of occupations. Pieceworkers earned between 13 and 25 percent more than time workers. This cannot be due to self-selection, since firms using time rates have the possibility of firing the least efficient workers and of keeping the most efficient ones.
12. A typical example of this is the recent case of an tax employee who received bonuses linked to the percentage of taxpayers' queries answered. He maximized it by systematically throwing out any query left unanswered by evaluation time. In terms of our model, the externalities generated by failing to constrain all aspects of behavior were probably greater than the reduction in shirking due to the use of market processes.
13. Intertemporal suboptimization is also a problem. Subsidiaries are not free-standing entities, and are not generally quoted on local stock markets. There is therefore no easy way to evaluate the impact of the subsidiary manager's present decisions on the subsidiary's future profit stream. If the manager is rewarded on the basis of annual profits, he or she can be expected to maximize present income at the expense of future profits by a variety of stratagems, such as cutting R&D budgets, or cutting employment and jeopardizing long-term government relations.
14. An exception is the work of Ouchi (1979, 1981a). Ouchi pointed out that firms could monitor the performance of their employees on the basis of either behavior or output. His explanation of the choice between these two modes is, however, different from the one used here. For him, 'a bureaucratic form of organization succeeds because it replaces complete forms of contracting with a single incomplete contract, which is the employment contract' (Ouchi 1981a, p. 416). He does not make the link between shirking and cheating (see for example 1979, p. 836).

15. K. Eisenhardt (1985) found commission payments and straight salary to be substitute forms of compensating salesclerks.
16. Sometimes socialization is extended to the whole labor force. For example, Nissan spent $63 million to send 383 employees of its US assembly plant to see its Japanese operations and to be indoctrinated in the company 'way of doing things' (C. Lawrence 1983).
17. In the 1890s, for example, when steamship travel from the UK to Australia took a month, the chief executive of the Australian subsidiary of the London-based Bank of Australasia ran his business with full autonomy. He was not asked to visit the London head office, and neither did he receive visits from London directors (Blainey 1984).
18. Differences in tax rates between countries may make it advantageous to use transfer prices which differ from arm's-length prices. As a result, a subsidiary's reported profits may diverge from its real profits. Rewarding managers on the basis of these reported profits will have strong disincentive effects. One solution is to keep two sets of books, one for the tax authorities, and the other to judge the profitability of the subsidiaries and to reward their managers. The latter record the profits obtained by using unbiased transfer prices (Brooke and Remmers 1970).
19. See also C. T. Taylor and Silberston (1973, Chapter 7).
20. Egelhoff finds a significantly positive correlation between output control and centralization, and no significant correlation between the extent to which subsidiaries are staffed with expatriates and both centralization and output control. The first set of results may be explained by the way output control is measured. The second set of findings may come from the difficulty of keeping the desired level of control constant when observing the mix of methods used to control foreign subsidiaries.

8 Information-processing Theory and the Multinational Corporation*

William G. Egelhoff

The MNC is probably the most complex form of organization in widespread existence today. Operating across products and markets, nations and cultures, it faces problems and situations far more diverse than even the largest domestic firms. With the increasing globalization of business, a rapidly growing level of economic activity now depends upon this form of organization. Thus the MNC is an important entity for scholarly study both because its influence is growing and because it presents organizational problems that lie at the forefront of organization theory and challenge the capacities of existing theory.

MNC research of an organizational nature has focused on two primary topics:

1. What kinds of organizational design contribute to effective MNC performance and under what strategic and environmental conditions is one form of design preferable to another?
2. How have MNC organizational designs changed and evolved over time and what factors cause or explain this evolution?

The principal concept associated with the first type of research has been the concept of *fit* (between organizational design and strategy or environment). Work has centered around how to measure fit and how to relate such fit to performance (Stopford and Wells 1972; Franko 1976; Daniels, Pitts and Tretter 1984). Most MNC research has used some

* An earlier version of this chapter was presented at the workshop on Organizational theory and the Multinational Corporation at INSEAD on 1–2 September 1989. The author wishes to thank David Whetten, John Daniels, Andrew Van de Ven, Michael Gerlach and Susan Schneider for their helpful comments. A later version appeared in the *Journal of International Business Studies*, 22 (September 1991). This chapter is the third version.

form of correlation technique to relate organizational design to a variety of strategic and environmental variables. Generally, little attention has been given to developing an abstract theoretical framework that could explain or support hypothesizing the relationships. A noteworthy exception is Herbert's (1984) proposed set of relationships between four types of strategy and a variety of organizational characteristics based on resource flow considerations. While research studies frequently discuss why certain fits might contribute to effective MNC performance, fit in MNC research has tended to be expressed more in empirical generalizations than in theoretical terms. That is, the primary reason for anticipating certain fits in MNCs is not that any abstract theoretical framework can explain why and when they should exist but that they have been found in the past. This chapter will argue that information-processing theory is an attractive candidate for extending MNC research to include such a theoretical framework.

The second type of MNC research effort, how MNC organizational designs change and evolve, has largely produced a documentation, rather than a theory, of the evolution of MNC structure over time (Pavan 1972; Stopford and Wells 1972; Dyas and Thanheiser 1976). Contingency relationships developed with cross-sectional data have not been tested longitudinally. Evolution has generally been measured only with a limited number of case studies. Existing notions about what has caused MNC structure to change and evolve over time are relatively simple and tend to lack empirical support. The basic evolution of international business form or strategy has generally been explained in economic terms (Vernon 1971; Kindleberger 1973; Stevens 1974; Hymer 1976). As evidenced in the various stage models of organizational growth (Stopford and Wells 1972; Dyas and Thanheiser 1976), it is generally presumed that organizational structure has followed the evolution of MNC strategy and environment.

This brief overview of organizational research on the multinational enterprise has identified where the frontiers of such research might lie today. Throughout the present chapter, which will develop and discuss an information-processing perspective of MNCs, we will evaluate how such a perspective might support future research on these issues.

THE CONCEPTUAL FOUNDATIONS FOR AN INFORMATION-PROCESSING PERSPECTIVE OF ORGANIZATIONS

The general idea that it would be useful to view organizations as information-processing systems seems to have several sources. A number of theorists have sought to understand organizations by describing them as communications systems, decision-making systems or systems that have to cope with uncertainty. Although definitions of these concepts vary, and for certain purposes the distinctions may be important, they can all be subsumed under the broader notion of information processing. Information processing in organizations is generally defined as including the gathering of data, the transformation of data into information, and the communication and storage of information in the organization (Galbraith 1973; Tushman and Nadler 1978).

Theorists interested in viewing the organization from an information-processing perspective have taken environmental uncertainty as the key contingency concept. Thompson (1967, pp. 10, 13) presents the conceptual argument for the importance of uncertainty:

> We will conceive of complex organizations as open systems, hence, indeterminate and faced with uncertainty, but at the same time as subject to criteria of rationality and hence needing determinateness and certainty . . . .
>
> With this conception the central problem for complex organizations is one of coping with uncertainty. As a point of departure, we suggest that organizations cope with uncertainty by creating certain parts specifically to deal with it, specializing other parts in operating under conditions of certainty or near certainty. In this case, articulation of these specialized parts becomes significant.
>
> We also suggest that technologies and environments are major sources of uncertainty for organizations, and that differences in those dimensions will result in differences in organizations.

Thus, Thompson suggests that uncertainty arises from certain characteristics in the environment and the technology facing an organization, and that differences in uncertainty somehow lead to differences in the organization's design.

Galbraith (1969, 1973, 1977) added further conceptualization to Thompson's general framework and developed a much more operational framework and model that has generally been referred to as an information-processing approach to organizational design. He rigorously defined the concept of uncertainty in terms of information processing: 'Uncertainty is the difference between the amount of information required to perform the task and the amount of information already possessed by the organization' (Galbraith 1977, p. 36). There is thus a relationship between the amount of uncertainty faced by an organization and the amount of information processing that must go on in an organization. Effective organizations are those that fit their information-processing capacities (for gathering, transforming, storing and communicating information) to the amount of uncertainty they face.

Galbraith also specified the relative information-processing capacities of different organizational design features. These features are listed below, in order of increasing information-processing capacity (Galbraith 1973, p. 15):

(a) rules and programmes;
(b) hierarchical referral;
(c) goal setting;
(d) vertical information systems;
(e) lateral relations.

Where conditions are routine and simple, rules and programmes can be used to absorb the relatively small amount of uncertainty facing the organization. For example, how foreign subsidiaries will set up their accounting systems is usually specified in a set of rules from the parent headquarters (HQ) describing the chart of accounts and various closing and reporting dates. Such rules absorb a good deal of uncertainty and eliminate the need for other forms of parent–subsidiary information processing. When uncertainty increases, exceptions must be referred up the hierarchical authority structure for decision-making. When information-processing requirements threaten to overload the management structure, goal setting and planning allow more decisions to be made at lower levels in the organization as long as they are within the plan. This relieves the information-processing load on the hierarchical structure.

When such steps are no longer adequate, various vertical information-processing systems that increase the organization's information-processing capacity can be attached to the hierarchical structure. These systems frequently include computer-based information systems and staff groups and tend to increase the capacity for centralized information processing. When uncertainty and information-processing requirements are very great, the use of lateral relations allows more information processing to be decentralized so that the more limited information-processing capacity at higher levels of the organization is not overloaded. Lateral relations mechanisms include direct contact between individuals, liaison roles, task forces, teams and matrix designs. Thus Galbraith's model suggests a more operational framework for linking quite a number of organizational design features to the level of uncertainty or information-processing requirements facing an organization.

Uncertainty and information-processing concepts have served as the basis for a substantial number of empirical studies (Burns and Stalker 1961; Lawrence and Lorsch 1967; Galbraith 1970; Duncan 1973; Van de Ven, Delbecq and Koenig 1976; Tushman 1978; Egelhoff 1982; Kmetz 1984). It will be helpful to summarize these views in what might be called 'the general information-processing approach to organizational design'. As shown in Figure 8.1, this general approach or model is a summary of the Galbraith (1973) and Tushman and Nadler (1978) models. It is also consistent with the conceptual approaches used in the empirical studies mentioned above.

Figure 8.1   The general information-processing approach to organizational design

On the one hand, the impact on an organization of its strategy and the environmental factors with which it chooses to deal can be expressed in terms of the information-processing requirements they create. On the other hand, the potential of the organization to cope with these requirements can be expressed in terms of the information-processing capacities furnished by its organizational design.

The strategic and environmental conditions include all those factors external to the organization's design that influence the information-processing requirements of the organization. These include technology, size, environmental change, environmental complexity, subunit interdependency and goals. Similarly, the different features of an organization's design (such as structure, degree of centralization, planning and control systems and interpersonal communication patterns) must also be measured or expressed in terms of the information-processing capacity they provide.

Measuring fit between such dissimilar phenomena as strategic and environmental conditions on the one hand and features of organizational design on the other has troubled organization theory ever since the emergence of contingency theory. Aldrich has stated that: 'we know the physics of air, water, and light to which flying, swimming, and seeing creatures must conform. We need much better knowledge of organizational types and appropriate environments before we can do as well in understanding organizational change' (1979, p. 45). Information-processing theory suggests that information processing may be the missing 'physics' that can help us to understand better the critical conformities between organizational types and environments and the impact of such conformities on organizational survival and change. The information-processing perspective calls for translating strategic and environmental conditions and organizational design features into their respective information-processing implications. Then it will be easier to measure fit between information-processing requirements and information-processing capacities, which are more comparable phenomena.

An important assumption underlying the information-processing perspective is that the quality of information-processing fit constrains organizational performance and survival. This assumption is more likely to be valid for large, complex organizations operating in difficult environments (competitive, heterogeneous, changing) than it is for small organizations operating in benign environments (low competition, homogeneous, stable). If information-processing fit is not constraining on performance, it makes more sense to organize around some other principle that might be constraining. An alternative example might be how to fit or satisfy the desires of local governments (a political perspective) or how best to motivate employees (a motivation perspective). Obviously it is desirable that the basis for evaluating organizational fit be stable over an extended period of time. It seems reasonable to assume that for large, complex organizations, such as MNCs, the limits of information-processing capacity are frequently reached or exceeded by information-processing requirements, and that the difficulty in realizing information-processing fit consistently constrains performance in such organizations.

Before proceeding, it is useful to evaluate the proposed framework against more cognitive views of organizational information processing which have recently become prominent. Cognitive theory views organizations as systems that learn (Fiol and Lyles 1985; Ginsberg 1990) and interpret their environments (Daft and Weick 1989). Information processing is primarily represented in terms of the cognitive abilities of organizational members (either individually or collectively) to learn, make sense out of, and make decisions for an organization, when influenced by a variety of factors such as values, beliefs, culture and differences in power (Wood and Bandura 1989). Environmental conditions may still be the stimulus for the occurrence of information processing, but the emphasis is on explaining how information processing is influenced by what goes on in the heads of individuals (psychological determinants) and between individuals (social–psychological determinants).

By contrast the proposed perspective, which has sometimes been referred to as a logistical view of organizational information processing (Huber 1982), views organizations as systems that need to balance the organization's information-processing capacities against the information-processing requirements inherent in its strategy and environment. Fit is equated with good organizational performance and survival, and misfit with poor performance and failure. Information processing is largely represented in terms of the capacities of different kinds of organizational structure and process to transfer information within an organization, to move it across the boundaries of an organization, and to access specific kinds of knowledge and decision making capabilities needed to transform data or information. This view focuses primarily on how information processing is influenced by organizational characteristics, independent of the individual characteristics of the organization's members. The cognitive view, on the other hand, focuses primarily on how information processing is influenced by the psychological and social–psychological characteristics of organizational members.

The two perspectives should be viewed as complementary, and not contradictory, explanations of organizational information processing. The cognitive perspective largely addresses the question of how strategic decisions are made. It argues that much of the input or influence is cognitive and that strategic decisions are not merely, or even primarily, determined by organizational and environmental considerations. The unit of analysis tends to be the strategic decision or strategic issue (Dutton and Jackson 1987). From a population ecology perspective such strategic decisions become a source of variation and change in an organization and its position in its environment. The logistical perspective of information processing, on the other hand, does not attempt to explain the source of organizational or strategic variation or change. It tries to explain the information-processing capacities inherent in an organization's design and generally evaluates these against requirements for information processing inherent in an organization's strategy or environment. This evaluation of fit and misfit between organizational characteristics and environmental conditions responds to the selection mechanism in a population ecology perspective and explains change not in terms of strategic decisions, but in terms of differential selection by competitive forces in firms' environments. Thus the two perspectives have different arguments and a different purpose.

Information Processing as an Abstract Intervening Concept

With the exception of some of Galbraith's case studies (1970, 1977), the information-processing perspective has been used primarily in more micro-level studies, where the units of analysis are either individuals or small groups. Such studies have managed to measure directly such aspects of information processing as the frequency of oral communications between work groups (Tushman 1978), the extent to which policies and procedures, work plans, personal contact and meetings are used to coordinate members of work teams (Van de Ven, Delbecq and Koenig 1976), and the structure of groups during decision-making (Duncan 1973). For more macro-level studies, such as those focusing on the parent HQ–foreign subsidiary relationship in MNCs, the difficulty of directly measuring such detailed information-processing phenomena between very large subunits of an organization necessitates a different approach to operationalizing the information-processing perspective.

Instead of attempting to measure information processing directly, macro-level studies must use information processing as an abstract intervening concept to aid in positing relationships between directly measured characteristics of an organization's design and its strategy and environment, both of which have identifiable information-processing implications. This approach is already reflected in the general information-processing approach to organizational design shown in Figure 8.1. The solid lines indicate that strategic and environmental conditions and organizational design features are directly measured variables, while the broken lines indicate that information-processing requirements and information-processing capacities are abstract variables that can only be derived from measured variables.

For the information-processing approach to advance, what is needed is a more precise translation of the measured contextual and design variables into the abstract information-processing concepts that are so useful for general theory building. This translation should be easier to accomplish if one first identifies the dimensions of information processing that are important to the type and level of organization being modeled and then constructs decision rules for mapping measured contextual and design variables on to these dimensions.

Multidimensional Measures of Information Processing

Most existing research that has sought to use an information-processing perspective to link organizational design to various strategic and environmental conditions does not rigorously specify the dimensions that are being used to measure and evaluate information-processing capacities and requirements. For example, consider the case of a bank that as a result of a growth strategy faces a sharp increase in the number of checks it must clear. Obviously such a strategy has led to increased requirements for information processing. Galbraith (1973) has indicated that increased information-processing requirements frequently need to be met by the addition of lateral information-processing systems, such as more face-to-face communications, matrix structures, cross-functional committees and task forces to an organization. Yet it is doubtful that these information-processing mechanisms address the requirements associated with the increased load of check clearing. Instead, an expanded computer system, which Galbraith regards as a vertical information-processing system, seems better able to provide the kind of information-processing capacity needed to cope with the increased requirements for check clearing.

The bank's growth strategy may also call for the development of new financial products and services. This also increases requirements for information processing within the organization, and this time the kind of information-processing capacity provided by cross-functional teams and matrix designs seems more appropriate than that provided by an expanded computer system. Both strategies lead to increased information-processing requirements for the bank, but somehow the kinds of information-processing capacity needed differ, and exactly what dimension or dimensions define this difference is not clear.

There are a number of empirical studies that generally match suitable information-processing mechanisms to the different information-processing requirements and discuss a number of reasons for the suitability of the match. Some important examples are Galbraith's (1977) analysis of the information-processing requirements associated with Boeing's development of the 747, Van de Ven, Delbecq and Koenig's (1976) analysis of the differing task requirements found in an unemployment agency, and Tushman's (1978) analysis of the differing information-processing requirements facing development groups as opposed to research groups in an R&D laboratory. While such discussions often hint at how one information-processing requirement differs from another, however, this difference is not rigorously defined by any specification of what dimension or dimensions consistently differentiate one type of information processing from another.

In other words, most studies do not directly address the issue of whether one, two, three or four dimensions are needed to distinguish one information-processing requirement from another (or the capacity of one information-processing mechanism from another). Information-processing requirements and capacities are not mapped onto some prespecified multidimensional framework; instead, information-processing is used in a looser, less rigorous way that only implicitly, rather than explicitly, distinguishes among types of information processing.

An important exception to this complaint can be found in the work of Daft and Lengel (1986) and Daft and Macintosh (1981). These studies distinguish between equivocality reduction and uncertainty reduction in information processing and attempt to define the relative capacities of a variety of information-processing mechanisms for handling both types of information-processing requirements.

Our view is that at the macro level of large, complex organizations, other dimensions of information processing may also be useful – perhaps even more useful than uncertainty and equivocality – for measuring and evaluating information-processing requirements and capacities. At the macro level, information processing can readily vary in terms of subject and in terms of organizational purpose and perspective (Egelhoff 1982). It can also vary in terms of being relatively routine or non-routine within an organization and in terms of the nature of the interdependency shared by organizational subunits involved in an information-processing event. Following this view, the next section will illustrate how existing organization theory and research in a number of areas provides useful guidance for constructing explicit multidimensional frameworks for measuring information processing.

DEVELOPING AN INFORMATION-PROCESSING PERSPECTIVE OF MNCS

This section will use the information-processing concepts already discussed to develop an explicit framework for analyzing and understanding organizational design in MNCs. Deciding which dimensions to use in measuring information processing requires some judgment, but the general criterion should be to select dimensions that best reflect the information-processing limitations of the various features of organizational design for the strategic and environmental context in which they must operate (in this case, the complex and dynamic environment faced by most large MNCs).

Structural Dimensions

The first set of dimensions reflects the purpose and perspective of information processing (whether it is strategic or tactical) and the subject or content of information processing (whether it deals with product matters or company and country matters). Both require some explanation and conceptual development.[1]

The *purpose and perspective of information processing* can be defined in terms of whether it is primarily strategic or primarily tactical. The conceptual distinction between these two concepts comes from the strategic management literature. Ansoff (1965) refers to operating, administrative and strategic decisions in organizations. Tactical information processing combines the first two categories and deals with the large volume of relatively routine day-to-day problems and situations confronting an organization. The decision-making perspective required to handle these situations tends to be relatively narrow, and it usually exists at the middle and lower levels of management. Strategic information processing attempts to deal with a much smaller volume of relatively non-routine, and usually more important, problems and situations. These problems deal with the fundamental position of the organization in its environment and usually involve changing this position. Thus, strategic information processing has a different purpose and requires a different perspective from tactical information processing. It addresses higher level organizational goals, is broader in scope, and usually has a longer time horizon.

Research suggests that different levels of an organization's hierarchy tend to process different kinds of information and have different purposes for processing information (Landsberger 1961; Thomason 1966). Mintzberg (1979, p. 54) states that 'the issues each level addresses are fundamentally different', and notes that strategic decisions generally involve members of the 'strategic apex' or top management of an organization. Since the majority of tactical decisions do not involve members of the strategic apex, tactical and strategic information processing tend to occur at different levels of an organization. The association of tactical and strategic perspectives with different levels of an organization presupposes that hierarchy exists in most MNCs. Recent literature suggests that MNCs may be becoming less hierarchical (Hedlund 1986; Bartlett and Ghoshal 1989). To the extent that an MNC is less hierarchically organized, it becomes more difficult to generalize about where strategic and tactical perspectives exist in an organization.

The framework also reflects the *subject or content of information processing* and distinguishes between information processing for product matters (product and process technology, market information) and information processing for company and country matters (finance, tax, legal, government relations, human resources). Subject knowledge or specialization tends to vary horizontally across organizations, and different organizational structures tend to cluster it into different subunits. Using these distinctions, four types of information processing are developed, as shown in Figure 8.2. The four types are generally not

SUBJECT OF INFORMATION PROCESSING

Company and country matters   Product matters

	Company and country matters	Product matters
Tactical	Tactical information processing for company and country matters Example: Evaluating how and when to raise money in international money markets	Tactical information processing for product matters Example: Deciding on a routine change in the price of a product
Strategic	Strategic information processing for company and country matters Example: Deciding on the company's position *vis-à-vis* foreign government pressures for local ownership in foreign subsidiaries	Strategic information processing for product matters Example: Deciding on the long-range level of R&D support for a major product line

PURPOSE AND PERSPECTIVE OF INFORMATION PROCESSING

Figure 8.2   The structural dimensions of information processing

substitutes for each other since they tend to address different problem areas that require different types of knowledge and different perspectives of the organization and its goals.

This set of information-processing dimensions distinguishes the organizational locus of different kinds of knowledge and different kinds of decision-making capabilities. It helps to identify which parts of an organization need to be linked together in order to solve a given problem or address a specific decision-making situation. In other words, these dimensions are useful for measuring the structural aspects of organizations and understanding their implications for information processing.

Process Dimensions

Another set of dimensions is needed, however, to measure and distinguish differences in the ways in which information is gathered, processed, stored and exchanged. Such information processing occurs within and between the organizational subunits and levels that have already been identified. This second set represents the process dimensions of information processing. Here we will distinguish between routine and non-

routine information processing and sequential and reciprocal information processing.

There is a substantial literature supporting and describing the distinction between *routine and non-routine information processing* (Simon 1977;
Daft and Macintosh 1981; Daft and Weick 1989). Routine information
processing deals with inputs that are frequent and homogeneous. It
transforms them under conditions of high certainty and assumes that
goals and means–ends relationships are well known. Information-processing mechanisms that most efficiently provide routine information-
processing capacity are rules and programs (including organizational
policies, standard operating procedures and standard methods), formal
single-cycle planning systems (where there is no feedback from a later
stage of the process to an earlier stage), post-action control systems
(where feedback occurs after the controlled activity or time period is
completed; Newman 1975), and most computer-based information
systems. Non-routine information processing deals with inputs that are
either unique or infrequent and heterogeneous. It transforms them under
varying degrees of uncertainty about goals and/or means–ends relationships. Information-processing mechanisms that provide non-routine
information-processing capacity are hierarchical referral; some vertical
information systems, such as planning staffs; multicycle, interactive
planning systems (where information developed in later stages of a
planning process can feed back to earlier stages); steering control
systems (where feedback occurs before an event is completed; Newman
1975); and most horizontal or lateral information systems (direct
contact, task forces and teams, integrating roles and matrix designs).

The distinction between *sequential and reciprocal information
processing* reflects the kind of interdependency that exists between the
parties to an information-processing event. This distinction is based on
Thompson's (1967) typology of the three different forms of interdependence that can exist between organizational subunits (pooled, sequential
and reciprocal). Information processing is sequential to the extent that
information flows in a predetermined direction across parties to an
information-processing event. Information processing is reciprocal to
the extent that information flows back and forth between parties in a
kind of give-and-take manner that has not been previously determined.

Figure 8.3 shows the four types of information processing that emerge
when the routine–non-routine and sequential–reciprocal axes are combined. A specific information-processing event is also provided to
illustrate each type. In order to understand better the logic employed,
we will discuss one of these events further.

Consider the event where it is necessary to decide on a routine change
in the price of a subsidiary's product. Since this event occurs frequently

INTERDEPENDENCY BETWEEN PARTIES TO
AN INFORMATION-PROCESSING EVENT

		Sequential	Reciprocal
ROUTINISM OF AN INFORMATION-PROCESSING EVENT	Routine	**Routine–sequential information processing** Example: Deciding on a routine change in the price of a product	**Routine–reciprocal information processing** Example: Deciding how to handle and expatriate manager's request for reassignment back to the parent company
	Non-routine	**Non-routine–sequential information processing** Example: Exploring the possibility of selling a customer products not available in the local subsidiary, but available in another subsidiary	**Non-routine–reciprocal information processing** Example: Deciding on the long range level of R&D support for a major product line

Figure 8.3   The process dimensions of MNC information processing

and the kind of things that need to be considered (e.g., effect on volume and gross profit, relationship to competitors' prices) is well known, information processing is routine. And since the information inputs of the various parties to this event (subsidiary marketing manager, subsidiary CEO, HQ marketing manager) can be combined serially in order to arrive at an informed and responsible decision, information processing will tend to be sequential (probably represented by a flow of memos between the concerned parties). In process terms this is simple hierarchical referral (or information processing through the chain of command), which is a commonly used routine–sequential information-processing mechanism in organizations.

However, in order to describe this event more fully, we need also to consider its structural dimensions. Recalling the previous set of information-processing dimensions described in Figure 8.2, it is obvious that this event deals largely with product-related knowledge as opposed to company-related and country-related knowledge (if host government approval for the price increase were required, the latter might also be involved). In this case the subsidiary marketing manager provides information about the increase and its relationship to competitors' prices as well as the anticipated impact on margins and sales volume. The subsidiary CEO merely checks the proposal for broad consistency with his or her budgeted sales and profit targets and goals concerning the subsidiary's competitive position. The proposal is approved at a relatively low level in the HQ marketing group, where it is again checked for consistency with broad goals for the product line, and more specifically checked against the price in other subsidiaries whose markets might interact with this particular subsidiary's. Since this kind of decision is not expected to alter significantly the position of the product line in its competitive environment, the perspective that these managers tend to apply is tactical rather than strategic. In summary, this event largely requires tactical information processing for product matters.

This identification or measurement has largely structural implications. It pinpoints which subunits or individuals in the organization need to be involved in the information-processing event (those that can contribute the right kinds of knowledge and capabilities). The previous identification or measurement, however, has primarily process implications. It helps to identify which information-processing mechanisms (processes) are most suitable for linking together the specific subunits or individuals that possess the necessary knowledge and capabilities.

The Information-Processing Capacities of Structure

The location in an organization of specific kinds of knowledge and capabilities is strongly influenced by the organization's formal structure. Research on MNC structure (Brooke and Remmers 1970; Stopford and Wells 1972; Franko 1976; Hulbert and Brandt 1980; Egelhoff 1982) has helped to identify where different kinds of knowledge and capabilities tend to be located in the four elementary structures used to organize international operations. Table 8.1 provides a summary of the location of information-processing capacities in each structure.

A worldwide functional division structure means that the functional activities in a foreign subsidiary report directly to their respective functional divisions in the parent. Tactical information-processing capacity for company and country matters tends to lie in such functional divisions as finance, human resources, tax and government affairs, both at the parent HQ and at the foreign subsidiary levels. Similarly, tactical product-related information-processing capacity tends to lie in the R&D, manufacturing and marketing divisions found at both levels. This structure should facilitate tactical information processing between the parent and foreign subsidiaries so long as the processing can take place within a functional area. Tactical information processing across functions, however, will be difficult (and will require non-hierarchical processes) since the structure does not facilitate communication between divisions at either the subsidiary level or the tactical levels of the parent.

Table 8.1 Location of information-processing capacity in the four elementary MNC structures

	Types of information-processing capacity			
Type of structure	Tactical information-processing capacity for company and country matters	Strategic information-processing capacity for company and country matters	Tactical information-processing capacity for product matters	Strategic information-processing capacity for product matters
Worldwide functional divisions	Company and country-related functional divisions of parent HQ (e.g., finance, human resources) Similar functional divisions of foreign subsidiaries	CEO and executive committee of parent HQ	Product-related functional divisions of parent (e.g., R & D, manufacturing, marketing) Similar functional divisions of foreign subsidiaries	CEO and executive divisions of parent HQ
International division	International division HQ Foreign subsidiary HQs	Higher management of international division HQ Higher management of foreign subsidiary HQs	Domestic product divisions (outside of international structure) Product divisions of foreign subsidiaries	Higher management of domestic product divisions (outside of international structure) Higher management of product divisions of foreign subsidiaries
Geographical regions	Company and country-related management and staff of regional HQs Domestic and foreign subsidary HQs	Higher management of parent corporate HQ Higher management of regional HQs Higher management of domestic and foreign subsidiaries	Product-related management and staff of regional HQs Product divisions and domestic and foreign subsidiaries	Higher product-related management of regional HQs Higher management of product divisions of domestic and foreign subsidiaries
Worldwide product divisions	Foreign subsidiary HQs	Higher management of foreign subsidiary HQs	Parent product division HQs and domestic product operations Product divisions of foreign subsidiaries	Higher management of product division HQs Higher management of product divisions of foreign subsidiaries

Since the formulation of business strategy requires a cross-functional perspective, strategic information processing cannot readily occur within a foreign subsidiary or even at lower levels of the parent HQ. Only at the CEO and executive committee level does a cross-functional or general management perspective exist, and only at this level does the structure facilitate multifunctional information coming together. While non-hierarchical information processes might be employed to bring such information together at lower levels of the organization, there is still a problem regarding the lack of a general management perspective at such levels in a functional division structure. Thus, subunits in foreign subsidiaries cannot generally participate in or make direct inputs to the strategy-formulation process. This centralization of strategic information processing means that processing capacity is limited (only a few people at one level of the parent are involved) and it is difficult for new information about the environment to enter the process.

With an international division structure, all foreign subsidiaries report to an international division that is separate from the domestic operations. Brooke and Remmers (1970) found that this structure tends to facilitate information processing between the parent and foreign subsidiaries, while at the same time it hinders information processing at the parent level between the international division and the domestic operations. Product knowledge tends to be centered in the domestic divisions, while knowledge about such company and country matters as international finance and foreign political conditions is centred in the international division. Consequently, parent–subsidiary information-processing capacity is relatively high for company and country matters and relatively low for product matters. There is a general management or strategic apex at both the subsidiary and international division levels. Thus strategic as well as tactical information processing can take place between a subsidiary and the international division, but it will center around company and country matters rather than product matters. In order to connect foreign subsidiaries to the centers of product knowledge in the domestic product divisions, non-hierarchical information processes must be used.

A geographical region structure divides the world into regions, each with its own headquarters. Each HQ is responsible for all of the company's products and business within its geographical area. The regional HQ is the center of the company's knowledge about company and country matters within the region. Most regional HQs also contain either product or functional staffs to provide coordination for product matters across subsidiaries in the region (Williams 1967). There is a general management or strategic apex at both the subsidiary and regional HQ levels. As a result, this structure facilitates a high level of all four types of information processing between a subsidiary and its regional HQ. The information-processing capacity between a foreign subsidiary and domestic operations or a subsidiary in another region is low. The only structural mechanism for coordinating across regions is the corporate HQ, and most regional companies tend to have relatively small corporate managements and staffs (Egelhoff 1982). Thus largely non-structural or non-hierarchical information processing should be established if, for example, product technologies and strategies are to be coordinated between regions (the former requires largely tactical information processing; the latter, strategic information processing).

A worldwide product division structure extends the responsibilities of the domestic product divisions to cover their product lines on a world-wide basis. Under this structure, there is a tendency to centralize product-related knowledge and decision-making capability in the parent product groups and to decentralize non-product knowledge and decision-making to the foreign subsidiaries (Brooke and Remmers 1970). Consequently, the capacity for processing information on company and country matters tends to be concentrated in the foreign subsidiaries, while the parent HQ tends to have a product orientation. Product-related tactical and strategic information-processing capacities, on the other hand, tend to be highly developed at both the foreign subsidiary and parent product division levels. The product divisions in the foreign subsidiaries are directly connected through the hierarchy to the centers of product knowledge in the parent. For each product line, there is a strategic apex at both the subsidiary and parent product division levels, which facilitates strategic information processing at both levels for product matters.

As can be seen in the above discussion and in Table 8.1, formal structure significantly influences where specific types of knowledge and decision-making capability reside in large organizations. The four dimensions of information processing employed in Table 8.1 seem a useful framework for describing these differences in MNCs. The specific locations of knowledge and decision-making capability are consistent with previous research findings concerning the influence of formal structure on information flows in organizations. The author has used a framework similar to that expressed in Table 8.1 to develop hypotheses about strategy–structure relationships in MNCs. These hypotheses were empirically tested using a sample of 34 elementary structure MNCs and 15 matrix and mixed structure MNCs, representing both US and European firms (Egelhoff 1988a, pp. 61–128). The testing tended to support the framework. Thus, research to date seems (1) strongly to support the assumption that formal organizational structure has a major influence on the location of knowledge and decision-making capability in organizations, and (2) to provide reasonable support for the logic used in developing the specific framework shown in Table 8.1. Formal structure is not the only determinant of the location of knowledge and decision making capability, however, and there can be significant variation between companies with the same structure.

The Capacities of Information-Processing Mechanisms

Having created a kind of directory of where knowledge and capability tend to lie in an MNC, we need to produce an analogous directory of the kinds of information-processing mechanism that can be used to access and connect the various sources of knowledge and capability. Figure 8.4 provides such a directory by showing the different information-processing capacities of Galbraith's information-processing mechanisms as well as others that are frequently used at the parent–foreign subsidiary level of analysis in MNCs.

	Sequential information-processing capacity		Reciprocal information-processing capacity
Routine information-processing capacity	Rules and programmes (H) Single-cycle planning (H) Post-action control (H) Stand-alone computer systems (H)		Integrated data-base computer systems (H)
	Vertical information systems: assistants; clerical staff; and planning staff (M)	Steering control (M) Multi-cycle, interactive planning systems (M)	
Non-routine information-processing capacity	Hierarchical referral (L)		Horizontal information systems: direct contact (L); task forces (M); teams (M); integrating roles (L); matrix designs (M)

Note: The letters in parentheses indicate relative volumes of information processing capacity: H = High, M = Medium, L = Low.

Figure 8.4   The capacities of information-processing mechanisms

It is important to realize that the routinism and interdependency axes are Gutman-like scales. Thus, mechanisms capable of providing non-routine information processing can also provide routine information processing; mechanisms capable of providing reciprocal information processing can also provide sequential information processing, but usually at a lower volume and/or at a greater cost than mechanisms specifically designed to cope with more routine or sequential information-processing requirements.

Mechanisms that are specifically designed to provide routine–sequential information processing include rules and programs, single-cycle planning processes, post-action control systems and stand-alone computer systems. As Figure 8.4 indicates, these mechanisms provide relatively high volumes of information processing and do this at relatively low cost when compared to other mechanisms. Other forms of vertical information systems, such as assistants, clerical staffs and planning staffs (Galbraith 1973), can usually handle more non-routine information processing than the preceding mechanisms but also tend to provide largely sequential information processing. Hierarchical referral, such as the referral of an exceptional or non-routine event up the hierarchy and the transmission of a decision back down, provides a two-way flow of information that also tends to be sequential. Since managerial hierarchies can easily become overloaded, this mechanism provides a relatively low volume of information-processing capacity and usually does so at a relatively high cost.

Computer systems with integrated data bases (such as airline reservation systems) that can be simultaneously shared by many users provide more reciprocal information processing, but largely for predetermined routine events. Galbraith (1973) identified a number of mechanisms that tend to provide horizontal or lateral information processing across subunits or individuals: direct contact between individuals, task forces and teams; integrating roles; and matrix designs. These mechanisms facilitate information inputs being made in a flexible, give-and-take manner among all parties to the information-processing event and, consequently, these mechanisms are the primary providers of non-routine–reciprocal information processing in organizations.

Several mechanisms are shown at the midway point of both axes in Figure 8.4, indicating that they fall between the two extremes already presented. Steering control systems (such as interim reviews by parent HQ of a foreign plant's start-up) clearly provide more reciprocal information processing and can handle more non-routine situations than post-action control systems, such as annual reviews of a subsidiary's sales and profits (Newman 1975). Multicycle, interactive planning systems also provide more nonroutine and reciprocal information processing than single-cycle planning systems. Obviously, all locations in Figure 8.4 are approximations. Information-processing capacities can vary considerably depending on the exact design of a mechanism, how it is implemented, and how it interacts with other aspects of an organization. Yet the generalizations expressed in Figure 8.4 are both useful and necessary if one wants to build a more systematic theory about information processing in organizations.

The reader will probably have noticed that there may be some positive correlation between the routine–non-routine dimension and the sequential–reciprocal dimension when the two are used to measure actual information-processing mechanisms. Thus many mechanisms seem to fall along a single dimension (the 45-degree diagonal in Figure 8.4). Mechanisms that provide reciprocal information-processing capacity seem to be able to handle non-routine situations, and mechanisms that only provide sequential information-processing capacity seem to be confined most frequently to handling routine situations. It is useful here to recall that Galbraith (1973) originally ranked his information-processing mechanisms along a single dimension, in an order roughly similar to that which occurs along the diagonal in Figure 8.4. Galbraith did not explicitly identify the routine–non-routine or the sequential–reciprocal dimensions as underlying his ordering, but simply referred to information-processing mechanisms as varying from low to high. At a minimum, Figure 8.4 helps one to understand better the differences that underlie Galbraith's general ordering of information-processing mechanisms. Daft and Lengel (1986) developed a similar ordering of information-processing mechanisms based upon the relative amounts of equivocality reduction and uncertainty reduction capacity a mechanism can provide.

The multidimensional framework in Figure 8.4 represents a significant extension of Galbraith's one-dimensional ordering, however, and both the routine–non-routine and the sequential–reciprocal dimensions need to be retained as conceptually distinct, even if information processing in organizations frequently reveals some correlation between them. There are three reasons supporting this argument. First, some important mechanisms do seem to lie off the diagonal and thus to contradict a one-dimensional ordering. Second, new information-processing mechanisms may be developed that will lie increasingly off the diagonal (this seems especially likely in the computer-based information systems area: Huber 1990). And third, many of the indicated mechanisms can be altered to vary along one dimension without necessarily varying along the other. For example, rules and programs can be altered to fit different contingencies or even turned into guidelines (which leaves the implementer with greater flexibility in responding to an information-processing event). Both options increase the non-routine information-processing capacity of this mechanism without changing the fact that it provides only sequential information processing between the creator and the implementers of the rule or guideline.

The conceptual framework developed in this section defines four structural dimensions and four process dimensions that are to be used to measure information processing in MNCs. The framework provides a more explicit way to measure and define information processing at the macro level, where information processing is a useful intervening concept for evaluating an organization's fit with its strategy and environment. The following section will apply the framework to a currently important subject in international management: transnationalism. The purpose is to illustrate how the framework can be applied and also to demonstrate that it can provide meaningful new insight into complex organizational issues.

APPLIED EXAMPLE: THE INFORMATION-PROCESSING IMPLICATIONS OF TRANSNATIONALISM

Recently interest in new ways to organize and manage MNCs has been growing (Hedlund 1986; Perlmutter and Trist 1986; Prahalad and Doz 1987; Bartlett and Ghoshal 1989). Although details and terminology may vary, most of these proposals have at their core more multidimensional organizational designs and a wider variety of integrating and coordinating mechanisms than can usually be found in traditional designs. The new designs are responses to the need to compete with new strategies in an international business environment that is increasingly complex and competitive. Bartlett and Ghoshal (1989) call this new trend in strategy and organizational design 'transnationalism'.

Transnational strategies attempt simultaneously to realize (1) efficiency and economy through global-scale operations and global integration, (2) responsiveness to national and local differences through local differentiation, and (3) a high level of innovation worldwide through extensive learning and transfer of knowledge. Traditional strategies primarily emphasize only one of these. It is obvious, therefore, that transnational strategies create much greater requirements for information processing between parent HQ and foreign subsidiaries and among foreign subsidiaries than is the case under more traditional strategies. Depending on the specifics of the strategy (e.g., where does product knowledge have to be locally differentiated? where does it need to be globally integrated?) and the company's organizational structure (which, according to Table 8.1, provides a directory as to where different types of knowledge and decision-making capabilities are located), a variety of information-processing mechanisms (taken from Figure 8.4) can be employed to link together the relevant sources of knowledge and capability with the appropriate information-processing capacity (e.g., non-routine–reciprocal information processing). This is an information-processing picture of the flexible way that organizations will need to be designed in order to implement transnational strategies.

Bartlett and Ghoshal (1989) describe the key characteristics of transnational design as revealed by their research on companies that are moving in this direction: (1) assets and capabilities are dispersed, interdependent and specialized; (2) there are differentiated contributions by national units to integrated worldwide operations; (3) knowledge is developed jointly and shared worldwide. Other characteristics include flexibility, dropping the need for symmetry and consistency in designing HQ–subsidiary relationships, self-regulating systems, and a heavy dependence on company culture and shared values in facilitating coordination.

The information-processing framework developed in the previous section seems uniquely suited to analyze the new transnational designs that are now emerging in firms and provide useful insights into them. Four information-processing implications are particularly important to the future of transnational design.

The Role and Function of Formal Organizational Structure may be Changed

As discussed in the previous section, formal structure is important because it provides a basis for locating, maintaining and accessing different kinds of knowledge and decision-making capabilities. This is especially important in large, complex organizations such as MNCs, where the range of knowledge and decision-making capabilities is extremely wide. A key function of formal MNC structure is that managers across the company know where specific sources of knowledge and capability lie, the locations tend to be fairly stable, and managers are generally familiar with how to access them.

Compared to traditional designs, transnational designs will tend to locate knowledge and decision-making capability in a more eclectic manner that is at the same time more dynamic and subject to change. For example, the Australian subsidiary may replace the parent's R&D laboratory as the center of knowledge for a new generation of product technology. The company's foreign subsidiaries are familiar with monitoring and transferring new technology from the parent's R&D laboratory (several existing information-processing mechanisms already provide the necessary linkage) but not from the Australian subsidiary. New, non-hierarchical information-processing mechanisms will have to be developed. Several years later industry trends in some countries may favor yet another version of product technology that has been developed in the company's German subsidiary for use in the local market. Again, sources of knowledge and information flows will have to change. As the situation in this example becomes widespread, formal structure begins to lose its value as an accurate and stable directory of where knowledge and capability reside and how they can be accessed.

The design logic that underlies formal structure is hierarchy and symmetry. Transnational design gives up this logic in order to gain more flexibility. In the process, the organization loses some of its ability to locate and access knowledge and capability, due to the diminished role of formal structure. Thus transnational designs need to provide new information-processing capabilities that address this loss.

The Amount of Strategic Information-Processing Capacity for Product Matters must be Greatly Expanded

Of the four types of information processing identified in Figure 8.2, strategic information processing for product matters should increase the most under a transnational strategy. Under traditional strategies and structures, strategic knowledge and decision-making capability tend to be centralized at the upper levels of product division HQs and geographical region HQs. Only with a multidomestic or polycentric strategy does the locus of this information-processing capacity move to the subsidiary level and become diffused. Thus, most strategic decision-making for product matters tends to take place either through hierarchical referral or within strategic planning processes that are also hierarchically structured. As a result, there is frequently a great deal of similarity in strategic product planning across product lines and subsidiaries within a company.

An important characteristic of transnationalism is that it disperses product knowledge across foreign subsidiaries and reduces the concentration of such knowledge at the parent HQ and in home country operations. This should result in a much more complex, heterogeneous and less hierarchical strategic planning process in transnational firms. For some product matters, strategic information processing should occur directly between concerned foreign subsidiaries, with little or no involvement from parent HQ. Other matters will need to be coordinated globally through the parent HQ. Still other matters, those that primarily respond to local conditions, will be left to each subsidiary. Since these three information-processing events tend to supplement rather than replace each other, the amount and variety of strategic information-processing capacity for product matters will need to be greatly expanded in transnational as opposed to traditional MNCs.

These first two implications primarily stem from the impact of transnationalism on the location of knowledge and decision-making capabilities in MNC structures. They are the structural implications of transnationalism for information processing. The next issue deals with the primary process implication of transnationalism for information processing.

The Use of Non-routine-Reciprocal Information-Processing Mechanisms will need to be Significantly Expanded

Transnational designs require high flexibility in the way they link different parts of the MNC organization together. Bartlett and Ghoshal (1989, p. 2) state that 'companies see that they can gain competitive advantage by sensing needs in one country, responding with capabilities located in a second, and diffusing the resulting innovation to markets around the globe'. Thus a transnational firm seems to need unusually high amounts of non-routine–reciprocal information-processing capacity in order to respond to the variety of changing opportunities this strategy seeks to exploit. Figure 8.4 shows the various horizontal information-processing mechanisms that provide this kind of capacity. All are people-intensive in the sense that they employ large amounts of managers' and key employees' time. They are costly and difficult to control when contrasted with more routine and sequential information-processing mechanisms. An important issue that MNCs will have to face is the extent to which they are prepared to provide large amounts of non-routine–reciprocal information-processing capacity as they begin to embrace transnational strategies.

It is interesting to recall that matrix structures were once heralded as the inevitable design for coordinating more multidimensional international strategies (Stopford and Wells 1972; Davis and Lawrence 1977). However, many MNCs were forced to abandon matrix structures when they could not successfully implement them (Bartlett and Ghoshal 1990). Matrix structures (such as transnational designs) also require large amounts of non-routine–reciprocal information-processing capacity to coordinate and resolve conflict between the two formal hierarchies that constitute the matrix. Many MNCs adopted matrix structures without recognizing this fact or providing the required non-routine–reciprocal information-processing capacity. As a result, conflict was frequently not resolved through lateral information processing at lower levels (as it was supposed to be) but pushed vertically up the hierarchies to be resolved at the top by hierarchical referral. In some firms that abandoned matrix structures, such as Dow Chemical, the costs of duplication and conflict resolution seem to have outweighed the benefits. In others, such as Texas Instruments, the matrix structure resulted in more severe problems: the breakdown of information processing, the overcentralization of decision-making due to the organization's inability to resolve conflict at lower levels, and serious delays in making critical decisions.

MNCs face a similar problem if they adopt transnational strategies and designs but fail to develop the necessary non-routine–reciprocal information-processing capacities to make them work. Here the problem is not conflict resolution between two formal hierarchies, as it was with matrix structures. Instead, it is (1) conflict resolution between some non-hierarchically organized transnational activity and the traditional hierarchy that still exists and interfaces with the transnational parts of a company, and (2) the need continually to redesign and alter transnational relationships within a company. Both of these activities will be commonplace in transnational firms and will require an increased use of such non-routine–reciprocal information-processing mechanisms as direct contact and meetings, task forces and work teams, and liaison and integrator roles.

Bartlett and Ghoshal (1989) state that transnational firms need to rely primarily upon informal matrixing accompanied by high levels of commitment and shared values to achieve the necessary coordination. These qualities facilitate the kind of lateral, non-routine–reciprocal information processing we have been discussing but do not automatically ensure it will occur. Many firms may require significant changes to their culture and large scale OD (organizational development) interventions (team building, survey feedback, process consultation, grid organizational development) in order to develop the potential for high levels of non-routine–reciprocal information-processing capacity. The costs of these changes may be extremely high (in some cases even prohibitive) and clearly need to be weighed against the benefits of a transnational approach.

There will be a much Greater Need for Design Rules at All Levels of the Organization

A fourth implication of transnationalism is that the process of design itself is going to be a major problem. It must be flexible, emergent from the individual situation, and fitted to the opportunities and problems posed by a firm's technology and environment. Instead of largely imitating a well-known prototype, managers at various levels will require some kind of guidance on how to design transnational relationships, how to interface them with more traditional, hierarchical and symmetrical parts of the organization, and when to convert emergent and informal coordination to more formal and traditional coordinating mechanisms. In short, the transnational organization requires a widely understood set of design rules that can be used to implement the various complexities of a transnational strategy by helping to create suitable flexible designs. Organizing itself becomes a new technology that almost all managers in a transnational firm must master. Such is not the case in a traditional firm, where organizing is done infrequently by relatively few people.

At present, implementing transnational designs in MNCs appears to rely too much on the simple notions of informal matrixing and heavy doses of commitment and shared values among organizational members. More technical knowledge than this will be required to activate and maintain effective transnational designs. The information-processing model developed in the previous section provides both a design logic and a preliminary set of design rules that seem to address this problem. While other conceptual frameworks for design might also be useful, information processing seems to be one of the primary characteristics that differentiates a transnational approach from more traditional approaches to strategy and organizational design. More traditional approaches to change have typically called for structural change, which only indirectly leads to information-processing change. Transnational design generally bypasses structural change but calls for more direct changes in information-processing capacities both within and outside the existing formal structure of a firm. Thus there is a need within such firms for a more comprehensive design approach and a model based on an information-processing perspective of the organization.

Applying the information-processing framework and model to transnationalism produces new insight and understanding. At the present time, transnational design exists largely as an illustrated but not a conceptual form; it is explained by discussing examples of firms that are employing it. This section has demonstrated that the information-processing framework and model can provide a more conceptual and general understanding of transnationalism, one which is useful to practitioners and can serve as a base for further research and theory building.

CONCLUSION

This chapter has sought to develop an information-processing perspective of organizational design that can be used when studying large, complex organizations, such as MNCs. To date, most rigorous attempts to build theory with an information-processing perspective have taken place in micro-level studies, where the unit of analysis has been the individual or work group. By using information processing as an abstract, intervening concept to relate organizational design to the strategic and environmental conditions facing an organization, researchers can better evaluate fit between these two dissimilar and hard-to-compare sets of variables. The use of more explicitly defined multi-dimensional frameworks (such as the one developed in this chapter for MNCs) to measure both the information-processing capacities of organizational design and the information-processing requirements inherent in an organization's strategy and environment will add rigor to the measurement and evaluation of such fit.

It is probable that the information-processing perspective will be of greatest interest to researchers studying what organizational designs contribute to effective MNC performance and under what strategic and environmental conditions one form is preferable to another. In order to develop and extend further the information-processing model presented in this chapter, systematic empirical research is needed on the structural dimensions framework and the process dimensions framework described respectively in Table 8.1 and Figure 8.4. As indicated, some empirical research has already been done in MNCs on the structural dimensions of information processing, while support for the process dimensions framework rests largely on conceptualizations intended more for use at the micro levels of organizations and supported by research in settings quite different from the MNC. Research in MNCs also needs to identify and understand the capacities of new information-processing mechanisms, which Bartlett and Ghoshal (1989), Prahalad and Doz (1987) and others report are currently evolving in MNCs. It is probably reasonable to expect much more dynamism on the process side than on the structural side of MNCs. It is important for theory that new forms of information processing be identified and understood in terms of some conceptual framework, such as the one suggested here.

Although the study of how MNC organizational designs change and evolve may seem a less likely candidate for the information-processing perspective, there are possibilities for exploring the role that such a perspective might play in theories of change and evolution. To the extent that evolutionary change involves the maintenance of organizational fit during transition, the framework developed above might be useful. At the other extreme, serious organizational (information-processing) misfit might be equally interesting as it should lead to failure and a more revolutionary pattern of change. Thus the information-processing perspective would appear to be potentially applicable to theories about change and evolution as well.

Theory and science are increasingly lagging behind the advancement of art when it comes to the management of MNCs. Recent books and articles report on many new trends and management approaches that seem to be currently developing within MNCs, yet the identification (as well as our understanding) of these phenomena lies largely outside existing theory. Consequently, there is a pressing need for theory to catch up with practice, otherwise practice will be increasingly operating without theory. Only theory and science – not practice and art – provide the kind of abstract and generalized understanding that can be moved, with some reliability, from one situation to another and integrated with other theories of understanding.

Note

1. The discussion about the framework shown in Figure 8.2 is taken from Egelhoff (1982).

9 Assumptions of Hierarchy and Heterarchy, with Applications to the Management of the Multinational Corporation*

Gunnar Hedlund

The virtues of hierarchical organization – of matter, of life, of information, of human institutions – are mostly taken for granted. Analysts invoke the supposed virtues of hierarchy without much specification. An example is Galbraith's (1973) synthesis of the information-processing theory of organization design: the discussion is very detailed on most aspects of design dimensions, but hierarchy is left curiously anonymous. Hierarchical structuring is introduced as one of the first and most fundamental ways of improving the handling of information, but why it is among the first and fundamental is left unexplained.

Other authors go into greater detail, but hierarchy is not really questioned in a fundamental way. For example, in a 1968 article discussing the hierarchy of authority in organizations, Peter Blau focuses primarily on the number of levels in the hierarchy and related factors. He mentions, but does not pursue, a more ambitious project: to 'explain why organizations develop various characteristics, such as a multilevel hierarchy or decentralized authority' (Blau 1968, p. 454). A somewhat later article, however (Blau 1970), analyzes the relationships between differentiation, size of the organization and size of administrative functions, and thus approaches the more basic question of why there is hierarchy in the first place.

* An earlier version of this paper was presented at the workshop on Organizational Theory and the Multinational Corporation at INSEAD on 1–2 September 1989. The author wishes to thank W. Richard Scott, David Hawk, Bruce Kogut and colleagues at IIB, particularly Maria Bolte, Peter Hagstrom, Lars Hakanson, Dag Rolander and Karl Ahlander, for constructive criticism of earlier drafts.

211

The importance of formal structuring of tasks and managerial hierarchy as a way to coordinate work is, of course, treated in great detail in the contributions of the contingency school (Burns and Stalker 1961; Woodward 1965; Lawrence and Lorsch 1967; and many others), and by the Aston group. Although the word hierarchy is often used in these works, it is not sharply defined and neither are its opposite(s) or negations clearly stated, even when its functional equivalents are analyzed. Sometimes hierarchy figures as a part of a more encompassing term, such as in Weber's bureaucracy. Hierarchy is an element of a totality, and 'each element operates not in isolation but as part of a system of elements that, in combination, are expected to provide more effective and efficient administration' (Scott 1987, p. 42 in reviewing Weber 1946, pp. 196–204.) Thus although the concept is often used, most organization theorists seem to regard hierarchy as a primitive concept not requiring much further definition. Few authors have grappled explicitly with the fundamental issues of the nature of hierarchy (Simon 1962; Pattee 1970; Herbst 1974; Koestler 1978; Camacho and Persky 1988 are examples).

The first aim of this chapter is to contribute to a discussion of the fundamental assumptions underlying a non-tautological concept of hierarchy, thereby making it possible to suggest basic alternatives to it. The second aim is to apply one such alternative, which I shall term *heterarchy*, to the structure of MNCs.

This chapter discusses some theoretical justifications for hierarchy and the historical roots of the concept. It argues that Simon's (1962) widely quoted defence of hierarchy is of less relevance to human organization than we might think at first glance or infer from its acceptance among social scientists. The conceptions of the original inventor of the term, Dionysius the Areopagite, still serve as a guide to its meaning. If some of the assumptions in these two authors' arguments are challenged, hierarchy appears as less all-pervasive, and other structures can be suggested.

This rather abstract discussion will be preceded and followed by some considerations pertaining to the modern MNC. It constitutes a crucial arena for testing the viability of hierarchy. The complexity and size of such firms challenge hierarchical forms to deliver their promise of being an efficient mechanism for handling complex tasks. In the business strategy literature, the MNC is often seen as the latest, most complex stage in an evolution of structures logically related to the strategy of the firm. (See the important line of research initiated by Chandler 1962; significant contributions on MNCs are those by Caves 1971; Stopford and Wells 1972; Franko 1976; Galbraith and Nathanson 1978; Teece 1983; and Chandler 1986.) Also, some lines of research originating in economics take the view that the MNC is the general case, which a theory of the firm should discuss, and that simpler types of company should be treated as special cases (see Casson 1987).

Three initial caveats have to be mentioned. First, this chapter does not discuss all uses of hierarchy and does not pretend to be a comprehensive review of the relevant literature. It argues for a restricted meaning of the word, indicating a breakdown of a totality into parts, and the establishment of clear notions of levels of units, with 'upper' levels in some way being superordinate to others. Hierarchy is thus seen as one of many potential mechanisms to ensure the integrity of a totality; the mere existence of a totality does not in itself make it a hierarchy. This narrower definition conforms both to lay use of the term and to what organization theorists usually mean by it. However, it excludes some broader conceptions. Simon (1962, p. 88) explicitly includes systems 'in which there is no relation of subordination among subsystems', and he reserves the term 'formal hierarchy' for systems with subordination between levels of subsystems. Another broader view of hierarchy will not be discussed in detail here: transaction cost theory. In that tradition, hierarchy is the alternative to market, and a firm is by definition a hierarchy.[1] This study is more interested in the nature of the internal working of a system, where hierarchy is only one aspect, and where alternatives to hierarchy are conceivable *within* the firm. Therefore, although relevant and important discussions akin to those here appear in the debate on transaction cost theory (e.g., the contribution by Ouchi 1980), this stream of thought will be largely ignored.

The second caveat is that I shall focus on arguments for and against hierarchy that are couched in terms of efficiency rather than legitimacy or power. This does not mean that the latter are unimportant. On the contrary, unmasking some of the unjustified claims for the universality of hierarchy's efficiency will direct attention to those other sources for it.

Third, I have elected to treat one classical defense of hierarchy in depth rather than enumerate a number of contributions. The reasons are that Simon's (1962) paper is so widely quoted and rarely discussed in detail, and that it goes into greater depth than many others. My hope is that Simon's assumptions concerning hierarchy will prove to apply also in other uses of the concept. The focus on one single paper thus should be seen as a heuristic device to clarify existing concepts and generate new ones. The critical tone of the following discussion should be read in this light. The paper is selected not because of its weaknesses but because of its strengths: it is important, well-argued and consistent.

A consequence of the concentration on Simon's work is that the discussion will have to mirror his use of examples and parables. These may seem remote from the world of MNCs to some readers. In addition,

Simon's focus is on establishing general principles for the structuring and behaviour of systems, whereas this chapter's is more restricted. In this sense, the discussion will be broader than justified by the nature of conclusions sought, but it should still be of some interest.

STRAINS ON HIERARCHY IN THE MNC

Four observations from the practice of MNC management seem pertinent. Together, they suggest that alternatives to hierarchy are emerging.

First, firms are finding that clean, streamlined organization structures are difficult to design and particularly difficult to make work. The debate in theory as well as practice is mostly phrased in terms of what should be the primary dimension of structure, function, geography or product being the most common candidates. More and more MNCs are frustrated by such discussion. They need to coordinate along product lines *and* geographical lines *and* functional lines simultaneously.

The matrix structure, which is a way of institutionalizing ambiguity, was proposed and tried as a remedy for such ills. The summary judgement after a good deal of experience is fairly negative. The response in MNCs has been an increasing willingness to live with messy organization structures, happily blending dimensions and tolerating inconsistencies, overlaps and non-institutionalized ambiguities. The organization chart – a favourite example for most theoreticians of hierarchy – becomes distinctly unwieldy and non-hierarchical. Some important MNCs even refuse to publish an organization chart; some regard their lack of one with pride.

Second, and partly as a consequence of the demise of pure structures, control systems other than the formal structure of the firm gain in importance. Two aspects stand out: the design of systems for information flows; and mechanisms to encourage shared goals, consensus on strategies, and, generally, a strong corporate culture. Organizational memory and capacity for rapid transfer of information between units is helped by long careers within the same firm and systematic rotation of personnel. Information technology increasingly allows direct (rather than mediated through hierarchy) access to information on a real-time basis. A metaphor for this type of information processing is *the holographic corporation*, in which information about the totality is shared in each and every part of the firm.[2]

Third, as is obvious from the first two points, lateral communication becomes much more important than heretofore. Subsidiaries talk directly to subsidiaries, divisions to divisions, etc. Increasingly, the national subsidiaries are given *global* roles and are put in charge of supranational projects. The temporary international project team becomes a basic building block of the MNC. An interesting structural parallel to laterality is the tendency to use interlocking directorates as a means of coordination. The head of the German subsidiary may be on the board of the US company, or perhaps even of the French parent company.

Fourth, the very *raison d'être* of the MNC seems to be shifting. Theories of the MNC emphasize monopolistic, firm-specific advantages (Hymer 1960; Kindleberger 1969; Dunning 1977) and the necessity of internalizing the exploitation of such advantages (Magee 1977; Buckley and Casson 1976; Rugman 1980; Teece 1983; Casson 1987). The modern, established MNC is better described in terms of 'new' advantages having to do with scale and scope, learning and operational flexibility (Vernon 1979; Kogut 1983). Thus international reach in itself and the organization's competence in exploiting it become the sources of competitiveness, rather than any narrowly conceived product/market position. The point about the MNC is its flexibility in mobilizing resources, and it becomes impossible to pre-specify the crucial interdependencies. The information processing view of organization design, like transaction cost theory (Williamson 1975), assumes a given task or transaction with given processing needs. The modern MNC lives in the absence of these givens. Both Galbraith's and Williamson's hierarchies therefore do not really fit the bill.

Now, if hierarchy is starting to be modified or to become less relevant in the world of practice, how is it holding up in a theoretical analysis? Are the deviations from an ideal hierarchical model either exceptions or mechanisms complementing hierarchy in situations of particular kinds, as Galbraith, Thompson (1967) and the contingency theorists would argue? Or do they signify more basic problems with the model?

THE THEORETICAL JUSTIFICATION OF HIERARCHY: WAS TEMPUS REALLY SO STUPID?

Interestingly, all writers seem to experience considerable difficulty in defining hierarchy in terms of more primitive concepts. Simon (1962) says that a hierarchy is a system that is composed of subsystems, each of which is in turn hierarchically organized. This is obviously a circular definition, and Simon seems to perceive the need for further delimitation. Rather than providing an abstract definition, he gives a number of examples: human authority structures, the composition of matter, computer programs, etc. Later, Simon (1973, p. 5) goes one step further in definition:

'Hierarchy' simply means a set of Chinese boxes of a particular kind
. . . Opening any given box in a hierarchy discloses not just one box
within, but a whole small set of boxes; and opening any one of these
compound boxes discloses a new set in turn . . . A hierarchy is a
partial ordering – specifically, a tree.

The reference to boxes and trees is significant. It is as if the author
feels that more formal definitions lack meaning. Simon is very conscious
of the possibility that hierarchy is partly a reflection of the mind of the
analyst, and may be almost an a priori category through which we see
the world. In the discussion of 'nearly decomposable systems' (1962[3], p.
108), he notes:

The fact, then, that many complex systems have a nearly decomposable, hierarchic structure is a major facilitating factor enabling us
to understand, to describe, and even to 'see' such systems and their
parts. Or perhaps the proposition should be put the other way
around. *If there are important systems in the world that are complex
without being hierarchic, they may to a considerable extent escape our
observation and understanding.* (emphasis added)

Koestler (1978) also introduces the idea that hierarchy may be in the
eye of the beholder rather than in the object beheld but, like Simon, he
finds support for a less solipsistic view. This hesitation in drawing more
far-reaching conclusions from the insight into the epistemological
problems of hierarchy is somewhat disappointing. Indeed, one could
argue that Simon himself implicitly acknowledges the lack of meaning in
his definition of hierarchy. He characterizes 'complex systems' in general
as those 'made up of a large number of parts that interact in a nonsimple
way' (1962, p. 86). 'Hierarchic systems, or hierarchy' are systems
'composed of interrelated subsystems, each of the latter being, in turn,
hierarchic in structure' (1962, p. 87). Apparently, if we assume that the
'parts' in the first definitions can also be complex, this means that *all*
complex systems are hierarchic. Any discussion of the usefulness, or
probability, of hierarchic as opposed to non-hierarchic systems thereby
becomes irrelevant. As this study will try to show, much of Simon's
discussion does indeed implicitly assume a more restrictive conception of
hierarchy where there is a subordination between components and levels.
    Simon's important argument is that hierarchy is dominant in the
architecture of complexity because hierarchical systems have an advantage in evolution due to their construction from stable subsystems. The
conclusion is reached and illustrated through an example of two watchmakers, Hora and Tempus:

There were two watchmakers, named Hora and Tempus, who manufactured very fine watches. Both of them were highly remarkable, and the phones in their workshops rang frequently – new customers were constantly calling them. However, Hora prospered, while Tempus become poorer and poorer. What was the reason?

The watches the men made consisted of about 1,000 parts each. Tempus had so constructed this that if he had one partly assembled and had to put it down – to answer the phone, say – it immediately fell to pieces and had to be reassembled from the elements. The better the customers liked his watches, the more they phoned him and the more difficult it became for him to find enough uninterrupted time to finish a watch.

The watches that Hora made were no less complex than those of Tempus. But he had designed them so that he could put together subassemblies of about ten elements each. Ten of these subassemblies, again, could be put together into a larger subassembly; and a system of ten of the latter subassemblies constituted a whole watch. Hence, when Hora had to put down a partly assembled watch in order to answer the phone, he lost only a small part of his work, and he assembled his watches in only a fraction of the man-hours it took Tempus. (Simon, 1962, pp. 90–1)

After the parable follows a mathematical demonstration of the fact that Tempus practically never managed to produce a watch. Now, let us discuss the assumptions made in the example and the consequences for understanding complex social or social/physical systems. In turn, I shall consider the *nature of the system*, its *input*, its *throughput process*, its *output*, its *environment* and the *relations between the parts*. The discussion will proceed from the watchmaker example but will also relate to Simon's wider analysis.

First, let me consider *the system (the watch is a mechanical system)*. The parts have no meaning outside the watch, no projects or goals of their own. Another characteristic of the watch is that its behaviour is completely and uniquely determined by the structure and configuration of the parts. The former can be derived from the latter. There is no 'novelty through combination'. These two characteristics hint at different classes of systems, for which hierarchy has different meanings.[4]

Second, *the parts – the inputs to the production process – do not change and are viable over time*. A watch consists of certain parts. As the Swiss watchmakers were saying when the Japanese were introducing batteries into watches: 'That is not a watch – *eine Uhr ist eine*

Uhr.' Hierarchical breakdown of a process into 'stable intermediate forms' tends to conserve the original system and make it resistant to change. (This would be more obvious if the example included a watchmaking factory with many people rather than one single master; however, there are also advantages in terms of flexibility if subsystems can be 'sealed off' from each other and independently improved, as Simon asserts. This assumes, of course, that the sealing off does not compromise the quality of linkage between subsystems.)

Third, *there are no problems of coordination between parts and between processes of manufacturing the parts: the throughput process is given and stable.* In fact, all parts are assumed to fit together perfectly. Also, it is possible to store components and have them around waiting for assembly without deterioration. If Hora were a cook rather than a watchmaker, he would have to contemplate issues such as sour milk and fermentation.[5]

Systems that evolve without mutual coordination tend not to fit together easily. Thus, there is a big jump from Simon's example – which assumes perfect fit – and the conclusion that the evolution and viability of complex systems is due to hierarchies built on independently originated building blocks. If we assume that contiguity in space and time facilitates mutual accommodation, which certainly is the case in social systems, the architecture of complexity involves *un*stable, *jointly developed* components.

Simon, in my view, implicitly assumes a kind of foreknowledge of the total system on the part of the components, which have to know, as it were, to stop developing when they are designed so as to fit well into a totality. Thus, the teleological 'overtones of the watchmaker parable' (Simon 1962, p. 93) seem to be more than overtones. Hierarchization *is* important when there are partial results that '*represent recognizable progress towards the goal*' (Simon 1962, p. 96; emphasis added).

Fourth, *the product – the output of the process – is given: a watch.* Compare the situation where exactly what to produce has to be discovered or invented. When the final product is known, it is possible to break it down into parts. This will, however, unavoidably create obstacles to later change, if we assume some inertia in the system of clustering tasks. Hora would probably never have worked out how to make a watch if he had started by making a series of parts. This means that, at least for the kind of system the example is about, the stable intermediate forms *follow*, not precede, the more complex system.[6]

Fifth, *environment is interruption, which destroys only the system currently worked on, and then completely.* The first point about the influence of the environment is that, in the parable, it is a discrete interruption, not a continuous buzz of challenges (like a wind). The example also depicts a distinct rather than fuzzy intrusion, the appropriate locus of reception of which is problematic. Finally, the environment is seen as exactly an intrusion, not a source of livelihood and opportunity.

By changing the assumptions about the environment, one can easily imagine situations where Tempus would do better than Hora. A slightly crazy example may be forgiven, I hope:

> Imagine a crisis in the Swiss watch industry, which forces our two heroes to diversify into building houses of cards instead, in the traditional, elaborate Swiss style, for the enjoyment of tourists, on top of windy Alps. Hora follows his tried method of building the parts first, leaving 10 chimneys, 10 balconies, 10 roofs, etc. for later assembly. To his disappointment, he finds that by the time he has finished going through all components, the unpredictable gusts of wind on the mountain top have destroyed almost all his previous work.
>
> Tempus, on the other hand, finds that he can protect his gradually evolving creation through reinforcing each and every part's stability by combining them in the more solid structure of the entire house of cards. The creation stays up long enough to collect money from admiring Japanese with digital watches and cameras. Thus, Tempus thrives whereas Hora gradually becomes crazy, not understanding why houses of cards are different from watches.

Sixth, concerning *relations between parts, and between parts and whole*, three different aspects are of interest: the temporal ordering of development, the degree of coupling between parts and levels in the hierarchy, and the nature of order and ordering.

As for *temporality*, is it empirically true that the hierarchies we observe are the effects of experiments with concoctions of previously existing components? An absurd counterexample is the human body. Was there a soup of organs – hands, feet, livers, brains, eyes, etc. – that luckily got combined into the first human being, miraculously also supplied with the capacity for procreation? Obviously not. If Simon's view of evolution is correct, we should observe many *independent* components floating about: protons without neutrons, brains without heads, accounting departments outside firms. The theory may explain the existence of complex systems, but it does not explain the relative absence of independent intermediate forms. In this context, it may be worth noting that Chandler's (1962, 1977) work depicts the evolution of managerial hierarchies as much in terms of the breakdown and reorganization of complex into simpler forms as the other way around. The evolution of the multidivisional form in particular took the former shape.

Even if Simon's argument were to hold for biology and physics, in human systems *forethought can dramatically increase the speed of evolution* and decrease the need for hierarchy, as Simon notes in his discussion of the safe example (1962, p. 96). Sets of subsystems can be conceived simultaneously, and previous arrangements of components can be drastically altered as a result of learning. New complex systems often require new components. It is well known how big projects like the Apollo mission or a war effort can lead to advances in technology at a lower level. A stable superordinate form (a drawing or an objective) in these cases gives rise to intermediate ones, rather than the other way around.

Regarding *coupling*, Simon discussed the properties of *nearly decomposable subsystems*. 'Near decomposability' means that 'intra-component linkages are generally stronger than intercomponent linkages' (1962, p. 106). Sometimes this tendency is treated almost as a way of defining a hierarchy, as in discussing how clusters of interaction in human societies 'will identify a rather well-defined hierarchic structure' (1962, p. 88). In other sections, it is an empirical matter, as in the discussion of communication in organizations (1962, p. 103). Two questions seem to me to be worth raising in this context. First, it is not obvious that the natural decomposition of a system is invariant over time, or even unambiguous at a certain time. If a hierarchy is defined according to frequencies of interaction, there may be no stable hierarchy when interaction patterns are varied and varying. Second, measuring the strength of linkages is problematical. Frequency may be relevant for some purposes, whereas the *importance* of linkages may be more appropriate for others: for example, there may be more frequent interaction between a boss and his subordinates than between bosses. Nevertheless, the strategic weight of the latter may lead one to cluster the systems into bosses and subordinates, instead of the groups containing mixes of the two that Simon's discussion (1962, p. 106) of different frequencies of interaction at different levels of a social hierarchy seems to imply.

Finally, the example implies a *universal* and *one-way ordering*, so that the parts of the clocks are obviously subordinated to the whole, and do not serve as parts also in other systems. A small Chinese box cannot contain the larger one. This is a characteristic of nested, 'material' hierarchies. The gene is a part of – contained in – the cell, the cell in the tissue, the tissue in the organ, etc. Interestingly this hierarchy, where the gene is at the 'lowest' level, is turned upside down if we consider it as an information, rather than a material, system. It is a central dogma of genetic biology that information goes only from gene to cell, not the other way around. Thus the subordinate part in terms of substance is the governor in terms of communication. (The universality of the ranking breaks down even further when we consider that this central dogma is now challenged. It appears that genes are indeed influenced by their surroundings.)

My imputation of clear ordering as a crucial component of Simon's use of hierarchy contrasts with his explicit inclusion of systems without subordination in his definition. Most of his examples, however, deal with formal (i.e., with subordination) hierarchies. One could go one step further. In the definition of hierarchy, the critical words may be 'composed of' or – for 'complex systems' – 'made up of'. If A is composed of many Bs, we would normally argue that B cannot be composed of As. Thus, there *is* a sense of subordination given by the type of relation implied in the verbs used.[7]

*   *   *

It seems that most of the points raised above in trying to save Tempus' reputation can be related to three assumptions underlying Simon's example. The *first* is an assumption of *pre-specification* and *stability*. Input, production process and output are given and do not change over time. There is perfect harmony within the hierarchy, which is polluted only from the environment.

The *second* is an assumption of *instrumental* parts and their *additive influence* on the whole. The components do not have their own goals, and their contribution to the totality contains no surprises.[8] They are totally subordinated to the function of the total hierarchy and, finally, to the will of its master. The *third* is the *universality* and *unidirectional* character of the hierarchy. There are not many superordinate systems to which a given part belongs, and there is no confusion as to what the top level, defining the totality, is.

THE HISTORICAL HERITAGE OF HIERARCHY: IS DIONYSIUS THE AREOPAGITE STILL VALID?

It is interesting to note how closely the three sets of attributes summarized above conform to the essence of the first known use of the word hierarchy. Dionysius the Areopagite (or pseudo-Dionysius, as he is sometimes called) invented the word in the fifth century AD and 'defined' it in two treatises, on the celestial and the ecclesiastical hierarchy, respectively.[9] His pioneering contribution has, to my knowledge, never been noted in the field of organization studies. Dionysius presented the organization structure of heaven. A number of principles of hierarchy can be extracted from the texts, and they resemble those of Simon, as well as those implied in the structure of large organizations, to a striking degree.

Dionysius' hierarchy is *eternal* and *never-changing*. It is *perfect* and *harmonious*. It has *enemies outside* and needs to be protected by *secrecy and obscurity* from the uninitiated. The organization structure is *deep* (nine levels) and *unambiguous*. Order is clearly a vertical affair and a matter of *universal subordination*. A given angel is subordinated to his (her?) boss for all issues and purposes (no temporary project organization in heaven!). It is amusing to find that the principle of *not by-passing* the chain of command applies also to angels (but not to God). The purpose of it all is for the lower levels to *become as much like the highest* as possible. In ascending, it is important to 'cry out with never silent lips . . . the hymn of divine praise' (Dionysius 1981, p. 56). *Knowledge and perfection increase* as you move up the hierarchy, thereby justifying the *one-way flow* of communication from the top down. *The boss knows everything*, literally.

Dionysius' hierarchy differs in some respects from the watchmaker's. There is dynamism through scope for advancement, so that a part becomes a part on a higher level. The stark instrumentality of the clock mechanism is also moderated in a system where the entire order is sacred, and every component reflects some of this.[10] Undoubtedly the main principle, however, is '*vertical sealing off of units*'. The fall of an angel must not compromise the integrity of the superiors.

The parallelisms indicated may appear trivial. Is it not just normal that the meaning of a word such as 'hierarchy' is relatively consistent over time? Is it not even commendable that it has retained most of its original significance? My quarrel is not with the fidelity to historical usage: the problem is rather that what was explicit and central to Dionysius is hidden as a set of implicit assumptions with later authors. Hierarchy is 'technified' and 'neutralized', which in itself is strange for a word so loaded with history and sacrament (see Appendix to this chapter). In this way we have inherited a propensity to take the meaning of word combinations such as 'hierarchical classification system', 'organizational hierarchy' (literally: sacred order of tools), and 'hierarchy of goals' as self-evident. We thereby tend to blend and hide important assumptions and make them difficult to discern.

One additional assumption, a kind of 'meta-assumption', is stated rather clearly by Dionysius: 'Our hierarchy is a sacred *science, activity, and perfection*' (1981, p. 17; emphasis added). Thus there is a hierarchy of *knowledge* as well as of *action* and of *being*, and the three coincide. Big action flows from the top and generates little actions by lesser beings, endowed with only partial knowledge. We here get closer to why hierarchy has been such a magnet for organizational theorists. The corporation has been seen as an instrument for processing information and dividing up work. Information and work are broken down into parts and handled by special units. The breakdown of information coincides with the breakdown of action. The result is a triple chain of organizational positions, information and action. To generalize wildly: there are CEOs with brains, global and summarized information, and formulation of strategies at the top, and workers with legs or more limited brains, specific information, and implementation of tactics at the bottom.

For many firms today, it is obvious that this model applies less and less. Knowledge may be greater at the periphery and far 'down' the command chain. Instead new strategies are developed, or emerge in subunits. The locus of knowledge may not coincide with the locus of strategic initiative. In fact, managerial work consists largely of constantly rearranging structures and work processes so that knowledge and potential for action may meet. (Compare the discussion in Zeleny 1987. The distinction between different types of 'division of labour' goes in the same direction as my distinction between different hierarchical orders.) Scott (1987a, pp. 40–5), in summarizing Weber's theory of bureaucracy and the criticisms against it, makes the point that in Weber's time technical competence and position were highly correlated, whereas today this is no longer the case. The staff-line distinction is a recognition of this, but perhaps 'not so much a solution to the difficulty . . . as a structural recognition of the distinctiveness of the two sources of authority sloughed over in Weber's analysis' (Scott 1987, p. 44). My suggestion is to posit several 'lines', and expect the degree of overlap to vary between organizations, and the relative criticality of the lines to vary as well, also over time.

It is not only a matter of separate dimensions (knowledge, action, work) overlapping, but also of the structuring of each dimension. Today we doubt that knowledge is fundamentally reducible to single bits. We also start to question whether new patterns emerge from big causes, cascading out in a hierarchy of smaller effects. Chaos theory is beginning to emphasize large effects of small causes ('the butterfly effect'), and the practical impossibility of deducing the former from the latter. Common experience of how new strategies emerge seem often to fit such a dynamic, rather than the hierarchical derivation of means from overarching ends (compare to Mintzberg 1973, and Mintzberg, Raisinghani and Theoret 1976).

Analyses of the disadvantages of hierarchy and emphasis on the existence of more complex systems than the clock are of course common in the literature. 'Control losses' in hierarchies and optimal structures for varying complexities of problems have been empirically studied (Bavelas 1951; Blau and Scott 1962; Williamson 1964; Perrow 1979; and many others). The intention has been to pinpoint crucial aspects of hierarchy, which are so obvious that they may escape undetected, and the questioning of which gives rise to new conceptions of organization. Therefore, how can the signs that hierarchy is being modified in MNCs be related to the conceptual discussion?

THE MNC AND ASSUMPTIONS OF HIERARCHY: THE EMERGENCE OF A HIERARCHICAL MODEL

An implicit point of view in the preceding discussion has been to reason in terms of organizational effectiveness. Hierarchy's consequences, rather than its causes, have been the main preoccupation. Now this perspective will be explicitly applied. I will argue that the MNC is confronting a world which largely invalidates the fundamental assumptions of hierarchy and of its benevolent effects. In turn, let us discuss the four assumptions of: *pre-specified and stable tasks; instrumentality and additive influence by parts*; *unidirectionality and universality*; and, finally, the meta-assumption of *coinciding hierarchies of knowledge, action, and people*.

Pre-specification and Stability

In the ethnocentric and polycentric MNC (Perlmutter 1965), tasks are indeed rather clear and stable. It is natural to build a pyramid with easily definable distinctions between headquarters and subsidiaries. Ethnocentrism implies sequential interdependence (Thompson 1967). Knowledge and initiative reside in the center, and more operational tasks in the periphery. Polycentrism suggests another, but equally clear, division of tasks. Headquarters is at the center of pooled interdependencies, and acts as a monitor and portfolio manager. However, in the geocentric case, the task of any one unit is much more complex, unstable and intricately related to the tasks of other units. Interdependencies between 'center' and subsidiaries, as well as among subsidiaries, become reciprocal. A design strategy that simply recommends incorporating such interlinkages in the same unit does not help very much. Too much becomes incorporated, since reciprocal interdependencies encompass many organizational units. The same problems confront the analyst or designer trying to map the organizational structure through frequencies of interaction.

If organization is perceived as a hierarchy of *jobs* (as in Weber's bureaucracy), the modern MNC constantly upsets the hierarchy, since a long-term specification of the role of any one organizational unit is unfeasible. One might take the argument one step further. The very *raison d'être* of the MNC is constantly to rearrange jobs and transactions, utilizing its infrastructural advantages of globality. In this sense, the MNC becomes a *meta-institution*.[11] It should not be understood as a particular solution in terms of the governance mode of Williamson's transaction cost theory (1975, and particularly 1981). Instead, it is better understood as a mechanism for constantly *selecting* governance modes for an array of innumerable and changing transactions. The MNC becomes a *selection mechanism* rather than a *selected mechanism*. This type of meta-institution is what is required when tasks, information, technological interfaces, etc., cannot be pre-specified and must change at non-trivial speed.

The implication of all this is that no hierarchical ordering will be well suited to probable future tasks. Given the pernicious influence and indirect effects of any particular 'freezing' of basic structure, it seems reasonable to argue that hierarchy must *not* be seen as one of the first strategies to manage complex information processing demands, as it is in Galbraith's (1973) analysis. (See, for example, W. H. Davidson and Haspeslagh 1982 on the difficulties of implementing an organization according to global product lines.)

Most recent suggestions for more flexible MNC management (Bartlett and Ghoshal 1986; Doz and Prahalad 1986; Hedlund 1986; Nonaka 1990; R. E. White and Poynter 1990) bring up the necessary multi-dimensionality of the organization structure. The argument here is that we need to go one step further and question the whole idea of stable dimensionality in the hierarchy. To exaggerate a bit, we need to consider the formal structure of the organization last, not first, as far as its efficiency in carrying out its tasks is concerned. This is not 'simply' a matter of matrix organization (see Hedlund 1986 for a discussion of this point). There may, of course, be reasons *other* than efficiency for sticking to a permanent hierarchy: for example, the preservation of power for the top managers or the need to identify a centre of accountability demanded by parties external to the firm.

Instrumentality and Additivity

It is obvious that the subsidiaries of large MNCs cannot be seen only as instruments of the centre, the headquarters, the corporate group, or whatever. Influential frameworks of analyzing the MNC take the anchoring in a host country environment as the critical factor against which any ambitions for global integration have to be balanced (Doz 1979).

Systematic or synergetic, rather than additive, coupling of subsidiaries to the rest of the corporation is implicit in the conception of a geocentric MNC. In polycentrism, one market can be given up and you simply have a slightly smaller company. In many industries today it is impossible to consider strategies this way. Take away the US market, and you also influence scanning for R&D, competitive posture on third country markets, the supply of components, exchange rate vulnerability, etc. The same argument may also apply across product lines. This discussion, however, applies primarily within only moderately diversified firms. In very heterogenous organizations, the benefits of rich interaction are too minor to justify the efforts.

Human aspects reinforce the trend away from instrumental and additive views of the parts of the MNC. MNCs have some disadvantage *vis-à-vis* local companies in recruiting, a disadvantage that becomes further pronounced if and when the subsidiary becomes only a pawn in a superordinate game.

Unidirectionality and Universality

It is not uncommon in MNCs to speak of a distributed network of 'centres of competence'. Subsidiaries are (or become, or are made) specialized, and take on roles as global coordinators in some areas, whereas they may continue to be 'soldiers' in others. Multiple hierarchies shift between products and issues, and over time intersect. In the extreme, there is no visible overall apex. Any unit is both a coordinating and directing centre *and* a subordinated part, and the composition of roles changes often enough and overlaps to such an extent that a segregation into different hierarchical chains becomes impractical.

I shall not claim that any existing MNC resembles this extreme model. However, tendencies to assign global product mandates, tendencies to charge subsidiaries with new roles as strategic contributors, functional specialization over subsidiaries and countries, the use of international project teams, and the interlocking directorate type of management structures all move the MNC in this direction. (See, e.g., Hedlund 1980; Bartlett and Ghoshal 1986.) Obviously, such trends will be more visible in MNCs from small home countries.

Coinciding Knowledge, Action and People Hierarchies

Many of the previous points can be related to the breakdown of the Dionysian construction of mirroring structures of knowledge, action and 'social' (if such a term is allowed among angels) position. Because of differing market environments and organizational histories, technological expertise often does not coincide with superior position in the organizational hierarchy. Innovation is increasingly likely to be generated from localized and diffused but globally motivated action rather than from tightly coordinated strategies formulated at the core. It is not possible to reduce the sum total of organizational knowledge to a filing cabinet, a department or a computer program at the top.

The question then becomes what the function of top management really is. Blau argues that 'conditions in organizations that make the reliable performance of duties relatively independent of direct intervention by top management further the development of multilevel hierarchies', since then the problem that hierarchy can make the top executive lose touch will not matter so much (1968, p. 464). His argument assumes that some useful coordination task remains to be achieved, or that competition is inefficient enough to allow hierarchies to be established on 'non-rational' grounds.

Now, the development of information technology has opened up new vistas for working with distributed knowledge and reliable multifocal action,[12] without relying on layers of management for coordination. Managerial levels become unnecessary when information is available immediately (in time) and broadly (in physical and organizational space). It is now routine in advanced MNCs to have systems where individual sales orders are immediately fed into global logistical, manufacturing and financial systems, and where many decision routines are automated and decision variables jointly optimized. The consequence is a drastic simplification in the number of formal managerial levels. This type of advanced technology thus makes hierarchy unnecessary, rather than relieving it of its drawbacks, as in Blau's (1968) discussion.

Such practically complex but conceptually simple cases of information technology may cloud the wider picture, however. In the long run, the consequences of wide access and possibilities for experimentation in combining pieces of information are probably more important.[13] Multiple trial is the only way to explore the consequences of combinations of one technology with another, one set of competences with a market far away, etc. Information technology makes this possible on a global scale. The approach is considered common sense in research laboratories, small high-tech firms (see Bahrami and Evans 1987) and some professional organizations. Now, in much larger settings, it may be possible partly to substitute for the strict demands on physical proximity and intensive personal interaction by linking people and units through technical means.[14]

The organization in this perspective becomes an arena for creation and experimentation, rather than for the exploitation of given knowledge and other resources.[15] In a way, we are sketching the outlines and structural prerequisites of global, large-scale entrepreneurialism. Schumpeter's (1947) long-run hypothesis was that the institutionalization of entrepreneurship would slowly grind the capitalist machine to a stand-still, or at least result in a more mediocre capacity for change. However, technical advances may allow the design of institutions not envisioned by Schumpeter. It is significant that as late as 1973, when Galbraith writes about information systems and strategies for organization design, he explicitly calls for *vertical* information systems (my emphasis). Although he refers to probable incapacities for imagining new social systems, Galbraith buys into the Dionysian formula of knowledge as one hierarchy. (It is true, however, that he emphasizes lateral processes and structures in general.)

Arrow uses the important distinction between 'terminal acts' and 'experiments' developed by Raiffa and Schlaifer to contrast two very different kinds of decisions: 'decisions to act in some concrete sense, and decisions to collect information' (1974, p. 49). Arrow emphasizes the trade-off between efficient terminal acts and rich experimentation, and does not at all see hierarchy, or any other structure, as the obvious solution: 'The optimal choice of internal communication structures is a vastly difficult question' (1974, p. 54). In spite of this, in the chapter that follows this discussion he does not really take issue with the argument that 'since transmission of information is costly . . . , it is cheaper and more efficient to transmit all the pieces of information once to a central place than to disseminate each of them to everyone' (1974, p. 68). This is seen as the classical argument for 'authority'.

The 'polar alternative' for authority is claimed to be 'consensus' (1974, p. 69). Consensus is viable when interests and information are identical in a group. There are indeed many ways to move towards these conditions, by using modern technology and by intelligent redesign of incentive systems, including ownership structures. If, in addition to this, the modern organization has to shift the balance towards more experiments and fewer terminal acts, it is not at all obvious that information processing demands lead one to design authority structures. Of course, this is a familiar argument. The evidence is well summarized by Scott (1987a, pp. 151–4). It seems as if the idea of experimentation and information seeking is not really carried through in the debate on authority, the advantages of which are more posited than argued.

Arrow emphasizes religious beliefs in the acceptance of authority (1974, pp. 64–5 in particular). Perhaps biases of the kind introduced by Dionysius can explain why his list (1974, p. 77) of 'responsibility mechanisms' in modern organizations does not contain the conceivable alternative of responsibility to those governed, with an active role by the subordinates (e.g., as constituted by the board of directors). Such circularity goes against the grain of hierarchy, but is not often mentioned, in spite of the fact that it does not contradict any of the basic lines of the analysis of information processing demands.

As an aside, it is tempting to contrast the implications of an emphasis on experimentation with those of transaction cost theory. The boundaries of the firm (*not* the 'hierarchy'!) will be determined by consideration of *optimum range and intensity of experimentation*, rather than by minimum cost of transacting and producing. The function of boundaries is partly the same; to ensure internalization of rents discovered and created, to handle incentive problems, etc. Added emphasis is placed, however, on the tacit dimension of organizational competence (cf. Pavitt 1971). The many references to Polanyi's (1958) discussion of tacitness in economics and organization theory do not stress adequately that Polanyi was talking about *personal* knowledge. The analysis and the challenges become more complex if tacitness is seen at a social level. A global firm may be seen as an investor in technical and human communications infrastructure and codes, where the interpretative capability is largely firm-specific and tacit. By definition, tacit knowledge cannot be easily codified, and is thus less amenable for assignation in hierarchical knowledge structures. Consequently, if social tacit knowledge is important, it follows that hierarchy is at least problematical as a reflection of the distribution of competence in the organization (see Arrow 1974, pp. 55–6.)

ASPECTS OF HIERARCHY

I have argued that hierarchy can be challenged conceptually and theoretically, and some assumptions can be laid bare that make it seem less attractive as a design principle for certain kinds of systems and organizations. The modern MNC falls in the category of system not benefited by hierarchical conception. It has also been claimed that tendencies in MNCs illustrate adaptations based on assumptions alternative to those constituting hierarchies.[16] From all of this is emerging a notion of an alternative organizing principle, which I call *heterarchy*.[17] A heterarchy is by definition a more ambiguous creature than the hierarchy. Still, it is possible to define some aspects of heterarchy in a more formal way.

1. Components in a heterarchy are related along three primary dimensions:

knowledge, action and position of authority.[18] The dimensions of most actual organization structures (geography, product, function, technology, etc.) are only proxies for the primary dimensions. It is necessary, whenever one specifies an order, also to specify along which dimension the order applies.

2. Units in a heterarchy may or may not be ordered in the same way along the three dimensions. The rule, rather than the exception, will be that the orders do not coincide. Thus 'management by exception' becomes a strange principle in a heterarchy.

3. The order will vary over time and circumstance. A given unit will be both Chief and Indian. Diagrammatically, hierarchy in its simplest form can be contrasted with heterarchy thus:

	Hierarchy		*Heterarchy*	
	A	A	B	C
	B	B	A	B
	C	C	C	A

4. The order will not necessarily be transitive. The organization will often be circular (Ackoff, 1974). This is McCulloch's (1965) original idea developed in the 1940s, which is applied in Ogilvy (1977) and Schwartz and Ogilvy (1979). McCulloch hypothesizes that the human brain is so constructed that:

> Circularities in preference instead of indicating inconsistencies, actually demonstrate consistency of a higher order than had been dreamed of in our philosophy. An organism possessed of this nervous system – six neurons – is sufficiently endowed to be unpredictable from any theory founded on a scale of values. It has a heterarchy of values, and is thus internectively too rich to submit to a summum bonum. (McCulloch 1965, p. 43)

Later findings on the holographic properties of the brain point in the same direction as McCulloch's speculations. The most intelligent systems we know seem to be heterarchically organized. Again, schematically, we can represent the difference:

Hierarchy	*Heterarchy*
A	A
B	B
C	C
	A

Practical examples of heterarchical social systems are democratic political systems, employee share ownership, and many kinds of project councils and R&D boards in companies. In addition, computer programs have been described as heterarchical. (See Hofstadter 1980).

5. The relations between units in a heterarchy may be of several kinds: A may issue commands to B, evaluate B, hold knowledge of importance to B, include B as a constitutive part, etc.; this is a consequence of multidimensionality. But also within the confines of the dimension of, say, action, we can conceive of different types of ordering. Act A may be an instruction leading to act B (such as McCulloch's neurons firing messages to each other). Act A may also be superordinate more in the sense of confirming or catalyzing a whole set of acts B, C, D, etc. Much of the problem with Simon's discussion has to do with the fact that the type of relation between subsystems is not specified.

The hierarchical model, as observed in organizational practice, obscures the differences between kinds of relations and puts the command structure as the primary one. A result of recognizing these distinctions is that the notion of rank order and verticality in themselves become less relevant, and at least 'secularized'.[19] The sum total is to create a situation where 'management' is as much a horizontal as a vertical affair, and becomes part of *every* unit's and individual's task. If managerial competence is a scarce resource, this may lead to specialization of this function, as of every other job (cf. Williamson 1975, pp. 47, 52). However, it is not clear why managers should be 'above' those whose coordination needs they serve.

Hierarchy	*Heterarchy*		
A	A	B	C
B			
C			

6. A heterarchy is given cohesion and is protected from mere anarchy primarily by normative integration (Etzioni 1975). Shared objectives and knowledge, and a common organizational culture and symbolism are important mechanisms. Investments in communication systems, rotation of personnel, a bias for internal 'promotion' and other human resource management strategies become increasingly important. Simon (1989), in discussing the balance between markets and organizations, emphasizes employees' identification with the organization, and criticizes transaction cost analysis for neglecting such aspects. However, Simon in this same paper emphasizes

'specialization and the consequent hierarchization of authority' (1989, p. 22). This chapter has tried to argue that specialization does *not* necessarily lead to hierarchy.

Simon introduces the concept of 'docility' to characterize the attitude of individuals in organization. To be docile is to be tractable, manageable, teachable. He confesses that he is not entirely happy with the term (1989, p. 13). No doubt it paints a brighter picture of human nature than the references to shirking, cheating, moral hazard and opportunism in the property rights, agency cost and transaction cost literature. Still, there are the contours of a curiously passive creature in the word and its referents. Heterarchy will have to rely also on more active and assertive organizational identification. Scott (1987a, p. 34) notes that 'formalization makes allowances for the finitude of humans'. The same point is made concerning government in general and scientific work. It is worth noting that industry leaders now start wondering about how to tap into the positive sources of human motivation much more directly, perhaps to make allowances for the *infinitude* of human beings. For example, Jan Carlzon of SAS (1985) makes the distinction between two ways of managing: by *instruction*, by specifying *restrictions*, which makes it impossible for the managed to take responsibility; and by *information*, by specifying *opportunities*, which makes the employee take responsibility.

Instilling common interests can and should also take the form of material incentives. A heterarchical MNC would do well seriously to consider global employee ownership *of the 'parent company'*.[20] Bonus systems can be designed to encourage system-wide responses and responsibilities commensurate with responsibilities.

In summary, and at the risk of launching unwieldy catch phrases, heterarchy as an alternative to hierarchy may be characterized as:

(a)   multidimensional (knowledge, action and position);
(b)   assymetrically ordered along the dimensions;
(c)   temporary subordination and simultaneous sub- and superordination;[21]
(d)   non-transitivity, circularity;
(e)   horizontality;
(f)   normative, goal-directed integration.

The Beginning of New Metaphors for the Large, Complex Firm

It seems as if the modern corporation has reached the limits of useful borrowing of concepts from other fields. Hierarchy came from the church;[22] strategies, line–staff distinctions, divisions and many other things from the military; bureaucracy from the state. Is it not time that the private corporation invested in something on its own?

Blocking such progress are the half-digested techniques and metaphors of history and other fields of human effort. Scrutinizing 'hierarchy' was meant to indicate that the inheritance is not all to the good. The idea of heterarchy is partly to suggest formally definable aspects of alternative structures. It is also meant to imply a more encompassing notion of order, of which hierarchy is a special case defined by some rather strict assumptions. Heterarchy also aims to describe empirical reality – what actually goes on in the modern MNC – better than conceptions of hierarchy.

Other reconceptualizations of managerial activity are consistent with the drift of my argument. Nonaka's (1990) 'information creation' (as distinct from information processing) is a step in a more dynamic view of what companies do and what it takes to do it. Morgan's (1986) critique of various views of 'organization', suggesting 'imaginizations' as one possible alternative concept, is also related to my discussion of the limits of instrumentality and mechanism.[23] Static conceptions of environment–organization interaction have long been challenged, notably by Weick (1979). Such ideas are akin to stressing the action dimension of heterarchy, and debating possibilities of pre-specification of tasks. Peters and Waterman, in their 1982 study as well as in their more recent work, also point to a new set of guiding metaphors for corporate life.

These broad discussions lead also to questioning the nature of 'management'. A first indication that this word is as loaded with partly outdated meaning as 'hierarchy' is the etymology of the word. A quick search in the *Oxford English Dictionary* reveals that it originally had to do with breaking and training horses. (The word *manège* means the arena where horses go round and round, just like employees, with the trainer with the whip in the centre, just like the manager.)[24]

If the world of heterarchy seems too messy to be a practical alternative, it may be a comfort to contemplate the possibility that non-hierarchy seems to work better in practice than in theory. The brain functions, perhaps heterarchically, in spite of our inability to grasp its mode of coordination. The naturalness of hierarchy thus may be much more a product of mental and perceptual biases than we like to admit. The conception that order requires ordering may also be contrasted with the view of a Canadian tribe of Indians, described by Miller (1955) and discussed in Bouvier (1984). Hell for them is a horrible place 'where some human beings are in control of others'. (The Western hell, as we know from successful interrogation by the Holy Inquisition, is very neatly organized, also in nine levels.[25]) The tribe does not even have a word for hierarchy.[26] A final reflection is that in Western languages, it seems difficult to find translations of the Greek word. We rely on the latitude of imprecision given by a silent consensus not to engage in conceptual archaeology. The cost is, as I have argued, the unconscious adoption of a number of interesting but questionable assumptions and/ or the complete stripping of the concept of any precise meaning.

Appendix

It is well beyond the scope of this chapter and its author to speculate on the reasons for the shift in the meaning of hierarchy from sacred to secular. A review by Patrides (1973) contains a concise history of the concept and its use in philosophy and religion. Based on his analysis, my own hunch is that the Enlightenment and science destroyed the deeper basis of a hierarchy of beings. However, for political and personal safety reasons, at least the top of the hierarchy was preserved. (Giordano Bruno was burnt partly for associating the new idea of infinity with the possibility that there might not be any particular distinctions in creation: 'pantheistic immanentism'.) The illogic of this (keeping the top) did not escape the great minds of the time: Leibniz wrote that:

> Sir Isaac Newton, and his followers, have also a very odd opinion concerning the work of God. According to their doctrine, God Almighty wants to wind up his watch from time to time; otherwise it would cease to move. He had not, it seems, sufficient foresight to make it a perpetual motion. Nay the machine of God's making is so imperfect, according to these gentlemen, that he is obliged to clean it now and then by an extraordinary concourse, and even to mend it, as a clockmaker mends his work.[27]

Notes

1. However, Williamson (1975, pp. 41–56) does discuss the relative merits of peer groups and 'simple hierarchies'. The latter concept is not strictly defined, however. Chandler's (1962, 1977) analysis resembles that of the transaction cost analysts. 'Managerial hierarchies' are seen as replacing *markets*, and the evolution of the large firm is described largely as replacing small hierarchies with bigger, more complex ones. The alternative is seen as a 'federation of autonomous offices', so that coordination is assumed to require hierarchy and the concept becomes almost synonymous with internal organization in general (see Chandler 1977, pp. 1–12).
2. See El Sawy (1985) for the first, as far as I know, discussion of the firm as a hologram.
3. Note that in the following discussion the page references of Simon (1962) refer to the 1982 reprint of that volume.
4. Ackoff and Emery (1972) provide classifications in line with these ideas. Cf. also the discussion of 'nested hierarchies' on the one hand and those

of 'independently individuated entities' on the other in Depew and Weber (1985).

5. The watchmaker analogy is a very interesting one in that it pictures a world with a maker of perfect knowledge, a sort of omniscient God. His creation is frictionless and everything has its perfect place in it. Simon argues (1962, p. 93) that his theory assumes no teleological mechanism, 'in spite of the overtones of the watchmaker parable'. It seems that the parable of a watchmaker is irresistible for social as well as natural scientists. Cf. the remarks by Leibniz quoted in the Appendix and Dawkins' (1982) 'blind watchmaker'.

6. See the history of navigation. The concept of navigation, which assumes reliable timekeeping, led to frenetic efforts to design robust clocks. Evolution could not work with a stable, ready part.

7. It is tempting but not possible here to get involved in the question of whether language itself is necessarily hierarchically structured, and whether the difficulties of defining non-hierarchy might have to do with this.

8. It may be argued that Simon's argument is exactly about the importance of independently existing parts, with which evolution can then play. However, the example assumes that the clockmaker *manufactures* the parts. He is *not* in the position of evolution, at least a non-teleological kind of evolution, having to contend with a historical mess of components not particularly useful a priori for any design at all. A better example would be to consider a complete ignoramus stumbling around in a junkyard, trying to get something interesting put together.

9. The contribution of Dionysius is sketched in Hedlund (1988) which relies on the translation and commentary by Thomas L. Campbell (Dionysius 1981).

10. Of course, hierarchy literally is translated as 'rule through the sacred'.

11. 'Institution' is here used in a restrictive sense, 'markets' and 'hierarchies' in transaction cost theory being regarded as institutions. See also Hedlund (1986).

12. Cf. Prahalad and Doz (1985) and their 'multi-focal MNC'.

13. Hagstrom (1990) contains a discussion of un- and rebuilding and relocation of activities in MNCs as a consequence of modern information technology.

14. All experience tells us that this will not be *sufficient*. It needs to be complemented by close attention to global *human* communication systems. Nevertheless, 'organized anarchies', 'adhocracies', 'free-form organization', etc., become possibilities also for large organizations. These may come to resemble 'professional organizations'. Analyses of coordination mechanisms in such organizations are akin to much of my discussion above. See Scott (1965 and 1987a: pp. 236–9). Edgar Schein's work on the nature of managerial hierarchy in such contexts is also very relevant (see for example Schein 1985 and 1989).

15. See Hedlund and Rolander (1990) for further discussion of exploitation and experimentation strategies.

16. It is not the purpose of this chapter to give an empirical review of the evidence, so the propositions must here stand only as hypotheses and examples.

17. I first discovered the concept in Ogilvy (1977), who refers to McCulloch (1965) as his source of inspiration. See also my own discussion (1986).
18. I have here selected anthropocentric concepts. It is possible that the aspects of heterarchy in social systems are also characteristic of a wider class of systems.
19. Of course, there are deep cultural forces protecting the sacred aspects of hierarchy. The relativistic view of relations between parts here propounded is not readily subscribed to in societies where the essence of the society is exactly the sanctity of authority relations. My argument is basically in terms of efficiency, not legitimacy.
20. Note that family metaphors are very common in MNC parlance: *daughter* companies ask *mother* for money, come *home* for review, etc. It should be apparent that such a metaphor does not necessarily imply unambiguous subordination ('*sub*sidiaries').
21. Laurent (1978) notes how few books and papers there are on subordination rather than on management. Since the two concepts imply each other, their treatment should be more equal.
22. Of course, the military may also be cited as the source of hierarchy in substance if not in name. However, the insistence upon authority is complemented by emphasizing local, independent action in line with very overarching goals. The military is more hierarchic in peace than in wartime action (see, e.g. Arrow 1974, p.69.)
23. 'Organization' comes from 'organon' which means, among other things, 'tool'.
24. Chuang-tzu has a chapter on horses' hooves, which argues that even in the training of horses you should not 'manage' too much. Half of the horses will die, for example. In Western orthodoxy, such germs of more indirect leadership principles are conspicuously absent. Lao Tzu, of course, also gives many examples of the virtues of non-action by the ruler, spontaneous order and vitality, etc. Taoism may be the source of inspiration for new perspectives on management.
25. See Paine (1972) Chapter 7.
26. The general question of cultural bias in the concept and practice of hierarchy is, of course, a very complicated one which cannot be discussed at length here. Works by Hofstede (1980a), Laurent (1983) and Maruyama (1978) seem particularly relevant among modern authors. Weber's work on religion and its relation to capitalism and bureaucracy also provides ample material.
27. From *The Leibniz–Clarke Correspondence*, ed. H. G. Alexander, quoted in Patrides (1973, p. 444).

10 Procedural Justice Theory and the Multinational Corporation

W. Chan Kim and Renée Mauborgne

Increasingly global strategy has been recognized to be a key determinant of the success and survival of MNCs. This is traceable, in no small measure, to the non-trivial benefits recognized as flowing from global strategy which include global economies of scale and scope, reduced factor costs, worldwide learning and enhanced competitive leverage (e.g., Yip 1989).

In response, the task of identifying the substantive content of winning global strategies has come to dominate recent literature on the MNC. Academicians (e.g., Hout, Porter and Rudden 1982; T. Levitt 1983; Hamel and Prahalad 1985; Kogut 1985a, 1985b) have conducted extensive analyses on multinationals in search of the answer to the question, What is the ideal global strategy? The result is a wealth of winning strategic prescriptions for the multinational. A recent work by Ghoshal (1987) summarizes well the diverse studies on global strategy and provides a framework that can aid executives in understanding, formulating and analyzing the content of global strategies.

Notwithstanding the importance of identifying the content of effective global strategies, relatively little research attention has been paid to the equally important issue of global strategy execution. Perhaps this is because, as articulated by Kogut (1989, p. 387), 'it may be more easy to isolate the substantive strategic content of an international strategy than to define the operating systems to pull it off'. However, irrespective of the ease or difficulty of this task, questions of global strategy execution need to be more systematically addressed. Even the best of global strategies essentially means little if not effectively executed.

The overriding objective of this chapter is to introduce the theoretical tradition of procedural justice-based research (e.g., Thibaut and Walker 1975; Tyler and Caine 1981; Alexander and Ruderman 1987; Lind and Tyler 1988; Folger and Konovsky 1989; Tyler 1990) to multinational management in order to explore the ways in which procedural fairness can act as a catalyst to the effective execution of global strategies. Specifically, we explore the importance of procedural justice in the context of global strategic decision-making between the head office and subsidiary units. Our conviction that procedural justice may well be a construct of importance in the implementation of global strategies came (1) from our field observations that so many multinational managers care not only what the content of global strategies are but also how these strategic decisions are generated, and (2) from the theoretically argued salutary attitudinal effects associated with procedural justice judgements. Research in procedural justice theory indicates if the process by which decisions are made is viewed by those affected to be procedurally just, then the organizational members involved in the decision process exhibit the higher-order attitudinal forces of commitment, trust and social harmony as well as the lower-order force of outcome satisfaction.

Given that (1) the very nature of the strategic requirements increasingly characterizing global strategies – consummate cooperations among global units – makes the higher-order attitudes of commitment, trust and social harmony increasingly central to the effective working of global strategies (e.g., Hedlund 1986; Kim and Mauborgne 1991), and also that (2) the distinctive powers of hierarchy which could have traditionally been used by head office management to affect subsidiary compliance (namely, fiat and refined monitoring and appraisal capability) have dissipated within the multinational (e.g., Hedlund 1986, and Chapter 9, above; Ghoshal and Bartlett 1989; Kim and Mauborgne 1989, 1991), procedural justice clearly has great potential importance for the effective execution of global strategies.

First, this chapter traces the antecedents of social psychology theories of procedural justice and the relationship of procedural justice to the higher-order attitudes of commitment, trust and social harmony as well as outcome satisfaction. Second, it explores the applicability of procedural justice theory to the multinational and the ways in which it can act as a catalyst to the effective execution of global strategies. Third, it reviews our field study, which set out to provide an initial test of the role procedural justice can play in implementing global strategies. Finally, this chapter discusses the managerial implications of procedural justice in the multinational and outlines potentially fruitful research areas in which procedural justice can be applied in the future for the effective management of the multinational enterprise.

PROCEDURAL JUSTICE: ITS ORIGIN, APPLICATIONS AND CONSEQUENCES

The historical antecedents of procedural justice theory are grounded in the seminal work of Thibaut and Walker (Thibaut *et al.* 1974; Thibaut and Walker 1975, 1978; Walker *et al.* 1974). The starting point of Thibaut and Walker's work is a clear demarcation between the way decisions are made and the nature of those decisions. Contrary to the then established field of social psychology, however, Thibaut and Walker did not concern themselves with the way in which the content of decision outcomes influences individuals' reactions to relationships, social experiences and institutions. Rather, what preoccupied Thibaut and Walker was the way in which the process by which decision outcomes are reached exerts a powerful influence on human cognitions and behavior. This preoccupation led them to embark on a systematic study of the psychology of social decision-making processes.

This seminal work of Thibaut and Walker essentially represented a domain of social psychology that viewed the individual through a different, and in some respects new, lens. It regarded individuals as equally, if not more, concerned with matters of process than with the nature of decision outcomes. Accordingly, the central focus of Thibaut and Walker's analysis was how individuals' evaluations of ongoing social interactions are shaped by the dynamics of social interaction. Although there exist multiple aspects of social processes that may well influence, to a non-trivial extent, individuals' reactions to their social interaction, Thibaut and Walker concentrated on only one: judgements that procedures and social processes are just.

Accordingly, the field of procedural justice was created by Thibaut and Walker by merging an interest in the psychology of justice with the study of process. More concretely, procedural justice theory concerns itself expressly with the 'social psychological consequences of procedural variation, with particular emphasis on procedural effects of fairness judgments' (Lind and Tyler 1988, p. 7). It maintains that people react to decision outcomes in terms of the procedures by which those outcomes were arrived at and argues for the primacy of fair procedures *per se*.

Thibaut and Walker first explored the concern for procedural justice in legal and judicial settings: few domains have granted as much attention to questions of procedures and processes as has the law. This research provided the first unambiguous demonstration that variations in procedural justice *per se* indeed affect the attitudes and behaviors of those subject to a procedure. Specifically, Thibaut and Walker found that increases in procedural justice judgements result in the salutary attitudinal and behavioral consequences of heightened outcome satisfaction as well as better acceptance of and compliance with the resulting decision outcomes. This led Thibaut and Walker to conclude specifically that the exercise of procedural justice may well allow the legal process to 'bind up the social fabric and encourage the continuation of productive exchange relations between individuals', and generally that the property of being fair and just may well be an important requisite for any model of decision-making. Subsequent studies of procedural justice in legal settings have widely confirmed these findings of Thibaut and Walker (e.g., Lind *et al.* 1980; Tyler and Folger 1980; Casper, Tyler and Fisher 1988; Tyler 1988, 1990).

As the theoretical work of Leventhal (Leventhal 1980; Leventhal, Karuza and Fry 1980) brought to light, however, the scope of procedural justice judgments as a psychological phenomenon is not limited to legal issues; the concept can be extended to procedures in non-legal settings as well. This position, which has since been echoed even more strongly in the work of Lind and Tyler (1988), provided an invaluable bridge between procedural justice concerns and a breadth of social settings. In essence, it untied procedural justice theory from its bondage to the legal domain, thereby clearing the way for more diverse applications of procedural justice theory.

Stimulated by Thibaut and Walker's initial research and Leventhal's provocative assertion, procedural justice researchers seized upon the vast terrain now open to them and accordingly embarked on an increasing amount of studies on procedural justice in non-legal settings. Consistently these works have found that concerns of procedural justice extend to arenas as diverse as educational (e.g., Tyler and Caine 1981), interpersonal (e.g., Barrett-Howard and Tyler 1986), and political (e.g. Tyler and Caine 1981; Tyler, Rasinski and McGraw 1985) settings.

Most recently, questions of how employees react to organizational procedures in business settings have begun to attract the attention of procedural justice researchers (Greenberg 1987a). For example, both Greenberg (1987b) and Folger and Konovsky (1989) applied the concept of procedural justice to the procedures used in performance evaluations for promotions and pay raise decisions. In another study, Tyler (1989) traced the impact of procedural justice judgments on the reactions of 302 workers to corporate resource allocation and conflict resolution decision processes. And in the study of Sheppard and Lewecki (1987), executives' perceptions of procedural fairness were assessed in seven distinct 'role domains' of managerial activity, ranging from business planning to coordination activities. In addition, issues of procedural justice have been extended to labor dispute resolution procedures (Sheppard 1984), grievance processes (Fryxell and Gordon 1989), personnel procedures (e.g., Folger and Greenberg 1985; Alexander and Ruderman 1987) and lay-off processes (Brockner *et al.* 1987) in business settings.

Without exception, these studies have provided support for Leventhal's assertion concerning the generality of procedural justice concerns; people, be they executives, middle-level managers or lower-level employees, were consistently found to care a great deal about the justice of the procedures by which organizational decisions were reached. Further-more, these works have widely suggested that procedural justice is an even more permeating concern than Leventhal himself had thought. Beyond affecting the attitude of outcome satisfaction well established in legal settings, procedural justice judgements have been shown to have positive and unambiguous effects on the higher-order attitudes of commitment (e.g., Alexander and Ruderman 1987; Brockner *et al.* 1987; Tyler 1989), trust (e.g., Greenberg 1987b; Folger and Konovsky 1989; Tyler 1989), and social harmony (e.g., Alexander and Ruderman 1987; Tyler and Griffin 1989) in organizational members subject to decision processes.

Lind and Tyler (1988), expanding upon the work of Thibaut and Walker, offer interesting insight into why it is that increases in procedur-al justice result in favorable changes in important attitudes and behaviors of organizational members. Lind and Tyler assert that in forming important attitudes towards organizations, individuals implicitly adopt a long-term perspective of informed self-interest. A long-term perspective is taken because individuals recognize that social association, here the act of working together in an organization, requires that other people's outcomes and objectives sometimes be given priority and that their own desires sometimes be postponed or abandoned for all individuals to continue to engage in the social interaction. But what then leads individuals to believe that, over the long term, their interests will be reasonably served by a given organization? Lind and Tyler assert that the perceived procedural justice of an organization's decision-making prac-tices plays a powerful role in influencing this belief. If the procedures by which decisions are reached are perceived as fair, organizational mem-bers tend to develop a feeling of reassurance that their interests will be protected and advanced through the decision-making process. This leads individuals to believe that over the long term they will receive reasonable outcomes, even in the absence of short-term gains or repeated sacrifices over an intermediate time frame. Consequently the conviction that an organization's decision-making practices are procedurally just tends to foster loyalty to an organization, more harmonious relations, and generally positive attitudes toward the organization as a whole and the authorities involved.

PROCEDURAL JUSTICE AND GLOBAL STRATEGY EXECUTION

Applying the preceding arguments of procedural justice research to the global strategy issue of the MNC, it is our contention that if the process by which global strategies are generated is viewed by subsidiary top management to be procedurally just, this judgment of procedural justice *per se* may provide a potentially powerful, yet previously unexplored, avenue for implementing global strategies. This is traceable, in no small part, to the higher-order attitudes associated with procedural justice judgments. Although we have made this point glancingly in the introduction, it is worthwhile pursuing in greater depth why it is that the salutary attitudes linked with procedural justice (namely, commitment, trust and social harmony) have come to play an increasingly important role in the execution of global strategies.

As articulated by Ghoshal (1987), the literature on global strategy has produced a rich body of global strategic prescriptions for the MNC. Whereas the particular strategic moves advocated in the literature may be diverse, ranging from comparative advantage-based competitive advantage (e.g., Kogut 1985a, 1985b; Porter 1986) to cross-subsidization (e.g., Hamel and Prahalad 1985; Kim and Mauborgne 1988) to worldwide standardization (e.g., T. Levitt 1983; Yip 1989), it is our observation that a fundamental thread runs through and unites each of these prescriptions. The fundamental thread that we speak of refers to the underlying conditions necessary for the effective execution of each of the designed global strategies. Specifically, three fundamental requirements can be consistently discerned: (1) effective and efficient exchange relations among the nodes of the multinational's global network; (2) swift actions in a globally coordinated manner; (3) the increasing sacrifice of subsystem for system priorities and considerations.

This suggests that an essential task for the effective execution of the prescribed global strategies is to foster a sense of community in the organizations' global network of subsidiaries. If subsidiaries do not feel part of this community and therefore attempt to undermine the organization in the pursuit of their individual gain, the prescribed global strategies cannot work effectively. Hence, to the extent that the arguments of procedural justice research are applicable to our global strategy-making context, it follows logically that the exercise of procedural justice in the global strategy-generation process can act as a powerful catalyst for the effective execution of the intended global strategies. With this procedural justice, the higher-order attitudes of commitment, trust and social harmony – key features of the community – would be generated in subsidiary top management, the key catalysts for the effective implementation of global strategies.

Beyond this, what makes the issue of procedural justice particularly important in the case of the multinational is that the distinctive powers of hierarchy used to mobilize internal organizations and affect subsidiary compliance – namely, recourse to fiat and refined monitoring and appraisal capability (Williamson 1975) – have declined within the multinational. Recent research (e.g., Hedlund 1986, Chapter 9 in this volume; Ghoshal and Bartlett 1989; Kim and Mauborgne 1989) attributes this decline to subsidiary units' increasing accumulation of rich resources and competencies, the growing size, complexity and intersubsidiary linkages characteristic of most multinationals, and the non-trivial cultural and spatial distances separating head offices from overseas units.

The upshot of this is that the distinctive powers of internal organization, which used to prompt smooth and cooperative exchange relations, have become largely invalidated in the modern multinational. Instead, the emergence of a monitoring problem and mounting loss of control increasingly plague the MNC, making its transaction atmosphere less and less distinguishable from that of mere market-mediated exchanges. Under such circumstances, subsidiary units have a non-trivial degree of managerial discretion not only to engage in extensive self-dealings but also to bargain aggressively to maximize fully their own independent utility functions. According to Williamson (1975), in the absence of a sense of community or organic solidarity, the above conditions presage the emergence of increasingly calculative, utilitarian and frictional exchange relations among the subsidiary units of the MNC; or, put differently, exchange relations that are essentially perpendicular to the demands of global strategy. Hence we argue that if the higher-order attitudes of commitment, trust and social harmony are indeed affected by procedural justice in global strategy-making, procedural justice should be treated as a key strategic dimension for making a multinational an effective global competitor.

Although the issue of procedural justice has never been the subject of systematic inquiry in the global management literature, its importance is not without mention; the most notable is the work of Prahalad and Doz (1987), which identifies 'due process' in global strategic decision-making as a key dimension for building the ideal global organization in the future.

FAIR PROCESS EFFECT AND GLOBAL STRATEGY EXECUTION

Aside from procedural justice concerns, justice-based research has also suggested that decision outcomes themselves, which in our context would be the content of the resulting global strategies, are not without salutary effects on the attitudes of organizational members. Specifically, when the outcomes received by organizational members are viewed as favorable in that they exceed members' expectations or are judged to be fair and equitable compared with one's performance (e.g., Adams 1965; Walster, Berscheid and Walster 1973), decision outcomes have been found to influence organizational members' satisfaction with, and hence acceptance of, decision outcomes.

Although the direct impact of decision outcomes, as indexed by either outcome fairness or outcome favorability, has been generally shown to overshadow that of procedural justice on the lower-order attitude of outcome satisfaction (e.g., Tyler, Rasinski and McGraw 1985; Alexander and Ruderman 1987; Folger and Konovsky 1989;), researchers (e.g., Thibaut and Walker 1975; L. Walker, Lind and Thibaut 1979; Greenberg and Folger 1983) have increasingly demonstrated that organizational members' assessments of these outcome issues are strongly affected by perceptions of the procedural justice of the decision process. This is termed the 'fair process effect' (Folger *et al.* 1979). Specifically, the fair process effect can be defined as the tendency for perceptions of procedural justice to enhance perceptions of outcome fairness and favorability and hence to contribute both directly and indirectly to the outcome satisfaction of organizational members. Relatively strong evidence exists to support the pervasiveness of this effect. To illustrate, not only did Folger (1977) find, in a laboratory-type setting, that subjects who viewed a decision process as just perceived the same outcomes as fairer than those who viewed their decision process as less just, but the fair process effect has even been shown to inflate significantly subjects' satisfaction with, and acceptance of, outcomes viewed to be negative and unfair; that is, inequitable (e.g., Thibaut and Walker 1975; La Tour 1978).

The potential presence of this fair process effect in the global strategy setting highlights still further the profound role procedural justice can play in the execution of global strategies. This is because the best overall global strategy for the MNC often requires that subsidiary units sacrifice subsystem gains for system gains and can result in the distribution of asymmetric outcomes across subsidiary units with similar performance. Rephrased, the very underlying requirements of global strategy increasingly point to the violation of norms of outcome fairness and often result in the distribution of perceived unfavorable outcomes.

As subsidiary top managers who view strategic decision outcomes as inequitable or unfavorable may well be inclined to exercise managerial discretion to engage in foot-dragging, subversion or even the undermining of global strategic prescriptions, it is important to check the discontent that stems from these outcome distributions. Hence, if the exercise of procedural justice can indeed inflate subsidiary top managers' perception of the fairness and favorability of strategy outcomes, it can contribute non-trivially to subsidiary top managers' satisfaction with and acceptance of final strategic decision outcomes. More complete compliance with the resulting global strategies is then commonly to be expected.

Before we report the results of our field study, which examined the importance of procedural justice relative to that of decision outcomes – in our context the content of the resulting global strategies – on the higher-order attitudes of commitment, trust and social harmony as well as on the lower-order attitude of outcome satisfaction among key members of global units, we first explore the meaning of procedural justice in the global strategic decision-making context.

THE MEANING OF PROCEDURAL JUSTICE IN THE GLOBAL STRATEGY MAKING CONTEXT

What is it that leads subsidiary top management to judge a decision-making process to be procedurally just? While up until this point we have been arguing that the stream of procedural justice research may well be of some importance in global strategic management, we have not confronted the more basic concern of defining the meaning of procedural justice in the global strategy-making context. Despite the recent surge of literature on procedural justice, a review of the literature suggests that as yet no commonly agreed set of criteria has emerged to represent the domain of procedural justice. Rather, some variations have been found to exist in the use of procedural justice criteria across the diverse settings in which procedural just has been examined. In the light of this and the fact that the procedural justice notion had never been studied in our setting, we decided to follow in the footsteps of Greenberg (1986) and Sheppard and Lewicki (1987) and use an open-ended questionnaire to identify the components of procedural justice in the global strategic decision-making context. We felt that by so doing we would enhance our ability to identify effectively only those criteria relevant to procedural justice in our context.

Towards this end we distributed an open-ended questionnaire to 63 subsidiary presidents, which asked them to reflect back on their last annual strategic planning/strategy-making process between the head office and their national unit and to write down either the one most important factor that made that process seem particularly fair or the one most salient factor that made that process seem unfair. Using the unstructured Q-sort technique, we then sorted the 63 statements provided by the subsidiary presidents into homogeneous groupings. This was done to eliminate the duplicity, similarities and idiosyncrasies of statements.

Following the Q-sort procedure detailed in Kim and Mauborgne (1991), we reduced our 63 original statements to 16 statements, which collapsed into five distinct procedural justice components. These are: the extent to which bilateral communication exists between managers of head offices and subsidary units involved in global strategic decision-making; the extent to which head offices do not discriminate but apply consistent decision-making procedures across subsidary units; the extent to which subsidary units can challenge and refute the strategic views of head office managers; the extent to which subsidary units are provided with a full account for the final strategic decisions of the head office; and the degree to which head office managers involved in strategic decision-making are well informed and familiar with the local situations of subsidary units.

Having defined the meaning of procedural justice in the global strategy-making context, we explored with subsidary presidents what it is that makes each of these items valued highly by subsidary top management. Bilateral communication between head office and subsidary top management is valued because it makes subsidary executives feel that their point of view was expressed and considered in reaching strategic decisions. Consistent decision-making procedures across subsidary units are prized because they are thought to minimize behavior that participants define as shaped by politics and head office favoritism in the global strategy generation process. With respect to the ability of subsidary executives to challenge and refute head office strategic views, subsidary top management view this as central to bringing to light possible misperceptions or wrong assumptions made by head office management concerning national conditions or subsidary operations. Subsidary top management judge the provision of an account for final strategic decisions as critical because it provides subsidary executives with an intellectual understanding of the rationale behind ultimate strategic decisions; especially valued here is a sound explanation for why subsidary views may have been overriden. Finally, subsidary top management see the familiarity of head office management with the local situation of national units as important because it is seen to provide a basic proof of head office management's sincerity to set global strategies with maximum knowledge of the ramifications such actions are likely to incur at the subsidary level. Taken together, these five criteria lead subsidary top management to judge the global strategy generation process to be procedurally just.

It is interesting to observe that, in total, four of the preceding procedural justice components find strong support in the existing literature. The components of bilateral communication (e.g., Thibaut and Walker 1975; Leventhal 1980; Greenberg 1986; Folger and Konovsky 1989), consistent application of procedures (e.g., Leventhal 1980; Sheppard and Lewicki 1987; Tyler 1988), ability to refute decisions (e.g., Leventhal 1980; Alexander and Ruderman 1987; Sheppard and Lewicki 1987), and familiarity with the situation of individual units (e.g. Greenberg 1986; Folger and Konovsky 1989) are conceptually similar to procedural justice indicators found to influence procedural justice judgments across a fairly wide variety of settings. At the same time, the identification of provision of an account as an important determinant of procedural justice judgments, although not without some support in the existing literature (e.g., Bies and Shapiro 1987), has been sparsely used in current works on procedural justice. Moreover, whereas ethicality – the 'politeness' or 'morality' of interpersonal treatment exercised in decision-making – has been widely recognized in the literature to influence subjects' perceptions of procedural justice, subsidiary top managers did not recognize this as an important determinant of procedural justice in global strategic decision-making. One can conjecture, however, that although subsidiary top managers do not say politeness matters, should head office top management repeatedly violate norms of acceptable conduct and act abruptly in a rude manner, subsidiary executives might well identify ethicality as an important determinant of procedural justice. Overall, the open-ended questionnaire we employed seems to have allowed us to identify effectively the specific criteria used by subsidiary top managers to define what they perceive to be a fair procedure in global strategic decision-making.

Using these identified procedural justice criteria, our field study set out (1) to examine the direct effect of procedural justice *vis-à-vis* that of decision outcomes on the higher-order attitudes of commitment, trust and social harmony as well as on the lower-order attitude of outcome satisfaction in subsidiary top management; and (2) to test the theory of fair process effect: that is, the indirect effect of procedural justice through the mediator of decision outcomes on outcome satisfaction. The next section briefly outlines our field study and findings. We do not, however, elaborate the operational aspects of data, measurement and methodology to maintain the speed of our discussion; a detailed discussion on these operational issues can be found in Kim and Mauborgne (1991).

A SYNOPSIS OF OUR FIELD STUDY AND FINDINGS

The subjects of our field study were 142 subsidiary top managers from 19 multinationals. We studied subsidiary top managers' perceptions on decision outcome fairness and favorability as well as on the procedural justice of global strategic decision-making. We also studied subsidiary top managers' organizational commitment, trust in their head office management, social harmony between them and their head office management and their decision outcome satisfaction. Decision outcome here was defined as the strategic roles, responsibilities and resources allocated to their unit as a result of the annual strategic planning/strategy making process between the head office and their national unit.

Here, our analysis involved three steps. First, a regression analysis was used to see the effects of procedural justice and decision outcome fairness and favorability on the higher-order attitudes of commitment, trust and social harmony and on the lower-order attitude of outcome satisfaction. Second, usefulness analysis was employed to distinguish the unique contribution of the two constructs of our central interest – procedural justice and decision outcomes (fairness and favorability) – to the higher-order attitudes and outcome satisfaction. Finally, path analysis was undertaken to test for the direct and indirect effects of procedural justice and decision outcomes on the higher-order attitudes and outcome satisfaction; of particular interest to us here was testing the presence or absence of the fair process effect.

In conducting the above analyses, we introduced negative affectivity as a control variable so as not to pollute the pure relationships between the independent and dependent attitudinal variables of this study; negative affectivity, an individual's propensity to respond negatively irrespective of the situation, has been found to operate as a methodological nuisance in research designed to assess individuals' attitudes. As stated, a detailed discussion on the measurement of the variables used in the study can be found in Kim and Mauborgne (1991). The following is a brief summary of our findings.

Regression Analysis

Bilateral communication between head office and subsidiary managers, an element of procedural justice in global strategic decision-making, affected both the organizational commitment of subsidiary members ($p < 0.01$) and social harmony between managers of head offices and subsidiary units ($p < 0.05$). The head offices' provision of account for final decision outcomes significantly influenced both the organizational commitment of subsidiary members ($p < 0.05$) and outcome satisfaction ($p < 0.05$), while the subsidiary managers' ability to refute the strategic views of head office managers significantly affected trust in head office management ($p < 0.01$). The head offices' consistent application of decision-making procedures across subsidiary units significantly affected trust and social harmony between managers of head offices and subsidiary units ($p < 0.05$). In addition, trust in head office management was also influenced ($p < 0.05$) by head office managers' familiarity with the local situations of subsidiary units. On the other hand, the perceived fairness of decision outcomes significantly influenced both outcome satisfaction ($p < 0.01$) and trust in head office management ($p < 0.05$), but with outcome satisfaction being affected to a greater extent.

Usefulness Analysis

First, although the procedural justice concerns uniquely influenced all of the higher-order attitudes at the 1 percent acceptance level, the strategic decision outcome concerns influenced only one dimension of the higher-order attitudes, trust, at the 10 percent acceptance level. More specifically, although the strategic decision outcome concerns accounted for only 9.2 percent of the variance in trust, the procedural justice concerns accounted for not only 22.4 percent of the variance in trust but also 18.5 percent of the variance in organizational commitment and 14.9 percent of the variance in social harmony. Second, although the procedural justice concerns showed some incremental explanatory power for subsidiary managers' outcome satisfaction, accounting for 8.6 percent ($p < 0.10$) of the variance, the strategic decision outcome concerns explained about 10.1 percent more variance, accounting for 18.7 percent ($p < 0.01$) of the variance.

Path Analysis

A central limit of the preceding analyses is that they index only the direct effects of the independent variables; indirect effects are removed from the equation through statistical controls. Path analysis showed that subsidiary managers' perceived fairness of global strategic decision-making indeed had significant indirect effects on outcome satisfaction through the mediator of strategic decision outcomes, providing evidence for the presence of the fair process effect. Interestingly, there was also evidence of an indirect causal path from procedural justice to trust in head office management through strategic decision outcomes.

Overall, the results support our central hypothesis that if subsidiary top management perceives the global strategy generation process between the head office and their national unit to be procedurally just, the higher-order attitudes of commitment, trust and social harmony as well as the lower-order attitude of outcome satisfaction result. The results also showed that although the direct impact of strategic decision outcomes on outcome satisfaction overshadowed that of procedural justice, perceptions of procedural justice inflated perceptions of strategic decision outcomes and hence contributed indirectly to the outcome satisfaction of organizational members. Figure 10.1, the results of our structural equation model, visually presents the overall findings of our field study. The standardized path coefficients or beta weights shown in Figure 10.1 indicate the relative strength of the link represented by the arrow.

DISCUSSION AND CONCLUSIONS

The results of our initial field study, which set out to test the proposition that the procedural justice of the global strategy generation process can act as a powerful catalyst to the effective implementation of global strategies, confirmed our expectation, yielding positive and unambiguous evidence of the significance subsidiary top management attach to questions of procedural justice in global strategic decision-making. Procedural justice judgments were found to demonstrate positive and significant effects on the higher-order attitudes of organizational commitment, trust in head office management, and social harmony between head office and subsidiary top managers.

To the extent that multinationals can carry out global strategies only insofar as they are supported by subsidiary top management, the importance of these higher-order forces and hence of procedural justice in the global strategy generation process is made evident: organizational commitment is essential in order to inspire subsidiary top management to identify with the global objectives of the enterprise and to pursue them to the best of their ability; trust in head office management heightens the propensity of subsidiary top management to sacrifice subsystem for system and short-term for long-term priorities and considerations; social harmony serves to strengthen the social fabric and inspire ongoing exchange relations of the effective and efficient kind between head office and subsidiary top managers. That the distinctive powers of hierarchy traditionally used to mobilize internal organizations and affect subsidiary compliance (namely, recourse to fiat and refined monitoring and appraisal capability) have dissipated within the multinational (e.g., Hedlund 1986, Chapter 9 in this volume; Ghoshal and Bartlett 1989; Kim and Mauborgne 1989) heightens still further the importance of procedural justice in the global strategy-making process.

Our field study also found that procedural justice made a direct contribution to the lower-order attitude of outcome satisfaction. In other words, subsidiary top management experienced outcome satisfaction when they perceived the process through which global strategies were determined to be procedurally just. As predicted, however, the direct impact of strategic decision outcomes, as indexed by outcome

251

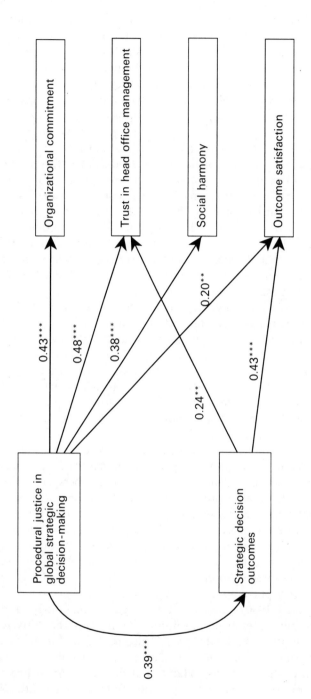

* The numbers next to the arrows are standardized path coefficients.
** p < 0.05
*** p < 0.01

Figure 10.1 Relationships among procedural justice, strategic decision outcomes, higher-order attitudes and outcome satisfaction*

fairness and outcome favourability, overshadowed that of procedural justice on the outcome satisfaction of subsidiary top management.

Perhaps more important, however, is our establishment that procedural justice in the global strategy-making process indeed produces a fair process effect. The presence of a strong fair process effect means that perceptions of procedural justice significantly inflate perceptions of decision outcome fairness and favourability, and they in turn contribute to the outcome satisfaction of subsidiary top management. What makes the presence of a fair process effect particularly significant is that not only is it impractical for multinationals to provide absolutely favourable decision outcomes to each of their numerous subsidiary units – in fact, the dynamics of global competition increasingly require subsidiaries to make sacrifices at the subsystem level – but that the best overall strategic choice at the global level may often lead to asymmetric decision outcome results across subsidiary units with similar performance and hence violate norms of outcome fairness. In other words, although outcome fairness and favourability can significantly contribute to the outcome satisfaction of subsidiary top management, the ability of multinationals to provide strategic decision outcomes that meet either of these two criteria has become increasingly limited by the intensity of global competition and the underlying requirements of global strategy. Hence perceptions of procedural justice become increasingly central to subsidiary top managements' perception of the fairness and favorability of decision outcomes, and consequently to their satisfaction with, and acceptance of, final strategic decision outcomes. More complete compliance with the resulting global strategies is commonly to be expected when procedural justice dominates.

All this having been said concerning the effects of procedural justice, it is worthwhile discussing briefly in what type of companies and situations procedural justice should matter most. From a company perspective we can conclude that procedural justice is likely to be of most importance in all those multinationals facing globalized competition and actively exercising global strategies wherein the need for extensive intersubsidiary exchanges and cooperations, for swift actions in a globally coordinated manner, and for the sacrifice of subsystem for system priorities and considerations ranks supreme. Specific examples of this might include: (1) multinationals actively pursuing a strategy of core competence building (Prahalad and Hamel 1990) wherein the knowledge, technology, and production skills cultivated in each subsidiary unit must be actively shared and continuously consolidated worldwide, and (2) multinationals aggressively exercising cross-subsidization across global units to out-manoeuvre global competitors (e.g., Hamel and Prahalad 1985). From a situational perspective, the exercise of procedural justice is likely to be of greatest value in multinationals' most powerful and resource-rich subsidiary units as well as in those subsidiary units that play a central but 'unfavorable' role in multinationals' global strategies (e.g., a subsidiary unit asked to drop prices and sacrifice its own revenue to parry a global competitor's move in another subsidiary's market). Rephrased, procedural justice is likely to yield the greatest gains in those subsidiary units where commitment, trust and social harmony are virtually indispensable to social order and the effective execution of global strategies.

In establishing the relevance of procedural justice to global strategy execution, we also explored the more basic concern of what leads subsidiary top management to judge a global strategic decision-making process to be procedurally just. In total, five procedural justice items were identified: the extent to which bilateral communication exists between managers of head offices and subsidiary units in global strategic decision-making; the extent to which head offices do not discriminate but apply consistent decision-making procedures across subsidiary units; the extent to which subsidiary units can challenge and refute the strategic views of head office managers; the extent to which subsidiary units are provided with a full account of the final strategic decisions of their head office; and the degree to which head office managers involved in strategic decision-making are well informed and familiar with the local situations of subsidiary units.

Beyond laying the foundation for the design of global strategic decision-making processes viewed as procedurally just, a few of the procedural justice factors identified are noteworthy in other respects. For example, of our five procedural justice factors, one, consistency, is slightly reminiscent of Bartlett and Ghoshal's (1986) 'United Nations' model of management. This suggests that a marginal trade-off relationship may exist between pursuing the recently advocated management model of internal differentiation and fully maximizing judgments of procedural justice. It is also interesting to observe that an overlap exists between some of the components of procedural justice and the factors that have been increasingly recognized as building an effective global organization in the existing literature. For instance, subsidiary top management's identification of bilateral communication as an important determinant of procedural justice is similar to Prahalad and Doz's (1987) notion of pluralism, which they view as critical to global learning and the effective balancing of a flexible country-specific perspective with a global cost-competitive one. Likewise, variants of one procedural justice component, ability to challenge and refute the strategic decisions of head office management, have recently been recognized as central to strategic renewal and the continuous coalignment of global strategies with the dynamic global environment (e.g., Bartlett 1986; Prahalad and Doz 1987).

Notwithstanding its merits in global strategic decision-making, procedural justice is not without its limitations. A potential cost of the procedural justice approach is that fair procedures may introduce inefficiencies in the decision-making process. For instance, the sounding of the head office's and subsidiary's multiple and perhaps contradicting perspectives can engender active and drawn-out debates to reconcile and incorporate the diverse perspectives into mutually agreeable strategies. Hence the attainment of procedural justice and the positive psychological consequences that result is not without its costs: attached to it is the price tag of a potentially slower decision-making process.

Several important questions and issues for future research arise from our study. The first concerns the cultural boundedness of procedural justice. Specifically, to what extent are the components of procedural justice identified here culturally loaded? Is there any significant difference in the meaning of procedural justice across different cultures? To what extent is the effect of procedural justice universal across cultural borders? To address these questions in a meaningful and conclusive manner, a study should have the requisite number of subjects with different cultural backgrounds such as French, German, British and Japanese cultural orientations.

The second issue concerns the possibility of different motivational consequences at different hierarchical levels in a given subsidiary. Although the subjects of our field study were limited to subsidiary top managers, subsidiary managers other than those in this top echelon can also be studied to understand the potentially different motivational consequences of procedural justice at different managerial levels.

A third avenue for future research concerns the procedural justice effect at different levels of aggregation: a single decision, the treatment of an entire company, the interactions between managers, and so on. Here the level of aggregation was limited to one discrete strategic planning/ strategy-making process, including both the formal and informal aspects, to lead respondents to reflect upon the same event in answering our questions. Hence, precisely speaking, the generality of our procedural justice findings beyond our global strategy-making context cannot be claimed. Thus direct comparisons of the effects of procedural justice across different levels of aggregation would be a fruitful task.

In examining perceptions of procedural justice, our field study limited its attention to the effect of decision process variables on procedural justice. It did not examine the effects of other intervening variables that may well affect managers' perception of procedural justice such as socialization in the company, length of career, education before and after joining the company, belonging to the same elite, and common external threats. A fourth potentially interesting avenue for future research might therefore be to assess how the perception of procedural justice is indeed affected by these and similar non-process variables.

A last extension of our field research, and one that we are currently pursuing, is to examine whether procedural justice in global strategic decision-making is capable only of producing salutary attitudes in subsidiary top management or whether the generation of these higher-order attitudes actually translates, in turn, into the salutary behavior of more forcefully implemented global strategies. One way to accomplish this task would be to include a measure of subsidiary top managements' compliance with final global strategic decisions as well as the attitudinal measures used in our field study. Such an examination would provide more conclusive proof of the practical worthiness of procedural justice for the effective implementation of global strategies.

Overall, this study suggests that for the mobilization of the MNC's global network of subsidiaries, researchers and management alike must become cognizant of the significant influence that the procedural justice of the global strategy-making process *per se* can have in shaping the attitudes and behavior of subsidiary top management. The image of subsidiary top management that has emerged in our field research is one of individuals highly concerned with the perceived fairness of the process through which global strategies are generated: that is, with the procedural justice of global strategic decision-making. However, research in the area of global strategic management has so far overlooked this potentially powerful dimension of procedural justice, focusing almost all of its efforts instead on questions of what winning strategic prescriptions for the multinational are. As a good global strategy means little if it is not supported by members of global units, the importance of procedural justice in global strategic management is made evident.

Looking into the future, we are strongly convinced that the application of the procedural justice concept to multinational management extends well beyond the limit context of global strategy-making. In fact, it is our contention that the effect of procedural justice may well be profound in a wealth of multinational strategic decision settings, such as the increasingly prevalent and important horizontal intersubsidiary exchange relations as well as the joint decision-making that occurs across globally dispersed functional and divisional activities. The title of the chapter reflects our growing conviction and optimism concerning the many fruits and rich managerial implications that can be borne through the further application of procedural justice theory to the multinational. It is our hope that this chapter will serve as a humble beginning for what we envisage as being a very long and fruitful road of studies on procedural justice in the multinational.

Part III

Organizational Culture and Norms

11 The Reproduction of Inertia in Multinational Corporations

Martin Kilduff

How do the members of a multinational organization organize them-selves each day to replicate the interconnections, the hierarchies, the problems and the routines with which they are familiar? It would be a mistake to assume that the taken-for-granted structures of everyday life such as interpersonal relationships, chains of command and exchange networks are re-formed effortlessly each day. In any large complex organization, such communicative structures only survive through constant use. Part of the use may be maintenance, as when friends telephone each other merely to 'touch base' rather than to exchange information. This skilled task of social reproduction is all the more difficult in the case of the MNC because it must be accomplished across national frontiers and cultural differences. In an MNC operating across many national borders with a variety of loosely coupled subsidiaries, a large amount of resources may have to be devoted simply to keeping routines and other structured behaviors reliable from day to day. Organizational inertia, from this perspective, is achieved only at great effort and cost (see, e.g., Hannan and Freeman 1984, p. 152).

This chapter will focus on the MNC as an especially interesting arena for research into (1) the formation of norms and routines, (2) the reproduction of such norms and routines across national and cultural groups, and (3) the consequences – especially those that are unintended – of this reproduction. As many writers have pointed out, the MNC is characterized by greater diversity and complexity than those organiza-tions operating within single national markets (see, e.g., Bartlett and Ghoshal 1989). Routines imprinted at the time of founding tend to persevere in all organizations (Stinchcombe 1965). However, persever-ance may be difficult to sustain in subsidiaries that are located in very different cultural milieus. Further, a set of behaviors that is taken for granted by the founder of the organization may be repeatedly challenged by newcomers from different cultural backgrounds. Coordination in any organization tends to be facilitated by common procedures and assump-tions. Such commonality may be more difficult to achieve and sustain in the MNC than in organizations operating within rather than across cultures.

In other words, inertia in the MNC does not occur by default, as a result of managerial complacency or as a natural consequence of growing organizational age and size. On the contrary, inertia is problematic: it is likely to be under continual challenge as subsidiaries open in new cultures and as the employee population becomes increasingly diverse. Paradoxically such challenges to taken-for-granted procedures may actually strengthen those procedures by leading to an explicit commitment by organizational members to adhere to what have hitherto been implicit norms (cf. Bettenhausen and Murnighan 1985). Relative to mononational organizations, the MNC may use more resources to ensure the reliable reproduction of routines. The MNC, then, faced with continual disruptions to its inertia, may be less tolerant of heterogeneous attitudes and behavior than organizations operating in more homogeneous environments. Anecdotal evidence suggests that some of the most successful MNCs, such as IBM, are the most rigorous in enforcing procedures and norms across cultural settings.

The MNC, then, is an especially interesting arena in which to study the production and reproduction of routines and the possible consequences of this reproduction for both individual and corporate actors. Although norm formation and perpetuation has been extensively studied in laboratory situations (e.g., Zucker 1977; Bettenhausen and Murnighan 1985), there has been little field work in organizational settings (but see Barley 1986 for an exception to this generalization). Recently structuration theory (Giddens 1984) has proposed that institutions reproduce themselves through the purposeful actions of knowledgeable agents. In a separate but compatible line of work, the enactment approach has described how individual routines produce complex organizational phenomena (Weick 1979; Abolafia and Kilduff 1988). The present study will approach the question of the reproduction of inertia in MNCs using both the structuration and enactment perspectives.

STRUCTURATION THEORY

Background

As formulated in the writings of Giddens (1976, 1984), structuration theory focuses on how knowledgeable actors draw upon rules and resources in their social interactions to reproduce complex social systems unintentionally. The theory draws upon the classic sociology of Marx, Weber and Durkheim as well as upon the contemporary literature on interaction routines (Goffman 1959) in trying to understand how people recreate the institutions of society.

For Marx, human beings 'make history, but not in circumstances of their own choosing' (quoted in Giddens 1984, p. xxi). Individual actors, pursuing their own ends, help sustain the very institutions of society within which they are constrained. It is this tension between voluntary, purposeful action, on the one hand, and institutional constraint, on the other, that structuration theory explores. From Durkheim, Giddens carries over the observation that an institution both pre-exists and outlasts the individuals who embody it at any particular moment. Institutionalized realities are social facts, according to Durkheim, that constrain individual action. Giddens adds an emphasis on the enabling properties of institutions. Social structures, such as language and bureaucracy, can imprison us in iron cages of outdated custom, as Weber has observed; but they can also enable us to communicate and to produce work efficiently.

To understand how human action is both constrained and enabled requires a focus on the routine, everyday behaviors of individuals. From Weber, Giddens adopts a strong emphasis on the meanings that actors place on the routines they enact, as well as a concern for the specific historical and geographical context within which action unfolds.

Analyses of meaningful situated action are best exemplified, according to Giddens, in the work of Erving Goffman. Goffman's writings carefully dismantle the apparently spontaneous flow of everyday activity into its routinized components. The organization, from Goffman's perspective, is composed of performance teams consisting of individuals who cooperate in staging routines (Goffman 1959, p.79). Goffman focuses attention on the dramaturgical aspects of routine interactions, the way teams stage displays to enhance their positions in competition with other teams. Successful performances require skilful use of sign equipment, such as clothes, furniture, cars, offices, and so on. Expert management of such sign equipment can help support the definition of the situation that team members are attempting to enact.

Team performances, no matter how well rehearsed, are fragile attempts to create social reality and are constantly subject to disruptions from unforeseen contingencies. Everyday routine performances are held to high standards of 'aptness, fitness, propriety, and decorum', by audience members (Goffman 1959, p. 55). Clearly, notions of aptness, fitness, propriety, and decorum vary dramatically across national boundaries, suggesting a rich field for the investigation of performance failures in MNCs between teams from different national subsidiaries. Indeed, much of the interest in dramaturgical analysis is on the myriad ways that impressions, those 'delicate, fragile' things (Goffman 1959, p.

56), can be both created and discredited and how team members cope with unexpected loss of face.

Structuration Theory and Routines as Programmed Responses

The emphasis on routines and norms as personal resources used by conscious individuals in pursuit of their own ends that is found in the work of Giddens and Goffman is startlingly different from the usual treatment evident in the organizational behavior literature. The importance of routines in organizations was first extensively developed by March and Simon (1958), building on and reacting to the emphasis on the routines of manual labour evident in the scientific management tradition (e.g., R.W. Taylor 1947; see Kilduff 1991 for an extended treatment of the influence of Taylor on March and Simon). March and Simon depicted the organization as a nested set of performance programs. At any particular level in the organization, decision makers faced with problems could invoke a repertoire of programmed responses from which they could choose the response that seemed most appropriate. From this perspective, organizational participants appear to be controlled by routines, as March and Simon (1958, p. 142) observed: 'Most behavior, and particularly most behavior in organizations, is governed by performance programs.'

This view of organizational behavior as largely determined by performance programs was elaborated in Cyert and March, where the organizational decision-making process was explicitly modeled as a computer program (1963, p. 126). Not until the development of the garbage can model (Cohen, March and Olsen 1972) did the Carnegie School researchers appear to recognize that individuals and coalitions could use routines to further their own interests whether or not the major problems facing the organization were being solved.

The most recent development of the programmed model of organizational decision-making is due to Nelson and Winter (1982). Echoing March and Simon (1958), Nelson and Winter (1982, p. 128) assert that 'the behavior of firms can be explained by the routines that they employ'. But several points of similarity between Giddens's conception and that of Nelson and Winter emerge. First, unlike the Carnegie School researchers, Nelson and Winter emphasize that organizational routines are opaque, rather than transparent. People may be purposively enacting routines without being able to articulate precisely what the routines consist of, much as people may be able to speak complex sentences without being able to explain the rules governing their production. Second, because knowledge of routines is largely tacit, the replication of routines across organizational boundaries is problematic (Nelson and Winter 1982, p.

118). Third, routines in organizations are not the mere instruments of management control emphasized by March and Simon (1958). Instead, as Giddens would agree, the set of routines in an organization represents a negotiated settlement of competing interests, a truce between potentially conflicting definitions of the situation.

Organizational inertia, then, is a function not merely of a market demand for reliability and accountability (cf. Hannan and Freeman 1984), or a consequence of imprinting at the time of founding (cf. Stinchcombe 1965), but may also be a consequence of the balance of internal tensions within the organization: 'Adaptations that appear "obvious" and "easy" to an external observer may be foreclosed because they involve a perceived threat to internal political equilibrium' (Nelson and Winter 1982, p. 111).

Despite some similarities between Giddens's theory and the Nelson and Winter model, the structuration approach remains unusual in suggesting how the structured world of rules, regulations, norms and customs is created and recreated through the routine, day-to-day interactions of purposeful individuals. The theory builds on the classic works of Marx, Weber and Durkheim, but offers an interpretation that differs sharply from the functional synthesis proposed by Parsons (1937). Structuration theory, unlike much of the modern organizational culture literature, does not accept the Parsonian notion that actors internalize the shared values upon which social cohesion is said to depend. Structuration theory offers a more paradoxical explanation of the replication of social institutions, as the following discussion will show.

STRUCTURATION THEORY AND THE MNC

Language is a favorite analogy used by Giddens to illustrate how interacting individuals reproduce institutions: a competent speaker of French unwittingly helps to reproduce the language itself as he or she engages in conversation. Further, the language that is reproduced is an institution that has preceded and will survive the speaker. The rules of language production are opaque, even though competent speakers tend to obey these rules unerringly. Competent speakers can always tell you what they are trying to say, and why they are saying it, even though they cannot always explain the rules that make speech possible.

A MNC is also an institution that is reproduced in the interactions of knowledgeable actors. The MNC, like a language, can precede and survive the particular individuals whose interactions serve at any given time to reproduce it. The actors can always provide rationales for why they are doing what they are doing. They have theories about the institution and their relationship with it. From a structuration perspective, the actions of top managers, as much as those of the lowest subordinates, express underlying rules that may be opaque in their operation. Further, the individually motivated actions of participants in an institution such as a multinational serve to reproduce patterns of social relations of which the participants themselves may not be aware.

The emphasis of the theory, then, is on the recursiveness of institutionalized reality, in contrast with the linear nature of each individual's life. Individual lives are linear in the sense that people age and die, whereas the institutions to which they belong may continue to be enacted by new generations of participants. The work of the MNC is continually recreated as employees engage in routinized exchanges that enact the familiar characteristics of the institution. The enacted routines, then, are the intended result of individual actions. Indeed, as part of the intentional reproduction of routine, actors reflexively monitor both their own activities and the activities of others. Each person is engaged in a skilled performance at work, in concert with others. Actors are alert to deviations from the expected performances and will intervene to repair slippage from expected enactments, as Goffman (1957) has shown.

From a structuration perspective, language is situated action in the sense that language use is embedded in local contexts of meaning. The reproduction of language is only possible through the activity of specific speech communities, within each of which speakers have mastered 'the circumstances in which particular types of sentences are appropriate' (Giddens 1987, p. 200). The reproduction of language is likely to vary across speech communities in accordance with local variations in contexts of meaning. Indeed, this phenomena is observable empirically in, for example, the differences in dialect and usage between communities located in neighboring counties in England.

The parallel between a language and an institution such as an MNC is not merely a fanciful metaphor. In a very real sense, an institution is expressed in its language use. March and Simon (1958, p. 166) may have been the first to have observed the reality-defining power of organizational vocabularies: 'The world tends to be perceived by the organization members in terms of the particular concepts that are reflected in the organization's vocabulary . . . The particular categories and schemes of classification it employs are reified and become, for members of the organization, attributes of the world rather than mere conventions.'

One of the most obvious facts about MNCs is that subunits in different countries tend to employ different languages. The implication of the present discussion is that the attempt to maintain adherence to the same concepts across language boundaries is likely to prove extremely difficult to the extent that such concepts are embedded in the language patterns of particular speech communities. Within the same multinational enterprise, managers from different cultural backgrounds maintain culturally based frames of reference and resist the homogenizing effects of organizational membership (Hofstede 1980a and b; Laurent 1983). When cultural differences are reinforced by language differences, fidelity to concepts and standards promulgated by corporate headquarters may be imperfect. Further, even if organizational members all accept the importance of a concept such as customer service, the interpretation of this concept is likely to vary widely. Discrepant interpretations of organizational norms can find support in the social networks through which norms are diffused (Krackhardt and Kilduff 1990).

Network members, drawing on shared normative frameworks, continually monitor interpersonal behavior. This monitoring can also be thought of as an individual difference variable (Snyder 1974, 1979). Some people are high self-monitors, in that they can skilfully adapt their behavior to the role demands of whatever setting they enter. Other people are low self-monitors, in that they prefer to enact roles that are relatively invariant across social settings. Low self-monitors are relatively insensitive to the social cueing of expected performance. In an MNC that is concerned with replicating similar institutional procedures across different cultures, such as a fast food chain, the low self-monitor who lacks sensitivity to local demands might be an appropriate candidate for transfer across cultures. For the MNC that seeks to shape its subsidiaries to the perceived demands of each culture, a high self-monitor would be the appropriate candidate for transfer.

From a structuration perspective, a role in an organization is best understood as a range of prerogatives and obligations that the incumbent can activate (Giddens 1984, p. 84). The actor has discretion with respect to the aspects of the role he or she wishes to express. There is always the possibility of a skilled performer reinterpreting the role demands in a creative way to the benefit or the detriment of other actors in the system. In an MNC, for example, a creative CEO can interpret the role demands to balance stakeholders' interests in terms of fundamentally realigning away from a core business, such as oil, and towards a potential high-growth business, such as electronics. This creativity in role interpretation disrupts the reproduction of inertia and can threaten the survival of the organization even as it opens new opportunities (Tushman and Romanelli 1986).

The knowledgeability of actors in a system such as an MNC is a fundamental tenet of structuration theory. Actors have a theoretical understanding of why they are doing what they are doing and can provide rationales or accounts if asked. The knowledge of actors includes a knowledge of the social conditions within which they act, such as the hierarchy of power relationships, for example. But actors also have a tacit, practical knowledge that is evident in their actions even though they are not able to articulate it. The distinction between the two types of knowledge is related to the familiar one between espoused theories and theories-in-use (Argyris and Schon 1978).

The espoused theories of organizational actors are expressed in accounts of action. From the structuration perspective, such accounts are themselves actions, designed to maintain social worlds (Garfinkel 1984; Heritage 1987). Accounts are social constructions in the sense that they retrospectively interpret events in the light of normative expectations. The presentation of accounts is, from this perspective, part of the reflexive monitoring that sustains ongoing social reality. An account can be a weapon in the effort to maintain an interpretive and normative base for future action.

Theories-in-use are expressed in actions that can have both intended and unintended consequences. A major focus of structuration theory is on the unintended consequences of action and the way these consequences feed back into the system to constrain subsequent actions. For example, the CEO of a diversified multinational may respond to calls for clarification concerning how the decentralized decision-making system works by issuing detailed guidelines to subsidiaries and monitoring their implementation. But this clarification and this monitoring work to tighten HQ control over decision-making rather than loosen it. Thus, by clarifying the decentralized control policy, the CEO unintentionally undermines the policy.

It is important to emphasize that, from a structuration viewpoint, the unintended consequences of action do not have the latent function of system maintenance and integration suggested by functional theories. Whereas functional theories (e.g., Merton 1936) show how seemingly irrational acts are not so irrational after all if they are considered in terms of the whole system, structuration theory focuses on what economists have called 'perverse outcomes'. For example, suppose an MNC wants to reduce labor costs and decides to shift production from the USA to a developing country. Other MNCs are doing the same thing, however, with the result that the wages in the developing country begin a rapid escalation, whereas labor costs in the USA begin to decline in real terms because of oversupply. By relocating to the developing country, therefore, the MNC helps to cause the very phenomenon – wage inflation – that it was trying to avoid.

Another hypothetical example: suppose a French MNC tries to penetrate the Japanese market by hiring local managers for the Tokyo office who can speak the language and who know the culture. The company is unable to attract the best connected and most qualified applicants, however, because they prefer to work for the top Japanese companies. The MNC selects from an applicant pool significantly weaker than that of its rivals. The managers it hires are not as good as those of its major competitors. The result, therefore, is a deterioration in competitive position caused by the policy that was meant to prevent such a deterioration.

These perverse outcomes are triggered by the actions of knowledgeable actors but are unintended. Often such perverse outcomes are remote in time and space from the triggering actions. Furthermore, the unintended consequences are often part of a vicious circle that constrains subsequent actions. For example, as the competitive position of the Japanese division suffers because of inferior management, the applicant pool itself becomes less impressive since good applicants are not attracted to poorly performing companies.

Knowledgeable actors in the process of reproducing the structures of the corporation use resources, both material and authoritative. Material resources, such as money and machinery, are familiar enough to students of organizations. Authoritative resources are potentially much more illuminating as a focus of study in MNCs. Authoritative resources consist of the capability to harness the activities of human beings and result from the 'dominion of some actors over others' (Giddens 1984, p. 373). The MNC, its authority breaching the boundaries of nation states, invents for itself a governance structure that seeks to balance local demands and global vision, to paraphrase one of the recent books on the subject (Prahalad and Doz 1987). The ways in which this balancing act is maintained are fundamental to understanding the functioning of MNCs. Do subsidiaries of MNCs replicate the normative environment of their parent company, or do they adapt to the local environment in which they are geographically situated? Is there evidence of normative control from subsidiaries to headquarters?

The emphasis on the efforts of subordinates to control superiors is not accidental. In the structuration perspective, power is expressed in patterns of domination, and resources are the media through which power is exercised. Power in this formulation is not the sole prerogative of top management in the MNC. Subordinates also act to control superiors by managing resources in certain ways. For example, subsidiaries can control corporate headquarters by manipulating resource flows.

To understand resource flows and power relationships in any social system requires an analysis of two aspects of social structure: the patterns of social relations, on the one hand, and the underlying codes of meaning, on the other. The patterns of social relations can be conveniently thought of in terms of two kinds of social networks: (1)

the informal exchange relationships between interacting individuals, and (2) the relationships across space and time between, for example, structurally equivalent individuals or entities. In an exchange relationship, individuals influence each other through personal contact, whereas in a structurally equivalent relationship, competing individuals may influence each other through envy-driven emulation in the absence of any direct contact (Burt 1987). To take one example of how these concepts might apply to MNCs, suppose an MNC has acquired a diverse group of previously autonomous companies and grouped them into business streams for administrative convenience. Units within each stream are compelled to see each other as more or less equivalent *vis-à-vis* headquarters. A social relationship of competition may commence, despite headquarters' efforts to foster cooperation.

A second aspect of structure consists of the norms that frame social encounters. These generalizable procedures enable the enactment of everyday life and constitute what one might call the culture of the system. The structuration perspective focuses on the 'many seemingly trivial procedures followed in daily life' (Giddens 1984, p. 22) rather than on unusual rites and rituals. These procedures, it is argued, can have profound effects on social conduct.

The top management of some MNCs explicitly tries to manipulate the reproduction of the organization's culture. Indeed, a common recommendation of books aimed at top managers of MNCs is that they should intervene to change, mould or otherwise shape the culture of the organization. From a structuration perspective, however, the organization's culture is expressed in the interactions and interpretations of knowledgeable actors, not in company handbooks, seminars or CEOs' speeches.

The culture of the organization at any point in time can be understood as a set of social constructs negotiated among knowledgeable actors to anticipate and control the motivational and cognitive diversity in the organization (Krackhardt and Kilduff 1990; see also Wallace 1970, p. 36). Institutionalized traditions, set in place by the organization's founders, shape and are shaped by emergent beliefs and actions. The paradox is that freely interacting individuals tend to reproduce their version of the organization's culture, thus constraining the diversity of behaviors and cognition they allow themselves, often without any awareness of the constraints they enact. Management's attempts to disrupt radically taken-for-granted procedures in the name of 'culture change programs' are likely to meet with resistance and resentment from those whose routines are threatened (see, e.g., Siehl 1985). Organizational culture can only be an imperfect management control device because routinized procedures are transmuted and transmitted by social networks that operate outside the formal organizational socialization and reward system (Krackhardt and Kilduff 1990).

In the MNC, the potential for subcultures to flourish with the support of local networks is tremendous. Members of these subcultures may believe that they, and not management, are enacting the traditions set in place by the founders. Management intolerance or ignorance of the diversity of interpretations and behaviors can lead to unanticipated organizational conflict (see, e.g., Whyte 1951; Stoffle 1975). Given diverse cultural premises, the production of organization-wide routines may be difficult to achieve. The national origin of European managers, for example, significantly affects their view of what proper management should be (Laurent 1983). Latin managers, compared to managers from northern cultures, perceive authority, status and power as attached not to institutional elements, such as offices or functions, but to individuals (Laurent 1986). In fact Latin managers, compared to their Northern European counterparts, are significantly less likely to take norms and rules for granted in organizations (Kilduff and Anglemar 1989). The MNC is an arena in which implicit theories of organizing are bound to conflict. Such conflicts may undermine the taken-for-granted legitimacy of organizational routines.

The mention of the effects of books about MNCs on the actions of members of MNCs raises the final aspect of structuration theory that is important to the discussion: the double hermeneutic. This is the process by which the results of social science affect the knowledgeable agents who are its subject matter. In the case of MNCs the process is clearly evident. Books about MNCs containing distillations of research on MNCs are targeted precisely at the practitioners who served as subjects. It becomes unclear whether innovations in MNC development result from research-based suggestions or managerial practice. In any case, a rigid distinction between theory on the one hand, and subject matter by which theory can be tested on the other, seems hopeless. From this perspective, even such apparently irrelevant aspects of social science research as the literary prowess of the author can have significant effects on future attempts to replicate findings by increasing or decreasing the communication of implications to the subjects of study.

ENACTMENT AND STRUCTURATION

The structuration perspective suggests that routines are the key to understanding the functioning of any organization. These routines can be understood as programs or standard operating procedures (see, e.g., March and Simon 1958). But these programs may be only imperfectly reproduced. The possibility of random variation in the reproduction of routines is not explicitly addressed in Giddens' (1984) model, but it is part of the ecological model of action proposed by Weick (1979). Random variations can alter routines so that diffusion across large, loosely coupled organizations may be imperfect. Just as in the children's game in which a message is systematically garbled as it is whispered from ear to ear, so in the MNC a routine transferred from one department to another may be transformed by the time it reaches a division in another country.

From both the enactment and the structuration perspectives, iterated individual acts produce and reproduce structure. One aspect of the structure of the organization is the set of rules that underlies the repeated actions and interactions of individuals. The structuration perspective tends to take these repeated interactions for granted as a starting point from which to investigate the consequences of such interaction. But the enactment approach is much more interested in the evolution of such norms in arbitrary traditions (Weick and Gilfillan 1971), rational myths (Meyer and Rowan 1977), and national cultures (Kilduff and Anglemar 1989). From the enactment perspective, the same iterated behavior may occur for a variety of different reasons, and attention must be focused on the meanings attributed to behavior (Abolafia and Kilduff 1988). Apparent behavioral homogeneity can mask heterogeneous goals, assumptions and values (Weick 1979; Donnellon, Gray and Bougon 1986). The MNC, with its diverse mix of ethnic and national groups, offers an excellent arena in which to investigate the enactment, attribution and regulation of norm-based behavior.

The enactment perspective and the structuration perspective are similar in their emphasis on the micro-foundations of organizational structure in the purposeful behavior of individuals. Interacting individuals can create complex structures beyond the power of any one person to comprehend (Weick 1979). In Giddens' terms, a perverse outcome of individual action may be that it constrains one's future actions in ways that are neither anticipated nor welcomed. For example, Carlos is a graduate in biochemistry from the best university in Ecuador. To further his career, he obtains a job with a multinational pharmaceutical company that offers professional and career advancement far in excess of what domestic employers can offer. After two years of training overseas, however, he is sent back to Ecuador to negotiate with the Health Minister retail prices for a group of drugs urgently needed by the rural and urban poor in Ecuador. His corporate mission is to persuade the minister to agree to a high retail price for the drugs, and in this he is successful: his command of the language and culture, and his personal contacts inside the country combined with the professional training he has received, make him an ideal representative of the MNC to the host government. But what has he achieved? He has succeeded in furthering the interests of the MNC at the expense of the people in his own country. His victory is also his loss. After six troubled months, he resigns abruptly to pursue an academic career.

In enactment theory, actors are said to create the environment that then impinges on their subsequent actions (Weick 1979). By combining this insight with structuration theory's emphasis on the individual's involvement in the reproduction of routines, one understands how an actor such as Carlos can create the conditions by which the structure of the institution constrains his choices. Carlos pursues his own ends at the same time as he recreates the structures of the organization that both enable and constrain. He pursues his own career even as he negotiates a high price for the drugs. If he finds himself trapped, then he has, in a sense, trapped himself.

In Weick's model, retrospective sense-making can change the meaning of action and lead an employee like Carlos either to quit the company or to become transformed into an organizational man who sees the acquisition of high corporate profits from selling drugs to developing countries as completely ethical. There is also the possibility that individual or coalition action can force changes in rule-based behavior (Abolafia and Kilduff 1988). Carlos could succeed in changing the strategy of the MNC. Drugs could be donated to developing countries as a way of gaining international goodwill. The enactment perspective, relative to the structuration perspective, is more optimistic about the possibility of changing vicious circles through modifications in cognitive attributions and behavioral routines.

The transmission of routines in multinational organizations is problematic because such routines are embedded in the interactions of specific individuals in specific places. Structuration theory suggests that the institutional authority of the MNC itself is an outcome of the everyday routine behavior of organizational participants who may or may not have internalized the values and norms promulgated by the top management team. Indeed, a central paradox exposed by both the enactment and structuration approaches is that organizational participants can actively participate in the reproduction of institutional arrangements with which they may fundamentally disagree. Within the international management literature (see Walter and Murray 1988 for a summary), one dimension of this problem has been pursued: namely, the headquarters–subsidiary balance of power: the pulls of the subsidiary to enlarge its autonomy and the countervailing efforts of the headquarters to maintain or increase control. The structuration approach suggests that the rational actor arguments used to explain headquarters–subsidiary relations can be subsumed within a larger, ongoing set of dynamics that make maintenance of MNC patterns problematic.

SUGGESTIONS FOR A RESEARCH AGENDA

There are two focal points where research on norms and routines in MNCs can make a powerful contribution to the further development of the structuration and enactment paradigms and where the paradigms can guide research of critical importance in understanding the MNC as a complex organization. First, given the enormous power of MNCs to transform the earth and the lives of its people, a set of questions of broad popular (as well as scholarly) interest concerns the formation of norms and routines in MNCs. What are the norms and routines that govern behavior in these huge entities? From where do these norms and routines come? Is it possible to infer the rules that govern the routines? How are the norms and routines reproduced across national boundaries, and what kinds of distortions ensue? Different cultural groups within MNCs are likely to espouse quite different theories about management and organizing (Hofstede 1980; Laurent 1983, 1986). Do these different espoused theories reflect different routinized practices? If such behavioral differences exist, what are the consequences of these differences? What are the conditions leading to high fidelity of reproduction of routines? To what extent are routines that appear startlingly different merely simple transformations of an underlying structural pattern? The research focus must not be on what top management declares the organizational philosophy or culture to be but on the norms that are expressed by workers throughout the organization in both their behavioral routines and in their accounts of action.

There are many ways to study the diffusion of norms from the headquarters to new subsidiaries. Certainly an ethnographic treatment of the diffusion process would reveal much about the possible mutations that norms might undergo in new settings. A social network analysis of the diffusion process would help embed norm transmission in ongoing patterns of relationships and might reveal the extent to which the normative order and the social order overlap.

The second research focus is on the apparently spontaneous social interactions between organizational teams in MNCs. These social interactions can be deconstructed into their routine dramaturgical elements (the realm charted by Goffman, Giddens and Weick under the rubric of impression management, structuration and enactment). This is also the realm of management decision-making, organizational stratification, internal labor markets, leadership and culture.

Within the MNC, each subsidiary can be considered a performance team. The preliminary step in a research effort would be to examine the identities and relationships of these teams. What kinds of routine performances are teams enacting for each other? How are impressions being managed? Are there interesting variations in the use of sign equipment?

As a way of understanding the pervasiveness of scripted behavior, a study of breaches of expected actions is instructive. Such breaches can reveal organization-wide coalitions whose interests may be strikingly opposed, even though their espoused theories are similar (Kilduff and Abolafia 1989). What kinds of performance disruption can be observed, and what do these reveal about the staged nature of social reality? What kinds of slippage can be observed between back and front regions? What kinds of rewards are teams performing for?

Taking a more macro-perspective on the routinized performances being enacted by teams in MNCs might lead to the question, 'Of what results are teams unaware, in terms of consequences that are set in motion by their own enactments?' Research on unintended consequences looks at how unforeseen events are triggered. These unintended events can, in their turn, circumscribe future actions because the actors remain unaware of the process they are enacting.

For example, one could analyze how an ecological disaster attributed to an MNC, such as the explosion of a chemical plant in a developing country, was the unwanted result of a series of apparently trivial routine decisions (see, e.g., Perrow 1984). Disasters blamed on MNCs may be unintended consequences, remote in time and space, of routine decisions taken in cultural contexts very different from those in which the decisions are implemented. Similarly, one could examine how an institutionalized practice, such as the cultural domination of an MNC by one ethnic group, was sustained not only by the actions of the dominant group but also by the actions of the subordinate.

Alternatively, one could trace over time how a cumulated series of events (e.g., the serial acquisition of a diverse group of previously autonomous companies) is derived from a rather trivial and accidental occurrence. In such a case, the accounts that people give retrospectively (e.g., the attribution to a diversification strategy), can be profitably compared to the circumstances of the first acquisition.

Finally, and perhaps most ambitiously, the researcher can ask, 'How is team activity embedded in and constitutive of the larger systems of meaning that collectively identify the MNC?' These larger systems include the political, structural and cultural systems, as well as the technical systems of production. March and Simon's (1958) image of the organization as a nested set of routine performances can be used to define the ultimate aim of a study of MNC routines: to show how sets of purposeful behaviors interlock and interact to produce the complexity and diversity that distinguish this particular organizational form.

CONCLUSION

This brief review of structuration and enactment paradigms has two surprising implications for research on MNCs. First, the outpouring of books and articles offering advice to managers of MNCs can itself be a focus of a research effort aimed at understanding the knowledgeability of agents in MNCs. As a realm of discourse, the managerial literature constantly recreates the double hermeneutic between discourse and practice. The analysis of how this discourse affects the reproduction of institutionalized practices in MNCs would itself be a valuable exercise.

The second implication of this review is that MNCs can be interesting arenas for theoretically driven research. But there can be no sociological or psychological theory of the MNC itself. MNCs are interesting because of the diversity and complexity of their routinized reproductions. However, social reproduction itself, and the structures of everyday life that enable and constrain it, are features of every social system.

12 The Flow of Culture: Some Notes on Globalization and the Multinational Corporation*

John Van Maanen and André Laurent

As this collection of essays suggests, organizational theorists are just getting around to the serious study of the MNC. As of yet they have not had much time for culture, but when culture does enter into the emerging representation of the MNC, it does so often as an all-purpose variable used to account for many of the problems faced by MNCs. Such firms by definition do business in different countries under vastly different conditions throughout the world; they must therefore enter into relations with people – as customers, employees, suppliers – from distinct national (and other) cultures who may have quite different ideas as to what the organization and their roles in relation to it are all about. This multinational character creates varying degrees of cultural complexity, confusion and conflict when individuals and groups who do not share the same underlying codes of meaning and conduct come into contact with one another. These troubles may persist over time and even become amplified, thus leading to a good deal of distrust, disorder, hostility and the unravelling of corporate or local agendas. Organization theory applied to the MNC becomes then a search for those organizational forms that might obviate, mediate or otherwise soothe local interests in favour of corporate ones.

At the same time, organizational theorists are quick to point out the various incentives and advantages of operating on a transnational scale: markets to exploit, labor pools to tap, information sources to develop, and so on. Thus, in the very process of doing business internationally, a firm may also discover new ways of doing things and new things to do that make use of the varied cultural backgrounds of its members,

*   We have received a good deal of aid, comfort and criticism from the unlucky readers of an earlier draft of this chapter. We have tried to be reasonably responsive to this friendly fire. Comments from Tony DiBella, Gideon Kunda, Jane Salk, Ed Schein and Eleanor Westney have been particularly helpful.

suppliers and customers. Cultural diversity is a resource for the firm. Organization theory applied to the MNC then becomes a search for organizational forms that preserve and capitalize on local knowledge, skill and interest.

More than form is at issue, however. As many organizational theorists are only too happy to point out, an MNC also has a cultural character of its own (e.g., Ouchi and Wilkins 1985; Schein 1985; Bartlett 1986; Fine 1985). Here, the now hackneyed phrase 'corporate culture' enters the analysis of multinationals as a way of indicating a sort of culture-of-cultures. The phrase carries a kind of hope and glory that is appealing to some theorists, for it suggests that culture operates as a bonding device holding an organization together: the superglue that connects structural elements of a firm to its economic, political and social strategies and, ultimately, to the results it obtains from the marketplace (e.g., Deal and Kennedy 1982; Ott 1988; D. Davidson 1989).

Our view of culture is not quite so bold. We do not, for example, equate culture with homogeneity of thought and action across a diverse collection of people. Such a condition, were it to exist, might well indicate a lack of culture rather than a presence. Culture is a differentiating device as much as it is an integrating one. It is a means of marking differences and establishing boundaries, not obliterating them. Culture concerns systems of meaning, ideas and patterns of thought. It represents more a model *for* the behavior of members of a given group than a model *of* their behavior (Goffman 1974, p. 41).

All of this is to suggest that to consider seriously what culture is and what it is not takes us well beyond the usual leisure of the theory class in organization studies, where concepts are turned into variables and measurement proceeds apace. Culture is most distinctly not a variable in any conventional sense. If anything, it is more a sensitizing concept for organizational theorists, akin to the biologist's use of the term 'life' or the physicist's notion of the term 'force'. It is central to the study of organization(s) but remains elusive. Once captured by a definition, it seems always to escape. This is not, however, for lack of effort.

CULTURE AS PROCESS AND PRODUCT

The study of culture – organizational or otherwise – has a reasonably long history. It is also a contentious history with a vast proliferation of approaches, empirical studies, concepts, theories and legendary figures (heroes and villains). Although most scholars today would probably agree that culture comprises symbols through which alternative patterns of conduct are more or less encoded and, with some slack, produced, there is no orthodoxy to be found.[1] Virtually all the old definitions and theories surrounding culture are still commingling with the new. But if we follow the Wittgensteinian principle and look not for the lexical meaning but for the way the term culture is used in scholarly practice, two usages are apparent (Peterson 1990). One treats culture as a process, the other as a product.

Culture as a process is an approach that derives from anthropology and sociology. It regards culture for the most part as codes of conduct embedded in or constitutive of the social life of a given group whose boundaries may be distinct or (increasingly) ambiguous, fixed or dispersed. Researchers within this intellectual tradition speak of the culture of a nation, a tribe, a corporation, a gang, a profession, an ethnic enclave or a common pursuit followed by such nominal groups as surfers, tourists, evangelists or drug dealers. Such codes are found by enthnographic observation, attitude surveys, content analysis of key documents or studying patterns of cultural choice.[2]

Culture as a product is an approach that comes from the humanities, literary criticism in particular. It treats culture as something created; the result of individual or group activities that carry distinct symbolic properties with certain meanings attached for certain groups. Students of 'high' culture look to the products of artists, scientists, intellectuals, architects, and so forth. Students of 'low' culture look to the products of the media, advertising, fashion, fads, movies, television, and so on. Various interpretive approaches – historical studies, deconstruction, semiotics, hermenutics, etc. – are used to uncover how the studied signs operate, what they teach, and how they use or are used by those exposed to them (Van Maanen 1990b).[3]

To a large extent, these two approaches to culture rarely overlap. Those who study symbols do not ordinarily concern themselves with the social organization standing behind cultural productions, and those who examine production activities are relatively unconcerned with what such productions mean to those who consume or witness them.[4] This is a pity, since even a modest convergence of interest between the two would add considerable depth to the empirical work going on in either domain. In the organizational research community, for example, it would be of more than passing interest to have a study that examined the products put forth by some of the celebrated, supposedly exemplary, organizational cultures. More relevant to our purposes here, however, would be the study of the influence the products or services offered by an MNC have on the host culture(s) in which that MNC operates. From our perspective, culture needs to be treated as both process and product. This is not easy.

Part of the difficulty in bridging these approaches lies in the mystery surrounding the elusive mantra that is culture itself. Process or product, it is a loose concept that refers to the marking and classifying of the experienced world. It is as much a socially organized process as it is a collectively validated result. When located within a group, it provides members with images of their basic concerns, principles, ethics and bodies of manners, rituals, ideologies, strategies and tactics of self-survival, including certain notions of good deeds and bad, various forms of folklore and legends, and a set of ideas that allows something of a 'consciousness of kind' to emerge such that rough boundaries of demarcation can be drawn between (and among) members and non-members. Culture is socially-organized meaning and a product of interaction. When interaction is tied to space, so too is culture.

The carriers of culture are individuals, and it is axiomatic among cultural theorists that culture is learned. The way we give logic to the world begins at birth with the gestures, words, tone of voice, noises, colors, smells and body contact we experience; with the way we are raised, washed, rewarded, punished, held in check, toilet trained and fed; by the stories we are told, the games we play, the songs we sing or rhymes we recite; the schooling we receive, the jobs we hold, and the careers we follow; right down to the very way we sleep and dream. Our culture is what is familiar, recognizable, habitual. It is 'what goes without saying'.

The tacit character of culture suggests that we are perhaps most aware of it when standing on or near its boundaries. When we speak of 'our' culture, we often do so in terms of what it is not, in terms of contrast. At a societal level, when a Frenchman remarks that 'American children are spoiled and impolite', he is referring not to American children *per se* but to the French conception of child-rearing and how the proper child ought to behave within French society. Likewise, if an American claims 'the French are rude and never let one finish their sentences', she is putting forth American rules for conversation. It is at the boundaries that cultural premises are brought into awareness. In this sense, only at the meeting places between cultures – where there is a breakdown, hitch or hiccup – does one become alert to both the similarity (what one shares with others of one's own culture) and difference (what distinguishes one from those of other cultures) expressed by the always relational notion of culture.

Culture Here, There, Everywhere

Modern society complicates the study of culture. Indeed, the twentieth century marks the end of a world that could, with some truth, be seen as a mosaic of separate cultures or societies with sharp, well-defined edges. Advanced urbanization, expanded literacy, bureaucratized work relations, forms of mass communication, geographic and economic mobility and the emergence of the nation-state are the surface features of such modernity. Advanced industrial societies contain a head-swirling mix of cultural groupings, from those grounded in ethnic and kinship identity to those resting on the mutual love of a particular labor or leisure. The deep structure of modernity seems to contain the idea that modern societies are cut loose from both their past and other societies not so modern (the un(der)developed world). Collectively, these societies contain countless cultural forms that interpenetrate one another.

Such interpenetration can be seen as a cultural flow: the movement of cultural products and/or processes from a group familiar with them to one that is not. Much of this flow results in an increased awareness on the part of some people and occurs in a relatively free, unsponsored, reciprocal and rather spontaneous fashion in everyday life as differing cultural groups interact at work, in school, on the street, in shops, or in any place where people congregate. Modern society is such that people generally develop a fairly broad conception of other cultural processes and products by the same kind of listening, looking and learning as they do within their own cultural group(s). The flow here is rather diffuse, uncentered, and multichannelled (Becker 1982).

Culture also flows in a centered or command fashion. Some who have it wish to provide others with it. The flow here is relatively thin, often confined to particular narrow channels but nonetheless steady and frequently institutionalized. The state, for example, is an organizational form that tries – with varying degrees of success – to reach out towards its subjects and project the idea of a nation as a culture. Citizens are schooled in officially approved cultural matters normally associated with conceptions of history and tradition (conceptions that may in fact be spurious and quite controversial). Work organizations engage in an analogous process whenever their leaders set out deliberately to create a corporate culture to which members are to demonstrate fealty. The success of such culture building and transmission obviously depends on the history and traditions conveyed to particular clusters of recipients and the degree to which the state or the organization is a valued part of the life of its subjects.

Another centered flow of culture occurs in commercial spheres. Markets represent channels for cultural flows as products and processes of one cultural group are offered to members of another cultural group. Culture may move by command, but its reception is by no means assured or welcomed (Hannerz 1989). Of concern to us here is a basic socio-logical proposition that commodities or services sent forth by organiza-tions to consumers or users have value beyond whatever function they perform or whatever labor value is associated with their production (i.e.,

Granovetter 1985; Etzioni 1988; DiMaggio 1990). A part of this value lies in the cultural meanings associated with particular goods and services. Culture can therefore flow for fun, profit, edification or any other motive in our collective vocabularies.

An example of the reach cultural marketing can achieve is provided by MacCannel's (1976) fine ethnographic study of the contemporary tourist. He argues quite convincingly that objects in the modern world are increasingly invested with symbolic capital, so much so that even 'pure experience' can be marketed. Culturally-infused products that leave no physical trace – such as the 'fidelity' of a stereo, the 'style' of a restaurant, the 'feel' of a computer, the 'ambience' of a resort or the 'strong backbone, heady, full, complete, almost thick' properties of a vintage red wine – are all goods sold on the 'experience' they deliver.

Cultural Experience

This brings us (at last) to a degree of focus, for we are concerned here not only with the flow of culture but with the structure of cultural experience itself. The latter is, it seems, a hot item in the marketplace today and a topic of considerable interest to students of MNCs. Cultural experience is, of course, the stuff from which ethnographies presumably emerge, the stuff that tourists relentlessly pursue, and the stuff that is used to direct MNCs. It may also be what MNCs provide – knowingly or not – to customers in distant lands as well as to their employees who happen to be located in or sent to such lands.

Cultural experience contains, to follow MacCannel's (1976, pp. 23–4) lead, a certain hip or gamey (even sexual) connotation beyond its somewhat sterile ethnographic and market meanings. In brief, it implies the transformation of an original emptiness or skepticism on the part of a person or group into a belief or feeling that results from direct, first-hand involvement in a previously unknown, or at least partially unknown, social domain. Importantly, cultural experience in no way signals the gaining of competence in or a conversion to the social world in which the experience is initially marked. Rejection, distaste, amusement, ignorance and befuddlement are all possible outcomes of such encounters. However, such encounters do promote a kind of cultural awareness that was previously lacking.

Examples of cultural experience are not hard to locate. Conventional levels of analysis serve as guides. Driving along an interstate freeway in the USA might serve as a delightful individual experience to the visitor from Denmark; the more barren the better, since it would be 'more American'. Managers or technicians from the Netherlands working in Mexico City as representatives of an oil company subsidiary in that country partake in a cultural experience organized partly by their firm. Or, to reverse the flow, Japanese students sitting in a local sake bar watching American sitcoms on television may be having a cultural experience of a remarkable or, more likely, unremarkable sort. Certainly, in most of the world, few groups are immune to cultural experiences of this sort. What are we to make of them?

Two rough answers can be sketched out to these questions. Both must account for the organizer, the taker, and the channel associated with cultural experience. If we first examine the market as the channel of interest, a kind of global homogenization or integration theory surfaces as one answer. Cultural influences continuously pound away on the sensibilities of people such that eventually bits and pieces of whatever indigenous cultures are associated with their life fade out as they assimilate more and more of the exported meanings and forms. Over time, the local character of culture is increasingly driven out in favor of transnational symbolic forms originating elsewhere. Everyday life as an organizer of cultural experience must compete with more distant sources of cultural experience whose organizers seek to spread as widely as possible. The culture-conscious MNC systematically replicates itself wherever it goes, given its willingness to invest in such a project, by pounding away on those who work in its subsidiary units.

This is cultural imperialism pure and simple. The high-tech culture of the industrialized world, with powerful organizational backing, faces a more or less defenceless, small-scale variety of national and folk cultures whose members are slowly but surely lured or coerced into dependency. Homogenization comes from a center-to-periphery flow of cultural experience, bringing about something of a world culture that is, by and large, a version of contemporary industrial society. This is a zero-sum game where the loss of culture shows itself most distinctly in the least organized and powerless communities while the more organized and powerful grow increasingly similar, coming to shape, share and signal the world culture.

The global homogenization thesis has a good deal going for it, not the least its simplicity. But another answer to our question is possible. This answer shifts from the market and concentrates on the flow of culture in everyday life where a good deal of stability and local values persist. Cultural experiences that do not easily fold into the patterns of thought and action on this level are (1) unmarked entirely and thus have no influence, (2) rejected out-of-hand as culturally inappropriate and unattractive, or (3) eventually brought into line through transformations of one sort or another. Culture may still flow from the center outward, along a market channel, but there is a corruption down the line so that the core of the penetrated culture is left untouched. The local core may even be recharged, reinvigorated, and made more aware and assertive of its own perspective as a result of such contact, displaying its own inherent strengths and adaptive abilities in the face of alien ways. Everyday life thus colonizes the center (or market) rather than vice versa, reshaping the imported culture to its own specifications.

ORGANIZATION, CULTURE AND THE MNC

Both the homogenization and resistance theories are popular, and each has adherents in various scholarly camps. Both view the current expansion of MNCs in uneasy terms. Homogenization suggests the gradual decline of diversity around the globe through the growth of a highly rationalized and commodified world culture. The resilience of local culture perspective implies a Balkanized world order where mutual respect, understanding or common ground across cultures is not to be expected. Evidence for both views is readily available.

Some students of MNCs, for example, point to the relative success some firms have had in creating a centralized global operation, where control of the firm is securely in the hands of those enthroned at headquarters, and the look and feel of subsidiary activities throughout the world are quite similar.[5] Managers and employees alike share corporate aims and the local policies and practices of the firm are more similar than not. These homogenized MNCs take advantage of what is regarded as a convergence of consumer preferences worldwide, sophisticated information technologies, the economic benefits of scale economics and the corporate dedication and competence of a similarly trained and motivated workforce to keep in check far-flung subsidiaries, to distribute and sell common products throughout the world, and to keep decision-making in line with firm criteria originating in corporate headquarters. The power to ignore, bypass, or shape and mould culture is taken for granted.

Other MNC watchers have become enchanted with a more heterogeneous model of global operations, one more in touch with the cultural resistance scenario outlined above.[6] They point to the growing strength of the forces of localization, including the dependence of MNCs on host governments and the apparent stubborn objections of consumers in some markets to standardized products and practices. The disadvantages – economic and social – of large-scale production are highlighted, along with the needs of MNCs for cultural expertise in order to operate effectively in unfamiliar societies. The heterogeneous MNC becomes the model operation. Independent and relatively self-sufficient national (or subnational) subsidiaries are emphasized, and a highly pluralistic version of the MNC is the result. Authority is dispersed across the organization, and the culture flow from the centre outward is more or less constrained.

Qualifications and contingencies can be tied to both models. Most students would agree that all MNCs bear something of a cultural stamp that originates in the society where the organization was first designed (Laurent 1983, 1986). The greater the economic power of this society, the larger and older the organization, the more obvious the stamp (Chandler 1986). At the periphery, the older and larger the subsidiary, the more likely the unit is to be marked by local or country-specific modifications (Stopford and Wells 1972). MNCs involved in the manufacture and sale of global products are apparently more likely to suffer from strong, centralized, corporate controls than MNCs involved in numerous, regionalized, consumer product businesses (Robinson 1967). MNCs headquartered in small countries are apt to be less ethnocentric than those from large countries, and hence the flow of culture may be more symmetrical or reciprocal (Hedlund 1986). Certainly complexity of the organizational form itself enters the picture since the total number of ties between the center and periphery may act as a constraint on the center's ability to tighten any or all links (Nohria and Ghoshal 1989).

What comes out of such studies is the notion that MNCs are virtually always faced with choice situations. They can, if senior managers wish, work towards a highly centralized operation on a global scale and attempt with more or less success to rein in subsidiary operations through the construction of a 'strong' corporate culture designed and communicated from the center outward. Or they can choose to cut loose operations on the periphery, allowing subsidiaries relatively great flexibility in terms of policy and procedure. Most popular now are various mixed models: firms can therefore learn to 'think locally and act globally' or 'think globally and act locally', depending on the kind of strategic models that are used by the managers who direct the activities of the firm (Prahalad and Doz 1987). The homogeneous parts of the MNC develop in response to intensive corporate socialization, rapid transfer and rotation of managers across selected units of the firm, strict reporting and evaluation procedures tied to common reward systems, elaborate corporate-wide rituals organized to promote feelings of commonality and shared purposes, and so on. The heterogeneous parts of the MNC adopt such practices from each other and encourage local autonomy. It is really all a matter of following the formula.

The problem for cultural theorists of all this commonsense organization theory is that it either trivializes culture by reducing its relevance to something which is thought to be fully under the control of a few and exported, if necessary or desired, to the many, or it enshrines culture as impenetrable, unique, unfathomable, always local and essentially time-less and omnipresent. Our view of culture is that it is always rubbing against other cultural processes and products. This calls out for a considerably more nuanced view of the workings of MNCs.

A revisionist perspective directs attention to specific cultural interaction sites in the firm where different marking, classifying and meaning-making devices are put to work in particular places at particular times. High variability is quite likely to be the result of such a focus with the exceptional and peculiar showing up in contrast to either the local autonomy stories or those of homogenization. Such particularity, however, would leave us as ethnographers with only a collection of highly diverse stories to tell. So given our aims here, some attention needs to be paid to an overall conceptualization of the flow of culture that incorporates a sense of the general.

To this end, we shall tell a tale that reaches for the general in its depiction of just how one culture attends to the imports of another. The level of analysis is relatively broad, dealing with national or societal culture, but the considerations that enter at this level are relevant all the way down the chain of cultural groupings. The story concerns a common practice of MNCs: namely, the packing-up of an operation and product developed at home and shifting it lock, stock and barrel elsewhere, across a cultural boundary. The hope always is that it will perform as well (or better) in its new surroundings as in the old. Examples are everywhere: Volvo goes to Russia, Mitsubishi comes to Palo Alto, Club Med goes to Paradise. Our story concerns the exporting of Disneyland, a product (and cultural experience) of some fame, into a new and culturally distinct context.

MICKEY GOES TO TOKYO[7]

At first glance, Tokyo Disneyland is a physical and social copy of Disneyland in Southern California: a clone created 6000 miles away and perhaps something of a cultural bomb dropped on perfect strangers. The castle, the flags, the rides, the entertainment, the orderly waterways and impeccably clean grounds, the ever-smiling ride operators and Disney characters that prance about charming the old and young alike; even the crowds, the traffic, the smog, the lengthy waits for attractions, the summer heat, the suburban sprawl surrounding the park, all seem in harmony with the spirit and letter of the 35-year-old original. Even the gate receipts for this detailed replica met and exceeded expectations from the day the Tokyo park opened. Walt's world travels well, it seems; so well, in fact, that another version, again a copy, is set to open outside Paris in 1992.

Global homogenization appears to be working here; culture is flowing from the West to the East quite smoothly and easily. Tokyo Disneyland is a transplant clean and clear, one that has been fully accepted and welcomed in all its pop culture American glory by its Japanese hosts. On the surface, at least, the culture codes at work and on display at Disneyland move gracefully into a vastly different societal context and perform the same wonders they perform at home. For observers of the MNC, this may seem a fortunate turn of events since it provides a rather visible, happy and public stage on which to examine the cultural exchange process. Moreover, it is virtually a pure case of emulation and adoption given that, before the park opened, Disney officials had relinquished direct control of their Japanese counterpart. This is *not* a case, therefore, of the center forcing itself on the periphery or a case of a more or less helpless, dependent subsidiary in an economically impoverished land facing the cultural order of the West (or East) and being offered a take-it-or-leave-it choice, which in most respects is no choice at all. This *is* a case of a highly autonomous, nominal subsidiary that asks for and receives a duplicate organization and then, after cutting itself loose from the parent, manages the enterprise by choice in a fashion that mirrors the center and reaps rather sizeable rewards in the host society as a result.

Tokyo Disneyland is perhaps a glimpse of the coming world culture, a commodified, mechanized and highly standardized mass culture built on the Coca-Colonizing forces of Western, particularly American, consumer values. The increased traffic in culture and the apparently asymmetric transfer of meaning systems and symbolic forms give way to an empire of signs ruled by those who produce and export the world's most desirable goods and services. This is a sort of context-free reading of the Japanese fascination with American popular culture and the universal desire for the bland sort of cultural experience a visit to Disneyland provokes. Indeed, Disney products and images have long been part of a world culture and are virtually impossible to escape anywhere. Mickey Mouse cartoons are seen in Balinese villages amid rice paddies and oxen (Myerhoff 1983). Children's candies are sold in Italy wrapped in packages adorned with the familiar cast of Disney characters (Iyer 1988). Disneyfication operates with an apparent vengeance in Latin America where millions upon millions of Donald Duck comic books are distributed (Dorfman and Matterlart 1975). In many respects, the Disney corporate logo of the globe with mouse ears is hardly an idle boast.

Context-dependent explanations for the workings of culture flow seem antiquated, or even downright quaint, when employed to explain the success of Tokyo Disneyland. Japan is a prime player in the world economy, highly sophisticated and self-conscious culturally, careful, almost xenophobic, about the importation of things foreign, and the possessor of one of history's oldest, most subtle cultures founded on a sense of exclusivity, hierarchy and obligation (Benedict 1946; Nakane 1970; Fukutake 1981). Japan is certainly not a cultural dumping ground for the West or likely to respond well to the more vulgar gruntings of American individualism and its associated colonial, paternal and patriotic images. Yet, when Disney officials expressed an interest in providing some home country attractions, such as a 'Samurai Land', to replace one of its American attractions or a ride and narrative based on the classic Japanese children's story 'The Little Peach Boy', the Japanese partners in Tokyo Disneyland resisted strenuously and insisted on a duplicate American version, thus retaining (presumably) the cultural purity of the original (Brannon 1990). The streams of visitors would then seem to validate the idea that Disney's cultural products and experience work in the same way across two radically dissimilar contexts, effectively and effortlessly transcending cultural boundaries.

This is certainly the spin put on the story by corporate officials. Consider the comment by a public relations spokesman at Tokyo Disneyland: 'We really tried to avoid creating a Japanese version of Disneyland. We wanted the Japanese visitors to feel they were taking a foreign vacation by coming here and, to us, Disneyland represents the best America has to offer.' (quoted in Brannon 1990). Such remarks explicitly suggest that the Japanese managers of Disneyland believe they have created a replica, and implicitly they suggest that the imported Disney version retains its original influence and meaning. The market conquers all in this sterling tale of an excellent company and product; however, if we look somewhat closer and in more detail – beyond the sales figures and surface similarities of the two parks – certain interesting contradictions to this presumed unproblematic one-way flow of culture begin to appear. We shall start at headquarters, move briefly to Florida where the second Disneyland was built (thereby providing a degree of choice for the Japanese partners in the amusement trade), and then stop at our destination, Tokyo Disneyland, to consider its cultural position and product.

Disneyland first opened its gates in July 1955. It has been a remarkable economic success and become something of a national institution. One student of American culture notes that the definition of 'good parents' in the USA turns, in part, on whether or not Mom and Dad have visited Disneyland with their children (Real 1977). Its appeal to foreign visitors as an 'authentic' American site representing the best the country has to offer, is apparent in this quote from an editorial in the normally dyspeptic and reserved London-based publication *The Economist*:

'Builders, architects, city planners, managing directors should all be forced in chains if necessary to find out from Mickey Mouse how one can create an environment in which laughter flourishes and well-being created. If Mickey Mouse were elected mayor, the efficiency of local government would increase by several hundred percent' (quoted in Harrington 1979).

Disneyland is, in this view, a product: part cinema, part tourist site, part shopping mall, part museum, part stage production, part playground, part shrine, part ceremony, part spectacle, part festival, and so on. It has been subject to countless assessments of culture critics who, although not always impressed by its wonders, do manage to agree on a number of unifying themes standing behind the product (themes that seemingly integrate and make meaningful a visit to the park on the part of the millions that crowd the grounds each year).[8] Most begin by noting the order, safety and cleanliness at Disneyland and the marked contrast these features bear in relation to contemporary urban life in America (Schickel 1968; Marin 1977; Myerhoff 1983). The rectangular grid of the city is replaced in the park by graceful, curved walkways. Motorists become pedestrians. The drab industrial and metropolitan landscape is replaced by bright colored buildings done up in ebullient and whimsical forms and covered by sumptuous ornaments and thousands of twinkling lights that turn night into day. The crowded, disorderly, fear-inspiring city scenes of ordinary life are transformed within the park to obedient, friendly queues and the peaceful strolling of people kept secure by unarmed, unobtrusive, yet ever-present and smiling park police. Work clothes give way to leisure garb. Adults take the role of children on rides designed to rekindle youthful memories while children take on adult roles by driving snarling miniature automobiles on toy freeways, exploring deep space and making the family decisions about what to do next. The frontier town of yesteryear is no longer dusty, dirty and rather formless but becomes prim, tidy and 'what it should have been' by virtue of its scrubbed, freshly-painted, simple and sweet look.

In the American context, Disneyland is a topsy-turvy world that highlights in its physical and social design a long string of semiotic contrasts that set the park off as a sought-after cultural experience for patrons: work/play, adult/child, dirty/clean, poverty/wealth, dangerous/safe, rude/civil, cold/warm, routine/festive and so on (King 1981; Gottdiener 1982). These contrasts of America/Disneyland create the differences on which the park's claim to be 'the happiest place on earth' rests. To bring off the claim requires the banishment of all signs of decay, crime, confusion, discontent, pain or struggle in the park's design and the reduction wherever possible of social and stylistic diversity on the part of customers and employees alike.

The layout of the park conveys a high degree of thematic integration well known to visitors. Dominating the landscape from the center is Sleeping Beauty's Castle with streets radiating outward, Versailles-like, into the four lands, each representing something of a distinct stage of life: Fantasyland for early childhood where the attractions are small scale and built on mythical, imaginary fables quite familiar to American children; Frontierland for adolescence where cowboy tales of the Wild West are re-enacted through the hourly shooting of the glum desperado by the smug sheriff, and summertime romps recreated on Tom Sawyer's Island; Adventureland for young adulthood where a test of courage against the strange and savage is presented as an Indiana Jones trek up-river into the dark, unexplored territories of the world; and Tomorrowland for adulthood where the dream of science and technology conquers all and personable robots cavort alongside humans.

The castle and hub of the park is reached by a walk through Main Street, an imaginative (but pickled) recreation of a mid-Western railroad town at the turn of the century full of quasi-Victorian shops selling modern merchandise. Between Adventureland and Frontierland lies New Orleans Square which, Walt Disney claimed 'is just like the 1850s original Vieux Carré but a lot cleaner' (Lowenthal 1985, p. 321). And in the backwoods of Disneyland sits Bear Country and its reminder of the rural, 'hayseed' relatives of the Mom and Pop entrepreneurs who made it to Main Street.

To the American visitor, each of the lands and constituent elements fit rather well-worn and comfortable mythical and historical narratives. Fantasyland, for example, embodies the classic children's literature of the West that has been culturally stripmined by Disney via films, books and television programs. The verbal and visual images of Perrault, Collodi, Milne and Barrie are now thoroughly familiar as Disney's Cinderella, Pinocchio, Winnie-the-Pooh and Peter Pan. In Frontierland, a Frederick Turner version of America is conveyed by its relentless westward-ho imagery of rugged individualism and hardships overcome. Adventureland reminds visitors of the exploration saga of a Stanley and Livingstone sort as they journey through a lush, tropical jungle where elephants wave their trunks on cue and headhunting is still in style. The stories are conventional, stereotypical American versions of their world and its inhabitants.

This mythology underlying Disneyland images and narratives is a form of what Myerhoff (1983) usefully labels 'hyperculture', a collective form of expression that overstates and overclarifies some cultural interpretation. There is certainly nothing subtle to Americans about Disneyland. The stories told in and by the park are exaggerated, inflated versions of events, aggrandized to the point of parody. Thus, when the summer-long bicentennial parade was staged at Disneyland in 1976, who should appear at the head of the parade bearing drums and fife straight from the *Spirit of '76* painting by Willard but the three symbols of the American Revolution, Mickey Mouse, Donald Duck and Goofy. The imagination provided at Disneyland is complete. Little room is left for the spontaneous or disarrayed. Lavish panegyric productions are staged to evoke both patriotism and nostalgia. Iconography is worked out in minute, common denominator detail such that the partaker of gloom in the Haunted Mansion is, for instance, greeted by willows (for sadness), twisted oaks (for transitory life), dark, podlike vehicles (for departure) and black- clad attendants (for morticians). Seemingly nothing is left to chance: each rock, tree and plant in the park is numbered and assigned a proper role.

The communicative work that takes place inside the park serves to distinguish Disneyland from other (and earlier) theme parks. In contemporary America, Disneyland emerges as an island of calm sanity and safety in troubled times. The forces of decay are arrested, sexual innuendoes are all but banished, alcohol is taboo, evil is overcome, the innocent prevail, disorder is tamed, the future is clarified, the past cleaned up and, in general, the perverse world of doubt, fear and unfair competition outside the gates is held at bay. Turn-of-the-century amusement parks in America performed much the same kind of symbolic work, but the reversals were different, almost an inversion of the symbolic work at Disneyland. Old parks developed from the background of a relatively stern Victorian heritage that stressed self-control, rationalism, industriousness and delayed gratification, and thus worked to create feelings of spontaneity, intensified emotion, release and a scornful, mocking attitude towards the culture outside the park (Kasson 1978; Harris 1990).

Two emblematic attractions at Disneyland – also found at Tokyo Disneyland – serve nicely as concrete instances of the hypercultural statements found in the park and will help to illustrate and unpack something of the cultural experience the park offers to its American customers. First, consider the tame imagery presented by 'It's a Small World', an attraction first built by Disney for the New York World's Fair in 1964 and then rebuilt a year later at Disneyland. The cuteness and adorableness that permeates every amusement in the park is particularly clear in this attraction. The patron enters a castle-like structure through a large and elegant topiary garden of plant life shaped into animal forms. One rides in small boats through a cartoon-like array of moving dolls dressed in native costumes to represent a selected variety of world cultures. The dolls spin and sing repetitively what is surely one of the most nauseating tunes of all time, 'It's a Small World After All'. The dolls portray the 'Children of the World' in miniature. They are uniform in size, appearance and mannerisms except for marginal differentiations of race, nationality and dress. The marking is simple and redundant, cultural signs that Americans have long been accustomed to through children's literature, movies, television and comic books. Holland is coded by tulips and bells, Japan by fans and kimonos, India by temples and saris. The faces are, however, basically Anglo-Saxon, even when intended to signal Chinese, Latino or Arabic. The facial markers are mere hints that point to the possible existence of differences but, since the differences are so slight, they could not possibly be taken to be of serious consequence. A sort of insidious ethnocentricism is obvious in the infantilization of the world's cultures where all human differences are superficial and benign. Americans are notably absent in this display except as passive observers of the scene, blissfully drifting past the world of young, diminutive, ebullient, bright-eyed, innocent and lovable 'Others'.

If Small World is a hypercultural message of simplicity and harmony, of sweet differences and unity in the world, the Adventureland 'Jungle Cruise' is less reverential and more explicit about some of the world's cultures. The racial themes and imperialist mentality of the late nineteenth and early twentieth centuries are built into this attraction, from the scenic constructions on the banks of the river to the words and phrases of the animated spiel that accompanies each cruise. The voyage departs next to a pile of plastic human skulls, beneath shields, spears, totems and other symbols of some nameless but faintly menacing region beyond white settlement. The adventure consists mostly of short takes of mechanized people of color and wildlife as encountered in the river and along its banks. One scene places five members of a safari atop a pole with a horned rhinoceros threatening to impale them from below. The members of the party are four Africans who stare minstrel-like at the animal beneath them, faces glazed with fear and eyes protruding. At the very top of the pole, furthest from the rhino and danger, is perched the white safari leader.

Disneyland is, of course, made up of thousands upon thousands of hypercultural statements. Any one sign may give way to diverse readings but, when bundled all together, the teachings are abundantly clear. The overt messages and themes come back to the same concerns: friendliness, optimism, the civilization of the frontier, the ultimate victory of good over evil, the beauty and power of America, the importance of efficiency, cleanliness, order and courtesy, the importance of staying in line (figuratively and literally), the triumph of modern technologies (particularly transportation technologies), and so forth. What is celebrated at Disneyland and what is being taught come together under labels such as patriotism, cultural superiority and the trivialization of differences across the globe. America shines and spreads its light on the world, and the exotic is reduced to familiar terms. All this is packaged in a fashion that is thematically consistent, rather banal, closely scrutinized and controlled, and licensed by broad middle-class values of harmony and order.

The same production is replicated as 'The Magic Kingdom' in Orlando, Florida. The second park opened in 1969, and now, with its peripheral attractions (the Epcot Center, MGM-Disney Studios and numerous Disney-owned and operated hotels and fun zones adjacent to the park) the total complex in Orlando outdraws Disneyland. Walt Disney World is, in fact, second only to Washington, DC, in the number of tourists it attracts within the USA each year (*Time Magazine*, 25 April 1988; Birnbaum 1989). Its construction, however, sets Disneyland apart as the 'original', giving it the measure of authenticity that only a copy can provide.

The copy is not perfect. The scale is larger and some attractions, such as the Matterhorn bobsleds, are still found only at Disneyland. The Magic Kingdom lacks the intimacy of Disneyland but, when combined with the other tourist sites at Walt Disney World, it becomes part of an activity menu that lengthens the average visitor's stay to a matter of days rather than hours. Modest changes within the park are visible as well. Sleeping Beauty's Castle is replaced by the bigger, more photogenic and splendid version, Cinderella's Castle. Some of the rides, such as Big Thunder Mountain, are longer and slightly more harrowing. Others are thin replicas, such as the Pirates of the Caribbean, which is much more elaborate, lengthy and entertaining at Disneyland. Still, despite small changes, the cultural experience for American visitors to the two parks must be much the same. The context does not shift radically and visitors seemingly do not notice much difference – beyond scale – in the two parks (Sehlinger 1985; Birnbaum 1989). What the park in Walt Disney World provides, however, is a measure of choice for those about to construct yet another copy of Disneyland.

Disneyland went international in 1983 with the opening of its Tokyo operation. On the surface it claims to be a near perfect copy of the Disneyland production minus a few of the original's attractions. There are some recognized modifications, but these are imports selected from The Magic Kingdom instead of Disneyland (e.g., Cinderella's Castle and the Mickey Mouse Theater). In terms of organizational control, it is as decentralized as they come; the Oriental Land Company, a Japanese development and property management firm, took full control shortly after the park was built and now provides Walt Disney Enterprises with a rough 10 percent cut of Tokyo Disneyland's profits from admissions, food and merchandise sales. A small American management team ('Disnoids') remains in Japan as advisers and consultants to keep the park in tune with Disney doctrine, and the firm hires a handful of non-Japanese employees, mainly Americans, as 'cast members' (entertainers, crafts people and characters) strategically scattered throughout the park. The question we now raise concerns the flow of culture from the West to the East. To what extent does Tokyo Disneyland mean the same thing to its new patrons as it means to its old?

In a nutshell, Tokyo Disneyland does not work in the same way as its American counterpart. Although certain principles of cultural flow hold steady, the meaning of the forms that flow shifts significantly, and whereas an American strolling through Frontierland may be gently reminded of a romanticized and nostalgic view of his or her past, the Japanese patron ambling through Westernland can have no such cultural experience. This is not to say that the symbols and Disney narratives are meaningless in the Japanese context. Such a view could not begin to explain the popularity of the park which is, in 1991, expected to outdraw Disneyland by nearly one million customers. But what does appear to be happening is the recontextualization of the American signs so that the Japanese are able to make them their own. This process may be highly general and something of the norm for cultural transformations.

Most observers of modern Japan note the country's penchant for the importation of things foreign, from public bureaucracies (Westney 1987) to fashion (Stuart 1987) to popular sports (Whiting 1977). In fact, Japan's widescale adoption of things American is now something of a universal cliché. The choice of imports is, however massive, highly selective. From this perspective, the consumption of foreign goods in Japan seems less an act of homage than a way of establishing a national identity by making such imports their own through combining them in a composite of all that the Japanese see as the best in the world. Some of this conspicuous consumption correlates with significant increases in per capita disposable income and what appears to be a new and more relaxed attitude among the Japanese toward leisure and play (Emmott 1989; Fallows 1989). But, whatever the source of this omnivorous appetite, the Japanese seem unworried that their cultural identity is compromised by such importation.

Not to be overlooked, however, are the subtle, sometimes hidden, ways in which alien forms are not merely imported across cultural boundaries but in the very process turned into something else again, and the indigenous and foreign are combined into an idiom more consistent with the host culture than the home culture. Two features of the way Disneyland has been emulated and incorporated in the Japanese context are apparent. Each suggests that Tokyo Disneyland takes on a rather different meaning for workers and customers alike in its new setting.

First, Disneyland is made comfortable for the Japanese in ways that contrast with its California counterpart. In some ways, the fine tuning of the park's character follows a domestication principle familiar to anthropologists whereby the exotic, alien aspects of foreign objects are set back and de-emphasized, replaced by an intensified concern with the more familiar and culturally sensible aspects (Douglas 1966; Wallace 1985). Thus the safe, clean, courteous, efficient aspects of Disneyland fit snugly within the Japanese cultural system and can be highlighted. Disneyland as 'the best of America' suits the Japanese customer with its underscored technological wizardry and corporate philosophy emphasizing high quality service. Providing happiness, harmony and hospitality for guests by a staff that is as well-groomed as the tended gardens is certainly consistent with Japanese practices in other consumer locales (Vogel 1979; J. Taylor 1983; Dore 1987). The legendary *sotto voce* of the Japanese service provider is merely a modest step away from the 'people specialist' of planned exuberance and deferential manners turned out by the University of Disneyland in the USA, at least in theory if not in practice (Van Maanen 1990a). And *Imagineering*, a smart Disney term used to designate the department responsible for the design of park attractions ('the engineers of imagination'), is used in Japan – as in the USA, without a touch of irony or awareness of contradiction.

If anything, the Japanese have intensified the orderly nature of Disneyland. If Disneyland is clean, Tokyo Disneyland is impeccably clean; if Disneyland is efficient, Tokyo Disneyland puts the original to shame by being absurdly efficient, or at least so says *Business Week* (12 March 1990). Whereas Disneyland is a vision of order, sanitized, homogenized and precise, Tokyo Disneyland is even more so, thus creating, in the words of one observer, 'a perfect toy replica of the ideal tinkling, sugarcoated society around it, a perfect box within a box' (Iyer 1988, p. 333). One of the charms of Disneyland to American visitors is the slight but noticeable friction between the seamless perfection of the place and the intractable, individualistic, irredeemable and sometimes intolerable character of the crowd. In the midst of its glittering contraptions and mannerly operatives are customers strolling about wearing 'shit happens' or 'dirty old man' T-shirts. Tourists in enormous tent dresses and full-Cleveland double-knit outfits share space in the monkey car of Casey Jones's Circus Train with tattooed bikers, skinheads and Deadheads. Obese men and women wearing short shorts mingle and queue up with rambunctious teenagers on the make, all to be crammed on to hurling clockwork bobsleds and sent on their way for a two-minute roller-coaster ride. Elderly retirees with seasonal passes sit serenely on Main Street watching gum-snapping, stringy blonde women dressed all in black being cuddled by their slobbering, leather-clad boyfriends heavily burdened by metal chains and stomping boots. Park police – dressed as US marshals or tin-horn cops – chase down the little criminals of Disneyland on Tom Sawyer's Island or Main Street as irate parents screech at their offspring to wipe the chocolate off their faces and keep their hands off the merchandise. Some parents manage to curb their youngsters' wanderlust by attaching them to a leash; others simply track them down after several ear-shattering screams fail to bring them in. For the Disneyland patron, such contrasts give life to the park and provide a degree of narrative tension.

In Tokyo, the shadow between the ideal and reality is not so apparent. Adults and children bend more easily toward the desired harmonious state, and out-of-order contrasts are few and far between inside (and, perhaps, outside) the park. This is a society where the word for *wrong* means 'different' and 'the nail that sticks out is the nail that must be hammered down' (Bayley 1976; Kamata 1980; M. White 1987). To the extent that there is order in Disneyland, it is welcomed as a contrast to the outside world; order in Tokyo Disneyland is expected and largely taken for granted, so that the park glides effortlessly rather than lurching self-consciously towards its fabled efficiency. Iyer (1988, pp. 317–18) summarizes his visit to Tokyo Disneyland in the following way:

> There was no disjunction between the perfect rides and their human riders. Each was as synchronized, as punctual, as clean as the other. Little girls in pretty bonnets, their eyes wide with wonder, stood in lines, as impassive as dolls, while their flawless mothers posed like mannequins under their umbrellas. [They] waited uncomplainingly for a sweet-voiced machine to break the silence and permit them to enter the pavilion – in regimented squads. All the while, another mechanized voice offered tips to ensure that the human element would be just as well planned as the man-made: Do not leave your shopping to the end, and try to leave the park before rush hour, and eat at a sensible hour, and do not, under any circumstance, fail to have a good time.

Such failures to have a good time are rare partly because of the way Tokyo Disneyland has rearranged the model to suit its customers. Despite its claims as a duplicate, a number of quite specific changes have taken place and more are planned. The amusement park itself is considerably larger than Disneyland (124 acres to 74). As a result, it loses some of the intimacy that is so uncharacteristic in its Southern California setting and instead gives off a feeling of conspicuous spaciousness rather unusual in greater Tokyo, where it seems every square inch is fully utilized. Disneyland's fleet of Nautilus-like submarines is missing, perhaps because of Japan's deep sensitivity to all things nuclear. There are few outdoor food vendors in the park but there are over 40 sit-down restaurants, about twice the number of those in Disneyland. It is considered rude to eat while walking about in Japan (the munching of popcorn in the park being apparently the only exception).

Several new attractions have been added in Tokyo, each quite explicit about which culture is, in the final analysis, to be celebrated in the park. One, incongruously called 'Meet the World', offers not only a history of Japan but an elaborate defence of the Japanese way. In this regard, it is not unlike Disneyland's 'Meet Mr. Lincoln', where visitors are asked at one point to sing along with the mechanical icon a passionate version of 'America the Beautiful'. In Meet the World, a sagacious crane guides a young boy and his sister through the past, pausing briefly along the way to make certain points such as the lessons learned by the Japanese cave dwellers (the importance of banding together) or the significance of the samurai warrior ('we never became a colony') or the importance of early foreign trade ('to carry the seeds offered from across the sea and cultivate them in our own Japanese garden'). Another site-specific attraction in Tokyo Disneyland is the 'Magic Journeys' trip across five continents, which culminates, dramatically, in the adventurer's return to 'our beloved Japan where our hearts always remain'.

Another altogether fascinating yet unique attraction to Tokyo Disneyland is situated inside Cinderella's Castle and is organized as a tightly packed mystery tour through a maze of dark tunnels, fearsome electronic tableaus and narrow escapes. Groups of about 15–20 persons are escorted through this breathless 13 minute adventure in the castle by lively tour guides who, in the climactic moment of the tour, select a single member of the group to do battle with evil. The chosen hero or heroine is provided with a nifty laser sword and, backed by inventive special effects and timely coaching from the tour guide, manages to slay the evil sorcerer just in the nick of time. The group is thus spared, free again for further adventures in the park. The attraction ends with a mock-solemn presentation of a medal to the now bashful group savior who leads everyone out of the exit after passing down an aisle formed by applauding fellow members of the mystery tour.

It is hard to image a similar attraction working in either Disneyland or Disney World. Not only would group discipline to ensure that all members of the tour would start and end together be lacking, but selecting a sword bearer to do battle with the Evil One would quite likely prove to be a considerable test for a tour guide when meeting with a characteristic American chorus of 'me, me, me' coming from children and adults alike. The intimacy, proximity and physical, almost hands-on, interaction between customers and amusement sources found in Tokyo Disneyland are striking to a visitor accustomed to the invisible security and attention given to damage control so prevalent in the US parks. Tokyo Disneyland puts its guests within touching distance of many of its attractions, so that a customer who wished to could easily deface a cheerful robot, steal a Small World doll or behead the Mad Hatter. This blissful respect for the built environment at Tokyo Disneyland allows ride operators to take an exhibitory stance to their attraction rather than a custodial one, which is often the perspective of Disneyland operatives (Van Maanen and Kunda 1989).

Other distinctly Japanese touches include the white gloves for drivers of the transportation vehicles in the park, a practice drawn from the taxi and bus drivers in Japan; name tags for employees featuring last names rather than first names; a small picnic area just outside the park for families bringing traditional box lunches to the park, a reminder of family customs in Japan and a compromise with the Disney tradition of allowing no food to be brought into the park; and subtitles in Japanese for most of the street and attraction signs. All ride soundtracks and spiels are, of course, in Japanese, and one American visitor reports considerably more ad-libbing on the part of Japanese ride operators compared to their American counterparts (Brannon 1990).

Such concessions to the Japanese guest contrast with the proclamation of a pure copy. One might argue that such changes are minor adjustments in keeping with the fundamental marketing techniques of both capitalistic societies (namely, tailoring the product to its audience). But it is also important to keep in mind that even the notion of consumer capitalism in the two contexts varies systematically.

Main Street, USA, for example, has become in Tokyo the World Bazaar. Little remains of the turn-of-the-century mid-Western town of Walt's slippery memory. The World Bazaar is quite simply an enormous, modern, up-scale shopping mall where many of the products (and possibilities) of the five continents are brought together in a post-modern Disney collage that is distinctly Japanese. Few modest trinkets are on sale at the World Bazaar; instead, costly, high-status items are offered, all bearing an official Disney label and wrapped in Tokyo Disneyland paper suitable for the gift-giving practices of the Japanese (as outlined by Brannon 1990). Frontierland's presentation of the continental expansion of the USA has given way to Westernland, which is apparently understood only through the Japanese familiarity with the Wild West imagery of American movies, television and pulp fiction. Thus to the same extent that nostalgia, patriotism and historical narratives provide the context of meaning for visitors to Disneyland, visitors to Tokyo Disneyland are made comfortable through devices of their own making. Although the structure may appear quite similar, the meaning is not.

The second feature of the emulation process in Tokyo Disneyland runs counter to some of our more optimistic (or, at least, calming) beliefs about the workings of cultural flows. Tokyo Disneyland serves as something of a shrine in Japan to Japan itself, an emblem of self-validating beliefs in the cultural values and superiority of the Japanese. Disneyland serves as such an American shrine, but it is, of course, America that is celebrated. How is it that a painstaking near-copy of what is undeniably an American institution – like baseball – can function to heighten the self-awareness of the Japanese?

The answer lies in the workings of culture itself for it is a differentiating device, a way of marking boundaries. Tokyo Disneyland marks cultural boundaries in a variety of ways. One already mentioned is the outdoing of Disneyland in the order-keeping domain. The message here is simply, 'Anything you can do, we can do as well (or better).' One of the characteristic features of modern Japan is its drive toward perfection, and it has built a Disneyland that surpasses its model in terms of courtesy, size, efficiency, cleanliness and performance. Were the park built more specifically to Japanese tastes and cultural aesthetics, it would undercut any contrast to the original in this regard. Although Disneyland is reproduced in considerable detail, it is never deferred to entirely, thus making the consumption of this cultural experience a way of marking the boundaries between Japan and the USA. Japan has taken in Disneyland only, it seems, to take it over.

Consider, also, another cultural flow analogous to the way Disneyland itself treats the foreign and exotic. Tokyo Disneyland maintains, indeed amplifies, self-and-other contrasts consistent with Japanese cultural rules. Only Japanese employees wear name tags in the park; the foreign (Western employees) do not. Americans hired to play Disney characters such as Snow White, Cinderella, Prince Charming, Alice in Wonderland, Peter Pan or the Fairy Godmother are nameless, thus merging whatever personalized identities they may project with those of their named characters. Other Westerners employed as craftsmen (glass blowers, leather workers, etc.), dancers, magicians, musicians or role-playing shopkeepers also remain tagless. Musicians play only American songs, ranging from Broadway production numbers such as 'Yankee Doodle Dandy' put on the large stage settings of the park to twangy, country and western tunes such as 'Stand By Your Man' played in a fake saloon of Westernland. During the Christmas season, songs such as 'Rudolph the Red-nosed Reindeer', 'Silent Night' and the 'Hallelujah Chorus' of Handel's *Messiah* are piped throughout the appropriately festooned park as a portly American Santa Claus poses for snapshots with couples and families who wait patiently in long queues for such a photo opportunity. That the *gaijin* (literally, 'outside person') employees ordinarily speak only English while playing their roles furthers their distinctiveness in the setting. Mary Yoko Brannon (1990) writes of these practices:

> Rather than functioning as facilitators of the Disneyland experience like their Japanese counterparts, gaijin employees are put on display. Gaijin cast members are displayed daily in a group at the place of honor at the front of the Disneyland parade, and gaijin craftspersons are displayed throughout the day at their boxed-in work stations not unlike animals in cages at the zoo.

The same general practice is followed at Disneyland where, of course, the roles are reversed and the 'others' are constructed out of different cultural building blocks. Just as blacks are notable at Disneyland primarily for their absence from the productions and the work force, Koreans are conspicuously absent in Tokyo Disneyland (victims, it seems, of the racial politics of Asia). Villains of the Disney narratives produced in the USA seem always to speak and act with vaguely foreign personae and accents, typically – but not always – Russian or German; evil in Tokyo Disneyland is represented by *gaijin* witches, goblins and ghosts whose accents are distinctly non-Japanese. Such a practice of sharply separating *gaijin* from society mirrors other Japanese cultural productions, such as the popular television shows devoted to portraying *gaijin* stupidities (Stuart 1987) or the practice of limiting the number of baseball players on professional teams to two *gaijin* players per team (Whiting 1989). The outsiders may be accorded respect but they are not to come too close, for the culture provides no easy space for them. One does not become Japanese any more than one can eat steak with chopsticks.

These contrasts in meaning across the two parks could be extended considerably. The point, however, is not to enumerate all the amplifications, reversals or twists in meaning but to note their rather pervasive presence. The perspective we wish to establish is that the Japanese cultural experience in Tokyo Disneyland is akin to a 'foreign vacation' with a number of comforting homey touches built in. The perfect copy of Disneyland turns out to be anything but perfect at the level of signification. If Disneyland sucks the difference out of differences by presenting an altogether tamed and colonized version of the people of other lands (who are, when all is said and done, just like the good folks at home in Los Angeles or Des Moines), Tokyo Disneyland celebrates differences by treating the foreign as exotic, its peoples to be understood only in terms of the fact that they are not Japanese and not, most assuredly, like the good people of Osaka or Kyoto. In this regard, both parks are isolated by a belief in their own cultural superiority. Perhaps it would be asking too much of a commercial enterprise to question such a belief since the corporate aim in both settings is, in crude terms, to build and manage an amusement park to which people will come (and come again) to be run assembly-line fashion through its attractions and stripped of their money.

In the cracks, however, Tokyo Disneyland offers some intriguing lessons in culture flow beyond the mere fact of its existence. First, the representation of 'the best in America' in Japan breaks some new ground and contributes modestly to what might be called post-modernism by combining cultural elements in new ways and then allowing customers and workers alike to develop the logic of their relationship. Thus Mickey Mouse, a symbol of the infantile and plastic in America, can come to stand for what is delightful and adorable in Japan and can be used to sell adult apparel and money-market accounts. This is not simply a matter of the Japanese appropriating Mickey but rather signals a process by which a selected alien import is reconstituted and given new meaning.

Second, such cultural flows are ongoing matters. Mickey Mouse has been hanging around Japan for a long time, and his current cultural status has a history. Working out the cultural meaning of Tokyo Disneyland is also a long-term affair. Many of the distinctly Japanese characteristics of the park were absent when the gates were first thrown back. Learning is occurring on both sides of the cultural divide. Interestingly, EuroDisneyland, set to open in 1992 in Marne-La-Vallée, 32 kilometers east of Paris, is much less a duplicate of Disneyland in its design than Tokyo. Part of this difference is due to the insistence of the French government that the park will have a number of decidedly French touches and another part is due to Disney's own marketing work and best guesses as to what will play well with the 310 million Europeans within two hours' flight time of Paris. A result of this still-early culture flow is the transformation of Tomorrowland into Disco-veryland, reflective supposedly of the more ambivalent attitude Europeans take towards scientific progress compared with Americans, although Disneyland officials claim the change is being made to allow the park to make use of the tales of French author Jules Verne (Sassen 1989). In either case, a degree of cultural sensitivity seems to be operating in EuroDisneyland, so that the blending of culture may be more noticeable than is the case in Japan.

Third, not only are cultural meanings worked out rather differently in a new setting compared to the old (and such adaptation takes time) but, as culture flows continue, people on both sides of the border become more aware of their own culture (and its contradictions) as they increase their awareness of the other culture (and its contradictions). The traffic flow is messy but, as culture moves back and forth, people on both sides may discover new ways to do things that might not be apparent from either culture. People are not passive in relation to culture as if they merely receive it, transmit it or express it; they also create it, and new meanings may eventually emerge as cultures interpenetrate one another. The notions of family entertainment, safe thrills and urban leisure will surely never be the same in Japan since Tokyo Disneyland has appeared on the scene.[9] A recent poll in Japan, for example, reported that over 50 percent of the Japanese adults, when asked 'where they experienced their happiest moment in the last year', responded by saying, 'Tokyo Disneyland' (Iyer 1988).

On the other hand, the view that cultural influence moves strictly along the tracks of massification – mass media, mass production, mass marketing and mass consumerism – ushering in a global culture that spells the eclipse of national and local cultures is certainly discredited by Tokyo Disneyland. As anthropologists have long known, this view is naive to the point of banality. Although, as Westney (1988, p. 6) wisely notes, 'our understanding of the emulation process is painfully inadequate', we nonetheless know that the myth of inevitable conformity when culture flows are directed from a center outward is, whatever the level of analysis, just a myth.

A useful term that may have the correct connotations is suggested by Hannerz (1989) and Rosaldo (1989), who use the notion of 'creolization' to describe the ongoing historically cumulative interrelatedness between interacting cultures, in particular among cultures where one or several may at the moment have the upper hand in terms of social and economic power. Thus, although the dominant Disney parent had the clout to bring the subordinate Tokyo Disneyland to life, the daughter organization in our tale of two cultures infused the park with its unique and highly localized personality. Creolization may be a rough metaphor, but it nicely captures the fact that cultures, like languages, can be of mixed, rather than pure and highly distinct, character (Holm 1988, pp. 13–68). Creole cultures emerge and develop as people actively take part in bringing about a synthesis of codes such that cultural affinities between interacting people increase as each is better understood by the other, thus facilitating a passage of more cultural imports and exports: 'l'appetit vient en mangeant'. ('Appetite comes with eating'). With creolization, a kind of openendedness might hold so that participants in mixed cultural contexts need not sacrifice their social heritage or local knowledge but may become competent in an openended, multicultural enterprise that is marked by reciprocal cultural flows. The American and Japanese observe each other at Tokyo Disneyland (and Disneyland), and whereas the Americans may mythologize and learn from the splendid service provided at the park, the Japanese may honor and learn from the ingenuity and charm of the park design and attractions. In the process, both may open themselves up so that culture flows back and forth more freely, and new ways of doing things come forth.

THE STRUCTURE OF CULTURE

What does all this culture mongering about the amusement trade have to do with the altogether serious and usually grim MNC? We think, quite naturally, a good deal. The connection begins with the very definition of a multinational firm. To take an all-purpose definition: 'The MNC is the quintessential case of the dispersed firm with individual components located in a number of autonomous political units. These organizational sub-units or subsidiaries are often embedded in highly heterogeneous environmental conditions and have developed under very different historical circumstances' (Ghoshal and Nohria 1990, p. 322). Such a definition features complexity, differentiation and implicitly, at least, suggests a good deal of variation in terms of the relations that hold between and among organizational units of the center and the periphery. Cultural diversity is a given. Within this context, a good deal of debate takes place as to what structural form best suits the MNC, and in pursuing this question the debate takes into account a rather long (and growing) list of contingent conditions: market, industry, strategy, governmental policies, consumer trends, and so forth.

On this list is 'corporate culture' which, in terms of reach or range, can be seen to stretch from a weak to a strong culture. Strong cultures are those that allegedly limit subsidiary discretion; direct firm actions from the center; export similar management practices, products and administrative routines from corporate headquarters to subsidiaries; and, in general, exercise considerable control and discipline over the operations of all units comprising the firm. Weak cultures are presumably everything the strong cultures are not. Their principal characteristic would seem to be local autonomy and relative freedom for subsidiary units.

The appeal to managers, and to a degree to organizational theorists, of the so-called strong culture standing behind the MNC is obvious. An organization with a culture of its own that inspires loyalty to a common pursuit would presumably reduce local peculiarities, promote uniform practices and, most optimistically, transcend all those annoying, culturally induced behavioral differences that result from maintaining operational outposts throughout the world. In theory, strong cultures can be encouraged by a variety of mechanisms such as the regular and relatively swift rotation of personnel to and from the centre and around the subsidiaries, encouragement of long-term employment within the firm, extensive use of headquarters-programmed training and development activities to help build a strong sense of identity and commitment to the firm on the part of employees, common management systems for performance appraisal and reward practices, extensive international seminars that bring members of the periphery together regularly and enhance the spread of common objectives, the use of common language throughout the firm, and so forth. This is a sort of Holy Roman Empire version of the MNC such that if it operated according to plan, a marketing manager of, say, a corporation headquartered in Paris would feel just as comfortable working in Hong Kong, Nairobi or San Francisco. Ouchi's (1981b) dream of the 'clan' form of organization nicely conveys this strong-culture perspective.

At the other end of the continuum sit those MNCs supposedly sporting weak cultures at the center and thus promoting independence on the part of some, if not all, subsidiaries. Perlmutter's (1965) polycentric forms of organizing fall here and feature such characteristics as highly differentiated management practices across subsidiaries, low levels of personnel rotation, small corporate staffs, little sustained contact between headquarters and peripheral units, and so on. Loyalty adheres to the local unit to which one is assigned, and whatever attachments individuals have toward the MNC itself are primarily instrumental and calculative.

As implied by the mechanisms supposedly associated with each organizing mode, culture, strong or weak, is a matter of social engineering. Ethnocentricism – whether from the center or from the periphery – can be rooted out or built in. It is all really a matter of managerial choice. Even mixed modes or designer organizations especially tailored to meet global business demands are possible such that strong cultures with multiple centers – the 'postmodern, holographic, heterarchy' of Hedlund (1986) or Perlmutter's (1965) 'geocentric organization' – emerge as normative possibilities.

There is perhaps some truth to these ideas of managerial discretion. At the extreme one could in theory perhaps blow away annoying local peculiarities by staffing the outposts of all operations with functionaries from headquarters and then locking them up so that no contact and corruption of plans and practices could ooze in from the local sites. Or, conversely, one could lock out headquarters officials and dictates. Endless variations on these strategic designs can be (and are) put forth. All represent a rather tired working-out of the dubious postulates of structural-functionalism (a view arguing that similar structures produce similar behavior).

This functionalist perspective on the MNC overemphasizes form or appearances and pays inadequate attention to the meaning or substance of behavior. Our 'Mickey Goes to Tokyo' tale was put forth to try to undercut such a view. Culture is not social structure. To consider the proper structural configuration of the MNC in terms of the corporate culture seen to be encouraged by such a configuration or to situate the study of MNCs within a context that subordinates (or elevates) localism, ethnicity or national culture to macro-social forces such as authority systems, rationalization, universalization or market forces would be to rehash stale debates. We set out to deal with culture as it is symbolically constructed, represented, understood and used by a group. This sidesteps the definitional problems posed by a search for a structural model of the MNC as a specific form of social organization. Organizational structures do not in themselves provide meaning for people; this is why so many organizations designed to create culture or community as a cure for fragmentation, conflict, underachievement or alienation are doomed to failure.

Culture is an ordinary word that, when imported into organizational studies, causes enormous difficulty. A good part of this difficulty is that culture implies simultaneously both difference and similarity: a group of people who (1) have something in common with each other that (2) distinguishes them from other people. The use of the term is, in fact, always occasioned by the desire or need to express such a relational idea. Pushed into service in the world of organizations, boundary problems surface immediately. The problems are, for example, not simply, 'Are those working for company X different from those working for company Y?' but, 'How different is a company X engineer from another company X engineer?' In other words, is the boundary dividing one company from another more meaningful to an employee than the boundary that distinguishes him or her from another within the same firm or an engineer from a sales representative, or a field service engineer from one in product development, or a headquarters-based engineer from a Paris-based engineer, or a Paris-based engineer from a Tokyo-based engineer, and so on. As one moves 'down' the scale towards the domain of day-in and day-out associations, the referents of the boundary become less apparent to the outsider until they may become entirely invisible (Van Maanen and Barley 1984).

However, as one moves down, the referents may also become more important to company members for they relate increasingly to the more intimate parts of their life, and perhaps refer increasingly to the more substantial and experiential aspects of their cultural identities that are, in fact, multiple. Conversely, as one moves up the scale, culture is approached more as a rhetorical front. When CEOs refer to their firm as 'a family', or government leaders refer to the 'European Community', or British officials lay claim to the cohesion among Pakistanis, Scots,

Canadians, Welsh, Tanzanians and the English in the name of 'the Commonwealth', they may often be regarded as indulging in rhetoric and stating an aspiration that is all too obviously missing in what is commonly called reality. But when workers in a machine shop talk of 'their group', ride operators at Disneyland speak of 'their crew', stockbrokers mention 'their club' or R&D managers denote 'their project', they may refer to an entity, a felt reality, invested with all the sentiments attached to friendship, kinship, citizenship, colleagueship, neighborhood, familiarity, jealousy, envy and rivalry as they inform the social processes of everyday life. At this level, culture is more than an oratorical abstraction; it hinges crucially on feeling and consciousness.

CORPORATE CULTURE REVISITED

We would not argue that it is inappropriate to talk of corporate culture, but rarely will such a product and process refer to what is peddled to stockholders and the business press. Official versions of corporate culture usually emerge from a self-conscious managerial effort to discover and reconstruct a heritage and identity for the firm; perhaps it is part of a search for authenticity and a felt need to contrast one's own organization with others of too similar ilk. Such a history serves as a collective counterpart to individual memory, and both are highly selective renditions of the past. By claiming a culture, the past can be fumigated, cleaned up and an ever so nice history developed. As Sontag (1979, p. 22) writes, 'Just wait until now becomes then and you'll see how happy we were.' Corporate culture in this sense is little more than a version of how corporate officials would like their organization to appear. Using the culture construct to frame such efforts is often an attempt to legitimize a rather problematic claim.

More serious portraits of corporate cultures reveal a far more interesting, complicated and divisive world than that put forth by managerially loaded accounts.[10] Such studies increasingly focus on the 'organization of diversity' and present few portraits of womblike cultures surrounding an obedient society of saints. Culture in the raw is lively, contentious, unpredictable. Strong culture is achieved only by great efforts, and then it is problematic since strong culture flowing from the top (or center) may embargo progress, retard change or deny differences and, by filtering out undesirable elements, create a kind of collective blindness. Weak culture is more a matter of allowing cultures at levels below corporate headquarters to go their own way, sometimes in splendid isolation, coordinating activities only when precious resources are threatened. Culture is everywhere and always relevant in organizational life, but there is no obvious or natural level of analysis from which to observe.

Organizations, like societies, are sometimes mistakenly deemed to have a totality or consensus because of their small size, low level of structural differentiation, acceptance on the part of most of the group of a relatively few models of action, highly stable environments in which habits and routines continue to work well, and/or isolation from other groups. When culture emerges from face-to-face interaction among a group of people who, for example, do not move around much and have little contact with outsiders, it is simple to think of culture in consensual terms; too simple, in fact. Such a view is misleading because consensus is, in many ways, a form of death at the group level since it cannot provide a group with alternatives, dynamics or the imagination required for meeting shifting conditions. Culture is a differentiating device in organizations, a way of marking differences within and between groups all the way up and all the way down the analytic scale. Any social organization highly differentiated at the structural level – such as MNCs – but homogeneous on the level of culture would be emptied of all cultural meaning.

SOME FINAL WORDS

With this review in mind, what are we to make then of the role that culture plays in the MNC? Five points are worth making. First, the effect of culture on performance, particularly economic performance, is probably drastically overestimated. At the international level, for example, whatever country is on top at the moment seems always to make too much of it by moralizing about the cultural reasons for their own success (Fallows 1989). Until the last decade, Westerners observing East Asia usually concluded that its culture(s) could never adapt to modern industrial capitalism. Confucianism, the willingness to sublimate the individual's interest to the group, the role allowed to elders, the respect for the past – all traits now cited to explain the economic boom in East Asia – were used earlier to explain why these countries could never catch up. The once prominent psychologist David McClelland (1961) proposed (without reservation) that what many of these countries needed was a massive hit of 'N-ach' (an induced trait that would alleviate underdevelopment by indoctrinating natives with an 'achievement oriented' motivation). This doctrine is not far from some of the more simple-minded Bushisms, Thatcherisms or Reaganisms of more recent times, although such bromides are now directed more to the layabout natives of America or England than to the enterprising natives of Korea,

Japan or Taiwan. The tables have turned, and the West is today the recipient of stern lectures from its most Significant Others in the East as to how Westerners can recharge their economies by adopting some of the profound cultural wisdom of the East: for example, 'Stop loafing and get a job.' Similar discourse goes on in organizations as the worth of a corporate culture rises and falls with its economic success. The champ-to-chump transformation of many of those sterling corporate cultures celebrated by Peters and Waterman in 1982 – and mourned by Peters in 1987 – is a case in point.

Second, even if a correlation between economic performance and strong corporate culture were to exist, it is not clear what it might mean. Corporate culture in the MNC can be strong in at least two ways. One version contains all the elements of an old, colonial, ethnocentric model whereby the centre merely replicates itself in its subsidiaries. This model, like its close relatives in governmental, religious and military domains, seems always to contain the seeds of its own destruction. Another, more sophisticated, version suggests a sort of globalized corporate culture building on the cultural differences and knowledge represented in subsidiary operations but essentially transcending them by drawing all parts of the MNC together in pursuit of common goals. Such goals are not necessarily imposed from the center and shipped to the periphery, but develop from interaction among those in diverse sectors of the MNC. There are, of course, enormous practical and analytic difficulties with such a model, not the least being the very high level of abstraction at which it is cast. But such a model may very well represent the best advice available to the managers of MNCs given the fact that research on the cultural side of MNCs still remains largely on the science fiction side of the house.[11]

Third, to the extent that the above global model emphasizes the slow, mutual acquisition of culture rather than simply trying to ram culture down through the corporation by means of coercive persuasion, it holds certain possibilities and potential. Coercive persuasion as cultural transmission puts great faith in agents – mother's brother, corporate trainers, business schools, top managers, Miss Gootch of Public School 39 – and the design of socialization settings and processes through which an agent's work is supposedly accomplished (Schein 1961). Corporate culture as something to be propagated from on high and effectively transmitted throughout the organization would represent a rather time-less, well-specified body of knowledge that everyone in the organization should, in theory, know.[12]

A focus on the acquisition of culture suggests, however, that no one gets it all (or needs it all). Acquisition occurs throughout the organization on far less than a one-to-a-customer basis. The flow of culture is ongoing, part of the political, social and economic life within (and certainly beyond) the firm and therefore always moving in several directions at once. The distinctiveness of the organization is then a matter of degree as cultural affinities across domains may be discovered along, for example, product, professional, geographic, divisional or personal dimensions. A concern for the acquisition of culture also seems in keeping with the multinational character of MNCs where employees do not renounce their various cultural citizenships when coming to work for the firm, but add to their cultural experiences (and, presumably, competencies) and those of the organization as a result of their participation.

An example is useful in this regard. Consider the foreign graduate students who currently attend MIT and INSEAD. Although these students might not describe themselves as 'competent' in English or French or in mainstream North American or French culture, they obviously are able to 'get by' in English or French and routinely observe many of the local conventions of behavior in either place. More to the point, they are able to contribute to their respective organizations in ways that go well beyond merely parroting back what they are told in the classroom. Increasingly, the goals of these institutions reflect the interests of their diverse student bodies, and these interests are overlooked only at the institution's peril.

Fourth, as to the impact of MNCs on the societies in which they operate, even the transcendent, global, participative, sensitive and cheerful MNC raises problems that cannot be casually dismissed. MNCs are powerful and resourceful actors on the world's stage, and they do disrupt, alter and influence the patterns of culture wherever they operate. So powerful are they that continuing to think in national terms may be a mistake. After all, capital now moves on computers across borders as if such entities as Japan, France, Brazil and the USA did not exist. In this global moment, perhaps it is foolish to worry about societal labels when Toyota meets the payroll in Tennessee and MacDonalds opens fast-food concessions in Beijing. The world is perhaps turning into one big marketplace, and the Great Wall is on its way to becoming the Great Mall.

MNCs clearly contribute to this process. As emissaries of the industrialized world, they spread a commodified culture everywhere. But Disney, as a cultural emissary from America, did not succeed – if, indeed, it cared – in subordinating the Japanese with Tokyo Disneyland. Our story shows evidence of little cultural erosion in Japan. But again, this tale has just one of many possible outcomes and we must be careful not to make too much of it, for the Japanese certainly possess the resources to preserve and protect their culture(s). This may not be true elsewhere if there are drastic imbalances in the resources of interacting parties. Were Disney, for some fanciful reason, to build a park in Burma or Equatorial Guinea, the local population might not be as able to recontextualize the meanings of Disneyland as the Japanese and might thus be swept away in an unceasing Americanization process to the delight of the homogenization theorist.

We doubt such a result. The resilience of culture constructed from a people's history, customs, and the materials of their everyday life throughout the world is not to be denied. Recontextualization may well be less predictable or effective than outright rejection. The resurgence of ethnic, religious, and national identities in the wake of colonialism and repression is one of the most obvious global trends in the late twentieth century. Perhaps such resurgence and the resulting differentiation and self-consciousness among cultures can be managed so that all cultures learn from each other and, slowly but surely through contact, exchange and an emergent form of creolization, grow more comfortable with one another. This might allow a kind of post-modern 'Utopia of differences' to be established on a global basis. Is this Utopia possible? This is as MacCannell (1976: xiv) notes, really a question for Professors Derrida, Lyotard and Baudillard. But since an answer (and a conclusion) is only a few keystrokes away, we shall provide one here. It is our fifth and final point.

Our sense is that whatever a Utopia of differences might mean and produce, it would ultimately depend on the ability of people of differing cultures to enter into a very deep dialogue with one another on an entirely equal footing. If, for example, the problems of an MNC are seen as obstacles that separate people of distinct cultural backgrounds and these obstacles are then treated first and foremost as objects of analysis to be understood rather than ignored, squashed, pushed aside or otherwise bulldozed over, then the possibility emerges that a deconstruction of cultures – 'ours' as well as 'theirs' – can occur, and a reconstruction based on the authentic and appreciated differences between and among people can develop. In this way, MNCs might contribute to the emergence of a world culture that reflects such a Utopia of differences.

This, alas, we think highly unlikely to take place anywhere, let alone within an MNC. The MNC is not in the deconstruction business. It operates in differing regions of the world for gain, not study. It operates by choice on those who often have no choice. As long as the idea of a common goal originating in some center and moving outward pervades the MNC, differences are likely to continue to be ignored, denied, covered up and otherwise regarded in mostly unfavorable terms. Such differences will continue to exist, of course, and will play themselves out in a variety of ways, but they will not be seen as a source of fundamental value and a mark of our common condition. There may be ways to manage these differences more respectfully and with perhaps greater appreciation as to what they may contribute to the organization as a whole. However, without confronting and altering the sense of self and other that runs deep and virtually everywhere in the MNC, such differences will not be understood.

Notes

1. Our view follows the 'interpretive turn' taken by many students of culture over the past twenty or so years. This perspective is set forth nicely by Geertz (1973) and is broadened by Rabinow and Sullivan (1987) and Rosaldo (1989). Such a view highlights the difficulties posed for native and analyst alike in 'reading' culture and thus treats culture as considerably more problematic, contentious and varied than earlier approaches. One result of this shift is that the functionalist view of a given social structure is seldom seen in current sociological or anthropological work beyond the four-color introductory textbooks. The functionalist view, emphasizing the 'replication of uniformity' approach to culture has given way to a more particularistic 'organization of diversity' approach to culture, wherein attention is paid to the contrasting habits, motives, customs, and so forth that coexist within or mark group boundaries (Wallace 1970). One implication to be drawn from recent cultural studies is that the homogeneity and monolithic nature of culture as portrayed in the classic ethnographic monographs was probably overdone (Marcus and Fischer 1986; Clifford 1988). Especially pertinent to the materials presented here is the observation that the common-denominator people so prevalent in the classic ethnographic texts on the remote and isolated societies of the world have become far less prevalent in contemporary texts since ethnographers have moved closer to home to do their work, where they perhaps know more of what is going on around them. Like the natives they study, current ethnographers have great difficulty stuffing the knowledge they gain of 'others' into simple categories. A brief summary of some of the twists and turns in ethnographic thought and practice is found in Van Maanen (1988, pp. 13–44).
2. A list of studies in this domain would be long indeed. Recent exemplary monographs within the relatively narrow range of organization studies include Jackell's (1988) treatment of US corporate managers; Biggart's (1989) look at direct sales organizations; Traweek's (1988) comparative analysis of how high-energy physics is conducted in the USA and Japan; and Halle's (1984) close study of a New Jersey chemical plant. Classic examples of such work are found in Gouldner (1954), Dalton (1959), and Becker *et al.* (1961).
3. Recent exemplars in this realm are not hard to locate. Some favorites of ours in the organizational studies domain include Gusfield's (1981) decoding of drunk driving enforcement practices in the USA, Latour's (1987) reading of the products of laboratory science, and Yates's (1989)

historical treatment of the social consequences of various office technologies. Broader examples of interpretive cultural work include Sahlins (1981), Leach (1976), and Wallace (1978). A good general introduction to this side of the cultural studies house in sociology is found in Becker and McCall (1990).

4. Notable exceptions include Manning's (1989) concern for the causes and consequences of the codes and practices of police dispatchers, Becker's (1982) treatment of the multiple worlds supporting the craft and social production of art, and MacCannel's (1976) wonderful ethnographic reading of modern tourists, tourist sites and the rapidly growing tourist industry. It is also worth noting in this regard that journalists are often interested in matching cultural practices to cultural products. Consider, for example, the social world created by trying to beat Las Vegas roulette as revealed by Bass (1985), the late 1960s life of the high-church priests of hippiedom and acid as chronicled by Wolfe (1968), and what 'getting-out-in-front-of-the-price-performance-curve' in the computer industry means to those who engineer the product as told by Kidder (1981). All three of these journalistic examinations involve a good deal of fieldwork and acute sensitivity to both sides of the cultural studies division identified in the text.

5. Global homogenization as played out in the MNC is something of an imperialistic call to order issued by headquarters. An unintentionally insightful example of just such a process is provided by Kuin's (1972) look at 'Unileverization', where the key to Unilever's economic success worldwide is said to be the adoption of a common language throughout the firm (English), intensive training, standard reporting formats, regular rotation of managers around the world, common goals and operating practices across subsidiaries, and the provision of long-term employment contracts for managerial and professional staff.

6. Global heterogeneity as cultural resistance no doubt takes many forms. In the case of the MNC it is perhaps best thought of as a noticeable drift by subsidiary units away from directions sought by headquarters. Such drift may be intentional or unintentional but the result is a degree of operational autonomy for subsidiary organizations. The management literature typically treats such drift as nearly pathological. It is ordinarily seen as a troubling problem about which something ought to be done (immediately). That so much attention is devoted to trying to regulate such drift suggests that the global heterogeneity scenario sketched out in the text is more than the wishful dream of those academic culture watchers who, it seems, are forever rooting for diversity. (See, for example, Edstrom and Galbraith (1977), Jaeger (1983), and Montagna (1990) for illustrative studies of policies and practices designed to increase the control of headquarters over drift-prone subsidiaries in the MNC).

7. The analysis that follows in the text is based on a number of methods, none of which are to be found in any respectable method textbook. Some are altogether opportunistic and retrospective, such as the lead author's 2½ year work stint as a ride operator at Disneyland in the late 1960s, his periodic visits to the US park(s), and, most recently, his three-day visit to Tokyo Disneyland devoted to checking out the 'findings' reported here. Although this sort of research-in-reverse is not recommended as a general

fieldwork strategy, it did prove valuable in this case and allowed a certain amount of representational fine tuning to develop in its wake. Mary Yoko Brannon helped mastermind this flying visit to Tokyo Disneyland in December 1990 and deserves a good deal of credit for whatever success was obtained. Former Tokyo Disneyland skyway operator and current University of Tokyo sociology student Yoji Inowa proved a skilful translator and guide in and out of the park. There is a good deal written about Disneyland, DisneyWorld, Tokyo Disneyland and Euro-Disneyland. We have drawn liberally from these materials as noted in the text and footnotes. A small part of the materials reported here was presented at the American Anthropological Association Annual Meeting in Washington, DC on 16 November 1989, at a session titled 'The Magic Kingdom' and organized by Maria Lydia Spinelli (see Van Maanen 1989).

8. Among the more engaging and challenging interpretations of the myth, magic, and mystery of Disneyland not mentioned in the text are Britton (1989), Eco (1986, pp. 20–56), Moore (1980), Real (1977, pp. 44–90), Shearling and Stenning (1985), Spinelli (1987) and Wolf (1979). This is but a drop in a very large bucket.

9. On this point, a sort of global tidal wave is seemingly building, since the amusement trade is growing very rapidly at the moment. Nine parks (including EuroDisneyland) are scheduled to open in Europe over the next few years. Japan has recently opened Sanrio Puroland ('Hello Kitty') and Tokyo Sesame Street. Sonyland is not far off in the future. Korea's Lotte World opened outside Seoul in March 1990. The current scramble to break the bank in the theme park business is reminiscent of the amusement boom that struck the USA just after Disneyland first opened to wild (and unanticipated) success. The boom was shortlived. Most of the parks built during that period have long since closed their gates. (See Kyriazi 1981.)

10. Of some studies we have not previously mentioned, Crozier (1964), Rohlen (1974), Buroway (1979), Powell (1985), Kunda (forthcoming) and Martin (forthcoming) are representative of rather complex 'corporate culture' portraits. Several anthologies have recently appeared containing a good deal of brief but inventive work: see, for example, Gagliardi (1990) and Jones, Moore and Snyder (1988).

11. There are, of course, enormous difficulties involved in conducting intensive, in-depth cultural studies of transnational organizations. Their intimidating size and geographic spread makes traditional ethnographic techniques appear helplessly inadequate. At the moment, however, the development of business case studies seems to be far and away the most common approach bearing evidence of the cultural character of the MNC. This situation should perhaps wake slumbering ethnographers for, however inadequate they may feel exploring the turf of the MNC, their methods are far superior to the reliance of most case writers on a plant tour, an overnight visit, a handful of interviews and the sanguine collection of company-produced documents.

12. This model assumes that culture can be transmitted in a reasonably uniform way such that individuals are either socialized or not. If socialized, the idea is that they will all behave in the same way under the same circumstances (Van Maanen and Schein 1979). Culture is

therefore provided on a one-to-a-customer basis, and customers have little choice as to what to accept or reject. Culture comes as a package deal. It is the case, however, that no one learns a culture in quite the same way, even within a single cultural tradition (T. Schwartz 1981; Wolcott 1982). Recognition of the inevitable slippage in any socialization programme has pushed theorists toward an 'acquisition' rather than 'transmission' model of cultural learning (Ochs 1988; Wolcott 1990).

References

Abolafia, M. L. and Kilduff, M. (1988) 'Enacting Market Crisis: The Social Construction of a Speculative Bubble', *Administrative Science Quarterly*, 33:2, pp. 177–193.

Ackoff, R. L. and Emery, F. E. (1972) *On Purposeful Systems* (Chicago: Aldine).

Ackoff, R. L. (1974) *Redesigning the Future* (New York: John Wiley).

Adams, J. S. (1965) 'Inequity in social exchange', in L. Berkowitz (ed.), *Advances in Experimental Social Psychology*, 2 (New York: Academic Press).

Aharoni, Y. (1960) *The Foreign Investment Decision Process* (Boston, Mass.: Harvard Graduate School of Business Administration).

Alchian, A. and Demsetz, H. (1972) 'Production, Information Costs, and Economic Organization', *American Economic Review*, 62, pp. 777–95.

Aldrich, Howard E. (1972) 'An organization–environment perspective on cooperation and conflict in the manpower training system', in Rosemary C. Sarri and Yeheskel Hasenfeld (eds), *The Management of Human Services* (New York: Columbia University Press).

Aldrich, H. E. (1976) 'Resource Dependence and Interorganizational Relations: Relations Between Local Employment Service Offices and Social Service Sector Organizations', *Administration and Society*, 7, pp. 419–54.

Aldrich, H. E. (1979) *Organizations and Environments* (Englewood Cliffs, NJ: Prentice-Hall).

Aldrich, H. E. and Whetten, D. (1981) 'Organization-Sets, Action-Sets, and Networks: Making the Most of Simplicity', in P. C. Nystrom and W. H. Starbuck (eds), *Handbook of Organizational Design* (London: Oxford University Press) pp. 385–408.

Aldrich, H. E. and Pfeffer, J. (1976) 'Environments of Organizations', *Annual Review of Sociology*, 2, pp. 79–105.

Aldrich, H. E., and Marsden, P. V. (1988) 'Environments and Organizations', in Neil J. Smelser (ed.), *Handbook of Sociology* (Newbury Park, Calif.: Sage Publications) pp. 361–92.

Alexander, S. and Ruderman, M. (1987) 'The role of procedural and distributive justice in organizational behavior', *Social Justice Research*, 1, pp. 177–98.

Allen, T. J. (1978) *Managing the Flow of Technology: Technology Transfer and the Dissemination of Technological Information within the Research and Development Organization* (Cambridge, Mass.: MIT Press).

Allison, P. D. (1984) *Event History Analysis: Regression for Longitudinal Event Data* (Beverly Hills, Calif.: Sage Publications).

Anderson, E. and Coughlan, A. T. (1987) 'International Market Entry and Expansion via Independent or Integrated Channels', *Journal of Marketing*, 51, pp. 71–82.

Anderson, E. and Gatignon, H. (1986) 'Modes of Foreign Entry: A Transaction Cost Analysis and Propositions', *Journal of International Business Studies*, 17–3, pp. 1–26.

Anderson, E. and Oliver, R. (1987) 'Perspectives on Behavior-based versus Outcome-Based Salesforce Control Systems', *Journal of Marketing*, 51, pp. 76–88.

Ansoff, H. I. (1965) *Corporate Strategy, an Analytic Approach to Business Policy for Growth and Expansion* (New York: McGraw-Hill).

Anthony, R. and Dearden, J. (1980) *Management Control Systems* (Homewood, Ill.: Irwin).

Aoki, M. (1988) *Information, Incentives, and Bargaining in the Japanese Economy* (Cambridge University Press).

Argyris, C. and Schon, D. A. (1978) *Organizational Learning* (Reading, Mass.: Addison-Wesley).

Arpan, J. S., and Ricks, D. A. (1986) 'Foreign Direct Investment in the U.S., 1974–1984', *Journal of International Business Studies*, 17–3, pp. 149–154.

Arrow, K. J. (1974) *The Limits of Organization* (New York: Norton).

Arrow, K. J. (1985) 'The Economics of Agency', in J. W. Pratt and R. J. Zeckhauser (eds), *Principal and Agents: The Structure of Business* (Boston, Mass: Harvard Business School Press), pp. 37–54.

Astley, W. G. and van de Ven, A. H. (1983) 'Central Perspectives and Debates in Organization Theory', *Administrative Science Quarterly*, 28, pp. 265–73.

Bacharach, S. B. and Aiken, M. (1976) 'Structural and Process Constraints on Influence in Organizations: A Level Specific Analysis', *Administrative Science Quarterly*, 21, pp. 623–42.

Bahrami H. and Evans, S. (1987) 'Stratocracy in High Technology Firms. Special Issue on Organizational Approaches to Strategy', *California Management Review*, 30:1, pp. 51–66.

Baliga, R. and Jaeger, A. (1984) 'Multinational Corporations: Control Systems and Delegation Issues', *Journal of International Business Studies*, 15:3, pp. 25–40.

Barley, S. R. (1983) 'Semiotics and the Study of Occupational and Organizational Cultures', *Administrative and Science Quarterly*, 28, pp. 393–413.

Barley, S. R. (1986) 'Technology as an occasion for structuring: Evidence from observations of CT scanners and the social order of radiology departments', *Administrative Science Quarterly*, 31, pp. 78–108.

Barley, S. R., Meyer, G. W. and Gash, D. C. (1988) 'Cultures of Culture: Academics, Practitioners, and the Prag-matics of normative control', *Administrative Science Quarterly*, 33, pp. 24–60.

Barney, J. and Ouchi, W. (1986) *Organizational Economics* (San Francisco: Jossey-Bass).

Barrett-Howard, E. and Tyler, T. R. (1986) 'Procedural Justice as a Criterion in Allocation Decisions', *Journal of Personality and Social Psychology*, 50, pp. 296–304.

Bartlett, C. A. (1979) 'Multinational Structural Evolution: The Changing Decision Environment in International Divisions', unpublished doctoral dissertation, Harvard Business School.

Bartlett, C. A. (1981) 'Multinational Structural Change: Evolution Versus Reorganization', in L. Otterbeck (ed.), *The Management of Headquarters–Subsidiary Relationships in Multinational Corporations* (Aldershot: Gower) pp. 121–46.

Bartlett, C. A. (1983) 'MNCs: Get Off the Reorganization Merry-Go-Round', *Harvard Business Review*, 61:2, pp. 138–46.

Bartlett, C. A. (1986) 'Building and Managing the Transnational: The New Organizational Challenge', in M. E. Porter (ed.), *Competition in Global Industries* (Boston, Mass.: Harvard Business School Press) pp. 367–404.

Bartlett, C. A., Doz, Y. and Hedlund, G. (eds) (1990) *Managing the Global Firm* (London: Routledge & Kegan Paul).

Bartlett, C. A. and Ghoshal, S. (1986) 'Tap Your Subsidiaries for Global Reach', *Harvard Business Review*, 64:6, pp. 87–94.

Bartlett, C. A. and Ghoshal, S. (1989) *Managing Across Borders: The Transnational Solution* (Boston, Mass.: Harvard Business School Press).

Bartlett, C. A. and Ghoshal, S. (1990) 'Matrix Management: Not a Structure, A Frame of Mind', *Harvard Business Review*, 68:4, pp. 138–45.

Bass, T. A. (1985) *The Eudaemonic Pie* (Boston, Mass.: Houghton Mifflin).

Bavelas, A. (1951) 'Communication Patterns in Task-Oriented Groups', in D. Lerner and H. D. Lasswell (eds), *The Policy Sciences* (Stanford University Press) pp. 193–202.

Bayley, D. (1976) *Forces of Order* (Berkeley, Calif.: University of California Press).

Becker, H. S., Greer, B., Hughes, E. C. and Strauss, A. (1961) *Boys in White* (University of Chicago Press).

Becker, H. S. (1982) 'Culture', *Yale Review*, 71, pp. 513–28.

Becker, H. S. and McCall, M. M. (1990) *Symbolic Interaction and Cultural Studies* (University of Chicago Press).

Beer, M. and Davis, S. (1976) 'Creating a Global Organization, Failures Along the Way', *Columbia Journal of World Business*, 11:2, pp. 72–84.

Bendix, R. (1956) *Work and Authority in Industry* (Berkeley, Calif.: University of California Press).

Benedict, R. (1946) *The Chrysanthemum and the Sword* (University of Chicago Press).

Benson, J. K. (1975) 'The Interorganizational Network as a Political Economy', *Administrative Science Quarterly*, 20, pp. 229–49.

Bettenhausen, K. L. and Murnighan, J. K. (1985) 'The Emergence of Norms in Competitive Decision Making Groups', *Administrative Science Quarterly*, 30, pp. 350–72.

Bies, R. J., and Shapiro, D. L. (1987) 'Interactional Fairness Judgements: The influence of causal accounts', *Social Justice Research*, 1, pp. 199–218.

Biggart, N. W. (1989) *Charismatic Capitalism* (University of Chicago Press).

Birnbaum, S. (1989) *Steve Birnbaum's Guide of Disneyland* (Boston, Mass.: Houghton Mifflin).

Blainey, G. (1984) 'The History of Multinational Factories in Australia', in A. Okochi and T. Inoue (eds), *Overseas Business Activities, Proceedings of the Fuji Conference* (University of Tokyo Press).

Blau, P. M. (1968) 'The Hierarchy of Authority in Organizations', *American Sociological Review*, 33, pp. 453–67.

Blau, P. M. (1970) 'A Formal Theory of Differentiation in Organizations', *American Sociological Review*, 35, pp. 201–18.

Blau, P. M. and Scott, W. R. (1962) *Formal Organizations* (San Francisco: Chandler).

Boddewyn, J. J. (1988) 'Political Aspects of MNE Theory', *Journal of International Business Studies*, 19:3, pp. 341–63.

Bohn, R. (1988) 'Learning in Noisy Manufacturing Environments: An Alternative to the Learning Curve', Working Paper No. 88-070 (Harvard Business School).

Bourgeois, J. (1979) 'Toward a Method of Middle-Range Theorizing', *Academy of Management Review*, 4:3, pp. 443-47.

Bouvier, P. L. (1984) 'Subjectivity and the Concept of Hierarchy: The Dominant Paradigm and the Prevailing Work System', in *Proceedings from the International Conference of the Society for General Systems Research*, June (New York).

Bower, J. L. (1970) *Managing the Resource Allocation Process* (Boston, Mass.: Harvard Business School Division of Research).

Bower, J. L. (1987) *When Markets Quake* (Boston, Mass.: Harvard Business School Press).

Boyacigilier, N. and Adler, N. (1991) 'The Parochial Dinosaur: Organizational Science in a Global Context', *Academy of Management Review*, 16-2, pp. 262–90.

Boyd, B. K. and McSween, C. B. (1988) 'Once More into the Breach: A Meta-analytic Review of the Relationship between Strategic Planning and Performance', Paper presented at the Annual Meeting of the Western Academy of Management (Big Sky, Mass. March 24–26).

Boyd, R. and Richerson, P. (1985) *Culture and the Evolutionary Process* (University of Chicago Press).

Brannon, M. Y. (1990) ' "Bwana Mickey": Constructing Cultural Consumption at Tokyo Disneyland', unpublished paper, School of Management, University of Massachusetts, Amherst.

Britton, D. (1989) 'The Dark Side of Disneyland', *Art Issues*, 4, pp. 13–22; 5, pp. 3–17.

Brockner, J., Grover, S., Reed, T., DeWitt, R., and O'Malley, M. (1987) 'Survivors' Reactions to Layoffs: We Get By with a Little Help from Our Friends,' *Administrative Science Quarterly*, 32-4, pp. 526–41.

Brooke, M. Z. and Remmers, H. L. (1970) *The Strategy of Multinational Enterprise* (New York: Elsevier).

Brown, M. and Philips, P. (1986) 'The Decline of the Piece-Rate System in California Canning', *Business History Review*, 60, pp. 564–601.

Brown, N. O. (1947) *Hermes the Thief: Evolution of a Myth* (Madison: University of Wisconsin).

Buckley, P. J. (1988) 'The Limits of Explanation – Testing the Internalization Theory of the Multinational Enterprises', *Journal of International Business Studies*, 19, pp. 181–93.

Buckley, P. J. and Casson, M. (1976) *The Future of the Multinational Enterprise* (London: Macmillan).

Buckley, P. J. and Casson, M. (1986) *The Economic Theory of the Multinational Enterprise* (London: Macmillan).

Burenstam Linder, S. (1961) *An Essay on Trade and Transformation* (New York: Wiley).

Burns, Tom and Stalker, G. M. (1961) *The Management of Innovations* (London: Tavistock).

Buroway, M. (1979) *Manufacturing Consent* (University of Chicago Press).

Burt, R. S. (1978) 'Stratification and Prestige Among Elite Experts in Mathematical Sociology Circa 1975', *Social Networks*, 1, pp. 105–58.

Burt, R. S. (1987) 'Social Contagion and Innovation: Cohesion Versus Structural Equivalence', *American Journal of Sociology*, 92, pp. 1287–335.

Burt, R. S., Minor, M. J. and Associates (eds) (1983) *Applied Network Analysis: A Methodological Introduction* (Beverly Hills, Calif.: Sage Publications).

Calvet, A. L. (1981) 'A Synthesis of Foreign Direct Investment Theories and Theories of the Multinational Firm', *Journal of International Business Studies*, Spring–Summer, pp. 43–59.

Camacho, A. and Persky, J. J. (1988) 'The Internal Organization of Complex Teams', *Journal of Economic Behavior and Organization*, 9, pp. 367–80.

Cantwell, J. (1989) *Technological Innovations and Multinational Corporations* (Cambridge: Basil Blackwell).

Capon, N., Christodoulou, C., Farley, J. U. and Hulbert, J. M. (1987) 'A Comparative Analysis of the Strategy and Structure of United States and Australian Corporations', *Journal of International Business Studies*, 8, pp. 51–74.

Carley, K. (1986) 'An Approach for Relating Social Structure to Cognitive Structure', *Journal of Mathematical Sociology*, 12:2, pp. 137–89.

Carlzon, J. (1985) *Riv Pyramiderna* (Stockholm: AB Bonniers).

Carroll, G. R. (1983) 'Dynamic Analysis of Discrete Dependent Variables: A Didactic Essay', *Quality and Quantity*, 17, pp. 425–60.

Carroll, G. R. (1984) 'The Specialist Strategy', *California Management Review*, 3, pp. 126–37.

Carroll, G. R. (ed.) (1988) *Ecological Models of Organizations* (Cambridge, Mass.: Ballinger).

Carroll, G. R. and Delacroix, J. (1982) 'Organizational Mortality in the News-paper Industries of Argentina and Ireland: An Ecological Approach', *Administrative Science Quarterly*, 27, pp. 169–98.

Carroll, G. R., Delacroix, J. and Goodstein, J. (1988) 'The Political Environments of Organizations: An Ecological View', in B. M. Staw and L. L. Cummings (eds), *Research in Organizational Behavior*, vol. 10, pp. 359–92 (Greenwich: JA1).

Casper, J. D., Tyler, T. R., and Fisher, B. (1988) 'Procedural Justice in Felony Cases', *Law and Society Review*, 22, pp. 483–507.

Casson, M. (1987) *The Firm and the Market* (Cambridge, Mass.: MIT Press).

Caves, R. E. (1971) 'International Corporations: The Industrial Economics of Foreign Direct Investment', *Economica*, 38, pp. 1–27.

Caves, R. E. (1982) *Multinational Enterprise and Economic Analysis* (Cambridge University Press).

Caves, R. E., Crookell, H. and Killing, J. P. (1982) 'The Imperfect Market for Technology Licenses', *Oxford Bulletin of Economics and Statistics*, 45:3, pp. 249–67.

Caves, R. E. and Mehra, K. (1986) 'Entry of Foreign Multinationals into U.S. Manufacturing Industries', in Porter, M. E. (ed.), *Competition in Global Industries*, pp. 449–82 (Boston, Mass.: Harvard Business School Press).

Chakravarthy, B. S. and Kwun, S. (1989) 'The Strategy-Making Process: An Organizational Learning Perspective', Working Paper, University of Minnesota Strategic Management Research Center.

Chandler, A. (1962) *Strategy and Structure: Chapters in the History of the American Industrial Enterprise* (Cambridge, Mass: The MIT Press).

Chandler, A. (1977) *The Visible Hand: The Managerial Revolution in American Business* (Cambridge, Mass.: Harvard University Press).

Chandler, A. (1986) 'The Evolution of Modern Global Competition', in M. E. Porter (ed.), *Competition in Global Industries* (Boston, Mass.: Harvard Business School Press) pp. 405–48.

Chandler, A. (1990) *Scale and Scope: The Dynamics of Industrial Capitalism* (Cambridge, Mass.: Harvard University Press).

Chandler, A. and Daems, Herman (eds) (1980) *Managerial Hierarchies: Comparative Perspectives on the Rise of the Modern Industrial Enterprise* (Cambridge, Mass.: Harvard University Press).

Channon, D. F. (1973) *The Strategy and Structure of British Enterprises* (Boston, Mass.: Division of Research, Graduate School of Business, Harvard University).

Child, J. (1973) 'Strategies of Control and Organizational Behavior', *Administrative Science Quarterly*, 18, pp. 1–17.

Clark, G. (1984) 'Authority and Efficiency: The Labor Market and the Managerial Revolution of the Late Nineteenth Century', *Journal of Economic History*, 44:4, pp. 1069–83.

Clifford, J. (1988) *The Predicament of Culture* (Cambridge, Mass.: Harvard University Press).

Cole, R. E. (1978) 'The Late-Developer Hypothesis: An Evaluation of its Relevance for Japanese Employment Patterns', *Journal of Japanese Studies*, 4-2, pp. 247–65.

Coleman, J. S. (1966) 'Foundations for a Theory of Collective Decisions', *American Journal of Sociology*, 71, pp. 615–27.

Contractor, F. J. and Lorange, P. (1988) *Cooperative Strategies in International Business* (Lexington, Mass.: Lexington Books).

Cook, K. S. (1977) 'Exchange and Power in Networks of Interorganizational Relations', *Sociological Quarterly*, 18, pp. 62–82.

Cook, K. S., Emerson, R. M., Gilmore, M. R. and Yamashigi, T. (1983) 'The Distribution of Power in Exchange Networks: Theory and Experimental Results', *American Journal of Sociology*, 89, pp. 275–305.

Crozier, M. (1964) *The Bureaucratic Phenomenon* (University of Chicago Press).

Crozier, M. and Friedberg, E. (1980) *Actors and Systems: The Politics of Collective Action* (University of Chicago Press).

Cvar, M. R. (1986) 'Case Study in Global Competition: Patterns of Success and Failure', in M. E. Porter (ed.), *Competition in Global Industries* (Boston, Mass.: Harvard Business School Press) pp. 483–515.

Cyert, R. M., and March, J. G. (1963) *A Behavioral Theory of the Firm* (Englewood Cliffs, NJ: Prentice Hall).

Daft, R. L. and Macintosh, N. B. (1981) 'A Tentative Exploration Into the Amount and Equivocality of Information Processing in Organizational Work Units', *Administrative Science Quarterly*, 26:2, pp. 207–24.

Daft, R. L. and Lengel, R. H. (1986) 'Organizational Information Requirements, Media Richness and Structural Design', *Management Science*, 32:5, pp. 554–71.

Daft, R. L. and Weick, K. E. (1989) 'Toward a Model of Organizations as Interpretation Systems', *Academy of Management Review*, 9:3, pp. 284–95.

Dahl, R. (1957) 'The Concept of Power', *Behavioral Science*, 2, pp. 201–15.

Dalton, M. (1959) *Men Who Manage* (New York: John Wiley).

Daniels, J. D., Pitts, R. A. and Tretter, M. J. (1984) 'Strategy and Structure of U.S. Multinationals: An Exploratory Study', *Academy of Management Journal*, 27:2, pp. 292–307.

Daniels, J. D., Pitts, R. A. and Tretter, M. J. (1985) 'Organizing for Dual Strategies of Product Diversity and International Expansion', *Strategic Management Journal*, 6, pp. 223–37.

Davidson, D. (1989) *Corporate Culture and Organizational Effectiveness* (San Francisco: Jossey-Bass).

Davidson, W. H. (1976) 'Patterns of Factor-saving Innovation in the Industrialized World', *European Economic Review*, 8, pp. 207–17.

Davidson, W. H. (1980) 'The Location of Foreign Direct Investment Activity: Country Characteristics and Experience Effects', *Journal of International Business Studies* 12, pp. 9–22.

Davidson, W. H. and Haspeslagh, P. (1982) 'Shaping a Global Product Organization', *Harvard Business Review*, pp. 125–32.

Davis, S. (1974) 'Two Models of Organization: Unity of Command vs. Balance of Power', *Sloan Management Review*, 16:1, pp. 29–40.

Davis, S. and Lawrence, P. R. (1977) *Matrix* (Reading, Mass.: Addison-Wesley).

Dawkins, R. (1986) *The Blind Watchmaker* (Harlow: Longman).

Deal, T. E. and Kennedy, A. A. (1982) *Corporate Cultures* (Reading, Mass.: Addison-Wesley).

Delacroix, J. and Carroll, G. (1983) 'Organizational Foundings: An Ecological Study of the Newspaper Industries of Argentina and Ireland', *Administrative Science Quarterly*, 28, pp. 274–91.

Delacroix, J., Swaminathan, A. and Solt, M. E. (1989) 'Density Dependence versus Population Dynamics: An Ecological Study of Failings in the California Wine Industry', *American Sociological Review*, 54, pp. 245–62.

Demsetz, H. (1988) 'The Theory of the Firm Revisited', *Journal of Law, Economics, and Organization*, 4:1, pp. 141–61.

Depew, D. J., and Weber, B. H. (eds) (1985) *Evolution at a Crossroads: The New Biology and the New Philosophy of Science* (Cambridge, Mass.: The MIT Press).

Depke, D. (1989) 'Suddenly, Software Houses have a Big Blue Buddy', *Business Week*, 3118, 7 August, pp. 68–9.

Deutsch, K. (1966) *The Nerves of Government: Models of Political Communication and Control* (New York: Free Press).

DiMaggio, P. J. (1986) 'Structural Analysis of Organizational Fields: A Blockmodel Approach', *Research in Organizational Behavior*, 8, pp. 335–70.

DiMaggio, P. J. (1988) 'Interest and Agency in Institutional Theory', in Lynne G. Zucker (ed.), *Institutional Patterns and Organizations: Culture and Environment* (Cambridge, Mass.: Ballinger).

DiMaggio, P. (1990) 'Cultural Aspects of Economic Action', in R. Friedland and A. F. Robertson (eds) *Beyond the Marketplace* (Chicago, Ill.: Aldine).

DiMaggio, P. J. and Powell, W. W. (1983) 'The Iron Cage Revisited: Institutional Isomorphism and Collective Rationality in Organizational Fields', *American Sociological Review*, 48, pp. 147–60.

DiMaggio, P. J. and Powell, W. W. (1991) *The New Institutionalism in Organizational Analysis* (University of Chicago Press).

Dionysius, the Pseudo-Areopagite (1981) *The Ecclesistical Hierarchy*, translated and annotated by Thomas L. Campbell (Lanham, Md: University Press of America).

Dobbin, F. R., Edelman, L., Meyer, J. W., Scott, W. R. and Swidler, A. (1988) 'The Expansion of Due Process in Organizations', in L. G. Zucker (ed.), *Institutional Patterns and Organizations: Culture and Environment* (Cambridge, Mass.: Ballinger).

Donnellon, A., Gray, B. and Bougon, M. G. (1985) 'Communication, Meaning, and Organized Action', *Administrative Science Quarterly*, 31, pp. 43–55.

Dore, R. P. (1973) *British Factory Japanese Factory* (Berkeley: University of California Press).

Dore, R. P. (1983) 'Goodwill and the Spirit of Market Capitalism'; *British Journal of Sociology*, 34:4, pp. 459–82.

Dore, R. (1987) *Taking Japan Seriously* (Stanford University Press).

Dorfman, A. and Matterlart, A. (1975) *How to Read Donald Duck* (New York: International General).

Douglas, M. (1966) *Purity and Danger* (London: Routledge & Kegan Paul).

Doz, Y. (1976) 'National Policies and Multinational Management', doctoral dissertation, Harvard Business School.

Doz, Y. (1978) 'Managing Manufacturing Rationalization within Multinational Companies', *Columbia Journal of World Business*, 8:3, pp. 82–94.

Doz, Y. (1979) *Government Control and Multinational Strategic Management: Power Systems and Telecommunications Equipment* (New York: Praeger).

Doz, Y. (1980) 'Strategic Management in Multinational Companies', *Sloan Management Review*, 21:2, pp. 27–46.

Doz, Y. (1986a) 'Government Policies and Global Industries', in M. E. Porter (ed.), *Competition in Global Industries* (Boston: Harvard Business School Press) pp. 225–66.

Doz, Y. (1986b) *Strategic Management in Multinational Companies* (Oxford: Pergamon Press).

Doz, Y., Bartlett, C. A. and Prahalad, C. K. (1981) 'Global Competitive Pressures vs. Host Country Demands: Managing Tensions in Multinational Corporations', *California Management Review*, 23:3, pp. 63–74.

Doz, Y. and Prahalad, C. K. (1981) 'Headquarters Influence and Strategic Control in MNCs', *Sloan Management Review*, 23:1, pp. 15–29.

Doz, Y. and Prahalad, C. K. (1984) 'Patterns of Strategic Control in Multinational Corporations', *Journal of International Business Studies*, 15:2, pp. 55–72.

Doz, Y. and Prahalad, C.K. (1986) 'Controlled Variety: A Challenge for Human Resource Management in the MNC', *Human Resource Management*, 25:1, pp. 55–72.

Doz, Y. and Prahalad, C. K. (1987) 'A Process Model of Strategic Redirection in Large Complex Firms: The Case of Multinational Corporations', in A. Pettigrew (ed.), *The Management of Strategic Change* (Oxford: Basil Blackwell).

Doz, Y. and Prahalad, C. K. (1988) 'Quality of Management: An Emerging Source of Global Competitive Advantage?', in N. Hood and J. E. Vahlne (eds), *Strategies in Global Competition* (London: Croom Helm).

Doz, Y., Prahalad, C. K. and Hamel, G. (1990) 'Control, Change and Flexibility: The Dilemma of Transnational Collaboration', in C. A. Bartlett, Y. Doz and G. Hedlund (eds), *Managing the Global Firm* (London: Routledge & Kegan Paul).

Duncan, R. B. (1973) 'Multiple Decision-making Structures in Adapting to Environmental Uncertainty: The Impact of Organizational Effectiveness', *Human Relations*, 26, pp. 273–91.

Dunkin, A. (1989) 'Now Salespeople Really Must Sell for Their Supper', *Business Week*, 3117, 31 July, p. 50.

Dunning, J. H. (1973) 'The Determinants of International Production', *Oxford Economic Papers*, 25:3, pp. 289–336.

Dunning, J. H. (ed.) (1974) *Economic Analysis and the Multinational Enterprise* (London: George Allen & Unwin).

Dunning, J. H. (1977) 'Trade, Location of Economic Activity and the Multinational Enterprise: A Search for an Eclectic Approach', in B. Ohlin, P. O. Hesselbom and P. J. Wiskman (eds), *The International Allocation of Economic Activity* (London: Macmillan).

Dunning, J. H. (1980a) 'Explaining Changing Patterns of International Production: In Defence of the Eclectic Theory', *Oxford Bulletin of Economics and Statistics*, 42, pp. 269–95.

Dunning, J. H. (1980b) 'Toward an Eclectic Theory of International Production: Some Empirical Tests', *Journal of International Business*, 11:1, pp. 9–31.

Dunning, J. H. (1981a) *International Production and the Multinational Enterprise* (London: Allen and Unwin).

Dunning, J. H. (1981b) *The Eclectic Theory of the MNC* (London: George Allen and Unwin).

Dunning, J. H. (1986) *Japanese Participation in British Industry: Trojan Horse or Catalyst for Growth* (Dover, NH: Croom Helm).

Dunning, J. H. (1988) *Multinationals, Technology and Competitiveness* (London: Unwin Hyman).

Dunning, J. H. (1988) 'The Study of International Business: A Plea for a More Interdisciplinary Approach', *Journal of International Business Studies*, 20-3, pp. 411–36.

Dunning, J. H. and Pearce, J. A. (1985) *Profitability and Performance of the World's Largest Industrial Companies* (London: The Financial Times).

Durkheim, E. (1933) *The Division of Labor in Society* (New York: Free Press).

Dutton, J. E. and Jackson, S. (1987) 'Categorizing Strategic Issues: Links to Organizational Action', *Academy of Management Review*, 12, pp. 76–90.

Dyas, G. P. and Thanheiser, H. T. (1976) *The Emerging European Enterprise: Strategy and Structure in French and German Industry* (London: Macmillan).

Eccles, R.G. (1981) 'The Quasifirm in the Construction Industry', *Journal of Economic Behavior and Organization*, 2, pp. 335–57.

Eccles, R. G. and Crane, D. B. (1987) 'Managing Through Networks in Investment Banking', *California Management Review*, 30:1, pp. 176–95.

Eccles, R. G. and White, H. (1988) 'Price and Authority in Inter-Profit Center Transactions', *American Journal of Sociology* (Supplement), 94, pp. 17–51.

Eco, U. (1986) *Travels in Hyperreality* (New York: Harcourt Brace Jovanovich).

Edstrom, A. and Galbraith, J. (1979) 'Transfer of Managers as a Coordination and Control Device in Multinational Organizations', *Administrative Science Quarterly*, 22, pp. 248–63.

Edwards, R. C. (1979) *Contested Terrain: The Transformation of the Workplace in the Twentieth Century* (New York: Basic Books).

Egelhoff, W. G. (1982) 'Strategy and Structure in Multinational Corporations: An Information Processing Approach', *Administrative Science Quarterly*, 27:3, pp. 435–58.

Egelhoff, W. G. (1988a) *Organizing the Multinational Enterprise: An Information Processing Perspective* (Cambridge, Mass.: Ballinger).

Egelhoff, W. G. (1988b) 'Strategy and Structure in Multinational Corporations: A Revision of the Stopford and Wells Model', *Strategic Management Journal*, 9:1, pp. 1–14.

Eisenhardt, K. (1985) 'Control: Organizational and Economic Approaches', *Management Science*, 31, pp. 134–49.

Eisenhardt, K. (1988) 'Agency- and Institutional-Theory Explanation: The Case of Retail Sales Compensation', *American Management Journal*, 31:3, pp. 488–511.

Eisenhardt, K. (1989) 'Agency Theory: An Assessment and Review', *Academy of Management Review*, 14:1, pp. 57–74.

Eisenstadt, S. N. (1966) *Modernization: Protest and Change* (Englewood Cliffs, NJ: Prentice-Hall).

El Sawy, O. A. (1985) 'From Separation to Holographic Enfolding', Paper presented to TIMS meeting, Boston, May.

Emerson, R. M. (1962) 'Power-dependence Relations', *American Sociological Review*, 27, pp. 31–41.

Emmott, B. (1989) *The Sun Also Sets* (New York: Simon and Schuster).

Etzioni, A. (1975) *A Comparative Analysis of Complex Organizations* (New York: Free Press of Glencoe).

Etzioni, A. (1988) *The Moral Dimension* (New York: Free Press).

Evan, W. M. (1967) 'The Organization-Set: Toward a Theory of Interorganizational Relations', in J. D. Thompson (ed.) *Approaches to Organizational Design* (University of Pittsburgh Press), pp. 173–91.

Evan, W. M. (ed.) (1976) *Interorganizational Relations* (Harmondsworth: Penguin).

Evans, P. E. and Doz. Y. (1989) 'The Dualistic Organization', in P. Evans, Y. Doz, and A. Laurent (eds) *Human Resource Management in International Firms* (London: Macmillan).

Fallows, J. (1989) *More Like Us* (Boston, Mass.: Houghton Mifflin).

Fama, E. F. and Jensen, M. C. (1983) 'Separation of Ownership and Control', *Journal of Law and Economics*, 26:2, pp. 301–26.

Fayerweather, J. (1960) *Management of International Operations: Text and Cases* (New York: McGraw-Hill).

Fayerweather, J. (1978) *International Business Strategy and Administration* (Cambridge, Mass.: Ballinger).

Fine, G. A. (1985) 'Negotiated Orders and Organizational Cultures', *Annual Review of Sociology*, 10, pp. 239–62.

Fiol, C. Marlene and Lyles, M. A. (1985) 'Organizational Learning', *Academy of Management Review*, 10, pp. 803–13.

Fischer, D. H. (1970) *Historians' Fallacies* (New York: Harper Colophon Books).

Flaherty, T. (1986) 'Coordinating International Manufacturing and Technology', in M. E. Porter (ed.), *Competition in Global Industries* (Boston, Mass.: Harvard Business School Press) pp. 83–109.

Fligstein, N. (1990) *The Transformation of Corporate Control* (Cambridge, Mass.: Harvard University Press).

Folger, R. (1977) 'Distributive and procedural justice: Combined impact of "voice" and improvement on experienced inequity', *Journal of Personality and Social Psychology*, 35, pp. 108–19.

Folger, R. and Greenberg, J. (1985) 'Procedural justice: An interpretative analysis of personnel systems', in K. Rowland and G. Ferris (eds), *Research in Personnel and Human Resources Management*, III (Greenwich, Conn.: JAI Press).

Folger, R. and Konovsky, M. (1989) 'Effects of procedural and distributive justice on reactions to pay raise decisions', *Academy of Management Journal*, 32:1, pp. 115–130.

Folger, R., Rosenfield, D., Grove, J. and Corkran, L. (1989) 'Effects of "voice" and peer opinions on responses to inequity', *Journal of Personality and Social Psychology*, 37, pp. 2253–61.

Fombrun, C. J. (1983) 'Attributions of Power Across Social Networks', *Human Relations*, 36:3, pp. 493–508.

Fouraker, L. E. and Stopford, J. (1968) 'Organization Structure and Multinational Strategy', *Administrative Science Quarterly*, 13, pp. 57–70.

Franko, L. G. (1974) 'The Move Toward a Multidivisional Structure in European Organizations', *Administrative Science Quarterly* 19, pp. 493–506.

Franko, L. G. (1976) *The European Multinationals: A Renewed Challange to American and British Big Business* (Stamford, Conn.: Greylock Publishing).

Freeman, J. H. and Boeker, W. (1984) 'The Ecological Analysis of Business Strategy', *California Management Review*, 26:3, pp. 73–86.

Freeman, J. H., Carroll, G. and Hannan, M. T. (1983) 'The Liability of Newness: Age Dependence in Organizational Death Rates', *American Sociological Review*, 48, pp. 692–710.

Freeman, J. H. and Hannan, M. T. (1983) 'Niche Width and the Dynamics of Organizational Populations', *American Journal of Sociology*, 88, pp. 1116–45.

Freeman, L. C. (1979) 'Centrality in Social Networks: Conceptual Clarification', *Social Networks*, 2, pp. 215–39.

Fruin, M. (1989) *Cooperative Structures, Competitive Strategies: The Japanese Enterprise System*, unpublished manuscript.

Fryxell, G. E., and Gordon, M. E. (1989) 'Workplace justice and job satisfaction as predictors of satisfaction with union and management', *Academy of Management Journal* 32:4, pp. 851–66.

Fucini, J. J. and Fucini, S. (1990) *Working for the Japanese: Inside Mazda's American Auto Plant* (New York: Free Press).

Fukutake, T. (1981) *Japanese Society Today* (University of Tokyo Press).

Gagliardi, P. (ed.) (1990) *Symbols and Artifacts* (New York: de Gruyter).

Galbraith, J. R. (1969) 'Organization Design: An Information Processing View', Working paper No. 425–69 (Sloan School of Management, MIT).

Galbraith, J. R. (1970) 'Environmental and Technological Determinants of Organization Design', in J. W. Lorsch and P. R. Lawrence (eds) *Studies in Organization Design* (Homewood, Ill.: Irwin), pp. 113–39.

Galbraith, J. R. (1973) *Designing Complex Organizations* (Reading, Mass.: Addison-Wesley).

Galbraith, J. R. (1977) *Organization Design* (Reading, Mass.: Addison-Wesley).

Galbraith, J. R. and Nathanson, D. A. (1978) *Strategy Implementation: The Role of Structure and Process* (St. Paul, Minn.: West).

Garfinkel, H. (1984) *Studies in Ethnomethodology* (Cambridge: Polity Press).

Gates, S. and Egelhoff, W. (1986) 'Centralization in Headquarters–Subsidiary Relationships', *Journal of International Business Studies*, 17:2, pp. 71–92.

Geertz, C. (1973) *The Interpretation of Cultures* (New York: Basic Books).

Gelsanliter, D. (1990) *Jump Start: Japan comes to the Heartland* (New York: Farrar, Straus, Giroux).

Gerschenkron, A. (1962) *Economic Backwardness in Historical Perspective* (Cambridge, Mass.: Harvard University Press).

Ghemawat, P. and Spence, A. M. (1986) 'Modeling Global Competition', in M. E. Porter (ed.) *Competition in Global Industries* (Boston, Mass.: Harvard Business School Press), pp. 61–79.

Ghoshal, S. (1986) 'The Innovative Multinational: A Differentiated Network of Organizational Roles and Management Processes', unpublished doctoral dissertation, Harvard Business School.

Ghoshal, S. (1987) 'Global Strategy: An Organizing Framework', *Strategic Management Journal*, 8, pp. 425–40.

Ghoshal, S. and Nohria, N. (1990) 'Internal Differentiation within Multinational Corporations', *Strategic Management Journal*, 10:4, pp. 323–38.

Ghoshal, S. and Bartlett, C. A. (1988) 'Creation, Adoption, and Diffusion of Innovations by Subsidiaries of Multinational Corporations', *Journal of International Business Studies*, 19-3, pp. 365–87.

Ghoshal, S. and Bartlett, C. A. (1990) 'The Multinational Corporation as an Interorganizational Network', *Academy of Management Review*, 15:4, pp. 603–25.

Giddens, A. (1976) *New Rules of Sociological Method* (New York: Basic Books).

Giddens, A. (1984) *The Constitution of Society* (Berkeley, Calif.: University of California Press).

Giddens, A. (1987) 'Structuralism, Post-Structuralism and the Production of Culture', in A. Giddens and J. H. Turner (eds), *Social Theory Today* (Stanford University Press) pp. 195–223.

Ginsberg, A. (1990) 'Connecting Diversification to Performance: A Sociocognitive Approach', *Academy of Management Review*, 15, pp. 514–35.

Goffman, E. (1959) *The Presentation of Self in Everyday Life* (New York: Doubleday).

Goffman, E. (1974) *Frame Analysis* (New York: Harper & Row).

Golding, A. M. (1971) 'Semiconductor Industry in Britain and the United States: A Case Study in Innovation, Growth and Diffusion of Technology', unpublished PhD dissertation, University of Sussex, Brighton.

Gottdiener, M. (1982) 'Disneyland: A Utopian Urban Space', *Urban Life*, 11, pp. 139–62.

Gouldner, A. (1954) *Patterns of Industrial Bureaucracy* (New York: Free Press).

Graham, E. and Krugman, P. (1989) *Foreign Direct Investment in the United States* (Washington, DC: Institute for International Economics).

Granovetter, M. (1973) 'The Strength of Weak Ties', *American Journal of Sociology*, 81, pp. 1287–303.

Granovetter, M. (1985) 'Economic Action and Social Structure: The Problem of Embeddedness', *American Journal of Sociology*, 91:3, pp. 481–510.

Greenberg, J. (1986) 'Determinants of Perceived Fairness of Performance Evaluations', *Journal of Applied Psychology*, 71, pp. 340–2.

Greenberg, J. (1987a) 'A Taxonomy of Organizational Justice Theories', *Academy of Management Review*, 12:1, pp. 9–22.

Greenberg, J. (1987b) 'Using diaries to promote procedural justice in performance appraisals', *Social Justice Research*, 1, pp. 219–34.

Greenberg, J. and Folger, R. (1983) 'Procedural Justice, Participation, and the Fair Process Effect in Groups and Organizations', in P. Paulus (ed.), *Basic Group Process* (New York: Springer-Verlag).

Gusfield, J. (1981) *The Culture of Public Problems* (University of Chicago Press).

Hagstrom, P. (1990) 'New Information Systems and the Changing Structure of MNCs', in C. Bartlett, Y. Doz and G. Hedlund (eds) *Managing the Global Firm* (London and New York: Routledge & Kegan Paul) pp. 164–85.

Hall, R. H., Clark, J. P., Giordano, P. C., Johnson, P. V. and Roekel, M. V. (1977) 'Patterns of Interorganizational Relationships', *Administrative Science Quarterly*, 22:3, pp. 457–71.

Halle, D. (1984) *America's Working Man* (University of Chicago Press).

Hamel, G. (1990) 'A Theory of Competitive Collaboration', doctoral dissertation, University of Michigan.

Hamel, G. and Prahalad, C. K. (1985) 'Do You Really Have a Global Strategy?'' *Harvard Business Review*, July–August, pp. 139–48.

Hamel, G. and Prahalad, C. K. (1989) 'Strategic Intent', *Harvard Business Review*, 67:3, pp. 63–76.

Hamel, G. and Prahalad, C. K. (1990) 'The Core Competence of the Corporation', *Harvard Business Review*, 68:3, pp. 79–91.

Hannan, M. T. and Freeman, J. (1977) 'The Population Ecology of Organizations', *American Journal of Sociology*, 82, pp. 929–64.

Hannan, M. T. and Freeman, J. (1984) 'Structural Inertia and Organizational Change', *American Sociological Review*, 49, pp. 149–64.

Hannan, M.T. and Freeman, J. (1989) *Organizational Ecology* (Cambridge, Mass.: Harvard University Press).

Hannerz, U. (1989) 'Scenarios of Peripheral Cultures', Paper presented at the Symposium on Culture, Globalization and the World-System, State University of New York at Binghamton, 1 April.

Harrigan. K. (1985) *Strategies for Joint Ventures* (Lexington, Mass.: Lexington Books).

Harrington, M. (1979) 'To the Disney Station', *Harper's* (January) pp. 35–9.

Harris, N. (1990) *Cultural Excursions* (University of Chicago Press).

Harrop, J.F. (1989) *The Political Economy of Integration in the European Community* (Aldershot: Gower).

Harvey-Jones, J. (1988) *Making it Happen: Reflections on Leadership* (Glasgow: Fontana-Collins).

Hayek, F. (1945) 'The Use of Knowledge in Society', *American Economic Review*, 35, pp. 519–30.

Hedlund, G. (1980) 'The Role of Foreign Subsidiaries in Strategic Decision-making in Swedish Multinational Corporations', *Strategic Management Journal*, 9, pp. 23–6.

Hedlund, G. (1981) 'Autonomy of Subsidiaries and Formalization of Head-quarters–Subsidiary Relationships in Swedish MNCs', in Lars Otterbeck (ed.) *The Management of Headquarter–Subsidiary Relationships in Multinational Corporations* (Aldershot: Gower) pp. 25–78.

Hedlund, G. (1986) 'The Hypermodern MNC: A Heterarchy?', *Human Resource Management*, 25, pp. 9–35.

Hedlund, G. (1988) 'The First Theory of Hierarchy: Contemplation of Its Pervasiveness in Modern Business Life', Institute of International Business, Research Paper 88/4.

Hedlund, G. and Rolander, D. (1990) 'Action in Heterarchies: New Approaches to Managing the MNC', in C.A. Bartlett, Y. Doz and G. Hedlund (eds), *Managing the Global Firm* (London and New York: Routledge & Kegan Paul).

Heenan, D.A. and Perlmutter, H.V. (1979) *Multinational Organization Development: A Social Architecture Perspective* (Reading, Mass.: Addison-Wesley).

Hennart, J.F. (1982) *A Theory of Multinational Enterprise* (Ann Arbor, Mich.: University of Michigan Press).

Hennart, J.F. (1988) 'Upstream Vertical Integration in the Aluminum and Tin Industries', *Journal of Economic Behavior and Organization*, 9, pp. 281–99.

Hennart, J.F. (1989a) 'Can the "New Forms of Investment" Substitute for the "old" forms? A Transaction Cost Perspective', *Journal of International Business Studies*, 10-2, pp. 211–34.

Hennart, J.F. (1989b) 'A Model of the Choice Between Firms and Markets', Working Paper, Wharton School.

Herbert, T.T. (1984) 'Strategy and Multinational Organization Structure: An Interorganizational Relations Perspective', *Academy of Management Review*, 9, pp. 259–70.

Herbst, P.G. (1974) *Socio-technical Design* (London: Tavistock).

Heritage, J.C. (1987) 'Ethnomethodology', in A. Giddens and J.H. Turner (eds) *Social Theory Today* (Stanford University Press) pp. 224–72.

Herriot, S., Levinthal, D. and March, J. (1985) 'Learning from Experience in Organizations', *American Economic Review. Papers and Proceedings*, 75, pp. 298–302.

Hill, C. W. L. and Kim, W. C. (1988) 'Searching for a Dynamic Theory of the Multinational Enterprise: A Transaction Cost Model', *Strategic Management Journal*, 9, pp. 93–104.

Hirsch, P. M. (1972) 'Processing Fads and Fashions: An Organization-Set Analysis of Cultural Industry Systems', *American Journal of Sociology* 77, pp. 639–59.

Hirsch, S. (1976) 'An International Trade and Investment Theory of the Firm', *Oxford Economic Papers*, 28, pp. 258–70.

Hofstadter, D. R. (1980) *Godel, Escher and Bach: An Eternal Golden Braid* (New York: Penguin).

Hofstede, G. (1980a) *Culture's Consequences: International Differences in Work-related Values* (Beverly Hills, Calif.: Sage Publications).

Hofstede, G. (1980b) 'Motivation, Leadership and Organization: Do American Theories Apply Abroad?', *Organizational Dynamics* (Summer) pp. 42–63.

Holm, J. (1988) *Pidgins and Creoles*, vol. 1 (New York: Cambridge University Press).

Homans, G. (1974) *Social Behavior: Its Elementary Forms*, 2nd edn (New York: Harcourt, Brace, & World).

Hoogvelt, A. and Puxty, A. G. (1987) *Multinational Enterprise: An Encyclopedic Dictionary of Concepts and Terms* (London: Macmillan).

Horst, T. (1972) 'Firm and Industry Determinants of the Decision to Invest Abroad: An Empirical Study', *Review of Economics and Statistics*, 54, pp. 58–66.

Hout, T., Porter, M. E., and Rudden, E. (1982) 'How global companies win out', *Harvard Business Review*, September–October, pp. 98–108.

Hrebiniak, L. G. and Joyce, W. J. (1985) 'Organizational Adaptation: Strategic Choice and Environmental Determinism', *Administrative Science Quarterly*, 30, 3, pp. 36–49.

Huber, G. P. (1982) 'Organizational Information Systems: Determinants of Their Performance and Behavior', *Management Science*, 28:2, pp. 138–55.

Huber, G. P. (1990) 'A Theory of the Effects of Advanced Information Technologies on Organizational Design, Intelligence, and Decision Making.' *Academy of Management Review* 15, pp. 47–71.

Hudson, R., Rhind, D. and Mounsey, H. (1984) *An Atlas of EEC Affairs* (London: Methuen).

Hulbert, J. M. and Brandt, W. K. (1980) *Managing the Multinational Subsidiary* (New York: Holt, Rinehart and Winston).

Hymer, S. H. (1960) *The International Operations of National Firms*, doctoral dissertation, MIT.

Hymer, S. H. (1970) 'The Efficiency (Contradictions) of Multinational Corporations', *American Economic Review*, 60, pp. 441–48.

Hymer, S. H. (1976) *The International Operations of National Firms: A Study of Direct Investment* (Cambridge, Mass.: MIT Press).

Iyer, P. (1988) *Video Nights in Kathmandu* (New York: Vintage).

Jackell, R. (1988) *Moral Mazes* (New York: Oxford University Press).

Jaeger, A. M. (1983) 'The Transfer of Organizational Culture Overseas', *Journal of International Business Studies*, 14:2, pp. 91–105.

Janis, T. I. (1972) *Victims of Groupthink* (Boston: Houghton Mifflin).

Jensen, M. C. and Meckling, W. H. (1976) 'Theory of the Firm: Managerial Behavior, Agency Costs and Capital Structure', *Journal of Financial Economics*, 3, pp. 305–60.

Jones, M. O., Moore, M. D. and Snyder, R. C. (eds) (1988) *Inside Organizations* (Newbury Park, Calif.: Sage Publications).

Kadushin, C. (1978) 'Introduction to Macro-Network Analysis', manuscript, Columbia University Teachers' College.

Kamata, S. (1980) *Japan in the Passing Lane* (New York: Random House).

Kanter, R. (1972) *Commitment and Community* (Cambridge, Mass.: Harvard University Press).

Kasson, J. F. (1978) *Amusing the Millions* (New York: Hill & Wang).

Kidder, T. (1981) *Soul of the New Machine* (Boston, Mass: Little, Brown).

Kilduff, M. (1991) 'Deconstructing Organizations', working paper, Pennsylvania State University.

Kilduff, M. and Abolafia, M. Y. (1989) *The Social Destruction of Reality: Organizational Conflict as Social Drama*, Working Paper No. 89/24 (Fontainebleau, France: INSEAD).

Kilduff, M. and Angelmar, R. (1989) *Shared History or Shared Culture? The Effects of Time, Culture, and Performance on Institutionalization in Simulated Organizations*, Working Paper No. 89/05 (Fontainebleau, France: INSEAD).

Kim, W. C. and Lyn, E. S. (1987) 'Foreign Direct Investment Theories, Entry Barriers and Reverse Investments in U. S. Manufacturing Industries', *Journal of International Business Studies*, 19-2, pp. 53–66.

Kim, W. C. and Mauborgne, R. A. (1988) 'Becoming an Effective Global Competitor', *The Journal of Business Strategy* (January–February) pp. 33–7.

Kim, W. C., and Mauborgne, R. A. (1989) 'Assessing the Administrative Forms for Managing the Modern Multinational', mimeo, The Michigan Business School.

Kim, W. C., and Mauborgne, R. A. (1991) 'Implementing Global Strategies: The Role of Procedural Justice', *Strategic Management Journal*, 12, Special Issue on Global Strategy, pp. 125–44.

Kimberly, J. (1975) 'Environmental Constraints and Organizational Structure: A Comparative Analysis of Rehabilitation Organizations', *Administrative Science Quarterly*, 20, pp. 1–9.

Kimura, Y. (1989) 'Firm Specific Strategic Advantages and Foreign Direct Investment Behavior of Firms', *Journal of International Business Studies*, 10:2, pp. 296–314.

Kindleberger, C. P. (1969) *American Business Abroad* (New Haven, Conn.: Yale University Press).

Kindleberger, C. P. (1973) *International Economics*, 5th edn (Homewood, Ill.: Irwin).

King, M. J. (1981) 'Disneyland and Walt Disney World: Traditional Values in Futuristic Form', *Journal of Popular Culture*, 15, pp. 116–40.

Klein, B., Crawford, R. and Alchian, A. (1978) 'Vertical Integration, Appropriable Rents, and the Competitive Contracting Process', *Journal of Law and Economics*, 21, pp. 297–326.

Klein, S., Frazier, G. L. and Roth, V. J. (1990) 'A Transaction Cost Analysis Model of Channel Integration in International Markets', *Journal of Marketing Research*, 27, pp. 196–208.

Kmetz, John L. (1984) 'An Information-processing Study of a Complex Workflow in Aircraft Electronics Repair', *Administrative Science Quarterly*, 29, pp. 255–80.

Kobrin, S. J. (1976) 'The Environmental Determinants of Foreign Direct Manufacturing Investment: An Ex-Post Empirical Analysis', *Journal of International Business Studies*, 7, pp. 29–42.

Kobrin, S. (1988a) 'Expatriate Reduction and Strategic Control in American Multinational Corporations', *Human Resource Management*, 27:1, pp. 63–75.

Kobrin, S. J. (1988b) 'Trends in Ownership of U.S. Manufacturing Subsidiaries in Developing Countries: An Interindustry Analysis', in Farok J. Contractor and Peter Lorange (eds) *Cooperative Strategies in International Business* (Lexington, Mass.: Lexington Books), pp. 129–42.

Kobrin, S. J., Basek, J., Blank, S. and La Palombara, J. (1980) 'The Assessment and Evaluation of Noneconomic Environments by American Firms: A Preliminary Report', *Journal of International Business Studies*, 11, pp. 32–46.

Kocka, J. and Siegrist, H. (1979) 'Die hundert groessten deutschen Industrieunternehmen im spaeten 19. und fruehen 20. Jarhhundert. Expansion, Diversifikation und Integration im internationalen Vergleich', N. Horn and J. Kocka (eds), *Law and the Formation of the Big Enterprises in the 19th and Early 20th Centuries* (Gttingen: Vandenhoeck & Ruprecht).

Koestler, A. (1978) *Janus – A Summing Up* (New York: Random House).

Kogut, B. (1983) 'Foreign Direct Investment as a Sequential Process', in C. Kindleberger and D. Andretsch (eds) *The Multinational Corporation in the 1980s* (Cambridge, Mass.: MIT Press), pp. 38–56.

Kogut, B. (1985a) 'Designing global strategies: Comparative and competitive value added chains', *Sloan Management Review* (Summer), pp. 15–28.

Kogut, B. (1985b) 'Designing global strategies: Profiting from operational flexibility', *Sloan Management Review* (Fall), pp. 27–38.

Kogut, B. (1988a) 'Country Patterns in International Competition: Appropriability and Oligopolistic Agreement', in N. Hood and J. E. Vahlne (eds), *Strategies in Global Competition* (London: Croom-Helm).

Kogut, B. (1988b) 'Joint Ventures: Theoretical and Empirical Perspectives', *Strategic Management Journal*, 9, pp. 319–32.

Kogut, B. (1989) 'A Note on Global Strategies', *Strategic Management Journal*, 10, pp. 383–9.

Kogut, B. (1990) 'The Permeability of Borders and the Speed of Learning Among Countries', *Globalization of Firms and the Competitiveness of Nations*, Crafoord Lectures (Lund, Sweden: University of Lund).

Kogut, B. (1991) 'Country Capabilities and the Permeability of Borders', *Strategic Management Journal*, 12, Special Issue on Global Strategy, pp. 33–48.

Kogut, B. and Chang, S. J. (forthcoming) 'Technological Capabilities and Japanese Foreign Direct Investment in the United States', *Review of Economics and Statistics*.

Kogut, B., Shan, W. J. and Walker, G. (1990) 'The Structuring of an Industry: Embeddedness Among Bio-technology Firms', Mimeo.

Kogut, B. and Zander, U. (forthcoming) 'The Knowledge of the Firm and the Replication of Technology', *Organization Science*.

Kolde, E. J. (1985) *Environment of International Business*, 2nd edn (Boston, Mass.: Kent Publishing Company).

Krackhardt, D. (1989) 'Graph Theoretical Dimensions of the Informal Organization', presentation at the European Institute of Business Administration (Fontainebleau, France: INSEAD).

Krackhardt, D., and Kilduff, M. (1990) 'Friendship Patterns and Culture: The Control of Organizational Diversity', *American Anthropologist*, 92, pp. 142–54.

Kreps, D. (1984) 'Corporate Culture and Economic Theory', working paper, Stanford Graduate School of Business, Stanford University.

Kuin, P. (1972) 'The Magic of Multinational Management', *Harvard Business Review* (November–December), pp. 89–97.

Kunda, G. (1992) *Engineering Culture* (Philadelphia: Temple University Press).

Kyriazi, G. (1981) *The Great American Amusement Parks* (Los Angeles: Castle Books).

Landsberger, H. A. (1961) 'The Horizontal Dimension in Bureaucracy', *Administrative Science Quarterly*, 6, pp. 299–332.

Latour, B. (1987) *Science in Action* (Cambridge, Mass.: Harvard University Press).

La Tour, S. (1978) 'Determinants of participant and observer satisfaction with adversary and inquisitorial modes of adjudication', *Journal of Personality and Social Psychology*, 36, pp. 1531–45.

Laumann, E. O, Glaskiewicz, J. and Marsden, P. V. (1978) 'Community Structure as Interorganizational Linkages', *Annual Review of Sociology*, 4, pp. 455–84.

Laumann, E. O., Marsden, P. V. and Prensky, D. (1983) 'The Boundary Specification Problem in Network Analysis', in R.S. Burt and M.J. Minor and associates (eds) *Applied Network Analysis: A Methodological Introduction* (Beverly Hills, Calif.: Sage).

Laumann, E. O. and Pappi, F. (1976) *Networks of Collective Action: A Perspective on Community Influence Systems* (New York: Academic Press).

Laurent, A. (1978) 'Managerial Subordinacy', *Academy of Management Review*, pp. 220–0.

Laurent, A. (1983) 'The Cultural Diversity of Western Conceptions of Management', *International Studies of Management and Organization*, 13, pp. 75–96.

Laurent, A. (1986) 'The Cross-Cultural Puzzle of International Human Resource Management', *Human Resource Management*, 25, pp. 91–102.

Lawrence, C. (1983) 'Nissan's Way', *Miami Herald*, 26 June, p. 5F.

Lawrence, P. and Dyer, D. (1983) *Renewing American Industry* (New York: Free Press).

Lawrence, Paul R. and Lorsch, Jay W. (1967) *Organization and Environment* (Homewood, Ill.: Irwin).

Lazarsfeld, P. F. and Menzel, H. (1969) 'On the Relation Between Individual and Collective Properties', in A. Etzioni (ed.) *Complex Organizations: A Sociological Reader* (New York: Holt, Rinehart and Winston), pp. 499–516.

Leach, E. R. (1976) *Culture and Communication* (Cambridge University Press).

Lehman, E. W. (1975) *Coordinating Health Care: Explorations in Interorganizational Relations* (Beverly Hills, Calif.: Sage Publications).

Lessard, D. and Lightstone, J. B. (1986) 'Volatile Exchange Rates Can Put Operations at Risk', *Harvard Business Review* (July–August), pp. 107–14.

Leventhal, G. S. (1980) 'What should be done with equity theory? New approaches to the study of fairness in social relationships', in K. Gergen, M. Greenberg, and R. Willis (eds), *Social Exchange: Advances in Theory and Research* (New York: Plenum Press).

Leventhal, G. S., Karuza, J. and Fry, W. R. (1980) 'Beyond fairness: A theory of allocation preferences', in G. Mikula (ed.), *Justice and Social Interaction* (New York: Springer-Verlag).

Levinthal, D. (1988) 'A Survey of Agency Models of Organization', *Journal of Economic Behavior and Organization*, 9, pp. 153–85.

Levitt, B. and March, J. G. (1987) 'Organizational Learning', *Annual Review of Sociology*, 14, pp. 319–40.

Levitt, T. (1983) 'The Globalization of Markets', *Harvard Business Review* 61:3, pp. 92–102.

Li, J. and Guisinger, S. (1990) 'Comparative Business Failures of Foreign Controlled Firms in the United States', paper presented at the Doctoral Consortium for International Management, American Academy of Management Conference (11–15 August), San Francisco.

Lincoln, J., Hanada, M. and McBride, K. (1986) 'Organizational Structures in Japanese and U.S. Manufacturing', *Administrative Science Quarterly*, 31, pp. 338–64.

Lind, E. A., Kurtz, S., Musante, L., Walker, L., and Thibaut, J.W. (1980) 'Procedure and outcome effects on reactions to adjudicated resolution of conflicts of interests', *Journal of Personality and Social Psychology*, 39, pp. 643–53.

Lind, E. A. and Tyler, T. R. (1988) *The Social Psychology of Procedural Justice* (New York: Plenum Press).

Lowenthal, D. (1985) *The Past is a Foreign Country* (University of Cambridge Press).

Luustorinen, R. and Welch, L. (1989) 'Internationalization: Evolution of a Concept', *Journal of General Management*, 14, pp. 34–55.

MacCannel, D. (1976) *The Tourist* (New York: Schocken).

McClelland, D. (961) *The Achieving Society* (New York: Free Press).

McCulloch, W. (1965) *Embodiments of Mind* (Cambridge, Mass.: Harvard University Press).

McManus, J. C. (1972) 'The Theory of the International Firm', in Gilles Paquet (ed.), *Multinational Firm and the Nation State* (Don Mills, Ontario: Collier Macmillan).

Magee, S. P. (1977) 'Information and the Multinational Corporation: An Appropriability Theory of Direct Foreign Investment', in J. N. Bhagwati (ed.), *The New International Economic Order: The North–South Debate* (Cambridge, Mass.: MIT Press), pp. 317–46.

Mahini, A. and Wells, L. T. (1986) 'Government Relations in the Global Firm', in M. E. Porter (ed.), *Competition in Global Industries* (Boston, Mass.: Harvard Business School Press), pp. 291–314.

Manning, P. K. (1989) *Signifying Calls* (Cambridge, Mass.: MIT Press).

March, J. G. and Olsen, J. P. (1980) *Ambiguity and Choice in Organizations*, 2nd edn (Oxford University Press).

March, J. G. and Simon, H. A. (1958) *Organizations* (New York: John Wiley).

Marcus, G. E. and Fischer, M. (1986) *Anthropology as Cultural Critique* (University of Chicago Press).

Marin, L. (1977) 'Disneyland: A Degenerate Utopia', *Glyph I*, Johns Hopkins Textual Studies (Baltimore, Md: Johns Hopkins University Press) pp. 50–66.

Martin, J. (forthcoming) *Harmony, Conflict, and Ambiguity in Organizational Cultures* (San Francisco: Jossey-Bass).

Martinez, J. and Jarillo, J. C. (1989) 'The Evolution of Research on Coordination Mechanisms in Multinational Corporations', *Journal of International Business Studies* (Fall) 20:3, pp. 489–514.

Mathias, D. (1978) *The Role of the Logistics System in Strategic Change*. unpublished doctoral dissertation, Harvard Business School.

Maruyama, M. (1978) 'The Epistemological Revolution', *Futures* (June) pp. 240–2.

Merton, R. K. (1936) 'The Unanticipated Consequences of Purposive Social Action', *American Sociological Review*, 1.

Meyer, J. W., and Rowan, B. (1977) 'Institutionalized Organizations: Formal Structures as Myth and Ceremony', *American Journal of Sociology*, 83, pp. 340–63.

Meyer, J. W. and Hannan, M. T. (1979) *National Development and the World System: Educational, Economic, and Political Change 1950–1970* (University of Chicago Press).

Meyer, J. W. and Scott, W. R. (1983) *Organizational Environments: Ritual and Rationality* (Beverley Hills, Calif.: Sage Publications).

Meyer, J. W., Scott, W. R., and Deal, T. E. (1983) 'Institutional and Technical Sources of Organizational Structure: Explaining the Structure of Educational Organizations', in J. W. Meyer and W. R. Scott (eds), *Organizational Environments: Ritual and Rationality* (Beverly Hills, Calif.: Sage Publications), pp. 45–70.

Meyer, M. W. and Zucker, L. G. (1989) *Permanently Failing Organizations* (Newbury Park, Calif.: Sage Publications).

Mezias, S. J. (1990) 'An institutional model of organizational practice: financial reporting in the Fortune 200', *Administrative Science Quarterly*, 35:3, pp. 431–57.

Miller, W. (1955) 'Two Concepts of Authority', *American Anthropologist*, 57, pp. 271–89.

Mintzberg, H. A. (1973) *The Nature of Managerial Work* (New York: Harper & Row).

Mintzberg, H. A. (1979) *The Structuring of Organizations* (Englewood Cliffs, NJ: Prentice-Hall).

Mintzberg, H., Raisinghani, D., and Theoret, A. (1976) 'The Structure of "Unstructured" Decision Processes', *Administrative Science Quarterly*, 21, pp. 246–75.

Mirrlees, J. (1976) 'The Optimal Structure of Incentives and Authority within an Organization', *Bell Journal of Economics*, 7 (Spring) pp. 105–31.

Mitchell, J. C. (1973) 'Networks, Norms and Institutions', in J. Boissevain and J. C. Mitchell (eds), *Network Analysis* (The Hague: Mouton) pp. 15–35.

Montagna, P. (1990) 'Accounting Rationality and Financial Legitimation', in S. Zukin and P. DiMaggio (eds), *Structures of Capital* (Cambridge University Press), pp. 227–60.

Monteverde, K. and Teece, D. J. (1982) 'Supplier Switching Costs and Vertical Integration in the Automobile Industry', *Bell Journal of Economics*, 13, pp. 206–13.

Moore, A. (1980) 'Walt Disney's World: Bounded Ritual and the Playful Pilgrimage Center', *Anthropological Quarterly*, 53, pp. 207–18.

Moran, T. H. (ed.) (1985) *Multinational Corporations: The Political Economy of Foreign Direct Investment* (Lexington, Mass.: Lexington Books).

Morgan, G. (1986) *Images of Organization* (Newbury Park, Calif.: Sage Publications).

Myerhoff, B. (1983) 'The Tamed and Colonized Imagination in Disneyland', unpublished paper. Department of Anthropology, University of Southern California.

Nakane, C. (1970) *Japanese Society* (Berkeley, Calif.: University of California Press).

Negandhi, A. R. and Baliga, R. (eds) (1980) *Functioning of the Multinational Corporation* (Oxford: Pergamon Press).

Negandhi, A. R. and Baliga, R. (1981) 'Internal Functioning of American, German and Japanese Multinational Corporations', in L. Otterbeck (ed.), *The Management of Headquarter Subsidiary Relationships in Multinational Corporations* (Aldershot: Gower), pp. 107–20.

Nelson, R., and Winter, S. (1982) *An Evolutionary Theory of Economic Change* (Cambridge, Mass.: Harvard University Press).

Newman, William H. (1975) *Constructive Control* (Englewood Cliffs, NJ: Prentice-Hall).

Nishiguchi, T. (1989) 'Strategic Dualism: An Alternative in Industrial Societies', unpublished dissertation, Nuffield College.

Nohria, N. and Ghoshal, S. (1989) 'The MNC as a Differentiated Network', unpublished paper, Harvard Business School.

Nohria, N. and Venkatraman, N. (1987) 'Interorganizational Information Systems via Information Technology: A Network Analytic Perspective', working paper No. 1909–87 (Sloan School of Management, MIT).

Nonaka, I. (1990) 'Managing Globalization as a Self-Renewing Process: Experiences of Japanese MNCs', in C.A. Bartlett, Y. Doz, and G. Hedlund (eds), *Managing the Global Firm* (London: Routledge & Kegan Paul).

Norman, R. (1976) *Management and Statesmanship* (Stockholm: SIAR).

North, D. (1981) *Structure and Change in Economic History* (New York: Norton).

Ochs, E. (1988) *Culture and Language Development* (New York: Cambridge University Press).

Ogilvy, J. (1977) *Multidimensional Man* (New York: Oxford University Press).

Ohmae, K. (1985) 'The Global Logic of Strategic Alliances', *Harvard Business Review*, 67-2, pp. 143–54.

Ohmae, K. (1990) *The Borderless World: Management Lessons in the New Logic of the Global Marketplace* (New York: Harper Collins).

Orru, M, Woolesey Biggart, N., and Hamilton, G. G. (1991) 'Organizational Isomorphism in East Asia: Broadening the New Institutionalism', in P. DiMaggio and W. W. Powell (eds), *The New Institutionalism in Organizational Analysis* (University of Chicago Press).

Ott, S. (1988) *The Organization Culture Perspective* (Reading, Mass.: Addison-Wesley).

Ouchi, W. (1977) 'The Relationship Between Organizational Structure and Organizational Control', *Administrative Science Quarterly*, 22, pp. 95–113.

Ouchi, W. G. (1978) 'The Transmission of Control Through Organizational Hierarchy', *Academy of Management Journal*, 21:2, pp. 173–92.

Ouchi, W. G. (1979) 'A Conceptual Framework for the Design of Organizational Control Mechanisms', *Management Science*, 25:9, pp. 833–48.

Ouchi, W. G. (1980) 'Markets, Bureaucracies and Clans', *Administrative Science Quarterly*, 25, pp. 129–41.

Ouchi, W. G. (1981a) 'A Framework for Understanding Organizational Failure', in J. Kimberly and R. Miles (eds) *The Organizational Life Cycle* (San Francisco: Jossey Bass), pp. 395–430.

Ouchi, W. G. (1981b) *Theory Z* (Reading, Mass.: Addison-Wesley).

Ouchi, W. G. and Wilkins, A. L. (1985) 'Organizational Culture', *Annual Review of Sociology*, 11, pp. 367–411.

Ozawa, T. (1980) 'Japanese World of Work: An Interpretive Survey', *MSU Business Topics* (Spring) pp. 45–54.

Paine, L. (1972) *The Hierarchy of Hell* (New York: Hippocrene Books).

Parsons, T. (1937) *The Structure of Social Action* (New York: McGraw-Hill).
Pattee, H. (1970) 'The Problem of Biological Hierarchy', in C. H. Waddington (ed.), *Toward a Theoretical Biology III* (Chicago, Ill.: Aldine), pp. 117–36.
Paul, J. K. (ed.) (1984) *High Technology International Trade and Competition* (Park Ridge, NJ: Noyes).
Pavan, Robert J. (1972) 'The Strategy and Structure of Italian Enterprise', doctoral dissertation, Harvard Graduate School of Business.
Pavitt, K. (1971) 'The Multinational Enterprise and the Transfer of Technology', in J. H. Dunning (ed.), *The Multinational Enterprise* (London: George Allen & Unwin), pp. 61–85.
Perlmutter, H. V. (1965) 'L'enterprise Internationale – Trois Conceptions', *Revue Economique et Sociale*, 23.
Perlmutter, H. V. (1969) 'The Tortuous Evolution of the Multinational Corporation', *Columbia Journal of World Business*, 4, pp. 9–18.
Perlmutter, H. V. and Trist, E. (1986) 'Paradigms for Societal Transition', *Human Relations*, 39:1, pp. 1–27.
Perrow, C. (1979) *Complex Organizations*, 2nd edn (New York: Random House).
Perrow, C. (1984) *Normal Accidents: Living with High-Risk Technologies* (New York: Basic Books).
Perrow, C. (1986) *Complex Organizations: A Critical Essay*, 3rd edn (New York: Random House).
Peters, T. J. (1987) *Thriving on Chaos* (New York: Knopf).
Peters, T. J., and Waterman, R. H. Jr (1982) *In Search of Excellence* (New York: Harper & Row).
Peterson, R. (1990) 'Symbols and Social Life', *Contemporary Sociology*, 19, pp. 498–500.
Pfeffer, J. R. (1981) *Power in Organizations* (Boston: Pittman).
Pfeffer, J. R. and Salancik, G. R. (1974) 'The Bases and Use of Power in Organizational Decision Making: The Case of a University', *Administrative Science Quarterly*, 19, pp. 453–73.
Pfeffer, J. R. and Salancik, G. R. (1978) *The External Control of Organizations: A Resource Dependency Perspective* (New York: Harper & Row).
Polanyi, M. (1958) *Personal Knowledge* (University of Chicago Press).
Porter, M. E. (1986) *Competition in Global Industries* (Cambridge, Mass.: Harvard Business School Press).
Porter, M. E. (1990) *The Competitive Advantage of Nations* (New York: Free Press).
Powell, W. W. (1985) *Getting Into Print: The Decision-Making Process in Scholarly Publishing* (University of Chicago Press).
Powell, W. W. (1988) 'Institutional Effects on Organizational Structure and Performance', in L. G. Zucker, (ed.), *Institutional Patterns and Organizations: Culture and Environment* (Cambridge, Mass.: Ballinger), pp. 115–38.
Poynter, T. A. and Rugman, A. M. (1982) 'World Product Mandates: How Will Multinationals Respond?', *Business Quarterly*, 47:3, pp. 54–61.
Prahalad, C. K. (1975) 'The Strategic Process in a Multinational Corporation', unpublished doctoral dissertation, School of Business Administration, Harvard University.
Prahalad, C. K. (1976) 'Strategic Choices in Diversified MNCs', *Harvard Business Review* (July–August), pp. 67–78.
Prahalad, C. K. and Doz, Y. (1980) 'Strategic Management of Diversified Multinatioal Companies', in A. Negandhi (ed.), *Functioning of the Multinational Corporation* (New York: Pergamon Press), pp. 77–116.

Prahalad, C. K. and Doz, Y. (1981) 'An Approach to Strategic Control in MNCs' *Sloan Management Review* (Summer) pp. 5–13.

Prahalad, C. K., and Doz, Y. (1987) *The Multinational Mission: Balancing Local Demands and Global Vision* (New York: Free Press).

Prahalad, C. K. and Hamel, G. (1990) 'The Core Competence of the Corporation', *Harvard Business Review*, 90:3, pp. 79–93.

Pratt, J. and Zeckhauser, R. (1985) 'Principals and Agents: An Overview', in J. Pratt and R. Zeckhauser (eds) *Principals and Agents: The Structure of Business* (Cambridge: Harvard Business School Press), pp. 1–35.

Provan, K. G., Beyer, J. M. and Kruytbosch, C. (1980) 'Environmental Linkages and Power in Resource Dependence Relations Between Organizations', *Administrative Science Quarterly*, 25, pp. 200–25.

Provan, K. G. (1983) 'The Federation as an Interorganizational Linkage Network', *Academy of Management Review*, 8, pp. 79–89.

Rabinow, P. and Sullivan, A. (eds) (1987) *Interpretive Social Science* (Berkeley, Calif.: University of California Press).

Ragin, C. C. (1987) *The Comparative Method* (Berkeley, Calif.: University of California Press).

Real, M. (1977) *Mass-Mediated Culture* (Englewood Cliffs, NJ: Prentice Hall).

Reibstein, L. (1987) 'Firms Trim Annual Pay Increases and Focus on Long Term', *Wall Street Journal*, 10 April, p. 25.

Ritti, R. R. and Silver, J. H. (1986) 'Early Processes of Institutionalization: The Dramaturgy of Exchange in Interorganizational Relations', *Administrative Science Quarterly*, 31, pp. 25–42.

Robinson, R. D. (1967) *International Management* (New York: Holt, Rinehart & Winston).

Robinson, R. D. (1978) *International Business Management: A Guide to Decision Making*, 2nd edn (Hinsdale: Dryden Press).

Robock, S. H., Simmons, K. and Zwick, J. (1977) *International Business and Multinational Enterprise* (Homewood, Ill: Irwin).

Rogers, E. (1971) *Diffusion of Innovations* (New York: Free Press).

Rohlen, T. P. (1974) *For Harmony and Strength* (Berkeley: University of California Press).

Rosaldo, R. (1989) *Culture and Truth* (Boston, Mass.: Beacon Press).

Rosenzweig, P. and Singh, J. (1991) 'Organizational Environments and the Multinational Enterprise', *Academy of Management Review*, 16:2, pp. 340–61.

Roumasset, J. and Uy, M. (1980) 'Piece Rates, Time Rates, and Teams', *Journal of Economic Behavior and Organization*, 1, pp. 343–60.

Rugman, A. M. (1980a) 'A New Theory of the Multinational Enterprise: Internationalization versus Internalization', *Columbia Journal of World Business* (Spring) pp. 23–9.

Rugman, A. M. (1980b) 'Internationalization as a General Theory of Foreign Direct Investment: A Re-appraisal of the Literature', *Weltwirtschaftliches Archiv*, No. 116, pp. 365–79.

Rugman, A. M. (1981) *Inside the Multinationals* (New York: Columbia University Press).

Sabel, C., Herrigel, G., Kazis, R., and Deeg, R. (1987) 'How to keep mature industries innovative', *Technology Review*, 90-3, pp. 26–35.

Sahlins, M. (1981) *Historical Metaphors and Mythical Realities* (Ann Arbor, Mich.: University of Michigan Press).

Sassen, J. (1989) 'Mickeymania', *International Management* (November) pp. 32–4.

Sayrs, L. W. (1989) *Pooled Time Series Analysis* (Newbury Park, Calif.: Sage Publications).

Schein, E. H. (1961) *Coercive Persuasion* (New York: Norton).

Schein, E. H. (1985) *Organizational Culture and Leadership* (San Francisco: Jossey-Bass).

Schein, E. H. (1989) 'Reassessing the "Divine Rights" of Managers', *Sloan Management Review* (Winter), pp. 63–8.

Schickel, R. (1968) *The Disney Version* (revised 1985) (New York: Simon & Schuster).

Schumpeter, J. A. (1947) *Capitalism, Socialism and Democracy*, 2nd edn (New York: Harper).

Schwartz, P., and Ogilvy, J. (1979) 'The Emergent Paradigm: Changing Patterns of Thought and Belief', *Analytical Report: Values and Lifestyles Program*, 7 (April).

Schwartz, T. (1981) 'The Acquisition of Culture', *Ethos*, 9, pp. 4–17.

Scott, W. R. (1965) 'Field Methods in the Study of Organizations', in J. G. March, (ed.), *Handbook of Organizations* (Chicago: Rand McNally) pp. 261–304.

Scott, W. R. (1983) 'Health Care Organizations in the 1980s: The Convergence of Public and Professional Control Systems', in Meyer and Scott (eds), *Organizational Environments: Ritual and Rationality* (Beverly Hills, Calif.: Sage Publications), pp. 99–113.

Scott, W. R. (1987a) *Organizations: Rational, Natural, and Open Systems*, 2nd edn (Englewood Cliffs, NJ: Prentice-Hall).

Scott, W. R. (1987b) 'The Adolescence of Institutional Theory', *Administrative Science Quarterly*, 32, pp. 493–511.

Scott, W. R. and Meyer, J. W. (1983) 'The Organization of societal sectors', in J. W. Meyer and W. R. Scott (eds), *Organizational Environments: Ritual and Rationality* (Beverly Hills, Calif.: Sage Publications), pp. 129–53.

Scott, W. R. and Meyer, J. W. (1989) 'The Rise of Training Programs in Firms and Agencies: an Institutional Perspective', Stanford University working paper.

Sehlinger, B. (1985) *The Unofficial Guide to Disneyland* (Englewood Cliffs, NJ: Prentice Hall).

Seiler, E. (1984) 'Piece Rate vs. Time Rate: The Effect of Incentive on Earnings', *Review of Economics and Statistics*, 66:3, pp. 363–75.

Shapiro, A. (1984) 'The Evaluation and Control of Foreign Affiliates', *Midland Corporate Finance Journal* (Spring), pp. 13–25.

Shearling, C. D. and Stenning, P. C. (1985) 'From the Panopticon to Disney World', in R. Ericson (ed.), *Perspectives in Criminal Law* (Toronto: University of Toronto Press), pp. 335–49.

Sheppard, B. H. (1984) 'Third-party conflict intervention: A procedural framework', in B. M. Staw and L. L. Cummings (eds), *Research in Organizational Behavior*, vol. VI (Greenwich, Conn.: JAI Press).

Sheppard, B. H., and Lewicki, R. J. (1987) 'Toward general principles of managerial fairness', *Social Justice Research* 1, pp. 161–76.

Siehl, C. (1985) 'After the Founder: An Opportunity to Manage Culture', in P. Frost, L. F. Moore, M. R. Louis, C. C. Lundberg, and J. Martin (eds) *Organizational Culture* (Beverly Hills, Calif: Sage Publications), pp. 125–40.

336   *References*

Simon, H. (1962) 'The Architecture of Complexity', *Proceedings of the American Philosophical Society*, 106, pp. 467–82.

Simon, H. (1973) 'The Organization of Complex Systems', in H. Pattee (ed.), *Hierarchy Theory* (New York: Braziller).

Simon, H. (1977) *The New Science of Management Decision*, revised edn (Englewood Cliffs, NJ: Prentice-Hall).

Simon, H. (1981) *The Sciences of the Artificial* (Cambridge, Mass.: MIT Press).

Simon, H. (1989) 'Organizations and Markets', Working paper, Carnegie-Mellon University.

Singh, J. V., House, R. J. and Tucker, D. J. (1986) 'Organizational change and organizational mortality', *Administrative Science Quarterly*, 31, pp. 587–611.

Singh, J. V. and Lumsden, C. J. (1990) 'Theory and Research in Organizational Ecology', *Annual Review of Sociology*, 16, pp. 161–95.

Snyder, M. (1974) 'The Self-Monitoring of Expressive Behavior', *Journal of Personality and Social Psychology*, 30, pp. 526–37.

Snyder, M. (1979) 'Self-monitoring Processes', *Advances in Experimental Social Psychology*, 12, pp. 85–128.

Sontag, S. (1979) *On Photography* (Harmondsworth: Penguin).

Spinelli, M. L. (1987) 'Disneyland and Old Sturbridge Village', Paper presented to the Northeastern Anthropological Association, Amherst, Massachusetts.

Stalk, G. and Hout, T. M. (1990) *Competing Against Time: How Time-based Competition is Reshaping Global Markets* (New York: Free Press).

Starbuck, W. (1983) 'Organizations as Action Generators', *American Sociological Review*, 48, pp. 91–102.

Steinbruner, J. (1974) *The Cybernetic Theory of Decision: New Dimensions of Political Analysis* (Princeton, NJ: Princeton University Press).

Stevens, Guy V. G. (1974) 'The Determinants of Investment', in J. H. Dunning (ed.), *Economic Analysis and the Multinational Enterprise* (New York: Praeger), pp. 47–88.

Stiglitz, J. E. (1987) 'Learning to Learn, Localized Learning and Technological Progress', in P. Dasgupta and P. Stoneman (eds), *Economic Policy and Technological Performance* (New York: Cambridge University Press).

Stimson, J. A. (1985) 'Regression in Space and Time – A Statistical Essay', *American Journal of Political Science*, 29:4, pp. 914–47.

Stinchcombe, A. L. (1965) 'Social Structure and Organizations', in J. March (ed.), *Handbook of Organizations* (Chicago: Rand McNally), pp. 142–93.

Stockey, J. (1983) *Vertical Integration and Joint Ventures in the Aluminium Industry* (Cambridge, Mass.: Harvard University Press).

Stoffle, R. W. (1975) 'Reservation-based Industry: A Case from Zuni, New Mexico', *Human Organization*, 34, pp. 217–25.

Stopford, J. M., and Wells, L. T., Jr (1972) *Managing the Multinational Enterprise: Organization of the Firm and Ownership of Subsidiaries* (New York: Basic Books).

Stopford, J. M., Dunning, J. and Haberich, K. O. (1980) *The World Directory of Multinational Enterprises* (New York: Facts on File).

Stuart, P. M. (1987) *Nihonsense* (Tokyo: The Japan Times).

Swendenborg, B. (1979) *The Multinational Operations of Swedish Firms* (Stockholm: Industrial Institute for Economic and Social Research).

Taylor, C. T. and Silberston, Z. (1973) *The Economic Impact of the Patent System* (Cambridge University Press).

Taylor, J. (1983) *Shadows of the Rising Sun* (New York: William Morrow).

Taylor, R. W. (1947) *Scientific Management* (New York: Harper).

Teece, D. J. (1980) 'Economies of Scope and the Scope of the Enterprise', *Journal of Economic Behavior and Organization*, 1, pp. 223–47.

Teece, D. (1983) 'A Transaction Cost Theory of the Multinational Enterprise', in M. Casson (ed.), *The Growth of International Business* (London: Allen & Unwin).

Teece, D. (1985) 'Multinational Enterprise, Internal Governance and Economic Organization', *American Economic Review*, 75, pp. 233–38.

Teece, D. J. (1986) 'Transaction Cost Economies and the Multinational Enterprise', *Journal of Economic Behavior and Organization*, 7, pp. 21–45.

Terpstra, V. (1982) *International Dimensions of Marketing* (Boston, Mass.: Kent).

Terpstra, V. and Yu, C. M. (1988) 'Determinants of Foreign Investment of U.S. Advertising Agencies', *Journal of International Business Studies*, 19:1, pp. 33–46.

Thibaut, J., and Walker, L. (1975) *Procedural Justice: A Psychological Analysis* (Hillsdale, NJ: Erlbaum).

Thibaut, J., and Walker, L. (1978) 'A Theory of Procedure', *California Law Review* 66, pp. 541–66.

Thibaut, J., Walker, L., La Tour, S., and Houlden, P. (1974) 'Procedural Justice as Fairness', *Stanford Law Review*, 26, pp. 1271–89.

Thomason, G. F. (1966) 'Managerial Work Roles and Relationships, Part I', *Journal of Management Studies*, 3, pp. 270–84.

Thompson, James D. (1967) *Organizations in Action* (New York: McGraw-Hill).

Tichy, N. M., Tushman, M.L. and Fombrun, C. (1979) 'Social Network Analysis for Organizations', *Academy of Management Review*, 4, pp. 507–19.

Tilton, J. (1971) *The International Diffusion of Technology: The Case of Semiconductors* (Washington, DC: Brookings Institute).

Tolbert, P. S. (1985) 'Resource dependence and institutional environments: Sources of administrative structure in institutions of higher education', *Administrative Science Quarterly*, 30, pp. 1–13.

Traweek, S. (1988) *Beamtimes and Lifetimes* (Cambridge, MA: Harvard University Press).

Tuma, N. B. and Hannan, M. T. (1984) *Social Dynamics: Models and Methods* (New York: Academic Press).

Tushman, Michael L. (1978) 'Technical Communication in Research and Development Laboratories: Impact of Project Work Characteristics', *Academy of Management Journal*, 21, pp. 624–45.

Tushman, M. L. and Nadler, D. A. (1978) 'Information Processing as an Integrating Concept in Organizational Design', *Academy of Management Review*, 3, pp. 613–24.

Tushman, M. and Romanelli, E. (1986) 'Organizational Evolution: A Metamorphosis Model of Convergence and Reorientation', in L. L. Cummings and B. M. Staw (eds), *Research in Organizational Behavior*, 7 (Greenwich, Conn.: JAI Press) pp. 177–222.

Tyler, T. R. (1988) 'What is Procedural Justice?: Criteria Used by Citizens to Assess the Fairness of Legal Procedures', *Law and Society Review*, 22:1, pp. 301–55.

Tyler, T. R. (1989) 'Using Procedures to Justify Outcomes: Managing Conflict and Allocating Resources in Work Organizations', Northwestern University working paper.

Tyler, T. R. (1990) *Why People Obey the Law* (New Haven, Conn.: Yale University Press).

Tyler, T. R. and Caine, A. (1981) 'The Influence of Outcomes and Procedures on Satisfaction with Formal Leaders', *Journal of Personality and Social Psychology* 41, pp. 642–55.

Tyler, T. R., and Folger, R. (1980) 'Distributional and procedural aspects of satisfaction with citizen–police encounters', *Basic and Applied Social Psychology* 1, pp. 281–92.

Tyler, T. R. and Griffin, E. (1989) 'Managing the Allocation of Scarce Resources: Using Procedures to Justify Outcomes', Northwestern University working paper.

Tyler, T. R., Rasinski, K., and McGraw, K. (1985) 'The Influence of Perceived Injustice on Support for Political Authorities', *Journal of Applied Social Psychology*, 15, pp. 700–25.

UNCTC (United Nations Centre on Transnational Corporations) (1988) *Transnational Corporations in World Development: Trends and Prospects* (New York: United Nations).

United Nations. (various years) *International Trade Statistics* (New York: United Nations Publications).

Van de Ven, A. H., Delbecq, A. L. and Koenig, R. (1976) 'Determinants of Coordination Modes within Organizations', *American Sociological Review*, 41, pp. 322–38.

Van de Ven, A. H. and Walker, G. (1984) 'The Dynamics of Interorganizational Coordination', *Administrative Science Quarterly*, 29, pp. 598–621.

Van Maanen, J. (1975) 'Police Socialization: A Longitudinal Examination of Job Attitudes in an Urban Police Department', *Administrative Science Quarterly*, 20, pp. 207–28.

Van Maanen, J. (1988) *Tales of the Field* (University of Chicago Press).

Van Maanen, J. (1989) 'Whistle While You Work', Paper presented at the American Anthropological Association Annual Meeting, Washington DC (November).

Van Maanen, J. (1990a) 'The Smile Factory', unpublished paper, MIT.

Van Maanen, J. (1990b) 'Trade Secrets', unpublished paper, MIT.

Van Maanen, J. and Barley, S. (1984) 'Occupational Communities', in B. Staw and L. L. Cummings (eds), *Research in Organization Behavior*, vol. 6 (Greenwich, Conn.: JAI Press), pp. 287–365.

Van Maanen, J. and Kunda, G. (1989) 'Real Feelings', in B. Staw and L. L. Cummings (eds) *Research in Organization Behavior*, vol. 11 (Greenwich, Conn.: JAI Press), pp. 43–104.

Van Maanen, J. and Schein, E. H. (1979) 'Toward a Theory of Organizational Socialization', in B. Staw and L. L. Cummings (eds), *Research in Organization Behavior*, vol. 1 (Greenwich, Conn.: JAI Press), pp. 209–69.

Vancil, R. (1973) 'What Kind of Management Control Do You Need?', *Harvard Business Review* (March–April), pp. 75–86.

Vernon, R. (1966) 'International Investment and International Trade in the Product Cycle', *Quarterly Journal of Economics*, 80:2, pp. 190–207.

Vernon, R. (1971) *Sovereignty at Bay: The Multinational Spread of U.S. Enterprise* (New York: Basic Books).

Vernon, R. (1979) 'The Product Cycle Hypothesis in a New International Environment', *Oxford Bulletin of Economics and Statistics*, 41, pp. 255–67.

Vogel, E. F. (1979) *Japan as Number One* (Cambridge, Mass: Harvard University Press).

Von Hippel, E. (1988) *The Sources of Innovation* (Oxford University Press).

Walker, G. (1985) 'Network Position and Cognition in a Computer Software Firm', *Administrative Science Quarterly*, 30, pp. 103–130.

Walker, L., La Tour, S., Lind, E. A., and Thibaut, J. (1974) 'Reactions of participants and observers to modes of adjudication', *Journal of Applied Social Psychology* 4, pp. 295–310.

Walker, L., Lind, E. A., and Thibaut, J. (1979) 'The relation between procedural and distributive justice', *Virginia Law Review*, 65, pp. 1401–20.

Wall Street Journal (1989) 'Euroman: As 1992 Approaches, the Old World Takes on a New Look', A World Business Supplement, 22 September.

Wallace, F. A. C. (1970) *Culture and Personality* (New York: Random House).

Wallace, F. A. C. (1978) *Rockdale* (New York: Knopf).

Wallace, F. A. C. (1985) 'Rethinking Technology "and" Culture'; Paper prepared for the Mellon Seminar on Technology and Culture, University of Pennsylvania, Department of Anthropology.

Wallerstein, I. (1979) *The Capitalist World Economy* (Cambridge University Press).

Walster, E., Berscheid, E., and Walster, G. W. (1973) 'New directions in equity research', *Journal of Personality and Social Psychology*, 25, pp. 151–76.

Walter, I., and Murray, T. (1988) *Handbook of International Business*, 2nd edn (New York: Wiley).

Warren, R. L. (1967) 'The Interorganizational Field as a Focus for Investigation', *Administrative Science Quarterly*, 12, pp. 369–419.

Weber, M. (1946) *From Max Weber: Essays in Sociology*, in H. H. Gerth and C. Wright Mills (eds) (New York: Oxford University Press).

Weick, K. E. (1979) *The Social Psychology of Organizing*, 2nd edn (New York: Random House).

Weick, K. E., and Gilfillan, D. P. (1971) 'Fate of Arbitrary Traditions in a Laboratory Microculture', *Journal of Personality and Social Psychology*, 17, pp. 179–91.

Weihrich, H. (1990) 'Europe 1992: What the Future May Hold', *The Executive*, 4:2, pp. 7–18.

Welge, M. (1987) 'Subsidiary Autonomy in Multinational Corporations', in D. Van Den Bulcke (ed.), *International Business Issues*, proceedings of the 13th annual meeting of EIBA, Antwerp.

Westney, D. E. (1987) *Imitation and Innovation: The Transfer of Western Organizational Patterns to Meiji Japan* (Cambridge, Mass.: Harvard University Press).

Westney, D. E. (1988) 'Isomorphism, Institutionalization and the Multinational Enterprise', Paper presented at the Academy of International Business Annual Meeting, San Diego, California (October) .

Westney, D. E. and Sakakibara, D. (1985) 'Competitive Study of the Training, Careers, and Organization of Engineers on the Computer Industry in Japan and the United States', MIT–Japan Science and Technology Program, MIT (mimeo).

White, M. (1987) *The Japanese Educational Challenge* (New York: Free Press).

White, R. E. and Poynter, T. A. (1985) 'Strategies for Foreign-Owned Subsidiaries in Canada', *Business Quarterly*.

White, R. E. and Poynter, T. A. (1990) 'Organizing for World-wide Advantage', in C. A. Bartlett, Y. Doz and G. Hedlund (eds) *Managing the Global Firm* (London: Routledge).

Wilkins, M. (1970) *The Emergence of the Multinational Enterprise: American Business Abroad from the Colonial Era to 1914* (Cambridge, Mass.: Harvard University Press).

Williams, C. R. (1967) 'Regional Management Overseas', *Harvard Business Review*, 45, pp. 87–91.

Williamson, O. E. (1964) *The Economics of Discretionary Behavior: Managerial Objectives in a Theory of the Firm* (Englewood Cliffs, NJ: Prentice-Hall).

Williamson, O. E. (1970) *Corporate Control and Business Behavior* (Englewood Cliffs, NJ.: Prentice-Hall).

Williamson, O. E. (1975) *Markets and Hierarchies: Analysis and Antitrust Implications* (New York: Free Press).

Williamson, O. E. (1981) 'The Economics of Organization: The Transaction Cost Approach', *American Journal of Sociology*, 87 (November) pp. 548–77.

Williamson, O. E. (1985) *The Economic Institutions of Capitalism* (New York: Free Press).

Williamson, O. E. and Ouchi, W. G. (1981) 'The Markets and Hierarchies Program of Research: Origins, Implications, Prospects', in W. Joyce and A. Van de Ven (eds), *Organizational Design* (New York: John Wiley), pp. 347–70.

Wilson, B. D. (1980) *Divestment of Foreign Subsidiaries* (Ann Arbor, Mich: UMI Research Press).

Winter, S. (1981) 'Attention Allocation and Input Proportions', *Journal of Economic Behavior and Organization*, 2, pp. 31–46.

Wolcott, H. F. (1982) 'The Anthropology of Learning', *Anthropology and Education Quarterly*, 13 (special issue).

Wolcott, H. F. (1990) 'Propriospect and the Acquisition of Culture', unpublished paper, University of Oregon, School of Education.

Wolf, J. C. (1979) 'Disney World: America's Vision of Utopia', *Alternative Futures*, 2, pp. 72–7.

Wolfe, T. (1968) *The Electric Kool-Aid Acid Test* (New York: Farrar, Straus & Giroux).

Womack, J. P., Jones, D. T., and Roos, D. (1990) *The Machine that Changed the World* (New York: Rawson Associates).

Wood, R. and Bandura, A. (1989) 'Social Cognitive Theory of Organizational Management', *Academy of Management Review*, 14, pp. 361–84.

Woodward, J. (1965) *Industrial Organization: Theory and Practice* (New York: Oxford University Press).

Yates, J. (1989) *Control Through Communication* (Baltimore, MD.: Johns Hopkins University Press).

Yip, G. S. (1989) 'Global strategy...in a world of nations?', *Sloan Management Review* (Fall) pp. 29–41.

Zald, M. N. (1970) 'Political Economy: A Framework for Comparative Analysis', in M. N. Zald (ed.), *Power in Organizations* (Nashville, Tenn.: Vanderbilt University Press), pp. 221–61.

Zeitz, G. (1980) 'Interorganizational Dialects', *Administrative Science Quarterly*, 25, pp. 72–88.

Zeleny, Y. M. (1987) 'Management Support Systems: Towards Integrated Knowledge Management', *Human Systems Management*, 7, pp. 59–70.

Zucker, L. G. (1977) 'The Role of Institutionalization in Cultural Persistence', *American Sociological Review*, 42, pp. 726–43.

Zucker, L. G. (1983) 'Organization as Institutions', in S. Bacharach (ed.), *Advances in Organizational Theory and Research*, vol. 2 (Greenwich: JAI Press), pp. 1–43.

Zucker, L. G. (1987) 'Institutional Theories of Organization', *Annual Review of Sociology*, 13, pp. 443–64.

Zucker, L. G., (ed.) (1988) *Institutional Patterns and Organizations: Culture and Environment* (Cambridge, Mass.: Ballinger).

Zucker, L. G. (1989) 'Combining Institutional Theory and Population Ecology: No Legitimacy, No History', *American Sociological Review*, 54:4, pp. 542–5.

Index

Netherlands 77, 78
  US MNCs in 117–21; imports and
    FDI 121, 122
network/networks 13, 80, 81
  centrality measure 96, 97–8
  differentiated 99–100
  external 87
  integrated 5
  mandated 83
  methodology 100–4; and
    density 103
  MNC as 85–7, 99–100
  relationships 36, 37–8, 41, 79
Newman, W.H. 194, 201
Newton, Sir Isaac 234
Nigeria 77, 78
Nishiguchi, T. 154
Nissan 71, 181
Nohria, N. 15, 34, 39, 44, 47, 83, 85,
    283, 301
Nonaka, I. 225, 233
Norman, R. 35
normative isomorphism 55, 100
norms
  formation 260
  individual internalisation 271
  and structuration theory 268, 270
  see also culture
North American Free Trade Pact 62
North, D. 142

Ochs, E. 312
Ogilvy, J. 230, 236
Ohmae, K. 5–6, 23, 66, 69, 102
Oliver, R. 166
Olsen, J.P. 37, 262
opportunism 89, 141, 159
organization theory 158–66
  and control 172
  and diversified organizations 11
  ethnocentrism of 6
  and international management
    research 113–16
  and management research 48–50
  and MNCs 1–2; research 6–10,
    11–14, 20–2
  organizing costs 159, 161–4, 165
  price and hierarchy 159–61
  recent developments 106–9
  see also agency theory; contingency
    theory; diversified MNCs;

ecology theory; procedural
    justice; transaction cost theory
organization-sets 56, 86–7
  and boundaries 104
  densities of interactions 89;
    across 91–3, 94, 95–8;
    within 90–1, 94–5
  and learning across borders 71–2
  organizational fields 56–7, 60,
    62–4, 76
organizations
  roles in 265
  vocabulary 264–5
Oriental Land Company 293
Orlando Disneyland 291
Orru, M. 73
Ott, S. 276
Ouchi, W. 29, 30, 167, 168, 175, 180,
    213, 276, 302
output control 181
ownership 81–2, 143
  advantages 139–40
  and power 82

Paine, L. 236
Pappi, F. 96
Parsons, T. 263
path dependent drift 138
Patrides 234, 236
Pattee 212
Paul, J.K. 90–1
Pavan, R.J. 150, 183
Pavitt, K. 229
Pearce, J.A. 24
performance
  and culture 305–6
  and elimination 109
  and fit 182, 183
  and organizational design 182, 209
  and training of CEOs 111
Perlmutter, H.V. 33, 43, 67, 80, 203,
    224, 302
Perrow, C. 224
Persky, J.J. 212
Peters, T.J. 135, 233, 306
Peterson, R. 277
petrochemical industry 90
Pfeffer, J.R. 11, 38, 58, 81–2, 95
Philips (N.V.) 77, 78, 79, 82, 88, 99,
    174